Leo Heaps was seconded from the Canadian Army to the British during World War II and found himself with the First Airborne Division. After the battle of Arnhem he organized part of the Dutch resistance, for which he was awarded the Military Cross.

After the war he went to Israel setting up mobile striking units in the new army and it was there that he met his wife. During the Hungarian revolution he was the head of a special rescue team to bring refugees across the border.

Eleven years ago he came to Britain where he has been successful in dividing his time between entrepreneurial activities, searching for rare works of art and writing.

Leo Heaps

The Grey Goose of Arnhem

Futura Publications Limited
A Futura Book

A Futura Book

First published in Great Britain by
Weidenfeld & Nicolson in 1976.
First Futura Publications edition 1977

ISBN: 0 8600 7509 5

Printed in Great Britain by
C. Nicholls & Company Ltd
The Philips Park Press
Manchester

Futura Publications Limited
110 Warner Road, Camberwell,
London S.E.5.

For Lieutenant Eric Davies, M.C.,
who danced his last ballet

CONTENTS

In the town of Ede, a section of German Panzers was billeted next door to the house on Torenstraat where Brigadier John Hackett recovered from his wounds after the battle of Arnhem. Early in December 1944, these troops requisitioned from a local farmer a large, grey goose which they began to fatten up in preparation for their Christmas dinner. Hackett told the three old maids who nursed him that he intended to steal the goose so they could have it for their own Christmas. Mien de Nooy, the eldest sister of the household, thinking of the safety of her hunted guest, sternly dismissed the idea. Nevertheless, the thought of that fat, succulent goose continued to haunt Hackett for several months. One way or another he was determined that the goose would evade the clutches of the enemy.

Finally the day came when the brigadier felt well enough to attempt his escape through the swamps of the Biesbosch. He asked the three maids to listen to the BBC nine o'clock news on a particular night in February. If he succeeded in crossing the enemy lines, the announcer would broadcast the code message: "The grey goose has flown."

PREFACE

After the battle of Arnhem came to an official end on September 26, 1944, another battle began. It was one of attrition, then escape for most of the 250 men hidden in the woods, fields and houses around Arnhem and Ede. It represented a war within a war, where individuals and groups assisted by the Dutch Resistance made some of the most remarkable escapes in World War II. All the characters who appear in this book, except a few, either escaped, tried to escape, helped those who did or died in the attempt.

Frankly, at the beginning I was not interested in writing this book. I had already published my story of Arnhem, *Escape from Arnhem*, twenty-eight years ago. Besides, journalists had written too many colourful accounts, historians had dissected the operation and I had no intention of reviving memories that I thought had perished. Then, by chance, I rediscovered some of the characters who had been my companions. They were a fascinating lot. Many had been the first commandos and paratroopers in World War II. In their own right they were a dedicated, ingenious and audacious band. There may never be others like them.

THE MEMORIAL

Just before 2.0 p.m. on September 15, 1969, Sergeant Keith (Tex) Banwell of the 10th Battalion stood ready at the open doorway. High overhead jets flashed by like silver darts in the sun so that the old DC-3 Dakota seemed to be standing still in midair.

Deep, warm memories surged through the mind of Banwell. The Dakota, now all alone in the sky, lumbered on towards Ginkel Heath. This would be his 650th jump. He looked sympathetically at the nervous faces of the young men standing behind in readiness, some of whom were a third his age. They had seen the plane for the first time shortly before they boarded the craft for takeoff in England. The Dakota belonged in a museum, in fact that is where it came from. It bore little resemblance to the giant, sleek CI-30E Hercules with its four turbo prop engines, presently used by the paratroops. The young paratroopers, in fact, were enacting a bit of history. But to Banwell, now a legend among the men of the 10th Battalion, everything seemed as real as the day it happened.

They came in peacefully over Ginkel Heath at exactly 2.0 p.m. and the plane sloped in towards the dropping zone as the red light changed to green. At that second the past swept suddenly before Banwell's eyes. He watched in silence as the port engine of his Dakota suddenly fell apart. Shrapnel struck the starboard engine and it spurted into flame. A Spandau opened fire from a clump of pine trees and the burst of bullets ripped the fuselage, almost cutting it in half. Six of the fifteen paratroopers lay dead on the floor. As the American pilot fought to keep the plane in the air, Banwell – at five hundred feet – stepped out and shouted to his men to follow. Most of the paratroopers struggled clear over the dead bodies to the doorway, as the Dakota became a flaming coffin, hurtling uncontrollably to the ground.

As Banwell floated down to Ginkel Heath to what he thought would be certain death on that afternoon long ago, the past events of his life had flashed before him. Now it happened once again. He pictured himself enlisting in 1931 as a private in the Coldstream Guards, fighting the Pathans and Kashmiries on the mountainous northwest frontier of India; operating in Arab dress out of the Kufra oasis in the sweltering heat of the Western Desert in 1942 – a member of the Long Range Desert Patrol; captivity in Tobruk, escape in a half-track, later imprisonment in Crete as a Commando and finally escape in a fishing boat to freedom in North Africa. Escape, capture, escape. That seemed to be the rhythm of his army life.

When Banwell landed alive in the knee-deep grass of the heath he had witnessed the strange charge of Lieutenant George Mackay, his platoon commander – a sight he never forgot – as he sprinted single-handed towards a Spandau mounted on top of a pile of logs on the edge of the field. The lieutenant turned around several times in a grotesque death pirouette and fell full of bullets on the grass. In the distance Banwell's Dakota crashed among the tall pines. Then Banwell, pinned to the ground by machine-gun fire, could not move more than a few hundred yards in any direction for two days. Eventually he managed to reach Division Headquarters at the Hartenstein Hotel with two survivors, Corporal Bill Cuttill and Private Ginger Whadcoat. Banwell wondered where his companions were now. All this and more passed before him in a matter of seconds. Time seemed to have gone out of sequence. Then the present returned.

The countryside was strangely, almost reverently silent. Ginkel Heath was empty, but along the jammed roads and pathways of Oosterbeek thousands of people waited expectantly, craning their necks upwards towards Banwell floating down through the bright autumn afternoon. The battle of Arnhem was exactly a quarter of a century old.

THE BEGINNING

The planners at the Supreme Headquarters of the Allied Expeditionary Force in Europe realized after the invasion of the Normandy beaches on June 6, 1944, that their armies had to reach the industrial heartland of Germany if they wished to quickly win the war. The German war machine was fed by the heavy industries in the Ruhr Valley. Therefore the Allied advance was designed to ultimately cut off the retreating German forces in north Holland and then to swing eastward to take the Ruhr. Field Marshal Bernard Montgomery had come to the conclusion that only a most daring plan could achieve the objectives.

In late August the plan was born. There were some people who raised their voices against the operation, but they were not vigorous voices. For it is difficult to contradict a conquering general flushed with a string of successive victories. Even General Dwight Eisenhower hesitated to object when his own Chief of Staff, Lieutenant General Walter Bedell Smith, warned him against Montgomery's plan. In August, Eisenhower reluctantly concurred with Montgomery. A final, paralyzing blow must be dealt the Germans. An airborne invasion would cut off the enemy retreat and shorten the war by many months. That, at least, became the grand strategy as the ground troops advanced across Europe. The Germans were retreating everywhere on the Western front. All that remained was the final lunge at the enemy's jugular to finish him off.

On paper the plan looked good. Invincible. The Allied First Airborne Army – under Lieutenant General Lewis Brereton and Deputy Commander, Lieutenant General Frederick Browning – would carry out the strike, which would be named Market-Garden. The American and British airborne forces would undertake the "Market" part of the operation. Meanwhile the ground forces of the Second British Army led by the tanks of Lieutenant General Brian Horrocks's XXX Corps would batter their way through to join up with the para and glider troops landing ahead of them. The ground operation became known as "Garden." Five years of German occupation of Holland looked as if it were finally coming to an end.

Confined to a life of grinding boredom in England since June, the men of the 1st British Airborne Division were impatient to fight. Major General Roy Urquhart's soldiers would have accepted any plan, no matter how hazardous, in order to enter the battle for Germany. The American 101st and 82nd Airborne divisions waited with equal impatience. The rapid advance of Allied armour caused the planners in Montgomery's headquarters to constantly alter the objectives. All during the summer after the Allied invasion of France, this great airborne army waited the signal to set off.

Some of the cancelled plans offered relief rather than disappointment, at least for Urquhart. The code names seemed to indicate the impetuous nature of the hastily conceived operations. "Wild Oats" became the order for Urquhart's division to land a few miles ahead of the Allied beachhead at the French town of Evercy after D-Day. As Urquhart said, "It would have been rather sticky." He was pleased when Evercy was overrun and his troops were not needed.

Then came the abortive plan for taking the concrete fortifications of St. Malo where the German Atlantic submarine fleet was based. "Raising Britanny," a reckless joint campaign with the French Maquis, never happened. "Hands Up", "Sword Hilt" and finally "Transfigure", where the British were to rendezvous with the Americans and thus take Paris, suffered the same fate as all the other cancelled plans. Allied headquarters kept projecting the waiting airborne army into operations ahead of the advancing armour all through France and Belgium. Week after week the troops went on the alert and then stood down again. Altogether sixteen operations were planned and cancelled during that hot, dusty summer of 1944 as the Allied ground forces thrust forward, and the Germans wearily retreated back towards the Homeland.

By September the frustration of the waiting troops, confined to barracks at the announcement of each new operation, mounted to unbearable proportions. The short leaves after each cancellation offered only temporary relaxation before the waiting started all over again. A kind of dull, fatal resignation set in among the airborne, who were now convinced they would never really be used. Perhaps the American divisions were more likely to be launched into battle than the British, whom Montgomery had decided to commit at the extreme limit of any strategic plan to block the fleeing enemy.

Then, suddenly, it happened. Operation Market-Garden scheduled for midnight on September 16 was not cancelled. By 5.0 a.m. the following morning, as a pink dawn spread across the green fields and country lanes of England, the first wave of troops was on the lorries and on the way to their predesignated aerodromes. By 8.0 a.m. the last of the transports rolled up to the fields where the grey gliders and Dakotas waited in position. The little villages, the stone-turreted castles and country estates where the troops had been billeted were suddenly empty. All that remained of the Airborne bases was the skeletal framework of the divisions – a few ground troops who would later follow overland as the rear party.

Eindhoven, Grave, Nijmegen and Arnhem became the Dutch towns selected as the main targets. They ran almost in a straight line south to north. The towns dominated major river barriers and canals whose vital bridges had to be secured for the passage of the tanks of the Guards Armoured Division that would come up from the south as the spearhead of Horrocks's XXX Corps. The armour drove on relentlessly from Belgium where it had crossed the Albert and Meus-Escant canals to rendezvous with the airborne carpet about to unroll before them.

Furthest to the south lay the town of Eindhoven, around which the 101st U.S. Airborne Division would land under command of Major General Maxwell Taylor. The 101st would then proceed north to take the bridges that spanned the Wilhelmina and Willems canals. Taylor's divisional objectives would extend north to the next barrier – thirty-five miles –

the long bridge at Grave that vaulted the sluggish water of the Maas. At Grave the 82nd U.S. Airborne Division led by Major General James Gavin would have a bitter struggle to dominate the main road that stretched another ten miles north to Nijmegen and thus also control the bridge on the river Waal. Therefore the two American airborne divisions would dominate the bridges over two canals and two wide rivers in preparation for Horrocks's advance. The Americans eventually secured their objectives, but not without days of bloody battle. However, one bridge remained to be taken. The bridge over the Rhine at Arnhem.

After the drop on September 17, news of the 1st British Airborne Division filtered back very slowly to Montgomery's headquarters. The reports from Arnhem were fragmentary, confused. No one knew if the British held this last link, without which the grand strategy would collapse. Something seemed to have gone wrong at Arnhem. It was as if all the strength, all the effort of the Allied attack had been expended with the taking of the first two bridges by the Americans. Meanwhile the tanks of the Guards Armoured Division pounded on north hoping to join up with the scattered para and glider troops at Arnhem.

It took two precious days for Urquhart to put down his entire division on the dropping zone of Oosterbeek. Eight miles east lay the bridge. On the first day less than two hundred men, consisting mainly of mixed troops, reached the town, the fulcrum where the Guards tanks were to turn eastward into Germany. Without the bridge at Arnhem, Market-Garden would have little to commend itself for the extravagant waste of life and material.

The battle for Arnhem and Oosterbeek began quietly on a warm, sunlit Sunday. It ended in catastrophe nine days and ten nights later on the shores of the Rhine for the two thousand men who were eventually ferried to safety over the river. Between the beginning and the end over nine thousand British soldiers were killed, wounded or lost. In the contracting crucible at the Hartenstein Hotel in Oosterbeek and on the ramparts of the torn bridge, the men of the 1st British Airborne Division made their last stand. They were overwhelmed by parts of several divisions of German troops. Tanks appeared unexpectedly, endless cascades of mortars rained down, while lack of food and ammunition hastened the end. Perhaps Arnhem might have been just another battle, forgotten among all the others of World War II, if those few scattered Englishmen had not resisted so stubbornly against great odds.

The 1st Airborne Division, made up largely of veterans, were among the very best soldiers Britain had. But the Arnhem operation could not succeed. The advancing Allied armour managed to link up with the Americans, but the tanks were stretched too thin to be effective. They were trapped too deep in the muddy meadows on the one slender road that sped like an arrow from Nijmegen to the Rhine. They could not reach the British defenders. When a small reconnaissance unit of Allied armour finally did struggle through to the south bank of the Rhine on September 20, the Germans had retaken the bridge at Arnhem. For three days a gallant force under command of Leiutenant Colonel John Frost had held it.

The battle of Arnhem is now over thirty years old. Already people are remembering it like Sevastopol, Dunkirk, and one day far ahead might even think of it as some kind of fiercely contested Thermopylae. Concentrated into a few days – intense, brutal, one-sided – it developed into more of an organized slaughter than a battle. The enemy had the advantage of numbers, tanks and terrain. The British were driven to preposterous acts of ingenuity to survive. The nine days they held out represented seven more than they were ordered to hold. Their stubborn endurance allowed others elsewhere to consolidate and hold their positions. Around the bridge at Arnhem and on the grounds of the Hartenstein Hotel at Oosterbeek the lifeblood of the 1st Airborne Division drained away. It was never again reformed. Perhaps that is the ultimate tribute that could be given to the men who once filled its ranks.

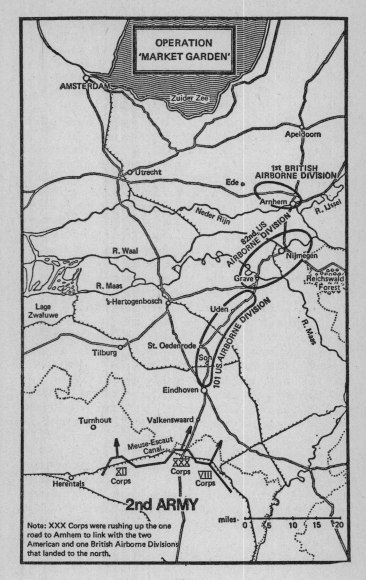

OPERATION 'MARKET GARDEN'

AMSTERDAM

Zuider Zee

Apeldoorn

Utrecht

Ede

1st BRITISH AIRBORNE DIVISION

Arnhem

R. IJssel

Neder Rijn

82nd US AIRBORNE DIVISION

R. Waal

Nijmegen

Grave

Reichswald Forest

R. Maas

's-Hertogenbosch

Uden

Lage Zwaluwe

R. Maas

St. Oedenrode

101 US AIRBORNE DIVISION

Tilburg

Son

Eindhoven

Turnhout

Valkenswaard

Meuse-Escaut Canal

XII Corps

XXX Corps

VIII Corps

Herentals

2nd ARMY

miles

0   5   10   15   20

Note: XXX Corps were rushing up the one road to Arnhem to link with the two American and one British Airborne Divisions that landed to the north.

20

THE EVADERS

The leader of the four men falling through the moon-filled sky called himself, for security reasons, Captain Fabian King. In his records at headquarters of the Special Air Service, at Moor Park near London, his real name was listed as Gilbert Sadi-Kirschen and his nationality, Belgian. Once he had been a lawyer in Brussels. The others were also Belgians. Corporal Jules Regner, a one-time circus acrobat, had been trained as a wireless operator. He escaped from a prisoner-of-war camp in Germany in 1940 and made his way to England by way of Russia. This would be his third mission with Kirschen behind enemy lines. Often the Dutch Resistance leaders would watch in amazement as Regner swung like a monkey on the rafters of a barn setting up the radio antennae. The other members of Kirschen's team were René Pietquin, a tough former miner, and Jean Moyse, a quiet, small corporal from Brussels.

Kirschen was convinced that the long, wearisome road of war that began for him with the humiliating capitulation of the Belgian Army in 1940 would soon end on a Dutch meadow on this September in 1944. His briefing had prepared him for the rapid overrun by the advancing Allied Second Army coming up from the south. The mission was expected to last for five days. He eagerly awaited the time when he could continue his law practice in Brussels. Four years before Kirschen had escaped from France after imprisonment by the Vichy Government in Marseille. Through Spain and Portugal he had slowly made his way to England where he joined that small, elite band called the Special Air Service. On this mission Kirschen had two objectives. He hoped to discover the bases for the new German V-2 rockets being launched against London and also to supply intelligence for the Allied airborne landing in Holland in the operation known as Market-Garden. Kirschen had arrived forty-eight hours before the airborne invasion would begin. He hoped the Dutch Resistance men were better organized than his French contacts on his last mission to the Ardennes.

The British pilot carefully deposited Kirschen and his men in the middle of the correct meadow with all twenty-four containers intact. The wireless set and generator suffered no damage. (Kirschen was a good deal more lucky than Dick Kragt – who used the code name of Franz Hals – had been. Kragt, sent out on a disorganized, ill-fated mission sponsored by Military Intelligence 9, commonly called IS9, parachuted down near Baasen, not far from the town of Ede in June 1943. He barely missed the church steeple, brushed against a large poplar tree and tumbled into a ploughed turnip field. All his equipment, including his radio set, landed many miles away and was lost and later retrieved by the Germans. According to Kragt, the impatient Canadian pilot switched on the green light ten minutes too soon because he had a date in London in three hours. Kragt's survival was due to his ingenuity and joining forces in the town of Emst with Joop Piller, a Dutch Jew. Kragt, without a wireless set, little money and a Colt .45, felt badly equipped to rescue evaders, which was his function. The paths of Kirschen, Kragt and the evaders were to cross many times. Although Kragt had little more than the clothes on his back with which to complete a complex mission, he had one enormous asset. He spoke Dutch fluently. And after Piller corrected some glaring mispronunciations and changed a faulty identification card that showed the Dutch lions facing the wrong way, Kragt could pass easily as a Dutchman.)

Kirschen's drop was perfect and unopposed. The reception committee was on the field to meet him with the correct flash-light code. A car with driver was waiting on a small, wooded lane near the dropping zone. Several Dutchmen quickly and efficiently gathered up the containers of equipment and buried the silken parachutes so that in a few minutes no trace of them existed. Kirschen was astounded at the unhurried efficiency of the Dutch, a pleasant contrast to the disorganized speed and delays he had experienced when he was dispatched on the mission. Only on the truck that took him to the airport at Keevil did he have time to explain the job to his team. Once at the airport, the poor weather and timing of the Allied advance caused a frantic delay of three days. Cancellation seemed a real possibility. The liberation of Belgium and the hope of soon returning home gave the mission a desperate sense of urgency. It could not last very long.

Kirschen introduced himself to Piet Een, the head of the reception committee, who took the Belgian team to a hunting lodge where the keeper enthusiastically broke open a bottle of cognac to celebrate the occasion. The next day the Resistance chief Lange Jean arrived, accompanied by a tall, gangling man in plus fours. Like Lange Jean, Roelof van Valkenburg spoke good English. Van Valkenburg and his girl friend Bep Labouchère were designated as Kirschen's liaison and courier respectively.

Kirschen took up residence at the farm of Wuf Langerwey, outside the village of Glindhorst. In the middle of a large meadow there were three shabby, unpainted chicken coops surrounded by overgrown grass. From the outside the three buildings looked exactly alike. However, Kirschen's chicken coop contained three comfortable rooms panelled with white acoustic boards. One room had a large bed with a feather filled mattress and quilt. A stove and sofa were in the living room and electricity and running water provided the Belgians with luxury they never before experienced behind enemy lines.

On September 16 hundreds of bombers flew overhead and pounded the German positions around Arnhem. Shortly afterwards Kirschen received the official news of Operation Market-Garden on his Jedburgh wireless set. The greatest airborne invasion ever undertaken had started. Meanwhile Van Valkenburg and Kirschen began to set up their intelligence-gathering system. Messages between the chicken coop on Langerwey's farm and Lieutenant-Colonel Ian Collins' office in the golf club at Moor Park near London began to flow daily.

Quickly the brief mood of relaxation that Kirschen felt in the luxury of his converted chicken coop faded away. A sudden message came from Collins, the GSO 1 at the Moor Park Airborne Headquarters, that communications had been unexpectedly cut between the 1st Airborne Division and the War Office. In the early hours of Wednesday morning, Kirschen, following instructions, sent Corporal Regner and the Dutchman Een in civilian clothes on bicycle to Oosterbeek to try and reestablish contact with the airborne troops.

At noon on September 17, before the armada of planes and gliders arrived, Edith Nijhoff, her husband Albert, her daughter Geraldine and son Gerald watched twelve Stirling bombers flying very low over their house. Mrs. Nijhoff felt certain the Ede barracks next door to her home were to be blasted. But the planes continued on their way. The Stirlings contained 186 men of the Pathfinder Company of the 1st Airborne Division commanded by Major Boy Wilson, who were to drop one hour ahead of the main force. They marked the dropping zone with orange smoke signals in advance of the division. Among the officers who jumped with the Pathfinders that day was Zeno, who in later years – while serving a prison sentence for murder – would write an absorbing personal account of the battle called *The Cauldron*.

The Stirlings were alone and unmolested. The sky that Sunday remained a startling deep blue, the air delightfully serene when suddenly Wilson gave the weird fighting cry of the division – "Waho Mohamet" – and tumbled out into space followed by his company. The Pathfinders descended into the gracious peace of the Dutch meadows, south of the railway tracks near the Wolfheze Hotel. Wilson began preparing the landing zones for the armada of paratroops and towed Horsa gliders that would stretch for more than 350 miles over Holland to the North Sea.

Among all the remarkable characters of the division, Wilson stood out almost alone for his daring. An ex-jockey, less than five feet two inches tall, he came to Holland at the age of fifty.

Deaf in one ear, he commanded a group of men as wild and uncontrollable as himself. By some remarkable coincidence Wilson had celebrated his birthday the day before. Few people knew his official age. But among those who did were his namesake "Boy" Browning, the commander of the 1st British Airborne Corps and Major Freddy Gough, commander of the Reconnaissance squadron, who at forty-three with his white hair, looked older than Wilson. In Wilson's force were twenty-five Jewish refugees recruited for their ability to speak German and their exceptional fighting qualities. For the purpose of this operation they had all changed their names and taken up new identities as MacPhersons, MacTavishs and MacLeods. General Roy Urquhart, the commander of the 1st Airborne Division, a proud Scotsman himself, made sure no one used the name of Urquhart.

As the Nijhoff family raced to greet the descending paratroops, they could see scattered forces of the Wehrmacht fleeting in disarray in carts, bicycles and cars to the east in the direction of Arnhem.

Berkenlaan 16, the Nijhoffs' home in Ede, was to become a private transit camp for evaders. Since 1940, the red-brick, terraced house had sheltered countless Jews and escaping airmen in its specially constructed attic compartments. Edith Nijhoff roamed the countryside by day, sometimes as a visiting tennis player, often as a Red Cross worker, and frequently could be seen driving a horse and cart piled high with sacks and old blankets. Underneath the sacks were escaping prisoners or Jews being transported from one hiding place to another. About a hundred yards up the street from her house on Berkenlaan, the Germans had a large barracks towards which Mrs. Nijhoff showed a contemptuous indifference. In spite of her furiously busy life, this bustling, middle-aged lady always had time to tend the flowers and plant the tulip bulbs in her meticulously kept back garden.

*

I floated down gently from heaven at 1.30 p.m. on Sunday, September 17. It could not be more delightful, I said to myself. No one fired at me and I could see no enemy. The sun shone, the fields of Wolfheze were bathed in warm light and the green meadow bloomed with large bursts of yellow sunflowers. The only sound was the steady drone of the clumsy grey Dakotas trailing long lines of statachutes like streamers of confetti.

> Feet together
> Shoulders round,
> Elbows in
> And watch the ground.

I chanted the little verse that Eric Davies taught me as the breeze carried me away from the dropping zone. Below, I saw my kit bag, which had broken loose from my leg, showering all my belongings over the countryside as it exploded on the ground.

By rights I should not be here – not that I needed an invitation, but I had come only because the Canadian Army was so anxious to see the last of me. I quickly pulled on one of the shroud lines to avoid a threatening dark wood of pointed pine trees. Successive commanders had branded me "not of officer calibre, no initiative, not aggressive enough," and I tended to agree. When the Canadian Army finally decided to discharge me and recall me as a private under the Mobilisation Act, I thought this was going a bit too far. My father said that since all my commanders had unanimously agreed I was not officer material, I should take their word for it and go to work as a labourer on my fat aunt Rosie's farm near Toronto. There I would be exempt from military service and could safely help the war effort. I rebelled at the idea of working in the manure and dirt. Even when a kindly brigadier took pity on me and gave me one more chance to qualify in the infantry. I failed. No one had ever failed before to qualify for the infantry. I should definitely not be here. When the British Army desperately needed junior officers to fill its depleted ranks, naturally I quickly volunteered along with several hundred other disgruntled Canadian subalterns. Already I had been thrown as cannon fodder onto the Normandy beaches. Fortunately I survived a slight wound and the aftermath of being mistakenly evacuated to England. Now the tough, kind veterans of the 1st Parachute Battalion had adopted me. I was very much a novice in their midst. Only Eric Davies knew this was my first jump.

Much to my amazement I crashed through the pine trees unscratched and landed gently on my feet on the mossy floor of the forest. Lieutenant Colonel David Dobie, my commander, had asked me to gather up transport and then to find him, since every other job in the battalion was filled. He would be somewhere on the river road on the way to the main Arnhem bridge waiting for me. I wondered whether I could find my friend Lieutenant Eric Davies, the ballet dancer. He would be with Dobie marching into the town. I would have been much more of a novice paratrooper without his many helpful explanations. (But the opportunity would come months later to reciprocate as he lay dying of gangrene in a small Dutch farm-house deep in enemy territory.)

After all the fuss and excitement, it seemed like a quiet war. Private William Watts, the batman allocated to help me gather up German transport, dangled from a bough of a tree. I threw him a knife and he cut himself loose. Men struggled out of the broken Horsa gliders and made off over the deep grass eastward towards Arnhem. I went north with Watts to the main Arnhem–Amersfoort highway, wondering whether I would really find any vehicles for my battalion. I had no platoon to command, no important job to perform and no illusions about my role. I had the feeling I was meant to keep out of the way while my battalion got on with the serious business of fighting a war.

My commander could not understand why a strange Canadian lieutenant should join his battalion a few weeks before they left for Holland. I did not bother to elaborate to Colonel Dobie how I had marched one day to the office of Major General K. C. Crawford, in command of airborne training at the War Office in London, and put my case. I had suffered from acute boredom in an infantry holding unit after being discharged from hospital upon my return from the Normandy beachhead, and I explained that I would like a quick and painless way into battle. I had chosen the paratroops. The General, who was over fifty, said he had parachuted into Normandy unbeknown to his superiors on D-Day. If he could do it, there was no reason why someone thirty years his junior could not do the same. I shook hands with Crawford and he said he would take care of the details. We had struck a perfect understanding. A week later the florid-faced colonel at my holding unit who had threatened to court-martial me for conduct unbecoming to an officer (I had on occasion disappeared when wanted for orderly duty), handed me my transfer. He was glad to get rid of me. I knew he would never court-martial me since it would bring attention to a comfortable job with as much good food, liquor and women as he had appetite for. He would do nothing to jeopardize his safety. That was how I found myself that evening looking for nonexistent transport in a strange land, searching for a commanding officer I never expected to meet again.

As darkness fell, Watts and I stumbled onto the grounds of the beautiful Wolfheze Hotel. The proprietor and his daughter opened a pre-War bottle of cold wine for dinner to celebrate their liberation and we decided to settle down to a peaceful, comfortable evening. Late that night the hotel proprietor graciously led me to a four-poster bed made with clean, white linen.

Within hours I awakened to the distant clatter of Bren guns answered by the sudden burps of German Spandaus. But that was not what had awakened me. My Dutch host shook my shoulder fearfully, bidding me to dress quickly and quietly. He pointed nervously outside my window where the silhouette of a long column of German infantry passed by burdened with guns and equipment. Watts and I waited until the last enemy vanished and then with a quick handshake and hurried goodbye, we made our sad departure into the starless night.

*

It could be said that the 1st Airborne Division was dominated by short and tall men. Because of their size they became prominent, noted for courage, daring, foolhardiness – indeed for their contempt of death. The two jockeys – Major Boy Wilson and Major Pongo Lewis – were tiny, even smaller than Brigadier John Hackett or Lieutenant Colonel David Dobie. The tall men were equally conspicuous. General Roy Urquhart stood six feet one and Brigadier Gerald Lathbury, when he did not stoop, was almost three inches taller. Major Digby Tatham-Warter counted himself among the tall ones.

The battle at the Arnhem bridge on the second day went from bad to worse for Tatham-Warter and his company. Elsewhere on the northern ramparts conditions were equally critical. Early morning mist clung thickly to the twisted steel girders of the bridge as German Panther tanks rumbled across from the south bank of the Rhine against light opposition. The tanks poked the long snouts of their 88 mm guns through the windows of the houses and fired at point-blank range, blasting out the defender with deafening explosions. The battle that had begun with a shining sun, a cloudless sky and little wind to trouble the dropping paratroopers had undergone a dramatic transformation in twenty-four hours. Tatham-Warter, whose three platoons were the only organized force to reach the bridge in strength, took warfare in a leisurely, matter-of-fact manner. However, he had not shown the same optimism as his commander, Lieutenant Colonel John Frost, who had packed his golf clubs in his luggage to follow in the rear party from Nijmegen. Frost would not be needing them for some time.

Quite clearly, Tatham-Warter knew something terrible had gone wrong from almost the very beginning. But still no one fully comprehended the situation. The idea that only A Company under Tatham-Warter and a fraction of Major Douglas Crawley's B Company had managed to come this far – out of a total of three battalions that started from Oosterbeek – seemed incomprehensible. C Company from Frost's battalion had disappeared altogether. The route Tatham-Warter had briefly opened to the bridge on the river road had closed in behind him like a self-sealing tube. The boisterous, genial Major Freddy Gough with two of his reconnaissance jeeps, a Royal Army Service Corps platoon with a captured lorry full of ammunition, some engineers and the Brigade Major Tony Hibbert, had somehow managed to reach the northern ramparts. Small avenues were open on the first day. After that these openings were clamped shut by the steel jaws of the enemy. Brigadier Gerald Lathbury, who had set out on the first day for the bridge with the General, failed to show up altogether.

After the second evening, Tatham-Warter watched in alarm as great fires consumed the clusters of houses on the north side of the Rhine, where the airborne troops had taken up positions. When Tatham-Warter fought in Africa and Italy he had always found good defence positions in the stony rubble of houses. At Arnhem, the houses simply burned down into charred, red-hot embers and the troops had to move from house to house to avoid being roasted alive.

Casualities mounted very quickly at the bridge. By the third night half the defenders were wounded or killed. Frost's second-in-command, Major David Wallis, was shot dead by a sniper. The loss of Wallis, an old friend, grieved Frost tremendously. Shortage of ammunition among the English began to tell. The enemy now moved with relative freedom, choosing their own time to cross from their position on the south side of the river over the Arnhem bridge to the north bank. The doomed men would see no more helpers stumbling by accident into the perimeter like the diminutive figure of Major Pongo Lewis on the second day. Behind Lewis miraculously had come the uncomprehending remnants of two platoons. A chink, just big enough to squeeze through, permitted Lewis and his men to pass before the jaw shut tight for them, too. But his support would do nothing to sway the battle and would only add to the casualities.

Tatham-Warter walked calmly around the battered positions

quite unconcerned about his personal safety, cheering the wounded and organizing his men in the shelled houses. Once, in anger, he poked his rolled-up umbrella – which he had picked up in a rubble heap – through a slit in a passing German armoured car, immobilizing the driver.

The expected arrival on Tuesday morning, the third day, of the Polish Parachute Brigade commanded by that fiery warrior General Stanlislaw Sosabowski, did not materialize on the south shore. It would, in any case, have been of little help. The Poles would have dropped right into the middle of the attacking German Panzers who were slowly eliminating the British and – by sheer weight of numbers and armour – becoming irresistible. But Tatham-Warter and Frost were further concerned about the news given by their prisoners from the 9th and 10th Panzer Division, who told how the two divisions were reforming in the Apeldoorn–Arnhem area. No airborne force had sufficient fire power to stand up to the weight of heavy armour. This depressing intelligence had never been fully transmitted during the pre-operation briefings. Also, there was no sight of the supposedly advancing British XXX Corps, which by now should have been in view. From the fragmentary radio reports from Division, Tatham-Warter deduced his own conclusions. He knew the fate of the troops was sealed.

A garbled radio report received on Major Tony Deane-Drummond's radio set before it lost contact with Division confirmed that the General was lost somewhere in the street fighting in Arnhem. Tatham-Warter did not know that Urquhart and his own brigade commander, Lathbury, were hiding in the attic of a house about a mile away. Neither could he know that Lathbury would soon be wounded and join him at the St. Elisabeth Hospital.

A particularly brutal assault on the third afternoon by Mark IV tanks barely beaten back with Piat bombs and anti-tank grenades, left the dwindling garrison at the bridge badly mauled. Tatham-Warter had been hit with shrapnel splinters and the seat of his pants blown off. But he did not feel amused.

The small force was reduced by half. There could not have been more than fifty men left on that third evening as dozens of houses burned through the night. Tatham-Warter thought the town burned sadly and magnificently. The roofs of the fine Dutch houses fell flaming into their own hollowed-out graves. Flames spread unchecked as Tatham-Warter climbed into an attic to watch the growing conflagration. The streets were as bright as daylight. He prayed the wind would not shift to the west, else they would all be burned out. The major wondered about the state of the civilians, many of whom still hid in the smoke-choked cellars. Then a light rain fell and there were a few hours of unexpected tranquillity as Tatham-Warter walked through the bitter stench of smoke to visit the remaining men of his company, who constituted two-thirds of the defending force.

Some minutes later Tatham-Warter heard a series of explosions further to the north of his position and a breathless runner came to inform him that his battalion commander, Frost, lay wounded – sprawled on the cobbled streets unable to move.

Frost had a deep, paralyzing pain in both legs and he dragged himself over the road towards the nearest house where Captain James Logan, the battalion medical officer, pulled him onto a stretcher. From here Logan took the commander to the Medical Aid Station. Frost's ankle and shinbone were shattered by shrapnel. He could not walk. As he lay on a litter in a cellar, Frost recalled an unreal conversation he had had a few hours earlier with Division Headquarters on the radio, one of the rare occasions when communications worked. He had been told a small patrol with ammunition and food was on the way through from Oosterbeek, but he did not believe it would succeed. He pulled himself onto an old ammunition crate and despondently put his head in his hands, knowing the end was near.

On that third day, Brigadier John Hackett, Commander of the 4th Parachute Brigade, had advanced barely a mile east towards the bridge. Over nine miles still separated him from his objective. A mile away Division Headquarters had been set up at the Hartenstein Hotel. The brigadier's advance on the bridge had been halted by more German troops and tanks than the determined Hackett could cope with.

By now the previous day's events appeared quite frivolous, insignificant by comparison. Then, thirty feet above the ground in the afternoon of September 18, Hackett's ash walking stick, purchased at Blands in Notting Hill Gate in London, slipped out of his hand and vanished into the deep grass of Ginkel Heath. He had followed his stick down and made a soft parachute landing in spite of the heavy anti-aircraft and machine-gun fire. As usual, he paid scarce attention to his own weapons. Personal firearms had little interest for him. He expected others, better trained in the use of weapons, to protect him. His walking stick had priority over his revolver. When a group of aged, frightened Wehrmacht soldiers approached the brigadier with their hands in the air, the irascible Hackett ordered them to stay where they were and consider themselves his prisoners. He would look after them when he found his stick. He retrieved it from the underbrush and then returned to the patient Germans.

There had been a small mix-up about the ash walking stick a few months back when Hackett misplaced it after a visit to his commander, General Roy Urquhart, in his caravan on the golf course at Moor Park. The next time the brigadier saw the stick, to his surprise, Urquart carried it. A large "U" had been carved deeply into the handle, which seemed to leave little doubt now about the ownership. Hackett's claims were dismissed by his superior with a kind but courteous authority that made it clear that the "U" stood for Urquhart for all time. Hackett promptly went out and bought another similar ash stick at Blands. He might have lost the first round in the battle of the walking sticks to his General, but he did not intend to lose the second to the Germans.

Now these incidents were all but forgotten as the methodical brigadier wondered what he could do to gather his scattered forces so he could relieve the beleaguered troops on the bridge. By evening Hackett was so occupied defending his position on all sides from heavy attacks that far from mounting an offensive his thoughts turned to consolidation and survival.

*

In the early morning of September 18, the second day of the battle, I had worked my way south with Watts over a railway track, through a meadow into the town of Oosterbeek. While last night there seemed to be Germans everywhere, today I could find none. I chose a well-tended garden in one of the luxurious villas facing the Oosterbeek–Arnhem road and stretched out on a canvas deck chair in the sun. No sooner had I made myself comfortable and sent Watts off to find some food, when the GSO2 Intelligence, Major Hugh P. Maguire, came over and said he had a job for me. Earlier I had made my presence known to him and told him where I could be found.

The job seemed quite straightforward. I had to take a jeep piled several feet high with ammunition, food and a #22 wireless set, a wireless operator and reach the Arnhem bridge. All I had to do was head straight down the road until I came to the town and then ask someone for the whereabouts of a Lieutenant Colonel Frost. According to the map Maguire spread out, the town was less than eight miles away. I went back into the garden and asked the thin, hungry-looking Dutchman in the golfing plus fours and chequered socks whether he would like to be my guide and interpreter. Unknowingly, I had made the best of all possible choices. I had chosen Charles Labouchère, an Intelligence agent who lived in Velp, a small town east of Arnhem. Labouchère spoke impeccable English. Maguire mentioned that the defenders at the bridge had been notified by wireless that relief would be on the way. In other words, I was expected. Before we left, Maguire ominously handed me a bullet-proof vest. I gave it to the Dutchman, who had meanwhile produced a World War I steel

36

helmet and the orange armband of the Resistance. Watts, hollow-cheeked and unworried, straddled the spare tyre on the rear. Labouchère sat on a box of compo rations. He held onto a Sten gun and tucked a spare magazine into his tweed jacket pocket. Squeezed in between the crates of food and ammunition, the wireless operator squatted with his head phones in position, trying to tune his set. I sat beside our driver, Martin. Maguire's last words to me were, "When you reach the bridge, don't forget to let me know."

We sped down the Utrechtse Weg for about ten minutes unhindered and then stopped before the railroad bridge that led into the western sector of Arnhem. A major from the South Staffordshire glider-borne regiment rose excitedly from a ditch and flagged us down. He asked me "where the hell did I think I was going." I told him. He looked incredulously at Labourchère in his plus fours, tweed jacket and night-pot helmet. I never did recollect the major's final advice, but it had something to do with notifying my next of kin. I told him I acted under divisional orders. He asked my name, smiled, bowed slightly and then politely, quietly bade me to continue. As I went under the railroad bridge he quickly jumped back into the ditch. I noticed several dozen other men flattened out alongside the road looking strangely at us as we roared by. From the high ground to the north, short, sharp cracks of German Spandaus could be heard. Several feet away, alongside me on the meadow that sloped to the Rhine, it seemed someone with a sharp, invisible rake drew long furrows along the earth. Under the embankment we had a certain amount of protection. But I could not understand why all along the Utrechtse Weg not a person could be seen.

Suddenly a paratrooper leapt out from the bushes and frantically held up his hands to stop and directed me between two small houses. My harassed battalion commander, David Dobie, stepped out of one of the houses to greet me. He asked how I arrived and why. He had forgotten all about the transport. He had no need for it. He said emphatically that the road ahead was blocked by the enemy. All of his officers except three were dead or wounded that morning from the machine-gun fire that came from the high ground to the north.

Eric Davies was among the wounded, some of whom lay by the side of the road. I went forward on foot to Dobie's most advanced position, about fifty feet further up the road to Arnhem. Three hundred yards south, barges were moored along the river back. When I returned to the jeep from the reconnaissance, Labouchère and the radio operator waited for me. Martin and Watts had meanwhile vanished.

The Dutchman and I went down to the river searching for an alternative route to the bridge. The Spandau up in the wooded, high ground to the north found us again. For an hour we did not move from behind a small mound of earth that offered protection. Finally we made a quick dash to our vehicle and gained the road before the German machine-gun could fix its sights. When I took the wheel of the jeep, I impulsively made my decision. I started the engine and turned east towards Arnhem instead of back towards where Dobie waited. I pushed the accelerator all the way down to the floor and the jeep leapt past our forward positions. Then, without warning, the steering wheel came off in my hands and the vehicle smashed uncontrollably into the embankment, hurtling us onto the grass and scattering all our supplies. About ten feet in front a steady, deadly stream of machine-gun bullets lashed the stretch of road where I would have been had I continued.

Labouchère had cut his leg, but not seriously. The wireless operator and myself were shaken but unhurt as we crawled out of the ditch back onto the asphalt. I bandaged the Dutchman's wound and we collected the equipment. The jeep lay on its side on the edge of the ditch without a steering wheel and I decided to leave it there. I thought then my mission had ended when a Bren-gun carrier suddenly came out from behind a narrow hedgerow and slid down onto the road. It stopped beside me, as if somehow the driver knew I wanted him. The Bren driver had nowhere particular to go, so I asked him if he would care to take me to the bridge less than a mile away. He calmly nodded his agreement and we transferred our supplies to the carrier.

Labouchère carefully, cautiously directed us north and eastward through a maze of small back streets towards the bridge. The scene now dramatically changed in a matter of minutes. Shattered buildings, overturned tram cars, dangling cables and broken telephone poles dominated the landscape. The splintering explosions of shell and mortars tore through the air, landing all around us. Occasionally I caught a glimpse of limp bodies sprawled over bushes or lying awkwardly on the littered road. The Bren-gun carrier, strangely immune to the destruction that surrounded it, kept going ahead.

From clear daylight near the river, the midafternoon turned into a deep, grey twilight filled with the smoky, sour stench of continuous explosions of 88 mm shells. About two hundred yards straight up Alexander Straat a long, slender gun mounted on a half track blazed away at some houses on my left and then swivelled in our direction. We turned quickly into a driveway where I had earlier seen some red berets, and stopped between two houses near the heart of the city behind the St. Elisabeth Hospital. Captain G. C. Roberts, the General's aide-de-camp, came out of one of the buildings off Zwarte Weg and asked me to follow him quickly inside.

General Roy Urquhart and Brigadier Gerald Lathbury were preparing to leave the house together through a back entrance when we met. Both men were anxious to move out from the cat-walk of streets into more open territory where they were less vulnerable. Barrel-chested, with hulking shoulders and a square tough face, all Urquhart's features and movements suggested great physical strength and determination. Lathbury – tall, stoop-shouldered and spare, mournful with sad, bloodhound eyes – gave the impression of nervousness, sensitivity and immense restlessness.

The General tried to reach his headquarters on our wireless set but it refused to work. He gave me several messages to give to the acting Divisional Commander, Brigadier P. H. "Pip" Hicks and his GSO 1 Operations, Lieutenant Colonel Charles

MacKenzie. I, in turn, informed him of conditions elsewhere. The General ordered me, with apparent good reason, not to proceed to the bridge. His messages to Division now had priority. Urquhart carefully stepped over the dead body of Major Peter Waddy lying on the back stairs and joined the impatient Lathbury and his aide, Roberts. The three men set off through the tangled garden to the north. The Bren-gun carrier swivelled about. The day was almost spent as we started off in the approaching dust hoping to find the route back to Divisional Headquarters.

*

At 1.0 a.m. on Tuesday morning of the second day, Major Tony Hibbert heard loud, then gradually fading shouts of "Waho Mahomet" coming from some buildings three hundred yards to the north of the bridge. He "felt a great exhilaration," as he believed it to be the long-awaited relief. But he did not know it was the last stand of the remains of a single platoon of the 3rd Battalion, which had drifted by chance into the bridge area and was now reduced to less than ten men. By the end of the day they would no longer exist. The cries grew very faint as they moved eastward and then died out altogether amid firing and shouting.

Hibbert, the Brigade Major of the 1st Brigade, had at the beginning tried to set up a Brigade Headquarters. But he arrived at the Arnhem bridge without his brigadier, Gerald Lathbury. His headquarters consisted of himself. He could not find anyone else. Hibbert did not expect to see Lathbury again.

With some amazement, at first light Hibbert observed the German artillery on the south side of the Rhine systematically knocking down every church steeple in Arnhem. "thinking, I suppose, we were using them as observation posts." Hibbert had thought all along that these same steeples were German observation posts and was relieved and also a little saddened by the destruction of these beautiful eighteenth-century buildings, their ornate stained-glass windows now shattered beyond repair. From time to time he could hear a bugle call sounding from the rubble of a house and answered by another nearby. This ingenious method of communication was part of Tatham-Warter's signalling system. Tatham-Warter did not trust radio communications in battle. The platoon buglers sounded their clear clarion calls to the incomprehensible astonishment of the enemy. They were always heard above the din and roar of the guns.

The painfully familiar pattern of the previous day began to repeat itself with more ferocious attacks. Through the broken windows in the attic of his house, Hibbert, about a hundred yards north from the bridge, watched the Germans rolling anti-aircraft guns into position on the south side of the river. Instead of pointing up into the sky, the guns were levelled at the shapeless piles of rubble on the north side of the bridge that had once been trim Dutch houses. Shielded in the remains of the houses were the few British defenders. On the cumbersome #22 wireless set Hibbert picked up some Canadian voices from the slowly advancing XXX Corps that were still in the Nijmegen area. He finally exchanged conversation with his contact at XXX Corps and quickly informed them that the Arnhem bridge still remained passable but would not be for long. He asked how soon reinforcements would be able to reach them. The reply came back slowly, "that they were putting in an attack to secure Nijmegen bridge and hoped to be there soon."

In his hourly reports, Hibbert wrote in his diary on the third day that "Two Mark IV tanks suddenly appeared round the corner and under cover, a 15 cm gun was unloaded and pointed directly at Brigade HQ." This was a hundred feet away. At this critical moment the #22 radio set broke down. Hibbert relied upon it to bring artillery support to bear on his targets. Quickly he evacuated the attic which minutes later received three direct hits, the shells coming from the south and passing out through the north. After a few minutes a British mortar from one of Tatham-Warter's platoons opened up on the German gun. When Hibbert looked for the 15 cm gun he saw a large crater in the road. The mortar bombs had detonated the gun's ammunition. The brigade major immediately moved to a building on the small square of the Domstraat. During the afternoon the Germans and British chased each other in and out of the gradually disintegrating houses to the north and west of the bridge. There were times when no one knew who occupied what house and frequently German and British troops would suddenly come face to face with each other shooting it out or retreating.

In the evening a Tiger tank drove leisurely down the main road to the Arnhem bridge from the north and passed Hibbert's brigade HQ, spraying it with machine-gun fire and pumping a large number of shrapnel-bursting 88 mm shells into the building. The routine chases from house to house, the deafening noise, the collapsing buildings, the carting away of wounded, the casual ignoring of the dead all became part of the daily routine. If you were lucky you awoke from a brief nap, shook yourself to make sure you were alive and carried on.

The dutiful Hibbert found a piece of paper and a stub of pencil, and in a brief lull wrote a report on the fighting of the first two days at the bridge. He rolled the paper into a capsule and entrusted it to the one small grey carrier pigeon he had carried with him into the town. Then he launched the frightened bird into the smoky night air.

The *Pie-Eyed Piper of Barnes* readied for take-off in the early afternoon of September 21, the fourth day of the battle of Arnhem. On the outside of the cockpit below the windshield the head of a drunken piper was painted in yellow and blue. The pilot, Flying Officer Jimmy Edwards of 271 Squadron, opened wide both throttles of the Dakota as he taxied for take-off over the grass runway of Down Ampney Airfield. In his spare time Edwards had become well known as the base comedian and entertainments officer. That morning he did not feel very humorous. His hangover had not yet worn off.

Edwards's commanding officer, Lieutenant Colonel Pierre

Joubert of the South African Airforce, told him at breakfast time that as he had already completed his two required missions to Arnhem, the third would be optional. However, Joubert was one plane short. Edwards volunteered to fill the vacancy. What he had seen of Arnhem from the air on his previous flights held a peculiar fascination.

Shortly after 1.0 p.m. the *Pie-Eyed Piper* became airborne and throttled down to its cruising speed of 110 mph. Flight Sergeant Knobby Clarke, the second pilot, sat beside Edwards but some minutes later went back to talk to the four dispatchers from the Royal Army Service Corps and to inspect the panniers of food and ammunition. Through the open doorway they could clearly see the familiar streets of Cirencester sharply defined in the sunlight from their altitude of 6,000 feet. Sergeant Sorenson, the wireless operator, and Sergeant Randall, as navigator, completed Edwards's crew.

On September 17 and 18, Edwards's Dakota had towed the fragile plywood Horsa gliders from Hicks Air Landing brigade. Edwards still retained nervous memories of the first lift to Arnhem. The glider he towed, overloaded with nine men and 7,000 pounds of equipment, prevented the Dakota from lifting as they came to the end of the runway. When the co-pilot excitedly shouted, "the plane won't get off the ground," Edwards yelled back, "get the bloody wheels up and it will." The wheels went up and the Dakota skimmed the tree tops with its glider in tow. Today Edwards felt a wave of relief without the weight of a glider to hold back the *Pie-Eyed Piper*. On D-Day, with the same crew, he had towed a glider of the 6th Airborne Division behind the invasion beaches. He did not consider these work-horse missions a noble role for his precious Dakota. After he left Cambridge in 1940 and joined the RAF, it seemed he had been assigned to every conceivable duty, but now for the first time he felt fully utilized. The weather on September 17 and 18 was good, the opposition from the air minimal, and he expected to be home today right after tea. On the floor at his feet he kept a thermos flask of hot tea and a pack of sandwiches.

As the *Pie-Eyed Piper* flew over the English coast, Edwards noticed suddenly that the usual heavy fighter protection had left his squadron. Not a single Spitfire or Typhoon could be seen above or below. He attributed the sudden departure of the fighters to the poor weather closing in over parts of Belgium where some of the aircraft were based. However, this lack of protection failed to disturb him. The Dakotas flew on course over the western part of Holland and then made a wide loop to the east and came back up north over the Maas and the Waal rivers. When they reached the Rhine, the *Pie-Eyed Piper* began its slow descent towards the airborne perimeter in Oosterbeek. Edwards could now clearly hear the intense, steady firing of guns from the ground and some of the bullets were coming uncomfortably close to the fuselage. The scene below confused him. A white Verey light flare shot up from the tennis court at the Hartenstein Hotel and barely missed the wing of the plane. Edwards thought it was some kind of signal but he had no idea what it meant. He did not know that someone on the ground was desperately trying to direct him to the correct dropping zone. A few moments later the four RASC dispatchers pushed out the panniers as the firing around the Dakota intensified considerably. Like most of the panniers that day, few from the *Pie-Eyed Piper* landed in the small British perimeter.

In a single panoramic view, Edwards saw the two sides posed for battle, as the Dakota swept across the British positions in Oosterbeek. He saw a solid line of enemy mortars and artillery pointed towards the Hartenstein Hotel, partially camouflaged by the woods. Self-propelled guns, tanks, machine-guns and mortars were all aimed at the grounds of the Hartenstein. Seldom had he been so glad to be in the air instead of fighting on the ground. He breathed a sigh of great relief.

After dropping all his supplies, Edwards turned the plane around for another look at the battle in spite of howls of protest from his crew. Some of the German ground guns were now pointing at the *Pie-Eyed Piper*. His curiosity now satisfied, Edwards slowly climbed to 10,000 feet to escape the barrage of shells and tracers that were coming after him. Around the Dakota a number of four-engined Mitchell bombers were flaming across the sky, struck by anti-aircraft fire and trailing black plumes of smoke before plummeting to earth. Several Dakotas from 271 Squadron burst into flames on either side. The war being fought below on that Thursday afternoon suddenly became quite personal to Edwards as the Dakota headed south across the Rhine for home. Edwards put on "George", the automatic pilot, opened the sandwiches and poured himself a hot cup of tea from the thermos flask.

A few minutes later he felt an uncomfortable jolt, heard a roar like a violent blast of wind, then several sharp cracks like the chop of an axe splitting wood. Sorenson, the wireless operator, was shouting wildly, but with the wind rushing in the open doorway Edwards could not understand him. Edwards did not require further explanation. A Focke Wulf 190 streaked out of the sun for a second pass at the helpless Dakota, cannons blazing as the shells ripped through the fuselage. Edwards put the plane into a steep dive, straining the already weakened wings as the *Pie-Eyed Piper* vanished into a cloud. When it emerged the Focke Wulf 190 was waiting. It came so close this time that Edwards saw the pilot's face. The black crosses on the wings flashed by at 400 miles per hour. No defence existed. The crew's fire power consisted of four Colt .45 pistols. Edwards had never fired a gun before. Now that the hydraulic system was punctured, the flaps and tail were almost unmanageable as cannon shells passed right through the plane. The two motors cut out. Three dispatchers lay wounded on the floor, unable to move.

Edwards gave the order to bail out while he remained at the controls. The second pilot and navigator jumped at 5,000 feet, but Randall and the single unwounded dispatcher could not move against the force of gravity as the *Pie-Eyed Piper* plunged into a steep dive. About 1,000 feet from the ground, Edwards managed to pull out the escape hatch over his head with one hand and level off the plane at the same time. The engines were belching black smoke and the rear of the fuselage

45

was on fire. In his mind Edwards had calculated his position about twenty miles east and south of Nijmegen. As a small forest loomed ahead, he pulled the wheel all the way back and hoped for the best. Luck stayed with him. The forest consisted of young saplings that bent under the weight of the aircraft. The plane ploughed over the top of the pine trees with Edwards standing on the seat, with one hand on the wheel and his head out of the escape hatch. Then Edwards was catapulted out as the unwounded dispatcher and Randall fell to the ground through the rear door. The Focke Wulf 190 had not completed its mission. It followed the Dakota down. And now once again it strafed the burning plane and the escaping crew. A few minutes later the fuel tanks exploded with the wounded dispatchers still inside and the *Pie-Eyed Piper of Barnes* was transformed in seconds into a blazing funeral pyre.

The co-pilot and navigator landed in German territory and were taken prisoner. Edwards and his remaining two crew members were found badly burned on the floor of the forest by a small band of Resistance men who kept them hidden most of the day. Later a local doctor, wearing a starched wing collar, tie and black suit came to the forest to treat Edwards's burned face. Before night fell the survivors were transported by car to the house of a priest. Next day Edwards met the advancing Allied troops.

On this day nine Allied supply planes were lost and sixty-two damaged. When the *Pie-Eyed Piper of Barnes* ploughed through the top of the forest of saplings near Nijmegen, Captain George Sykes of the 479th Fighter Group, U.S.A.F., led his formation of P-51 fighters on a sortie over the Arnhem area. An intense barrage of anti-aircraft fire struck his plane and the engine flamed and stalled. He bailed out and landed in the woods south of Ede. One of Bill Wildeboer's men found Sykes and hid him in the mental home at Wolfheze.

*

In the late night of the third day I lay down to sleep beneath some towering pine trees in the grounds of the Hartenstein Hotel, Division Headquarters. An orderly came out of the hotel shouting my name in the dark and said the General wished to see me immediately. I had acquired some notoriety in failing to reach the bridge and instead finding the General. Since then I had been typed as a man suitable for odd jobs or employment others were less inclined to undertake. In this highly improvised, improbable and most informal atmosphere my mobile patrol would report from time to time at Division Headquarters and take refuge there.

The same night I returned from my chance meeting with the General, Brigadier Hicks, the acting commander, had sent me back almost immediately into Arnhem to find Lieutenant Colonel Dobie and the commanders of the 2nd Battalion and the Kings Own Scottish Borderers. I was to order them to attack the bridge immediately. This was a terrible message to give. It became an order of annihilation, of self-destruction for the remains of the three battalions that were to advance while exposed to the levelled anti-aircraft guns of the Germans from across the Rhine. Labouchère, Martin and I went on to the attack in the dawn mist. We were able to extricate ourselves and limp back to the Hartenstein with three flat tyres to report on the carnage. That morning, Lieutenant Lloyd McKenna, the other Canadian paratrooper at Arnhem, disappeared in the attack with almost all the 3rd Battalion. I never discovered what happened to him. We had exchanged a brief, sad greeting in the morning mist before clouds of air-bursting shells drove us to cover.

The General had worked his way out of Arnhem on the previous day with his aide, Captain Roberts. Lathbury, partially paralysed by a wound in the spine, had been left with some Dutch Red Cross workers in the town. Now as I mounted the stairs into the hotel, I could see flames from burning buildings on the shores of the Rhine. Great banks of smoky clouds drifted back towards Hartenstein.

The General looked tired. I waited until he carefully finished examining the map on the table. He removed his earphones on which he had just picked up some faint signal from Frost's force in Arnhem and then quietly said, "How would you like to try and take supplies through to the men at the bridge? They can't hold on much longer." The General was a compassionate man, kind and composed under the most austere conditions. He pointed out with almost paternal tenderness that he could not order me to go. I had to accept with my own free will. I welcomed the opportunity to escape the python-like coil of German steel trying to squeeze the life out of the last defenders of Hartenstein. Whatever transportation and supplies I required would be provided from the dwindling vehicle pool and supply dump. In the darkened room, lit only by the stabbing beams of flashlights, I stood silently for a minute or two across the table from the General and his GSO 1, Lieutenant Colonel Charles MacKenzie. Then I left. As I went back out into the night, for some inexplicable reason I felt extraordinarily elated and flattered.

My little patrol, if successful, could hardly alter the course of battle. The General knew that. What had already happened at the bridge could not be changed; Frost and his men were doomed. But some troops still held on. And the General owed it to his men to help them if he could. The once beautiful garden of Hartenstein had become barren, moon-cratered. The hotel itself had been hit many times and was windowless, with large, jagged holes in the walls and roof. Casualties were mounting rapidly and the small cellar of the hotel was filled to overflowing with wounded and dying. The scene everywhere was one of monumental confusion, weariness and despondency. But in the heart of that confusion new men rose to calmly assume control as their superiors fell, so that somehow or other at every isolated engagement in every part of the Hartenstein front, leadership passed on down a chain of natural command.

The General offered no plan and gave no advice as I left him, but I knew no one could survive a mad frontal dash into

Arnhem. A solid wall of German armour blocked every passage eastward to the town. The Heveadorp ferry on the Rhine might still be working. It offered a faint hope.

My Dutch guide, Labouchère, had unfortunately left that night to seek shelter in a nearby house. His capture in my company would mean certain death. I had loaned him a fur-lined, leather jacket that once belonged to a Luftwaffe officer. In his plus fours and thin cotton coat he froze in the chilly nights of Oosterbeek. (When Labouchère came back the next morning to Hartenstein, I was gone. Twenty-five years later he offered to return the jacket.)

Captain Martin Knottenbelt, a commando and paratrooper of the Netherlands Army who had dropped on the first day, agreed to accompany me. His role until now had been to organize the Resistance forces after the airborne landing. But it had become too hazardous to formally mobilize them, although for several days he had been in contact with Piet Kruyff and Harry Montfroy at Arnhem as well as Bill Wildeboer in Ede. He had supplied those men with arms and a plan for immediate sabotage. Also, Knottenbelt had been informed of the existence of a telephone link from the PGEM power station near Arnhem connecting with the Nijmegen terminal. He was a man who could be of great help if we succeeded in penetrating the enemy lines. Knottenbelt had played a quiet but highly important role in the battle, creating a steady flow of intelligence from his Dutch contacts into Division Headquarters.

Lieutenant Johnny Johnson, the American liaison officer of the American 8th Air Force, also joined me. We had been operating together for several days. All his radar and radio equipment had been destroyed by mortars on the first day. I awakened two sleepy glider pilots from a neighbouring slit trench and asked them to join the force. Each had a Thompson submachine-gun that could be useful. Assistant Adjutant and Quartermaster General Lieutenant Colonel P. H. Preston found two jeeps that had not been immobilized by shrapnel.

Food and ammunition were loaded onto the vehicles and on top sat the glider pilots. At midnight I was ready to go.

*

On the night of the fourth day of the battle, Major Hibbert watched Arnhem burning brightly around the northern ramparts of the bridge and along the river. Clouds of sparks blown by the wind set fire to other houses nearby until it seemed that the town was being consumed by fire, raging, hissing, exploding into a massive display of destruction. There was no water. None to drink and none with which to put out the fire. Flames spread unchecked in every direction. And that night more than one Dutch family hiding in their cellars was roasted alive.

Next day at 10.0 a.m. one of the #22 sets picked up divisional forward network near the Hartenstein. The first words Hibbert heard were those of Brigadier Hackett, "remonstrating with the G.O.C."* He heard Hackett say "yes, but you must realize that we have no anti-tank guns." This did not sound very reassuring. When the General suggested to Hibbert that the bridge defenders should organize Dutch civilians to gather up food and ammunition from the scattered containers dropped by the Dakotas, Hibbert explained with considerable restraint that this could not be done. No one could move from a house on any of the streets in daylight without attracting fire from mortars, anti-aircraft guns, machine-guns and tanks. The civilian population were in hiding in their dark cellars for protection and would certainly not venture out. He could not blame them. Scarcely any food existed, ammunition was scarce and more than half the force had been wiped out. However, the Brigade Major did send back his official estimate of enemy casualties, which he had written down in his neat handwriting.

*G.O.C., General Officer Commanding, Major General Roy Urquhart.

8 half-tracks destroyed
6 Mark IV tanks
30 lorries destroyed
1 Tiger tank destroyed
120 prisoners taken
300-400 German casualties

By 1.0 p.m. that day, high velocity guns had begun ranging in on Hibbert's tiny Brigade Headquarters near the square. Captain B. Briggs and Lieutenant G. Cairns, with twelve men out of their small force of sixty, withdrew there from the eastern sector. Action then limited itself to officers leading bayonet charges with a dozen men or less; like the one led by Lieutenant Barnett directly onto the bridge where Hibbert observed the small force being mauled by tank and machine-gun fire, so that half Barnett's men were left dying under the twisted girders. When the General came on the air again in the afternoon, Hibbert wrote in his diary, "that far from coming to our aid they (at Division) would probably call on us for support." He learned then that the forward squadron of tanks from the Guards Armoured Division were mired in the mud north of Nijmegen. At this moment Hibbert, like Frost, realized the inescapable truth. He began to make plans for the troops under his command to break out from the encirclement during the coming night.

At 7.30 p.m. the Germans began methodically blasting down the walls of the houses with 155 mm and 88 mm guns from tanks and half-tracks. Phosphorescent shells then put the houses alight. The deafening crash of the shells stopped occasionally while the German infantry assaulted the last airborne strongholds. To Hibbert, the brutal, emerging pattern became clear. The enemy was stepping up the pace as if desperate to crush the last spark of life out of the British. Indeed, these were the exact orders given by General Wilhelm Bittrich, Chief of the 2nd SS Panzer Corps, who still retained a good part of the tanks from the remains of the 9th and 10th Panzer Divisions. Resistance at Arnhem must cease that night so the Panzer Divisions could give their undivided attention

51

to the British XXX Corps fighting to reach the south approaches to the bridge at Nijmegen. The bridge across the Maas at Eindhoven had already been captured by the 82nd U.S. Airborne Division. Over the single, muddy, slender road that stretched nine miles north from Nijmegen to Arnhem, tanks from the Guards Armoured Division slithered off the route into the mine fields. Success of the grand strategy, Hibbert knew, depended on the small, beleaguered force holding the bridge over the Rhine. And their hours were numbered.

When the Major went down to the basement of his Brigade Headquarters, where Captain James Logan and Captain D. Wright – with a medical section – had set up an aid post, he estimated there were more than 250 wounded jammed into the congested space. The situation was further complicated by the lack of water. Both doctors had been without sleep from the first day. At eight o'clock that evening the building burst into flames from several hits by phosphorous shells, and while the wounded were being treated in the cellar the wooden building above them burned fiercely. Hibbert arranged for the evacuation of the wounded to another house. But as they moved from house to house the phosphorous shells followed them. When the Major made a short reconnaissance to the north of the perimeter, some Germans driving a British jeep roared by, almost running him down. Tanks and half-tracks clattered up and down the streets unopposed. Every once in a while he observed fleeing figures in red berets stealthily moving from the cover of one burning building to another.

At midnight Hibbert evacuated what troops he could find to the local schoolhouse about a hundred yards further to the north. His force comprised two platoons, each of five sections with an officer in command of every section. The section commanders informed Hibbert "whereas nearly everyone in the school was armed, that the ammunition situation was very bad." Each Bren and Sten gun had but one magazine apiece. The men were also exhausted. Hibbert could find no more troops and concluded correctly that the remainder of the defenders had been overrun. Around the bridge, the buildings not already aflame were crumbling into hot, smouldering rubble. The burned houses for many hours became ovens of red embers. At midnight Hibbert spoke to all the officers and men he could find in the schoolhouse. He told them that they could hold out for about another six hours against all the tanks and Germans in the immediate vicinity with their ammunition. But they no longer commanded the bridge.

A few hours before dawn the bone-weary Hibbert waited with his men in the school. The time had come to leave the burning, smoke-filled town. On the last radio communication from Division before Frost was wounded, the General had said supplies were on the way. In whatever direction Hibbert looked, he could see no sign of that help. Nor could he imagine how anyone could possibly find a way through seven miles of German-occupied terrain to relieve them. Hibbert then released all his sections with instructions to find their way through the maze of walls, streets and houses westward to Oosterbeek the best they could. Hibbert himself commanded the last section.

When the Brigade Major cautiously tried to move out of Arnhem in the dawn, he found all routes westward blocked by Germans. At first light he advanced no further than the great shell-torn Protestant cathedral about three hundred yards north and west of the bridge. Accompanied by the indomitable correspondent Anthony Cotterill, Hibbert took refuge in the rear garden of an empty house. He put two of his men in a toolshed and barricaded the remainder in a bedroom. Major Denis Mumford "curled himself up in a wooden crate, while Anthony Cotterill and I plumped for the coal bin." That morning German infantry and tanks filtered unopposed between the burning buildings, approaching from the south, east and north and took possession of the bridge and all the town.

*

My second attempt to reach the bridge at Arnhem ended in dismal failure.

The disaster would have been more complete had the Germans been less lethargic and the hour not so late. My two jeeps had roared out of Hartenstein shortly after midnight down the dirt road to the Rhine. The tall Knottenbelt sat discontentedly beside me pouting, squinting through his thick-lensed, rimless spectacles into the cold mist. More than slightly sceptical of the whole scheme, Knottenbelt had rejected every plan I had offered but one – southward over the Driel ferry and then east along the south shore to Arnhem. We did not plan beyond that. His face, smooth and ruddy like a child's, showed no emotion. Although an Oxford graduate and highly Anglicized, Knottenbelt still spoke fluent Dutch. A successful commando in France, he had only recently parachuted behind the lines in Holland and returned to England a few months ago.

I had thought a mad dash down one of the roads to the north or east would have a better chance of success. A single jeep might crash through the ill-defined defences. But it would have been impossible we later learned, and probably suicidal. On the map by the lamplight of Colonel MacKenzie's desk in Hartenstein, it all looked quite possible. He told me the enemy was disinclined to fight in the dark. I would have liked to believe him. On the night of September 20, there appeared to be incalculable confusion at the Heveadorp ferry – equal to our own. The scarred beech trees that lined the way down to the river cast giant shadows across our path. Only the shattering roar of our jeeps broke the silence, announcing our presence to all who were interested.

We stopped about fifty feet short of the Rhine on the narrow asphalt road that sloped down to the ferry. Johnson thought he heard Welsh being spoken. In error he switched on the headlights and the beams shattered against the impenetrable mist. We could barely see the outline of the ferry. It listed at an awkward angle about fifty feet from shore. Some weird shouts came from the undergrowth on the side of the road shortly after the two glider pilots disappeared into the brush to investigate. I never saw them again. The Heveadorp ferry lay beyond our reach. A thick wire cable extending across the river controlled the movements of the boat through a system of wheels and gears attached to the deck. In the cold, squally night the swift-moving river looked decidedly unfriendly. If we succeeded in pulling the ferry to shore and putting the jeeps aboard we would then have to winch ourselves three hundred yards across the river to the south shore. A ramp on either end of the ferry could be lowered to load the vehicles. If we were to cross the river that night we would have to act quickly.

However, I was puzzled by the absence of a small band of our engineers and paratroops who were supposed to be guarding the Heveadorp crossing. Slit trenches on the side of the road were abandoned. A few Sten guns with empty magazines lay in the ditches. The mist on the road had become so dense I could barely see the jeep parked a few feet behind. Without warning a sapper from the engineering platoon stumbled out of the woods, dazed and lost, looking, he said, for some wounded companions. He told us of a German column that had attacked the crossing half an hour ago and was beaten back by hand grenades. The defenders of Heveadorp had withdrawn to the Hartenstein Hotel. We were by ourselves in the fog.

I decided to board the ferry and see whether it could be moved. I tucked my revolver into my jacket and swung out into the river along the steel cable. After a few feet the cable sagged from my weight into the icy water and I went under in the current, bobbed up again and continued. With my ballooning trousers dripping water I hauled myself aboard the steel deck. The mist completely obscured both Knottenbelt and Johnson waiting for me on shore. I took a good look at the thick steel wire that wound around a great steel drum that operated a series of gears. The winding and unwinding of the cable winched the ferry between the two shores. I released the lever that locked the drum and it spun wildly, uncontrolled, and the boat slipped further into the stream before I could wedge the lever into place again. For several minutes I struggled un-successfully with the mechanism, attempting to wind the jammed drum. I shouted for Johnson to help and in a few minutes, more agile and acrobatic than myself, he rose out of the mist and lightly pulled himself aboard. Both of us were incapable of turning the drum. By the shaded light of Johnson's flashlight we discovered the reason. The gears had been smashed. The ferry was destined to remain in the river for many more months. (However, my knowledge of the ferry's location would later prove important as well as being the cause of a personal disaster.)

Nothing more could be accomplished. We slid back down the cable to the shore and mounted our jeeps. Knottenbelt and Johnson felt as dejected as I did. The Germans rustling beside us through the underbrush kept a respectful distance, shouting and calling to each other. I reported my failure to Lieutenant Colonel MacKenzie at the Hartenstein, standing before him in a puddle of dripping water. He nodded sympathetically and told me to change my clothes. Nowhere in that dark, tense room could I see the General. It was just as well.

The sickening thud of mortars awakened me punctually at 9.0 a.m. on the attic floor of the Hartenstein Hotel the next morning. Mortars dropped by the thousands from every conceivable direction. In the attic, where I had been drying out, shrapnel flew in from all angles through the partially demolished room. I ran down the stairs with Johnson and discovered the Operations room had moved into the basement. Knottenbelt had vanished with his Dutchmen. All guides and local helpers were ordered to leave the division for their own safety. Labouchère, my guide, faded that morning into the anonymity from which he had been plucked.

In the cellar one had to tread carefully between the wounded who occupied all the available space. Morphine was being freely injected and many of the wounded lay in silent comas. That peculiar, decaying smell of septic wounds mixed with the putrescent odour of excrement became overpowering. MacKenzie ordered me to go around the perimeter with my jeep patrol plugging up holes in the defences with as much firepower as I could muster. Only one jeep worked. Mortar fragments had immobilized the engine of the other. Johnson and I took two Bren guns, ammunition and rations, and left the compound as mortars continued to blast through the grounds.

*

We drove south to the river to the Lonsdale force. This decimated band of survivors constituted the remains of the three battalions which had failed to reach the bridge. They had retreated to the shattered Oosterbeek church, a modestly constructed building overlooking a large grassy plain that extended to the shore of the Rhine. The ragged force was all that protected Hartenstein from the east and guarded the escape route for the division down to the river. If anyone had asked why I went to the river I could only answer by saying we were curious as to what lay on the other side. The mystery of what lay beyond the water would determine our fate.

Major Dickie Lonsdale, second-in-command of the 11th Battalion, dropped at Ginkel Heath on the second day of the battle in the early afternoon. The Dakota that carried Lonsdale was struck by anti-aircraft fire countless times. It received 287 punctures in the wings and fuselage. Lonsdale, hit in his right hand by a piece of shrapnel, lost his precious signet ring that had been handed down from his great-uncle, Lord Araghdale. He considered this a bad omen.

When I saw him in the Oosterbeek church, the wound in his hand that kept him for two days at Division Headquarters was still bandaged. In addition, Lonsdale had a bloody bandage wrapped around his head as he moved among his 175 men, who were all that remained after a particularly brutal German attack earlier that morning, which had thrown the force back to the church. Lonsdale and his men had retreated to the uncertain safety of the churchyard. That morning the major stood in the pulpit of the church and lectured to his troops on how to defend themselves while they cleaned their weapons in the pews. Lonsdale, always a brash, boisterous, outgoing character, had the independence and grim sense of humour that allowed him to rise to the occasion. For a few minutes Johnson and I sat and listened in amazement to his abusive, fighting sermon. When it ended the men in the pews wrung out their soaked clothes, picked up their guns and took up their positions around the church.

We passed through the last of the Lonsdale force in the afternoon, explaining we would be returning the same way within twenty-four hours.

While most of the glider pilots were under command of Major Boy Wilson, Staff Sergeant Alan Kettley was not. One week after he had jolted his Horsa glider to a stop on Ginkel Heath, Kettley settled down uneasily in the spacious eight-room house where he chose to make his last stand. He looked out to the north from a position about two hundred yards away from the Hartenstein Hotel. He knew the hotel was supposed to be his headquarters, but he had never seen the place nor did he really know in which direction to go if anyone ordered him to retreat – providing anyone could find him and his few men to give the order. But he did not believe anyone cared. The last seven days had melted together into one unending day, the events of which bore no relation to time. A particularly neat individual, Kettley always carried a pair of nail clippers wherever he went. Whenever a lull occurred in the fighting, he would take out his clippers and clean and pare his finger-nails. He hated the dirt and grime and his inability to wash. At least he could keep his nails clean.

On that beautiful day when he landed his glider on the heath, Kettley thought it would be a short and lovely war. Glider pilots were not supposed to remain with the troops longer than twenty-four hours. He had been tossed garlands of flowers by the civilian population and Dutch maidens had passed him cold beer. Kettley later joined a small group of men who started on their own marching towards the Arnhem bridge. Everyone seemed to be going that way on September 17, so he joined the march. When on the first night he met a paratroop private going in the reverse direction, Kettley, for no good reason that he could recall, accompanied him and found himself in trouble. Both he and the private were suddenly trapped into fighting for survival against a platoon of SS troops who chased them from one rear garden to another. Kettley finally escaped and returned to Oosterbeek alone, more confused about what to do than when he first landed.

When the glider pilot stumbled onto the Lonsdale force near Oosterbeek church several days later, he took a Bren gun away from a dead soldier and set up an observation post in the attic of a derelict house. After a few minutes he saw a German self-propelled gun with infantry approaching and called on an artillery officer in the next building to put down fire. The artillery officer had promised to call on his guns for support, but no artillery barrage followed. Kettley observed the self-propelled gun closely with his binoculars for several seconds and realized he looked directly into the barrel. A few seconds later the shell crashed into the building about a foot below him and he fell through the ceiling and landed half way down the stairwell, bruised but unwounded. He did not know until several years later, when he became partially crippled, that the fall of twenty-five feet had moved his pelvis two inches out of alignment.

Later in the day the sergeant transferred to another building, where he met a fellow pilot, Mac Gwynne. Gwynne frequently left Kettley alone in the house and engaged in his favourite pastime of hunting snipers in the woods, at which he had become expert. On one occasion Gwynne returned from his one-man war party carrying a German officer's epaulette as a trophy. On another, he found a dusty old gramophone in the living room debris and some Bing Crosby records that he played at full volume all through the day and night. Bing Crosby crooned uninterrupted to the Germans across the gardens and shattered houses of Oosterbeek until September 23. On that afternoon, a German Tiger tank pulled up on the street about fifty yards away and swung the muzzle of its 88 mm gun towards Kettley. It began pulverizing the top of the house, working slowly down towards the ground floor. Bing Crosby stopped suddenly in the middle of a bar from "When the Blue of the Night Meets the Gold of the Day." German infantry, who apparently never heard of Bing Crosby, appeared yelling obscenities and attacked the house. Kettley recalls a wire picket fence in the garden cemented into concrete foundations. The fence was too high to vault over and too strongly constructed to knock down. When the time came to escape Kettley, possessed by an unknown strength, tore out the fence with his bare hands and then dived into a slit trench in the next garden.

Sitting in the garden, Kettley discovered a lost, dazed lieutenant from the glider-borne troops. One arm hung limply at his side. The stump was bandaged, but the muscle and bone were exposed. Sickened by the sight, Kettley could not move for a few seconds. When he recovered, he helped the wounded officer to the regimental aid post near the Oosterbeek church, where the casualties were laid out in the garden. A stack of bodies about three feet high was piled one on top of the other like cordwood, and while the horrified Kettley watched, one of the bodies on top of the pile moved his hand to scratch his nose. When Kettley reported this to the medical orderly the body was pulled out of the stack and brought inside the first aid post. Many years later this ghoulish incident became Kettley's recurring nightmare.

The glider pilot had slung his Sten gun across his back when he helped the stricken lieutenant. When he suddenly looked at his gun he found the barrel twisted and useless from a direct hit by shrapnel. He discarded the Sten, picked up a rifle and a pouch of ammunition, and entered the nearest deserted house. A medical orderly, aimlessly leading ten walking wounded, asked Kettley if he would take the wounded off his hands since he had no idea what to do with them. Kettley put the men in the cellar of the house and told them not to move out. About noon a paratroop private showed up with a rifle but no ammunition and joined Kettley, who shared the few bullets he had. For a day and a half they sniped at any Germans they saw. From a copious supply of bottled fruit in the cellar, the men ate their first good meal in days. On the night of September 26, a peculiar, unnatural peace settled over the houses of Oosterbeek. About midnight a considerable mortar barrage fell further south near the river. Kettley thought hopefully that it must be Dempsey's Second Army coming across the river to rescue them.

But the next morning after dawn, through the broken front windows, the sergeant saw a German squad escorting a group of airborne prisoners along the road. With their two rifles, one grenade and six rounds of ammunition, Kettley decided not to engage the enemy. Later that morning platoons of Germans systematically searched each house in the street. When they came to Kettley's, the glider pilot called the wounded up from the basement and then went to the door to greet the surprised soldiers.

The one item Kettley did not surrender to the enemy was his nail clippers.

Tex Banwell managed to survive until the last day within the small defensive square that surrounded the divisional grounds of Hartenstein. Foraging for food one morning in the woods nearby with Company Sergeant Major Lashmore, an enemy machine-gun burst shattered the top of the first two fingers of his right hand. Banwell took cover and bandaged his fingers the best he could and then waited until dusk, when both he and Lashmore retreated to the protection of the Hartenstein Hotel.

On the morning of September 25, Major Hugh Maguire informed Banwell of plans for withdrawal of the division across the Rhine that night. Before midnight Lashmore and Banwell left on their own initiative south through the dark woods to the river searching for the embarkation area. Although they could hear the throb of motor boats and crash of mortars exploding upon the water close by, they were unable to locate the correct rendezvous. After an abortive effort to swim the river – which they found too swift to breach – they redressed and returned to the deserted grounds of the Hartenstein. Banwell hoped to find a pannier containing food and ammunition on which they could survive until they could make contact with friendly Dutchmen. For the last three days neither of the men had eaten.

In the thick woods near the Heveadorp ferry, they at last found a full food container. It hung by some shroud lines from a treetop. Banwell climbed up and cut it loose. It crashed noisily to the ground in the otherwise silent morning of September 26. As the two men anxiously tore open the metal pannier to get at the food, Banwell suddenly felt the uncomfortable barrel of a machine-gun thrust hard into the small of his back. A party of ten Germans encircled the two men. The sergeant slowly raised his arms, his right hand still swathed in the filthy, bloody bandage.

That afternoon a German doctor treated the wound and wrapped it in clean gauze. The following morning Banwell joined a growing procession of ragged prisoners marching north from Oosterbeek towards the prisoner-of-war compound in the warehouse at Stroe, fifteen miles away.

*

From our hiding place in the tall grass by the Rhine I could see no sign of our advancing troops across the river. The land looked silent. When Johnson and I retraced our steps at dusk, we took up quarters in one of the large deserted villas in Oosterbeek where the gardens blazed with brilliantly coloured flowers during the day. Our jeep was parked in the empty garage. The house, like all the other silent, deserted homes with their shuttered windows and half-finished meals upon the kitchen table, increased the sense of desolation. We walked back towards Hartenstein through a small, dark forest, whose latticework of pathways had become familiar ground. The Germans were less furtive now, more aggressive, and their snipers had advanced to the immediate vicinity of the hotel itself. An enemy sniper in green camouflage jacket dangled by one foot from a rope attached to a tree branch. When the wind blew the dead man swung slowly like a pendulum.

Martin, my driver, was left with the jeep in the garage. If we did not show up in twenty-four hours Martin had instructions to return to Hartenstein and, if necessary, abandon the vehicle. I intended to cross the river that night to contact the forward element of advancing XXX Corps and show them the way to the division. It is true no one asked me to go, but on the other hand I hardly expected anyone to stop me. When I broached the idea to Lieutenant Colonel MacKenzie, he raised no objections. He had become accustomed to my bizarre requests and wished me well in my self-appointed task.

In the evening of September 21, Johnson and I started for the Rhine in the direction of the Oosterbeek church. Now and then we stopped and listened to the German broadcasts from loudspeaker vans somewhere on the nearby streets. Showers of leaflets fell from the sky enumerating in alphabetical order the benefits of surrender, punctuated by depressing swing music on badly scratched records. Oosterbeek church had gaping holes torn in the roof since our last visit. All the windows were blown out. The ashen-faced defenders looked as battered as the building itself. In some trenches dead men shared space with the living. A tired machine-gunner waved good-bye as we departed from the lonely outpost by the narrow path over the meadow. A Dutch commando named C. P. Gobers, who had been part of Knottenbelt's team, joined us at the church and asked to come as our interpreter. At dusk we reached a long hedgerow about fifty feet before the Rhine. I asked Gobers to wait by the hedgerow to provide covering fire while Johnson and I slid on our stomachs the remaining distance, dragging along two life preservers we had brought with us from the Hartenstein Hotel.

Several dull, grey shapes began to take form on the river as we watched and waited. Soon we heard the splash of paddles as some of the Polish Airborne Brigade under Major General Stanislaw Sosabowski appeared in rubber dinghies out of the mist. Then came excited arguments and loud shouts in Polish as Sosabowski's warriors stormed by without paying the slightest attention to us. Eventually I found the officer in charge and told him to contact Gobers, who would lead them to our troops, otherwise his men might not survive the walk into Oosterbeek. (Gobers never met the Poles, all of whom became casualties or prisoners. He told me this when we met some days later at the prison camp at Stroe, where he was threatened with execution as a spy.)

In an empty dinghy we paddled across the Rhine in the company of two Poles, colliding with another dinghy in midstream going in the opposite direction. We apologized and continued to the shore. In the middle of a nearby field about a hundred men surrounded the figure of Lieutenant Colonel E. C. Myers, the Chief Divisional Engineer. Unbeknown to me he had been sent across to organize the Poles and ferry them over to support the defenders at the Hartenstein. In the centre of what looked like a football scrimmage in the dark, Myers swayed back and forth. A kind of debate was in progress. Myers had difficulty in making himself understood. I interrupted briefly to inform him of my plan to contact our tanks and infantry and lead them back. He nodded, and returned to the scrimmage.

That night Johnson and I slept on a pile of apples in a barn near Driel, to be awakened in the dawn by a Dutch farmer in clogs bearing hot cups of coffee. Later we waded on munching apples through the endless orchards in thick dew that rose steaming from the earth. Several hundred feet ahead infantry from the Dorset Regiment returned our friendly greeting from their slit trenches when at last we stepped out from the smoky apple trees into our own lines.

*

The veteran Sergeant Major Robert Grainger, a paratrooper from Hackett's 10th Battalion, fought with his men for possession of an empty mill near the landing zone at Ginkel Heath under command of Captain L. E. Queripel. Seven times the mill changed hands in twenty-four hours. Grainger, wounded in the ear by a bullet that passed through the side of his helmet, was evacuated with four other men on September 19, the second day of the battle, to Wolfheze Mental Hospital. The patients were still inside and their howls and cries added to the other more deadly sounds of war. The hospital had been bombed by the 8th American Strategic Air Force before the invasion to soften up the area. General Urquhart said he took the decision with a great reluctance after being misinformed by Intelligence that the home was used as a German troop headquarters. Fortunately the Strategic Air Force missed their target.

At the makeshift hospital the slightly wounded Grainger was given a bare room and a mattress and told by the nurse, known only as Mary, to pretend to be one of the inmates when the Germans came. Next day the Germans arrived to take over. Grainger and the other airborne wounded wrapped blankets around their bodies, put bandages on their heads and danced with the patients out onto the streets of the town. In a wild scene the patients grimaced, fought and leapt about in a weird ritual, entertaining the amused Germans. Grainger forgot his army boots were visible below the blanket, but happily no one noticed them. When the procession finally reached a small wood about two miles north of Wolfheze, the nurse told Grainger and his comrades to flee. They needed no second invitation. They took their leave with grateful thanks for Mary's help as the pathetic little procession wound its way down the road.

*

Lieutenant Colonel Gerald Tilly, commander of the 4th Dorset Infantry Battalion, stood with his hands on his hips under a sullen sky surveying the Rhine. Dark smoke bloomed like flower petals and then fragmented. A drab curtain of bursting anti-aircraft shells hung over Oosterbeek. The lumbering Dakotas ploughed through this field of flak, followed orders, descending to eight hundred feet, and jettisoned their containers miles from the airborne troops. We stood mute, silenced by this brave, useless sacrifice of British and American lives. Communications had failed. Casualties had grown so frightening on the supply drops that volunteers were now flying these sorrowful missions.

I showed Tilly the location of our forces, for he awaited orders on the exact hour of his assault over the river. It would take place within twenty-four hours. Johnson meanwhile reported to his rear headquarters near Nijmegen but would come back to meet me at noon for our return to Hartenstein that night. He came back exactly on time from Nijmegen and at dusk we went down to the river where I met Lieutenant Colonel MacKenzie. The General had sent him on a mission to the Second Army to explain our critical position and he was looking for someone to take him across the water. I asked if he would care to join me in my rubber dinghy still hidden behind the dike. MacKenzie gladly accepted the invitation and as soon as darkness fell the three of us launched out and crossed the river easily without incident. Since we saw no Germans on either side of the Rhine, we could not help but wonder why the waiting troops of the Second Army had failed to move forward with more speed to the rescue. The way seemed open.

MacKenzie took the path to Hartenstein while Johnson and I attempted to make our way silently through the deserted streets of Oosterbeek to the villa where we left Martin with the jeep. As we walked that night my hatred for the men responsible for issuing the hobnailed boot intensified. As standard equipment this boot must have caused the death of many men. Hobnails clattering on the cobblestones of Oosterbeek sounded like cow bells in that unearthly silence. Soldiers were forced to bind their boots with rags and pieces of clothing to deaden the ugly noise.

A quick search in the villa and adjoining houses failed to find our jeep or driver. During the previous day a Dutch youth reported the presence of German tanks not far down the road. The jeep and driver were gone and the garage door shut. Martin now joined that growing list of men who seemed to disappear without a trace at Oosterbeek. Back at Hartenstein the weary and dazed defenders waited hopefully for some sign of the relieving forces. The crowded corridors of wounded, the derelict grounds, the shattered equipment conveyed the unmistakable feeling that the end was near. I wondered whether my luck would desert me. There seemed nothing more for me to do. I spoke to MacKenzie and he granted permission to recross the river and assist the assault of the 1st Dorsets under Tilly. The defensive square was now more like a squeezed, narrow wedge. If someone did not show the assaulting infantry where to go they would miss Hartenstein altogether. For the last time we followed our own secret path through the weary Lonsdale force. No one challenged us this time. The defenders around the church stared at us with glazed eyes hoping we had some news, but there was none to give.

Across the Rhine in the town of Driel, we entered a house with a large feather bed conveniently prepared with white sheets. Johnson and I undressed, sank peacefully into the great feather mattress and instantly fell asleep. Before dawn I awoke to a powerful hand trying to break my neck, flinging me back and forth against the pillow. I tried to reach for my gun but the hand held me powerless with strength greater than mine. A huge figure standing above shouted abuse in Polish. When he stopped, I explained where I had come from. Major General Stanislaw Sosabowski released his grip, sighed, smiled wistfully and departed.

At daylight, Johnson, my constant compaion for four days, said good-bye and set off for the 82nd U.S. Airborne Division near Nijmegen. I would not see him again. Someone once asked me who was Johnny Johnson and I said someone I bumped into at an hotel in Oosterbeek. That is all I know about Johnson. There was no need to know more. And when I inquired if anyone knew about an American at Arnhem called Johnson, no one did.

Later that day I met Lieutenant Colonel Myers conferring with Lieutenant Colonel Tilly of the 4th Dorsets. We discussed the assault across the Rhine planned for midnight, September 24. I was to go with the first assault boat to show the men the way to Hartenstein. Then at a given signal on my flashlight, two great amphibian DUKWs laden with food and ammunition would be launched on the river to the ferry road at Heveadorp. No one asked what the vehicles would do once they arrived on the north shore or how they were expected to reach Hartenstein. The objectives of the infantry were equally obscure. We followed orders. About an hour before midnight I located the leading assault boat hidden behind the dike and sat down beside it. Private Fokes, who had escaped from the bridge at Arnhem by swimming the river two days ago, volunteered to come with me. Then I curled up alone in the deep, damp grass beside the craft and waited for midnight, wondering what lay ahead.

*

Major Digby Tatham-Warter – with some small lacerations on his backside – and his second-in-command, Captain Tony Franks – wounded in the ankle – were taken prisoner. At the St. Elisabeth Hospital they were briefly treated on September 21 by an English medical orderly. As Tatham-Warter said, "he intended to make his stay as short as possible." After dark on the first night in the hospital ward, he and Franks left their beds and put on their clothes. When the German nurses went out of the room both men climbed down from the window of the first floor and crawled through a garden on the side of the hospital, hiding eventually in the nearby pine woods at Mariendaal.

Stealthily they made their way east by north out of Arnhem with Tatham-Warter's escape compass consisting of two metal fly buttons placed one over another.* They reached the railway tracks a mile to the west of the St. Elisabeth Hospital and rested. Both soldiers were thoroughly exhausted. At dawn they saw a farmhouse silhouetted at the edge of the forest. Two days ago the Germans had fed them a ladleful of mashed

---

*A button compass was made from two fly buttons which when removed left a drafty opening, but when placed one over the other constituted a compass with two luminous dots pointing north.

potatoes and one slice of unbuttered black bread. They had not eaten since. The paratroopers lay in the undergrowth watching the farmhouse for some sign of life, but it was as quiet as a tomb. Tatham-Warter decided he could wait no longer and would knock on the door for help.

The owner turned out to be a frightened little lady who lived alone. Although shocked at the sight of the two unshaven, ragged airborne soldiers, she instantly assessed the situation. She led Tatham-Warter to a loft in a barn behind the house where both men covered themselves over with damp straw and tried to sleep. Soon the little old lady returned with platters of fried eggs and cheese, which the soldiers devoured with a savage appetite. When the men awakened wet and aching after an afternoon sleep, Menno de Nooy of the Ede Resistance visited them. He assured the evaders that from now on he would take care of them and they should no longer fear for their safety.

Lieutenant Ronald Adams commanded the mortar platoon in the 156th Battalion of the 4th Brigade. On the second day of the battle on September 18 he accompanied a disorganized advance of his battalion in the direction of the Arnhem bridge where almost all the platoon commanders were killed, most of the field officers wounded and half the men became casualties. Those who were left were strafed by two Messerschmidt 109s. A self-propelled gun later caught the men outlined on a ridge and picked them off like ducks at a shooting gallery. Instead of a defeated German army, Adams found the enemy on the offensive and very much alive. He had been informed that the only air power would belong to the Allies, instead he saw only German Messerschmidts. After the third day Adams joined the retreat from the bridge, which had become a rout. From the time he wrapped his boots in sacking after midnight on September 20 and broke out of his encirclement near the Wolfheze Hotel, he became an evader seeking a place to hide.

For several days Adams and Captain Tom Wainwright, a

company commander in the 156th Battalion, hid in the woods by day and moved silently by night searching for food and water. They travelled west and north constantly fleeing from German patrols or finding themselves suddenly, as they did after a week, ensnared among gun emplacements in a German artillery park. They subsisted on raw turnips and tomatoes and shivered in their damp forest beds, demoralized by their inability to extricate themselves from the web of German defences. Every few hundred yards they encountered more enemy and wondered how long it would be before they would come across a friendly Dutchman. On September 25 they sought refuge for the night in a damp greenhouse which grew flowers. Here they were discovered next morning by a Dutch boy. After a few hours the boy returned with his curious father to look at the two peculiar Englishmen hiding among the plants. The older man gave each of the evaders a coat to wear over their uniforms and vanished. In the dawn of September 26, the thunder of shells and mortars stopped. The silence, incomprehensible at first, soon became meaningful. Fighting had ceased on the north shore of the Rhine.

Major Anthony Deane-Drummond was second-in-command of Divisional Signals. A smallish man with blond hair and calm, blue eyes, he conveyed at first glance an impression of misleading innocence. Deane-Drummond, better known as an escaper than a signaller, had already made two daring escapes in 1941 from Italy. Once captured at the very last moment near the Swiss frontier, he tried again and almost got stuck as he wriggled in pouring rain under the barbed wire fence separating Italy from Switzerland. He finally succeeded after digging a small tunnel with his hands, in wriggling all the way through into Switzerland. It seemed Deane-Drummond always became stuck in small places.

When Deane-Drummond ran out of ammunition, eight hundred yards short of the Arnhem bridge on the second day of the battle, he had with him twenty survivors from the 2nd Battalion. The house they unfortunately chose to hide in some hours later became a German fortification with the enemy placing their machine-guns at all the windows on the top floor. There was only one safe place to hide. Deane-Drummond and three other soldiers bolted themselves into the lavatory and locked the door behind. For three days and nights the four men stayed there, taking turns sitting on the toilet. Every so often a German would come to use the lavatory but finding it locked would obediently depart. Nobody questioned the unusually long time someone was spending inside. On the fifth day, September 22, before dawn the four men took off their boots and crept out of the building. At first light they safely reached the bank of the Rhine, stripped off their jackets, and swam the three hundred yards of swollen river. But the Germans were waiting for them when they arrived on the far shore. The men were driven back by car across the Arnhem bridge into captivity.

Deane-Drummond joined the more than two hundred prisoners who marched from the Arnhem church to the grounds of a large home in the outlying district of the town. That afternoon of September 22, before the Germans were to make their roll of prisoners, Deane-Drummond found another small place to hide. A cupboard seven feet high, a foot deep and four feet wide fitted flush with one of the walls of the downstairs living room. Once the Major reversed the mortice lock on the cupboard door the opening could not be noticed. When he tried out the cupboard for size, he found he could stand up but could neither sit nor lie. The provisions he took with him into hiding consisted of a can of lard, one water bottle and a jam tin filled with more water. Deane-Drummond estimated he could hold out in this cramped space for at least seventy-two hours. He would urinate into an empty can that could be dumped between the walls. He stayed there standing continually for thirteen days. On the thirteenth morning Deane-Drummond stumbled out of the cupboard into the deserted room half-dead, blinded for several minutes by the light. When his sight returned, he opened a large french window at the end of the bedroom and fell below into the shrubbery. Later he staggered into an apple orchard where he ate apples until until he became violently sick. Then he stretched thankfully out on the hard ground and slept.

*

My eyes were wide open but I must have been sleeping as I gazed at a few stars buried deep in the clouded sky. Midnight had come. I walked down to the assault boat where the Dorset infantry lieutenant huddled nervously. The other boats with quiet, helmeted figures hunched alongside waited for me to push off. I did not feel melancholy. I did not feel unhappy: I was thinking of all the things I had to do when I touched down on the far shore. The feeble force that was poised to cross could hardly shift the balance of power. I yawned and boarded the canvas assault craft, crouching at the bow as we launched out into the inky river. I passed the sunken Heveadorp ferry whose bow jutted from the swirling water. Lieutenant-Colonel Myers had been shown the exact position of the ferry on the map. I considered this information important. If the DUKWs bringing the supplies were not be be swept against the sunken boat and wrecked in the night, Myers should know its position.

The assault craft touched bottom gently at the Heveadorp road and I disembarked, pointing the way to Hartenstein. A fat infantry lieutenant leapt past me to shore and with a weird screech, scrambled up the bank and was swallowed by the dark. Further down river other boats landed and men were scrambling up the slippery bank blindly searching for the airborne troops they were meant to reinforce. In the chaos and darkness it would be impossible for anyone unfamiliar with the terrain to find his way through the narrow, twisting paths to Division Headquarters. Twelve men had landed in my assault craft, now on its way back over the river. An artillery officer lay beside me on the small patch of road to direct the medium guns of XXX Corps. Fokes, the survivor from the 2nd Battalion, waited at my side, listening. Unmistakable German

72

voices drifted down the road. While three nights ago I had quite easily driven to the Heveadorp ferry with Johnson and Knottenbelt, tonight it would not have been possible. Not far ahead logs had been pulled across the road, barricading the access to Division. If I thought the road safe for the DUKWs I would signal to Myers with my flashlight and the three, large amphibian vehicles laden with supplies would then be launched. Under the most favourable conditions these clumsy amphibians would have difficulty mounting the muddy embankment. If I had any doubt about the plan, the Germans quickly made my mind up for me. A deadly, intermittent stream of machine-gun bullets forced us back into the water to our knees. I lay there not moving, the lower half of my body in the river and my upper half pressed down hard into the earth. The artillery officer beside me calmly called for support without response. When I looked again, the artillery officer had vanished.

Fokes undressed, preparing to swim back to the far shore. I asked him to give Myers a message that on no account should any vehicle be sent over. The Germans had mistakenly concentrated their main fire around the ferry road. If they had only known their opposition was a single Canadian soldier who should not have been there in the first place, perhaps they would have left me alone. I threw away my Sten gun and stuck my Colt .45 automatic in my belt. Slowly, inexorably the machine-gun fire, then the mortars forced me down, further back into the river. The bullets were clawing the earth inches above me. When the mortars began to crunch down twenty or thirty feet away, I knew it was time to depart. In a few seconds I would be perfectly ranged. I threw away the flashlight, removed my boots and trousers and slid away down into the unexpectedly warm water. Fragments of mortars screeched through the air over the little bridgehead where I had once been.

*

On the afternoon of September 25, Lieutenant Robert Hardy, a divisional signal officer at Hartenstein, fed the last bits of grain to the last carrier pigeon. Hardy wrote out his message and rolled it up to clip onto the foot of the bird. He envied the bird, which had the marvellous power to fly into the peace of the quiet English countryside. Hardy retained his sense of humour to the end. The final sentence of the message read, "great beard-growing contest going on in our unit, but no time to check on the winner." He then released the pigeon from an upper-storey window, but to his mortification the pigeon flew a few feet and then perched on a nearby ledge and defecated. No amount of coaxing could move him. A sudden mortar blast rocked the building and the bird soared off excitedly. He circled high above Hartenstein Hotel, homing north towards England.

Meanwhile, Lieutenant Colonel David Dobie, the commander of the 1st Battalion, was being treated for shrapnel wounds to his left eye and arm in St. Elisabeth Hospital. His battalion had been butchered by the seemingly inexhaustible supply of air-bursting anti-aircraft shells fired from across the river over open sights. What men remained were cut up from the Spandau machine-guns that ranged over them at will from the high ground to the north. They were routed – trapped in the web of streets and fences – and finally fled for their lives. Someone who was in the attack described it later as "the stricken flight of a bloody mob." Those who escaped the first wave of terror and kept their heads were taken prisoner. No one knew for certain how it all happened. Orders had been obeyed. Those who escaped to Oosterbeek joined the Lonsdale force around the quaint little church on the river meadow.

Dobie and his adjutant, Captain Nigel Groves, were marched by the Germans to St. Elisabeth Hospital with the walking wounded; dazed, uncertain as to what had happened or how exactly the catastrophe began. Wandering through the large, cavernous wards of the hospital, Dobie had time to collect his thoughts. The number of wounded and dying startled him. He found he hardly recognized anyone. He had no idea that the

4th Brigade Commander, John Hackett, lay almost dead in another ward of the hospital about to undergo major surgery.

The churned-up front lawn of the hospital was covered with soldiers lying on stretchers. Others less badly wounded sat about in a dazed condition waiting for medical attention. In two small adjoining rooms on the ground floor used as operating theatres teams of British and Dutch doctors worked around the clock. German guards kept a loose surveillance of the wounded prisoners, even walking at random through the operating theatres during major surgery.

In the afternoon of his first day at the hospital, a guard took Dobie's watch, and while he showed it to a German nurse Dobie walked quietly out of the large building and hid in some bushes at the main entrance to wait for night to fall. No alarm was given and no search followed and Dobie stayed there until dark. Then he crawled across the road and entered a partially demolished white house, where he barricaded the door in an upstairs bedroom and fell asleep in a state of exhaustion. Below in the cellar of the same house the Dutch doctor, Van Beusekom, and his family had taken refuge for the last five days. When Van Beusekom went upstairs next morning, he forced open the bedroom door and found the sleeping Dobie. The doctor looked at Dobie for a moment or two, awakened him and then quietly, efficiently, dressed the officer's wounds. Although the two men could hardly communicate with one another, Van Beusekom managed to convey the idea that his house was unsafe for both of them. A German artillery battery had installed one of its medium guns in the rear garden and the gunners frequently came to the house to ask for water.

That evening, September 26, the doctor surreptitiously moved Dobie to a second bombed-out house, where the colonel slept untroubled all through the next night. Arnhem was being quickly evacuated and to remain alone without adequate Dutch protection would be dangerous. Van Beusekom gave Dobie civilian clothes and the two men walked to the home of H. B. Bakker, a Resistance helper who lived with several evacuees. Part of the same house was a billet for

German troops. The normally talkative Dobie, frustrated by his inability to communicate with anyone in this alien surrounding, waited for the opportunity to move from Arnhem. To date he had travelled a total distance of fifty yards from the St. Elisabeth Hospital. Although Bakker's house had been an evacuee centre longer than most others, the Arnhem SS commandant told Bakker on October 2 that he and his refugees must immediately leave the town. Dobie now prepared himself the best he could for the second stage of his journey.

Lieutenant Donald Olliff of the 133rd Parachute Field Ambulance sat dejectedly on the ground, not totally understanding his predicament. He recalled vaguely jumping out of the Dakota on the afternoon of September 18 with fourteen other doctors and orderlies and remarking casually that the pilot had put on the green light too early. But all that made no difference now.

Olliff had struck his head on the earth in landing and, stunned by the shock, looked about dazedly at the odd surroundings of pine trees, tall grass and ditches full of rain water and wondered where he was. His harness had not been released. He punched the quick release and it fell off. Another doctor, Major Brian Courtney, the second-in-command of his company, shouted "to get moving." This rude greeting startled Olliff, who lifted his gangling frame awkwardly from the ground, gathered up some men and obeyed Courtney, moving in a south-easterly direction towards where he thought he would find the headquarters of his field ambulance unit. A heavily armed section of engineers passed by on the way to Division and Olliff was later to regret he did not join them instead of striking out on his own. As armament he carried a .38 revolver, which he had never used before. The medical orderlies who accompanied him had no weapons. Within a matter of minutes the doctor came across two Army Service Corps drivers, one of whom had a Bren gun and these men joined Olliff. By the time the doctor left the dropping zone a third bunch of stragglers from his field ambulance augmented the mixed band of men. Olliff now commanded a largely non-combatant, small private army numbering twenty-nine. Like most of the airborne troops who dropped north of the railway track that afternoon, Olliff only had a remote idea of where he was going or what he was to do. In the pine woods he heard German voices and caught fleeting glimpses of enemy on all sides. In fact, if he had not left England so recently and had not adjusted himself with greater rapidity to the situation, he would have realized that he was surrounded from the moment he bumped his head on the soft polder.

A strongly armed German patrol saw Olliff and fired. Caught unprepared, the medical men took flight, followed by the two Service Corps privates. After this brief encounter Olliff found refuge deeper in the woods, thankfully unpursued by the enemy and minus the Service Corps drivers who became separated. Later on in the day Olliff had occasional glimpses of a single SS soldier, who apparently had been stalking him since morning. The doctor suddenly doubled back unexpectedly on his tracks and caught the surprised German hiding on the floor of the forest with his Schmeisser machine-gun tucked in an awkward position under his body so he could not use it. For a moment the tall Olliff and the prostrate German were face to face looking uncomprehendingly at each other. The men silently glowered at one another for several minutes. Olliff quickly decided it would be more prudent to retreat than to kill a man in cold blood, so he made off in the opposite direction followed by his twenty-nine orderlies.

Before the campaign began the doctor was given the choice of carrying a Red Cross armband or a .38 revolver. He had taken the gun, although he now doubted the wisdom of the decision. For three days Olliff and his orderlies wandered aimlessly through the deep forests of beech and pine trees with the single purpose of evading capture. On the fourth day the men for the first time began to experience the anguish of thirst. They had already eaten the last of their twenty-four-hour rations and began to realize they were trapped, cut off from their troops and without any idea where they were. The way south to the division was blocked, the way east full of SS troops and armoured vehicles while northward they could still move, but if they travelled in this direction they would be leaving their own forces. Olliff decided the best chance for survival lay in remaining in the protection of the woods – provided they found water. Unknowingly he had led his men to the edge of the village of Otterloo, just ten miles north of the battle zone in Oosterbeek. Every so often the doctor, needing the confidence of additional advice, would confer with his Regimental Sergeant Major Bowe, Corporal Pimperton, Staff Sergeant Hare or Private Trevor Williams. Olliff told his men they had three days to find water before their health became seriously endangered.

In a country where dikes were built everywhere to keep back the water, the doctor thought it strange they should be driven from cover by the lack of it. On the evening of September 24 one of the medical orderlies found a fresh water spring in the forest and the men slaked their torturous thirst. This water miraculously refreshed everyone and lifted their spirits enormously.

Next morning Bowe was sent to reconnoitre a nearby farmhouse. During his absence the area had suddenly become active with German patrols and the men hid from view while a detachment of the enemy set up a machine-gun post a few yards away. Eventually for greater safety the medical men crawled off in another direction and Olliff hoped Bowe would somehow find them. Bowe eventually returned to report that the farmhouse belonged to a friendly Dutchman and they should go there immediately. The Dutchman fed the twenty-nine exhausted men fried eggs, cheese, thick slabs of black bread and butter, coffee and then contacted the Resistance. On September 25, Driekus van der Pol from Ede, known as Flip, led Olliff and his anxious band to Mossel, to the Jagersveld farm which had become a regular stopping place for evaders over the years. That same day the doctor met Roelof van Valkenburg, who led him to the chicken coop of Gilbert

Sadi-Kirschen at the Langerwey farm near Barneveld. And thus Kirschen met his first evader.

When Olliff told the SAS captain he had twenty-nine medical orderlies with him, the Belgian immediately wired Moor Park for instructions. They came the next day. The message read: "Advise evaders to hide up in farm and wait until spring." Spring in England was seven months away.

*

The water of the Rhine felt warm as I drifted easily far out into the swift stream. At the ferry crossing the Germans continued to aim an unending barrage of mortars which crashed down on the landing road. Factories flamed along the banks of the Rhine like burning pyres, and the river reflected the yellow smoky clouds. I swam westward with the current. A piece of driftwood struck me in the back and I reached out and held on. Perhaps half an hour later my feet touched bottom as I came back to the north shore. Unmistakable German voices and marching boots crushed the earth above me. A column of troops was going east. I crawled onto the grass and waited. German machine-guns arced long beads of red tracers overhead. The prospect of becoming a prisoner was not very appealing and I chose to push out again into the water. I suppose I thought if I stayed in the river long enough I would float out through Moerdijk to the sea. The idea was quite preposterous, but this is what I thought would happen. I do not know how many hours I floated in the Rhine, but I passed burning factories and houses on both shores. When the current deposited me again on the north bank I was many miles west of the Oosterbeek perimeter. The sky to the east had a tiny touch of pink that shone through the murk and smoke that obscured Arnhem.

Clothed only in my underwear, caked in mud, I rose dripping from the deep river like some prehistoric monster and slowly dragged myself up the slippery bank. My teeth chattered as I trotted up and down the shore to warm up. I felt I would freeze to death or die of pneumonia in some enemy hospital if I stopped running.

Before long I heard the summons I expected. A guttural voice of an older Wehrmacht soldier beckoned me towards him. Behind strode a pimply-faced youth from the SS with a cocked Schmeisser pointing at me. I could see he meant business. I went along quietly to the headquarters of the battle group a few hundred yards north where I was exhibited before several German officers, barefoot, shaking in my underwear and dripping water. A soldier finally offered me a blanket and a bed, and paralysed with cold and fatigue, I fell asleep.

Early on the morning of September 25 an Intelligence officer shook me rudely awake and quickly began to question me. My dog tag with my number, name and religion was gone. I really had nothing to say. Shortly afterwards the officer returned with underwear, a civilian shirt, trousers and a pair of grey woollen stockings. About an hour later a German quartermaster, plump officious and angry, arrived, poked a large Luger pistol into my back and ordered me to follow him out into the grey, sunless morning. As I limped north down a pebbly road in my stockings, encouraged by frequent jabs from the quartermaster's pistol, my feet became cut and bleeding. Still he excitedly poked me on, urging me for no apparent reason to hurry. On either side of the road columns of indifferent, weary infantry moving up to the river watched the spectacle without comment. The puffing quartermaster waved down a car and sweating from the exertion, commanded the driver to turn about.

At Wageningen, a few miles north of the Rhine, I was signed for by an orderly sergeant on September 25 in the late morning. Then the fat, sweating quartermaster who seemed to regard me as his personal property deposited me in a barrack room occupied by an SS colonel. Barefoot in a chair in the corner of the command post, sipping a cup of coffee, I watched the quartermaster heil Hitler and briefly vanish. The colonel surveyed a map on the table as three well-dressed, highly proficient company commanders entered, heiled Hitler and with barely a glance in my direction began their meeting.

Shortly the quartermaster came back and took me away with him. We travelled north by Kubelwagen through Ede until at sundown we arrived at a large army barracks outside Harskamp, encircled by a high barbed-wire fence. Beyond the barracks lay green and pleasant countryside and narrow cart tracks that dwindled into a dark forest. A hundred and twenty prisoners, mostly airborne and Dorset Infantry, shared my captivity. After many arguments and protests about my cut feet, a Dutch SS guard brought me a pair of rubber boots. They were ill-fitting, but they had one enormous advantage. They made no noise when I walked.

I dreaded the idea of spending any length of time in captivity. Above all, the odious effects of heavy, black German pumpernickel became intolerable. Suddenly in the middle of that first night, the Germans emptied out the prisoner camp and we trekked four miles further north to the warehouse at Stroe next to a rail siding. Bleak cattle coaches waited on the single track pointing east to Germany. As dusk fell on that second day, the German camp commandant singled me out and asked why I wore civilian clothes. My explanations were unacceptable. Henceforth I would be considered a partisan. Next morning three grey, camouflaged Spitfires, hopping low over the hedges, flew across our prison and then roared away. One by one they returned from a greater height, swooping like eagles upon the locomotive and blowing off the wheels with rockets. Kirschen had arranged this small diversion which would delay our departure.

Most of the officers and men were weary of war and some were actually looking forward to what they thought would be the peace and tranquillity of prison camp. One Oxford philosophy graduate praised the advantages of continuing his studies deep in the heart of Germany. Another in whom I had confided my plans to escape looked around at the double rows of barbed wire, the Alsatian dogs and guards and told me not to try if I valued my life. The truth was, I think that even then I valued my life less than my personal freedom. I found no recruits among the few officers I had met. Walking around the barbed-wire perimeter that afternoon I noticed two sergeants coming from the opposite direction, obviously examining the fence with a more than casual interest. One was Tex Banwell and the other Alan Kettley. These two men were immediately willing and ready to escape.

*

Brigadier Gerald Lathbury never had much of a brigade to command. From Barkston Heath, Lincolnshire, to the meadow at Wolfheze was a short, uneventful ride by Dakota. Lathbury noted the exact time of his parachute drop as 1404 hours. Everything went calmly and almost predictably, except the "coup de main" to be carried out at the bridge by Major Freddy Gough's reconnaissance jeeps mounted with Vickers machine-guns did not materialize. The brigadier had doubts about the idea from the beginning. When his personal jeep finally arrived by glider at 1520 that first Sunday, he went off with his Intelligence officer in search of the 2nd Battalion. He instructed his Brigade Headquarters to follow. Soon he overtook Lieuteant Colonel Frost's slowly moving companies. General Urquhart previously had communicated with Lathbury urging more speed to the bridge. Lathbury then urged all his battalion commanders to hurry. They in turn goaded on their companies. But in view of the nature of the countryside and the unexpected response of the enemy this persuasion did little good. One might say the buck stopped with Major Digby Tatham-Warter's forwardmost platoon.

Lathbury, to his annoyance, soon found himself tangled in battles of company strength and became further upset by the sudden appearance of the General in one of the Arnhem houses. The personal fortunes of Lathbury after he met the General deteriorated rapidly. A few hours later he was struck by fragments of bursting shrapnel that lodged in his left elbow and in his back near the spine. The brigadier fell partially paralysed, unable to move. Lieutenant Jeremy Cleminson, from the 3rd Battalion, and the General helped carry Lathbury into the cellar of a nearby house. Then the General and the other officers and men of his strange little entourage went on their way and left the wounded brigadier in the care of a Dutch family, uncertain of ever seeing him again. On September 19 the Dutch Red Cross found Lathbury and carried him by stretcher to the St. Elisabeth Hospital. The hospital had changed hands several times and had reverted in the last hours to German control. The brigadier felt quite sick and welcomed the sight of a bed with blankets and the prospect of a hot meal. One of his first acts was to tear off his badges of rank and throw them out the window. Before Major C. J. "Shorty" Longland of the 1st Brigade's surgical team operated on the brigadier, he looked at the results of his surgery performed two years before when Lathbury had been wounded on the Primasoli Bridge in Sicily. A few grenade splinters were removed then from Lathbury's bottom. And as Longland regarded his former handiwork he playfully smacked the bare rump and commented that he was well satisfied with the job. This sharp smack on the bottom snapped Lathbury out of shock.

When a particularly heavy bombardment opened up on the hospital next day, Lathbury decided the time had come to leave. He planned to walk out through one of the many interconnecting corridors of the building which the guards were unable to police. At midnight on September 25, about the time the airborne at Oosterbeek were escaping across the Rhine in the boats of Major Michael Tucker's 23rd Field Company of Canadian Engineers, Lathbury walked quietly out of his ward at the St. Elisabeth Hospital. Like Dobie, he hid in the garden. When he saw no one followed he went north to the railway track and crawled on his stomach beneath seven cattle coaches, still in a fair amount of pain from his wounds. Before dawn Lathbury came to a meadow near the Johanna Hoeve farm where dozens of airborne containers still littered the field. He picked up a tin of soup and put it into his tunic. Beneath a tree he sat down to rest in the rain feeling thoroughly tired and miserable. But simple things in nature

83

always had the power to make Lathbury happy. The sight of two green woodpeckers on a nearby branch hammering away together raised his spirits. Close by he caught sight of a squirrel scurrying for cover and soon an inquiring hedgehog appeared from the underbrush. Lathbury, a keen ornithologist, was particularly gratified at the peaceful sight of these small creatures going about their business in the midst of war. War seemed to have scarcely disturbed the order of nature.

The main building of Johanna Hoeve's farm had been burned. However, in the barn Lathbury found some bales of straw on which he lay down and went to sleep. He awoke late, the rain still falling, feeling weak, miserable and wet. The future looked very bleak.

Major Michael Tucker had commanded the 23rd Field Company of Canadian Engineers since its formation in Montreal. He was a dedicated man, an arch conservative in private life who upheld the order of past things. But in battle Tucker made his own rules. He would try anything once. At the headquarters of the 43rd Wessex Division near Nijmegen at about 6.0 p.m. on September 25, Tucker was informed unceremoniously that the evacuation of the 1st Airborne Division across the Rhine would be largely his responsibility.

Meanwhile in anticipation of his role, Lieutenant Russel Kennedy had discovered the perfect hiding place for the storm boats in an apple orchard behind the high winter dike. About two hundred feet north lay the lower summer dikes that sloped down through ankle-deep mud to the river. Tucker's sappers would cross the Rhine from a position east of the village of Driel at 9.30 p.m. that night. A detachment of assault boats further west would commence operations at forty minutes after midnight. Tucker had taken a good, long look at the river that afternoon in the drenching rain. It raged in full flood.

The night descended quickly, black and moonless. German shells and mortars were soon falling near Tucker's company in the orchard and straddling the road that led over the dikes to the launching place. One of the sappers wounded from mortar fire had to be evacuated. Tucker began the dirty job of hauling and shoving the boats over the dikes, which were now slimy oozing banks of deep mud. The Canadian major had fourteen, storm boats under his command, each with a crew of three. A fifty h.p. Evinrude outboard motor powered the flat-bottomed, plywood craft. Twenty feet in length and six foot in beam, the boats were built to carry fifteen fully equipped soldiers. In the mud, the rain and the dark, the fumbling engineers who clutched at the slippery hulls felt the half ton of boat weighed double. One at a time the storm boats were hauled to the river and slid down the mud bank to the water's edge.

Tucker had sent four boats with a Protestant padre to the west of Driel while he kept the French Canadian Catholic priest, Captain Jean Mongeon. Therefore the river that night on the south bank divided itself into two religious congregations with Father Mongeon destined to have by far the largest. Ten minutes before schedule, at 9.20 p.m., Tucker launched the first boat, which sank right off shore. Rocks and boulders had riddled the bottom with holes as the sappers tried to drag it to deep water. German mortar and shell fire cascaded down on the river at regular intervals. Bren gun tracers defined on each side of the Canadians the width of the beach head. German Spandau fire replied over the engineers' heads with that rapid, ripping sound peculiar to that gun.

The second and third boats Tucker launched were sunk by direct mortar hits and the men killed before they could move any great distance. The fourth boat started its big outboard and thunderously roared away across the inky, black Rhine. Twenty minutes later it returned overloaded with wounded airborne survivors. Father Mongeon and the sappers went to work carrying out the survivors on improvised stretchers made from greatcoats. Tucker had been told he would be evacuating only able-bodied men, but fortunately took the precaution of setting up a medical aid post behind the dike. Almost everyone in those first few overloaded boats was wounded, and Father Mongeon – under fire for the first time in his life – worked tirelessly. He carried cans of petrol down to the beach, ministered to the casualties and gave his coat to one of the half-naked paratroopers. As the wounded were brought back in ever greater numbers, the engineers stripped off their own jackets to cover the freezing soldiers.

By 3.30 a.m. all Tucker's boats were operating, but they were having trouble with the motors in the rain. Electrical circuits were suddenly cutting out and the engineers were servicing them on both shores and out in the middle of the Rhine. Lieutenant Johnny Cronyn controlled the boats on the south bank while Kennedy organized the evacuation from the enemy shore. Tucker ranged over the entire operation trying to limit the chaos, keeping track of the number of boats returning and making sure his men kept going. Bullets seemed to be passing "between his armpits and under his crotch" and Tucker could not understand why he was not hit. Every four minutes another boat roared over the open highway of river, the noise drowned by the deafening explosion of shells and gunfire. Corporal C. F. Smith's boat capsized in the middle of the Rhine with a full load aboard when a mortar bomb landed in the water beside it. Only four survived. Smith, who could not swim, floated to safety across the water like a bat on his open greatcoat and went immediately to work again in another boat. Sapper D. J. McCready returned towing a disabled craft in his wake when his motor suddenly stopped for the third time. McCready had twenty-five men in his boat, but by the time the motor restarted and he reached Tucker, four of them were alive.

At 4.0 a.m. the first signs of a pink, wet dawn slowly spread across the grey sky. Two boats – McCready's and Kennedy's – were still serviceable and they kept crossing the river without stop. In a wild dawn ride the tough, huskily built Kennedy piled thirty-six soldiers on top of one another. Those who could find no space inside clung to the outside of the craft. Somehow it crossed the river. Before day broke the airborne survivors were fighting for the last places in Kennedy's boat. He had to beat them off and threaten to shoot to avoid capsizing. McCready's last trip was fortunate. As he came back with twenty-five men, the boat, riddled with machine-gun bullets, sank just as it ground to a halt in the shallow water.

Kennedy started off from the south shore for his final journey at 5.0 a.m. the boat and the crew now visible from both sides in the misty, dirty-grey light. The lieutenant filled up his boat as fast as he could with survivors and then threw several dozen life preservers on the mud. When he went to start the motor he did not have sufficient room to pull the start cord and he had to shove some men away. Slowly he managed to bring the heavily laden craft back to the waiting hands of his comrades. At 0545 Tucker received orders to cease operations. When he completed his count that morning he calculated his boats had made 150 trips. Out of the approximate 2,200 men who returned, the 23rd Field Company transported over 2,100 of them. The square-built, slow-talking Tucker, whom no one could hurry, had done his job.

At dawn on September 26, Tucker and his Canadian sappers officially brought the battle of Arnhem to an end. But the rescue role of his engineers was only beginning.

THE FLIGHT

On September 24, Corporal Hayter, quite conscious, was carried by two Dutch stretcher bearers into one of the small, ground-floor operating rooms in the rear of the St. Elisabeth Hospital near the chapel. The patient had a rather large hole in his abdomen and some shrapnel wounds on his face and hands. However, his mind seemed fully alert. In fact he had an illusory feeling of well-being in spite of the pessimistic prognosis. He was expected to die.

Earlier that day SS Major Egon Skalka, making the rounds with the British doctor, Captain Lipmann Kessel, had pointed a finger at Hayter. He recommended euthanasia, his custom with all serious head and stomach wounds. Kessel, who had been operating almost steadily for eighteen hours, casually mentioned he might as well make an attempt to save the corporal's life. The corporal had twelve perforations in two sections of his intestine. One perforation was inclined to be lethal. Skalka did not know that the Jewish Kessel, in addition to having a special interest in Hayter, "had on his own private war with the Nazis."

The patient on the stretcher with the ashen-grey face, cleanly shaven except for a small, finely trimmed moustache, lay still before the massive injection of morphia. Quiet and defiant. A slender man, five feet six inches tall, he possessed an unusually powerful will to live. He had told Kessel he did not intend to die no matter what the doctor thought. The fatigued Kessel then went to work and performed the outstanding operation of his career, under what can only be described as primitive conditions. While he operated German guards in jackboots would wander into the operating theatre and peer curiously over the doctor's shoulder. The operation lasted almost three and a half hours. Kessel kept his promise and patched up his patient. As his fellow doctor, Theo Redman, said, "if Victoria Crosses were given to doctors, Kessel earned one that day." What few people knew was the corporal's true identity. The medical orderlies who carried the unconscious soldier to his bed recognized the man. It was Brigadier John Hackett, the commander of the 4th Parachute Brigade. When Kessel asked Hackett in later years if he could mention the incident in a report, Hackett wrote back, "My dear fellow, it is your stomach, not mine. You may do with it as you wish."

On September 24, at the St. Elisabeth, Hackett came within a dice throw of meeting the same fate as two of the men whom he admired most in his life. His adolescent hero, T. E. Lawrence, had influenced the brigadier ever since he studied the "greats" at Oxford, where it was "a close thing" whether he would become a don or a professional soldier. Orde Wingate had befriended Hackett in Palestine and Syria in 1939 when both men guarded the Trans Iraqian oil pipeline. Wingate had patrolled the pipeline with his Palmach troops from the Jewish settlements while Hackett commanded an Arab detachment. Both officers made sure their troops never met.

Lawrence and Hackett had a good deal in common. Both had attended the same university, admired the same classics, were deeply infatuated with the Middle East. Their natures were similar. Both were products of the close, academic community of pre-War Oxford. They were hard, ascetic characters, cold in their emotions, possessed of certain sharp academic brilliance, lonely, solitary figures who kept slightly aloof from the men around them. Both were really incurable romantics. Hackett might have easily been another Lawrence but he came to Arabia too late. However, his experiences in Holland would be almost as incredible and, in a personal sense, equally profound as those experienced by Lawrence in the desert. Lawrence and Wingate had died suddenly in accidental crashes. One on a motorcycle on a lonely stretch of country road in England, the Chindit leader when his plane dived unexpectedly into a jungle in Burma. Hackett probably thought his death, if it came in war, would be lingering, painful. But he refused to believe it was in the dice.

On September 18, the Catholic priest, Father Daniel McGowan, dropped with the headquarters of Hackett's 133rd Parachute Field Ambulance on Ginkel Heath. He had been spared the sacrilege of falling into battle on Sunday with the 1st Brigade and thus missed a more peaceful reception. But it had not made much difference. As he floated down from the sky fate had already begun irrevocably to direct the course of his existence. Before him lay two shattering personal experiences. The first would be of a deeply spiritual nature. The second would strike from without and could be considered an act of God. (McGowan, when he returned home long afterwards, shocked all his friends by renouncing the priesthood and marrying. Some years later polio totally paralysed him. The disability was so complete that a close friend and former medical officer prayed McGowan would not survive the horrible prospect of continuing to live as a vegetable.) As he come down upon the heath on that bright Monday afternoon, perhaps he would not have chosen to live out the day had he possessed the power to divine the future.

McGowan, although not a soldier, could easily see that all the exploding mortars, machine-gun firing and confusion of running men looking for their leaders signified nothing was going according to plan. With his Bible in one hand, he soon found more wounded to administer last rites to than he believed possible. They were all around, and more were dropping from the bursting mortars and shells. Much of the heath was ablaze and as soon as he could he set off with an orderly in a jeep to the Oosterbeek crossroads where the Vreewijk and Schoonoord Hotels were used as hospitals. Most of that night he assisted Captain Peter Smith, a surgeon who operated nearby in the surgery of a Dutch dentist. Many of the cases were bloody amputations. Sleep was out of the question. Next morning in the Oosterbeek Catholic Church McGowan said Mass to as many men as he could find who had time to listen.

93

As he walked alone that same evening along the road near the hospital, he suddenly found himself jostled by a swarm of Germans who took him prisoner, and then handed him thirty-five wounded British soldiers to look after. McGowan insisted his charges be given attention. They required food and medical care. After the Germans put in an attack against the British, the SS officer in charge met the persistent McGowan and provided food and transport to the Municipal Hospital on the north side of Arnhem. Here the grounds were stacked with dead airborne troops, neat piles of blood-soaked uniforms and pyramids of arms. McGowan met his friend, Father B. M. Egan of the 2nd Battalion. Egan was badly wounded in the back and legs. He would not die however and be buried by McGowan like many others in the grounds of the hospital.

On September 23, a German medical officer took McGowan to see the hundreds of wounded laid out on the marble floor of Queen Wilhelmina's palace at Apeldoorn. McGowan continued his methodical work of recording the dead and wounded. The many casualties in the palace overflowed to the nearby Franciscan hospital. McGowan always feared that sooner or later he would be shot for surreptitiously passing back to the Dutch Red Cross workers at the St. Elisabeth Hospital the location and names of evaders hiding in thickets around the battlefield.

The priest would frequently set out on his own, prominently displaying his dog collar to the amazed Germans, who allowed him to pass into remote parts of the battleground. Here he would find dead, wounded, or small groups of soldiers hiding, waiting for someone to direct them to safety. On these journeys McGowan would often meet Mrs. Edith Nijhoff dressed in her Red Cross gown driving her horse and cart. The priest secretly passed on the locations of the men he found to this remarkable Resistance worker, who later would pick up the hiding airborne. Mrs. Nijhoff would then put the men in the back of her cart, cover them in old sacks and take them home through the German lines to Berkenlaan 16 in Ede. She made countless trips in and around the battlefield, her old nag becoming a familiar sight to German soldiers, who scarcely paid any attention to the decrepit old wagon.

McGowan would usually arrange by some impertinent act to have himself abjectly apprehended by the Germans and driven back daily to the St. Elisabeth Hospital. Conveniently, transport was always provided when he was retaken prisoner. Altogether he was captured a total of twenty-three times for trespassing too close to German installations. Some evenings McGowan would spend time talking to the bedridden John Hackett. The brigadier, still known as Corporal Hayter, wanted to know what happened each day around Oosterbeek and McGowan supplied the information to satisfy his curiosity. Often McGowan would thumb a ride from the astonished Germans, who never doubted that this well-fed looking padre with the Red Cross armband performed some official mission. McGowan thus kept a full record of all casualties, the condition of those who still held out near the Hartenstein Hotel and acted as a link for the Resistance in their search for evaders.

One afternoon McGowan came across a shocking sight in a ploughed turnip field north of the railway tracks at Wolfheze. His friend, Doctor Gary Grayson, lay dead. With him were fifteen other men. This represented the entire regimental aid post of the 10th Battalion. For a few minutes the sight thoroughly sickened the priest, who could see the mortar gashes on the victims. Then he began the macabre duty of recording all their names in his notebook. A day later he was to find the body of Doctor John Batholomew at the crossroads where the Schoonoord and Vreewijk Hotels faced each other in Oosterbeek.

At the St. Elisabeth some of the congestion lessened with the shipment of wounded to Apeldoorn. In the hospital wards he met a bedridden fellow priest, B. J. Benson of the 1st Air Landing Brigade, who had his right arm amputated. Benson died at the hospital and McGowan performed the burial service on the grounds. On September 26, after the retreat of the division over the Rhine, McGowan began to look for the dead and wounded with renewed intensity. The enormous amount of litter that covered the battlefields never ceased to amaze him. He thought it looked like Piccadilly the day after New Year's. Every haversack had been opened, ransacked and the contents scattered over the grass. At the Schoonoord Hotel his chaplain's kit had been rifled and the contents strewn on the floor. As McGowan walked alone through silent Oosterbeek and into the woods near Hartenstein, he suddenly heard a plaintive cry for help from behind a clump of bushes. A small group of haggard, wounded airborne were calling to the priest. McGowan casually dropped his haversack containing food beside the bushes, wrote down the map reference and continued on his way. That night two Dutch Resistance men arrived to lead the evaders away.

Next day at the St. Elisabeth Hospital the priest, the wounded and some of the medical teams were transferred to the Queen Wilhelmina barracks at Apeldoorn in preparation for their shipment to Germany. That day McGowan met among others the doctor, Lieutenant Colonel Martin Herford, and together they planned their escape.

The little town of Opheusden, a mile south of the Rhine, became the focal point of the advance for Lieutenant Colonel Robert Strayer's 2nd Battalion of the 506th Parachute Regiment. At the end of September, Strayer's men occupied the most forward position in the United States 101st Airborne Division. The colonel had been with the division since its formation in Fort Bragg, North Carolina, in 1943 and had finally arrived in Holland by way of Italy and France. A wry, stringy man of medium height, he had won the respect of his men by a kind of precise, unspectacular gallantry. He represented one of the few non-West Point officers of field rank in the division. His superior, Colonel Robert H. Sink, could trust him with any important job and know that Strayer would not rest until the job ended successfully. But the regiment was tired. The whole division felt weary and frustrated. Like other troops, they had not been able to overcome the fierce

German counter-attacks and reach the trapped British who had held out at Oosterbeek.

A fragile American front, ten miles wide, extended north and south in the wasp waist of land between the rivers Rhine and Waal. Heavy casualties were suffered. In early October, during one fierce, short, bloody engagement, ninety-five men were lost in the apple orchards around Opheusden. Eventually the Germans stopped attacking when they saw that their tanks and infantry could not break through the American defence. The struggle for Opheusden went on over many dreary weeks before the lines were formally drawn on that small island between the rivers. In the fields below the dikes patrols of both sides met furtively in vicious combat in the dead of night. The regiment held the south bank of the river to Driel opposite Oosterbeek.

Strayer's decimated Headquarters Company was commanded by Lieutenant Fred Heyliger. People knew Heyliger only by the name of Moose. The men of his company hardly realized he had another name. The Moose lived up to the reputation of the powerful, bull-necked animal of the North American forests. Moose had a long, mournful face, a loping gait. To his battalion commander, "Heyliger looked and acted like a moose." The Moose did not like the idea of spending the winter with his company barricaded in the shell-torn houses around the river in tedious static warfare. Only the deadly crunch of the mortars, the wet and discomfort indicated the war continued at its own wearisome, unhurried pace.

Into October, Strayer's battalion carried out their monotonous daily duties of patrol and observation on the dikes. The nights were almost always cold and frequently mist and rain shrouded the forward posts on the river, where Heyliger spent a good deal of time looking across at the far, silent shore. Once or twice a week a small patrol in a rubber dinghy would paddle over the Rhine and, undetected, scout the enemy bank. But it seemed quiet, as unspectacular as the defences of the 506th Regiment. By the end of the second week in October, Strayer had reason to believe that all was not as quiet as it appeared.

Lieutenant Lynch, the regimental Intelligence officer, had been handed down curious reports from Division. It seemed the Dutch Resistance was hiding several hundred men on the other side of the Rhine. From what Strayer could surmise, most of these evaders were being collected in villages and farms that were some miles behind the enemy forward defences directly across the river from his own positions.

In the three-storey red-brick house at Torenstraat 5 in the town of Ede lived three maidenly sisters, Mien, Cor and Ann of the De Nooy family. They were part of a much larger clan of eleven children and had many close relations who dwelt nearby. All members of the family had one particular quality in common. They resisted unrelentingly the Germans during the five long years of occupation. Those members of the family who were not active Resistance fighters – like their nephew Menno – contributed in a less spectacular manner by hiding escaped prisoners or Jews or wanted Dutchmen. On the surface, the three maids represented the soul of propriety, obedience and Calvinism. But beneath the surface seethed a quiet rebellion that began in the early, dark days of occupation in 1940, when many of their countrymen lost faith and accepted defeat. The maiden aunts kept their hope. To the Germans, some of whom were billeted next door, the home of these three elderly ladies on Torenstraat seemed a harmless enough place, an unlikely hideout for men for whom the Gestapo and detested Green Police were searching. There were several penalties for hiding enemies of the Third Reich. Your house was destroyed, the occupants shot or sent to a concentration camp. When the battle of Arnhem ended, the enemy became more, rather than less brutal and initiated a reign of terror that grew senseless and more desperate as the days passed. Around Ede the Germans hunted unsuccessfully evading airborne troops. They knew they were in the vicinity carrying forged papers, dressed as Dutchmen and living in Dutch homes. But their enquiries met a wall of silence.

In Renkum on the Rhine, eight miles south of Ede, Johan

Snoek and his sister dwelt with their mother in a small brick house. Their mother was a sister of the three maids of Ede. Johan's brother Wim had been taken to a German prison and his fate remained unknown. Snoek's cousin, Zwerus de Nooy, known as "Blue Johnny" because of the blue overalls he always wore, had been a courier for the airborne troops at Arnhem. When conditions became unbearable in Renkum, the Snoek family moved to Torenstraat to join the three maids.

The De Nooy sisters were tight-lipped. They could be depended upon to the last to keep a secret. Ede, with its proximity to the battered town of Arnhem and the surrounding woods and farms, was ideally situated as a centre for hiding evaders. Bill Wildeboer, the Resistance leader of Ede, readied the sheep pens, haylofts and underground shelters in the woods. They were not comfortable but they offered some protection against the damp cold of the approaching winter. Early in October Menno de Nooy told his aunts to prepare themselves. They would be sheltering a badly wounded soldier whose identity he could not disclose. The Resistance would supply food and other necessities. Johan would be there to help if necessary. The news delighted the maids, who grew excited at the prospect of defying the Germans.

When Harry Montfroy witnessed the coil of German armour crushing the life out of the last, frail airborne defences, he decided it was his duty to save as many men as he could. With Pieter Kruyff, the Arnhem Resistance chief, he kept a special watch on the St. Elisabeth Hospital, where hundreds of casualties were transported each day from the battlefield. Some of the wounded remained there while others were sent north to the Wilhelmina Hospital at Apeldoorn or directly to Germany. By the end of September Montfroy and his Resistance colleagues organized an escape route from the hospital to the farmlands around Mariendaal. This would be a first emergency stop. From here evaders could be dispersed to more permanent accommodations, which would take a little time to prepare.

Montfroy had planted seventeen-year-old Zwerus de Nooy at the St. Elisabeth, where the soldiers knew him only by the name of Blue Johnny. Zwerus came daily with Hessel Prins bringing clandestine supplies of cigarettes and canned cherries stolen from a warehouse at a nearby rail siding. Corporal Alan Payne, one of the first of Lipmann Kessel's surgical team to be hidden near the hospital by Zwerus, was supplied with a bicycle with which he escaped on September 29 to Ede. Johnny seemed to be everywhere. When he did not help the wounded he acted as a messenger for Kruyff and Montfroy.

The four-storey, red-brick St. Elisabeth Hospital dominated western Arnhem. From a high embankment on the upper road it overlooked the Rhine. A solid complex of buildings had been gradually added over a century or more creating a labyrinth of high-ceilinged wards and innumerable small rooms. Zwarteweg, a narrow street flanked on one side by terraced houses where the General once hid, ran along its western extremity where a side courtyard gave access to the large, domed chapel above the morgue. A great front stairway within the building ascended the amphitheatre-like entrance to the empty upper corridors. The casualties were treated in the basement near the two adjoining operating rooms facing Zwarteweg where teams of British and Dutch doctors under Lieutenant Colonel Graeme Warrack performed their duties, dashing from one operating table to another.

The Dutch nurses and doctors were competent. They toiled alongside their British counterparts. The casualties arrived through the cobbled courtyard in Zwarteweg beside the chapel. Montfroy and Albert Deuss were using the morgue as a convenient hiding place for arms and explosives. Towards the end of September, when casualties filled the building to overflowing, space in the morgue was at a premium. Between the hospital, the chapel and morgue were connecting passages of which the Germans were ignorant.

Surgeons like Lipmann Kessel, Theo Redman and Shorty Longland operated almost the entire day until they were too tired to continue. They hardly rested. It was estimated that on any day more than two hundred operations, minor and major, were performed. The Germans supplied some penicillin and anaesthetic, but Kessel thought it of inferior quality. The hospital was not only a place where a multitude of wounded were cared for, but also a haven where old comrades met and valuable information was exchanged before men died or were taken away in trains to Germany. Plans were hatched here for escape. Although the St. Elisabeth became better guarded with time, the constant flow of traffic made it difficult to control the movement of soldiers and civilians.

In the bed next to Hackett lay the commander of his 10th Battalion, Lieutenant Colonel Kenneth Smyth. Suffering from multiple shrapnel wounds, Smyth was dying. These two badly wounded men lay side by side exchanging experiences of the battle. Hackett took notes of everything Smyth said with a grim sense of academic curiosity that never seemed to desert him. Although this appeared a frivolous occupation at the time, important information about the gallantry of soldiers was being recorded. Hackett's life was soldiering and recognition of bravery remained the supreme accolade a man could achieve. Towards evening on September 25, Smyth died of his wounds and Hackett lived on.

Shortly after Smyth's death a strange incident occurred. An officer whom Hackett had never met before approached him carrying an ash walking stick of the same kind the brigadier had purchased at Blands in Notting Hill Gate two years earlier. When he looked closer he saw the carved "U" for Urquhart cut into the handle. The officer proffered it to the overjoyed Hackett as a gift. He accepted the stick and put it beside him in the bed. One day he hoped to return it to the General.

*

On September 28, Charles Labouchère took the road that led through Oosterbeek in the direction of his home in Velp, three miles east of Arnhem. He joined a long procession of trudging refugees pulling their belongings on small, two-wheeled carts.

The citizens of Oosterbeek had been ordered to evacuate their homes on September 27 and were given twenty-four hours' notice. To disguise his appearance Labouchère pulled up his coat collar around his face and offered to assist two old ladies. (My Luftwaffe flying jacket had been hidden under the floorboards of a bombed-out house in Oosterbeek.) He felt he would be less conspicuous this way. That morning on either side of the road German soldiers were lined up watching closely the parade of civilians file by. Particularly, they searched for familiar faces like Labouchère who had been helping the British. Some of the ex-prisoners who had been held in the stockade at the tennis courts in Hartenstein would easily recognize the thin, tall Dutchman.

As Labouchère passed the enemy gauntlet wedged between the two old ladies, he buried his head in his chest and tried to make himself shrink below his conspicuous six foot three inches. Labouchère was not noticed. He felt sorrowful at the fate of his airborne friends whom he had felt duty-bound to serve. Also, he deeply regretted parting with the fur-lined Luftwaffe fighter-pilot jacket, which was all he owned to protect himself against the cold nights. He also wondered what had happened to me. Reports had circulated that I had been killed in the assault to relieve the bridgehead. For the time being my father would simply receive the standard communication that I was missing in action along with thousands of others.

*

When Tony Hibbert left the prisoner-of-war compound at "Bene Sita" in Velp at 5.30 p.m. on Saturday, September 23, he never intended to go as far as the terminal prison camp in Munich.

The three-ton truck with the high wooden sideboards sped along the road to Brummen. It contained all the officers rounded up in Arnhem when the end came for the defenders of the bridge. Hibbert's face was still coated with black dust left from the coal bin where he and Anthony Cotterill were captured. When he looked across the open truck past the other prisoners and saw his companion's blackened face he thought he looked like a chimney sweep. The day before, Cotterill's three notebooks – perhaps the most complete notes of the battle for the bridge – had been snatched away by one of the German guards. Cotterill had been the only correspondent to accompany the 2nd Battalion. But Hibbert still had his own notes and would continue to add to them in the weeks ahead. The diary would provide an extraordinary history of the battle and his evasion. But now the only thought on Hibbert's mind was escape. When the truck slowed down he gave a determined wink to his friend Major Dennis Mumford, who clearly received the message. At this prearranged signal the two men suddenly leaped over the side and set out in opposite directions as the truck entered Brummen. It took several minutes for the startled guards to react.

Hibbert landed hard on his knees, cutting his face and eye on the asphalt road. He rose and dashed into a small side street, his raincape flowing behind. In a matter of minutes in rapid succession he vaulted a fence, crawled through four gardens and lost himself finally in a series of connecting alleyways. A few moments later at a main road on the outskirts of Brummen, the major stopped dead in his tracks. Someone nearby whom he could not see was whistling a bar from "It's a Long Way to Tipperary." When he looked around to identify the whistler, he saw the shadow of the man disappear. Minutes later a German staff car pulled up on the road and several German officers jumped out and entered their headquarters. He had narrowly averted capture. Once more that day this anonymous Dutchman who surreptitiously tracked Hibbert warned him of the immediate presence of the enemy by whistling the same tune. Hibbert never met his invisible protector. Meanwhile one eye was blackened and closed and his face bloodstained. The fleeing soldier took refuge in a small wood as German troops searched the nearby countryside. At 7.30 that night Hibbert heard a truck start and roar off down the road, taking the search party with it. At the compound in Velp he had fortunately traded his hobnailed boots for a pair of rubber ones and this allowed him to move silently over the countryside. When night fell Hibbert hollowed a hiding place underneath a log pile behind a small farmhouse, and with a supply of apples from a local orchard, closed himself over with the wood until morning.

When dawn broke he felt crushed from the weight of logs that had been pressing down upon him all night. The house of wood had caved in before he awakened. Bruised and cut, dazed, he crawled out on to the floor of the forest and attempted to recover his strength. The major looked a pitiful sight. One eye was black and blue, closed completely, dried blood had caked on his cheeks, his knees were tender from the fall onto the road and he could barely walk from the pain in his back. But he was free. Moreover, he would not suffer the same end as some of the others who remained prisoner, nor like Mumford would he be recaptured, nor be shot and mysteriously disappear like the correspondent Tony Cotterell.

The morning sun came out and Hibbert lay around in the woods resting in its warmth, recovering slowly. By nightfall he felt a good deal better than he looked as he knocked on the door of the small farmhouse behind which he had hidden. When the suspicious farmer came to the door Hibbert tried to explain his identity by drawing a Swastika and a Union Jack side by side on a piece of paper and crossing out the Swastika. Eventually the major convinced the wary farmer he told the truth. The farmer's wife then brought the starving officer a plate of sandwiches and a large pot of coffee while her husband went in search of a local interpreter. After being visited all that day by many curious Dutchmen, eventually one of the members of the local Resistance cautiously made his appearance. Dick Tjeenk Willink briefly, thoroughly, interrogated Hibbert. Satisfied the Englishman did not lie, the Resistance man took him home to Burg de Wijslaan A 491, in Brummen. Hibbert was amazed to discover that after two days of travelling he had moved only half a mile from the place where he jumped from the truck. A lifelong association began with the helpful Tjeenk Willink, his brother Aart and his mother, with whom Hibbert stayed for three weeks.

The Tjeenk Willink home had two ingenious hideouts. Beneath the attic ceiling a fake floor had been designed big enough to fit in a mattress. Behind a cupboard in another room the wall contained a double partition, wide enough to hide a man. Hibbert could vanish quickly into either place at the first warning from the Tjeenk Willink family of the approach of the enemy.

Dick told Hibbert some disturbing news. In Brummen by chance, a German lorry going in the opposite direction filled with armed SS troops saw Hibbert, Mumford and several other prisoners leap from the truck. The SS lorry had stopped alongside the halted vehicle and an excited young SS corporal had turned his Schmeisser machine pistol at random on the officers and killed two of them outright and wounded two more. One of the dead was Cotterill.

*

In the evening of September 26 my own plan was ready. Our escape equipment had been carefully preserved and well hidden by the meticulous Kettley. It consisted of a useless silk escape map of Western Europe too small to read, a small box of matches, a button compass, a tin of chocolate, a grey German Army blanket that hung over my arm like a toreador's, and Kettley's nail clippers. By good luck I was not at first missed in the dismal prison yard of the warehouse at Stroe as the officers were counted in the dark. I stood between Kettley and Banwell, waiting to be taken aboard the cattle coach on the rail siding. Before me I imagined the thousands of Jews and slave labourers who had stood neatly in line in yards like this prepared to leave for their helpless slaughter in concentration camps, perhaps as demoralized and defeated as many of the men who stood here.

The Germans were counting the number of officers once again. Presently they came and ordered me under escort towards the front of the train. I just had time to watch Kettley and Banwell being pushed into one of the rear cattle cars already jammed full with prisoners. The cattle coach in front of me had been divided into two. About thirty officers stood, squeezed behind a paddock normally used for horses. On the other side, in a larger space, sat about ten SS guards with Schmeissers on their knees, warming themselves around a small, coal stove, eating thick wurst sandwiches. At the prospect of yet another prisoner being wedged in the already overcrowded space, the prisoners let out a howl of protest. I quickly nudged the guard. Another howl of protest erupted. Then the German rudely pushed me away with the butt of his rifle towards the wagon where the two sergeants had vanished.

In the dark interior I saw both Kettley and Banwell. A thin shaft of light entered from a single tiny porthole at the far end of the car. Sleeping, huddled figures littered the floor, unmoving. Most slept the deep sleep of the totally exhausted and wounded. They could have been dead. I stumbled towards my friends over the mass of bodies. Some of the prisoners awakened briefly, cursing me violently as they came alive. The train lurched forward and gathered speed as it rolled towards Apeldoorn. In a few hours we would be across the German border where escape would be difficult among a hostile population. Kettley began prying with his nail clippers around the edge of the porthole. No one paid any attention to his industrious activity. No one seemed to care.

Kettley had pried out the glass in a few minutes and he handed it back carefully to Banwell. The porthole opening was about eight inches in diameter and criss-crossed on the outside with many loose strands of barbed wire. I saw that we rolled along the top of a high rail embankment which sloped steeply down into wide treeless meadows. Overhead stars shone hard and crystalline. There was no moon. I felt now nothing could stop our escape. I grabbed the edge of the opening, braced my foot against the side and pulled with all the strength I possessed. At first nothing happened. Then a rotten board pulled loose in my hands and I tumbled back over the sleeping forms who swore, shouted, and flayed out in anger. For a second time I repeated the performance. This time suddenly and without warning a section of wood about three feet wide and eighteen inches high unhinged. Cool night air rushed through the stuffy, fetid interior. We became feverish with haste. Kettley with his clippers quickly sawed through the last strands of rotten barbed wire. When I asked for the last time if anyone wanted to come only a single man responded. But badly wounded in the leg, he would not be able to walk unassisted. Regretfully, we could not take him. We had to put as much distance as possible between the Germans and ourselves that night and a wounded man who would have to jump fifteen feet down a steep embankment would be a considerable hindrance. I crawled through the opening and stood briefly at the swaying juncture of the two cattle cars. Kettley and Banwell were to follow as soon as they say me jump. The train rounded a wide curve as I leapt into the dark.

Tumbling down the steep embankment I came to rest out of sight in the deep, cool grass. Another figure leapt a few minutes later followed by a second as the car clattered on towards Apeldoorn. The long swaying train seemed to go on forever. The last coach finally swept away into the night trailing a red light that blinked weakly in the blackness. A few of the guards sang "Lily Marlene." And their voices trailed over the fields long after the train vanished and only the distant throb echoed along the tracks.

From the wet grass my two companions rose and came to-wards me. We were exhilarated, triumphant. We clasped hands warmly in the moonless night and repeated an oath I used to make in Canada before a basketball game. It was the only one I knew. We would win. My plan was to head west and north, marching always towards the coast from where we hoped to steal a boat to cross the North Sea to England. I placed Kettley's two small metal buttons on top of one another and the luminous dots pointed north. With my German army blanket wrapped over my arm, Kettley and Banwell without a word fell in behind as we crossed over the embankment. Later, when I could locate Polaris in the luminous sky, we were able to steer our course by the stars. Before dawn we had to cover over twenty miles. However, we soon found our progress slowed in the deep dunes of the Stroeërzand, a small unexpected desert in the middle of Holland. Wadis and dry scrub surrounded us as we slowly waded on. But the dunes were safe, an unlikely place for a German patrol. Banwell, who was used to the sandy terrain of North Africa, silently brought up the rear, walking casually with his hands in his pockets. Several hours later we arrived at the main Amersfoort-Apeldoorn road, where we watched a heavily loaded convoy of canvas-covered trucks lumbering eastwards to Germany. When dawn came we sheltered in a small wood, covering ourselves with my army blanket. In the early morning the rain fell.

*

The attitude of the Germans towards the population of northern Holland after the defeat of the airborne force at Arnhem had been dictated by a number of events that had occurred earlier. One event in particular rankled the Germans. September 5, 1944, became known as "Mad Tuesday." When a false rumour that a large landing of Allied troops had taken place in northern Holland grew to gigantic proportions, panic seized the enemy. Everyone believed it. Soldiers and collaborators took to the roads by the thousands, fleeing east to Germany. Blind fear engulfed the Nazis before they realized they had been tricked. About the same time as this mad fear gripped the enemy, the three main Resistance groups formed a single organization known as Forces of the Interior under command of Prince Bernhard. Each group had its area of responsibility. The O.D. (Ordedienst), which consisted largely of ex-army men in charge of the restoration of law after liberation, the L.K.P. (Landeliske Knokploegen), the combat arm of the Resistance, and the saboteurs known as the R.V.V. (Raad van Verzet), were at last united.

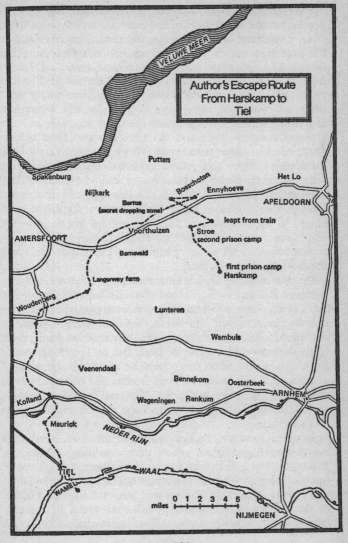

Author's Escape Route
From Harskamp to
Tiel

VELUWE MEER

Putten

Spakenburg

Nijkerk

Boschoten

Ennyhoeve

Het Lo

APELDOORN

Bertus
(secret dropping zone)

leapt from train

Voorthuizen

Stroe
second prison camp

AMERSFOORT

Barneveld

first prison camp
Harskamp

Langerwey farm

Woudenberg

Lunteren

Wambuis

Veenendaal

Bennekom

Oosterbeek

ARNHEM

Kolland

Wageningen

Renkum

Maurick

NEDER RIJN

TIEL

WAAL

WAMEL

miles 0 1 2 3 4 5

NIJMEGEN

Harry Montfroy remembered on that happy day in early September the weird flight of the Germans and their quislings as they swarmed eastwards down the road. They travelled in hand carts, on horses, staff cars, bicycles, in fact anything that moved. The sight made a deep impression. Anyone could easily have joined the confused mob on the road unnoticed. The idea took seed. Later, Montfroy hoped an occasion might arise when he could put the lesson to work for the Resistance. Before the middle of September the crazy scramble to leave Holland reversed itself and the Germans and their helpers returned. The bitter resentment felt by the enemy over their unnecessary flight and return exploded on the population after the 1st Airborne Division was evacuated over the Rhine.

Soon the Germans indulged in a last fling of unrestrained cruelty. Police Leader Hans Albin Rauter, the highest SS official in the land allowed his black-shirted troops and their underlings much individual discretion and they used that discretion in a spree of savagery against the population. And then the Resistance struck back.

On orders of the Dutch Government in exile in London, a National Railway strike was called in Holland for September 17. The response was total. Railways were paralysed throughout the country from mid-September until winter ended. In occupied Holland the strike caused slow starvation during most of the bitterly cold weather of 1944. But no Dutchman broke the strike. Little or no food could be moved to the areas of greatest need. Thousands of men, women and children starved to death in the towns and cities. Nineteen forty-four became one of the saddest winters of the war for the people of the Netherlands.

In late September, the Resistance ambushed a German staff car at Putten, killing an officer and wounding another. In retaliation five hundred and ninety men were transported to forced labour in German concentration camps. Five hundred and twenty died there. Putten was put to the torch. Earlier, in Amsterdam, the Resistance assassinated one of Rauter's high-ranking security officials. That same afternoon the SS troops grabbed twenty-nine hostages at random on the streets at the same place as the killing and executed them, leaving the bloody bodies on the pavement. From September 17 until the war ended no police informer, Nazi, or member of the Dutch NSB was safe from assassination. The SS Security men, Green Police, Dutch NSB and quislings took their revenge in their brief euphoric moment of victory after Arnhem. Later, as a security measure, the German High Command drove the Dutch from the towns and villages bordering the Rhine. There was a succession of deportations for forced labour. In the areas where the airborne evaders hid, the sad movement of civilians on the roads would create a diversion favourable for their escape. While the evaders prepared for their flight, occupied Holland erupted in deep turmoil.

On September 25, Menno de Nooy was summoned from Ede to a Dutch farmhouse in the Mariendaal woods where he found Digby Tatham-Warter with his second-in-command, Tony Franks. Franks still hobbled from his ankle wound. De Nooy took the two men a mile further north to the security of farmer Van der Ven's house, a more comfortable dwelling called "Nazareth" in the small, but dense Warnsborn forest. Here the two soldiers amused themselves every evening by cutting home-grown tobacco to make cigarettes or by playing cards with the farmer when it was safe to come out of their vaultlike secret room in the shed. A week later Tatham-Warter received a courier who carried a message from Gerald Lathbury. The brigadier lived in the neighbouring farm of Kleine Kweek, where the ruddy-faced Braafhart took great pride in displaying the high-ranking officer to all visitors. Lathbury wanted Tatham-Warter to know that he too had strolled out of the St. Elisabeth Hospital and was not far away.

On October 3, Bill Wildeboer, the Ede Resistance leader, called around to visit Tatham-Warter. He needed help. Widleboer, brave, solid, unimaginative, found it difficult to cope with the large number of airborne the Resistance were finding almost every day. These men required organizing and leadership. They were imposing an enormous burden on the resources of the local Dutch population. That afternoon Tatham-Warter, in civilian clothes, cycled with his new Dutch friend the ten miles into Ede to make his headquarters in Wildeboer's house on Lunterseweg 32.

The next day a barber, tailor and photographer were brought by the Dutchman to attend Tatham-Warter. The major's hair was trimmed and another, better-fitting suit supplied. The photographer took his picture and fingerprinted him. Then he received a false identity. Henceforth Tatham-Warter would be known as Peter Jensen, the deaf and dumb son of a lawyer from The Hague. He carried his identity card to prove it.

On October 2, a courier came to take Lathbury by foot from the barn of Mrs. Stark to De Lange Hut, the lovely country estate of the charming Miss Jeanne Lamberts, situated six miles due east of Ede. She spoke fluent English and greeted the brigadier warmly. A room in the attic, a razor, soap, a feather bed and access to a secret cupboard gave the officer a delicious feeling of security and comfort which he no longer expected. Private Bill Hogg joined the brigadier in the room and because of the cramped quarters slept on the floor with his feet stuck into an open cupboard. The Lamberts' home now harboured fifty-seven Dutch evacuees, Lathbury and Hogg as well as two recent arrivals, Privates Fred Brown and Fred Southall of the South Staffordshire Regiment. Lathbury draped his six-feet-four-inch frame over the small bed with considerable discomfort. However, his sense of confinement was made more endurable by the presence of the attractive Miss Lamberts, who had the capacity to arouse in Lathbury a feeling of well being. Attractive women had always played an important role in the brigadier's life.

Lathbury sometimes entertained himself by reading Tatham-Warter's interesting account of the battle of the bridge which Miss Lamberts's gamekeeper brought him one morning from Ede. The usually impeccably attired brigadier read Tatham-Warter's report dressed in his new Dutch clothes – striped black trousers that came up to his ankles, a green coat with a band on the back and brown, pointed, patent-leather shoes. Superficially Lathbury and Tatham-Warter had many qualities in common. Both were tall, lean men who paid excessive attention to their personal turnout. Equally determined soldiers, they could endure great hardship and had considerable powers of endurance. But Lathbury was a diplomat more than a soldier. Tatham-Warter was a soldier first and never very diplomatic. Lathbury recalled Tatham-Warter's drunken brawls in their North African mess where the major would occasionally smash up the bar-room furniture and engage in wild fist fights with friends that would be forgotten next morning. The major did not hold his liquor well, but after a night of drunken revelry he would return to his unit chastised and refreshed. The occasional booming of distant artillery that night told Lathbury the Second Army was still a long way off.

On October 6 a stolen German officer's car arrived with Wildeboer at the wheel to conduct Lathbury to his new quarters in Ede. In an hour they arrived at the home of Menno de Nooy on Brouwersstraat where he would now live. That afternoon the brigadier took his first short stroll with his host to a small shop in Ede to have his photograph taken for a false identity card. His new name would be Albertus Waterman, born in Amsterdam, May 28, 1898, with a fictitious address. It was a novel experience for the brigadier to step onto the road to allow German soldiers to walk on the pavement. That night Kirschen sent Lathbury a message from his chicken coop congratulating him on his escape, accompanied by a gift of a bar of chocolate. The brigadier shared the chocolate among the occupants of the house. And then news arrived from Wildeboer that Hibbert, Lathbury's Brigade Major, was hiding less than a mile away.

At the St. Elisabeth Hospital a solemn burial ceremony took place performed by the ubiquitous Catholic priest, Daniel

McGowan before he departed for Apeldoorn. Only those who could understand the rapidly read Latin missal knew McGowan recited a stream of gibberish.

For several days the Germans had been carefully stacking captured British arms and ammunition in a guarded storeroom within the hospital. Major C. J. Longland, now the senior medical officer, received an ominous, official grey envelope from the SS commandant in Arnhem on October 2. It stated that all arms were to be collected and handed over in two days. Next morning McGowan and Longland decided on their strategy.

Late that evening a burly pair of stretcher bearers entered the store room where the captured airborne weapons were kept while McGowan diverted the guards' attention. A few minutes later the bearers left with thick, lumpy shapes beneath the blankets. The guards were told the blankets concealed two British corpses on the way to their graves. A solemn-faced McGowan brought up the rear of the procession reading his Bible. On the stretchers were three Bren guns, a German Spandau, twenty Stens, several dozen grenades and two dozen full magazines of ammunition. In the garden two shallow graves had been hastily dug to receive the bodies. As the stretchers were quickly lowered the Germans looked on disinterestedly. They had seen the ceremony many times before and displayed no great curiosity. A burial detail stood back and saluted. McGowan crossed himself and mumbled an incomprehensible prayer. With unseemly speed the orderlies and Lipmann Kessel heaped earth onto the graves until they were completely covered. Two weeks later on a moonless night Pieter Kruyff, Harry Montfroy and three railway men came to the hospital graveyard. They exhumed the weapons and drove off with them on a butcher's bicycle.

By the end of the first week in October the shuttle escape service run by the Resistance between St. Elisabeth Hospital and the two farms, Nazareth and Warnsborn to the north, began to slow down for want of people. Those they had helped to escape were already hidden in lofts or forest trenches, while the other evaders were trying to find a way out on their own. Few of the latter would succeed in reaching the Allied lines.

At Apeldoorn, the captive doctors – Theo Redman, Martin Herford, Derek Ridler and Graeme Warrack – were running the William III Hospital. Warrack, as the chief divisional medical officer, had been in command there since September 26. When the St. Elisabeth closed on October 11, "Shorty" Longland and Lipmann Kessel joined him. The British medical staff were attending to over 1,300 of their own and with German doctors cared for another 1,500 enemy wounded. But as the prison trains transported the casualties deep into Germany near the eastern front, the hospital began to empty. Warrack wrote a letter to General Urquhart in England and gave it to the Resistance, which delivered it for him. As Warrack said, he had no intention of going to Germany and missing St. Andrew's Night in Edinburgh. Meanwhile, Kessel, Redman, Herford and the priest McGowan were hatching their escape plans.

On October 2 the SS Major Egon Skalka under orders from his superior drew up a schedule of casualties to be evacuated by train to Germany from the St. Elisabeth Hospital. All badly wounded would go. Among them would be the unrecognized brigadier, John Hackett. Hackett's stomach wounds, raw and discharging, required constant attention.

On the morning of October 3 a tall, well-built man with a deceptively soft, oval face approached the brigadier's bed. He wore a Red Cross smock and armband. In thick, broken English he said he had come from "Gerald." Piet Kruyff quietly slipped a small note written in Lathbury's own hand to Hackett. The note stated "this man can be trusted. You may put yourself in his hands." Kruyff, moreover, told Hackett he knew his identity and that he must follow his instructions if he valued his life. This would be the brigadier's only opportunity to avoid imprisonment in Germany. Arnhem and the adjoining land along the Rhine as far west as Wageningen was being evacuated of civilians. Kruyff told Hackett to be prepared to leave at 12.30 p.m. the next day when all would be ready. Then the Arnhem Resistance chief left, mingling with the throng of Red Cross workers and German nurses who moved among the wounded.

Kruyff controlled his team of non-political Resistance workers with a firm hand. Among Harry Montfroy, Albert Deuss, Nicolaas de Bode, Leo Blok, Joop Pillor, Albert Horstman, Alex Hartmann, Toon van Daalen and Menno Liefstink his authority was unquestioned. He spoke softly, asked the advice of his colleagues and kept the membership in his inner group limited to a few trusted friends. The nucleus originated from his intimate associates at the AKU textile works in Arnhem, where Kruyff had been a chief chemical engineer. By early October Kruyff's stature had so grown after the work of his group in the Arnhem battle that his authority now extended to major districts outside the town. Kruyff's men were all veterans of five long, hard years of German occupation. They knew every possible hiding place in the countryside and every man whom they could trust.

Shortly after first light on the morning of October 4, Montfroy left his usual sleeping quarters in the cellar of the Carmelite monastery a few miles to the north of Arnhem and set off by bicycle in the company of Leo Blok for St. Elisabeth Hospital. He made a wide detour along the paths in the Mariendaal Forest to the west so he could arrive at the St. Elisabeth shortly before noon, almost coinciding with the vehicle driven by Kruyff expected at the Zwarteweg. A dilapidated 1930 Fiat powered by a wood-burning engine drove up to the Zwarteweg and parked behind the Roman Catholic chapel at precisely twelve noon. Kruyff and Montfroy were now ready to put their plan into action. Montfroy would not forget the day. In one week it would be his thirty-fifth birthday.

Dressed as Red Cross workers, the men entered the side entrance of the hospital. Although very ill, the brigadier stubbornly refused to admit to himself or anyone else the serious nature of his wounds. This implacable will to resist irritated

Kruyff, who found Hackett even in his present state of health impossible to command. The strange illusion Hackett nourished about his well-being was quickly dispelled when Kruyff had to almost lift him out of bed. Although others were dying all around from wounds less serious, Hackett did not intend that this should happen to him. As early as 1933, when he felt war was inevitable, he decided that if he had to die it would be "much tidier to be killed as a professional than as an amateur." He must have been thinking of just how untidy his near fatal condition was when Kruyff called on that sunless day at the St. Elisabeth. For Hackett all action had to have a logical conclusion. But Kruyff could not supply all the answers.

Kruyff knew it would excite less attention if Hackett walked out of the hospital instead of being carried on a stretcher. The Dutchman had entered the ward dressed in his customary white smock, white helmet and Red Cross armband. Under the smock he hid a long, grey raincoat. Fortunately no German nurses were on duty, and the guards were being diverted by other Resistance workers. Hackett put the raincoat on over his underwear, slipped into his boots and shuffled slowly into a small side corridor unseen, through a door and into the morgue beneath the chapel. The brigadier held on grimly all the time to his ash walking stick. At the end of the morgue, the men entered another corridor and finally came out through a back entrance to the waiting Fiat on Zwarteweg. A moment later they were on their way.

Hackett sat silently in the car, his face a sickly ashen colour, uncomfortably seated in the back next to Kruyff. His instructions were to speak to on one until they arrived at their destination. In the town of Oosterbeek, Kruyff picked up two elderly refugees, a man and his wife. At the roadblock the German sentry quickly looked at the five occupants and waved the car on. The small vehicle bounced painfully over the rough road. Every bump made Hackett wince with agony from his wounds. No one who looked at him could doubt the pain he suffered during that fifteen-mile journey. Beyond the barrier the Fiat turned north towards the Wolfheze Hotel on the Ede road. Burned-out vehicles, scattered containers and unburied corpses littered the roadside. The signs of battle were still very much in evidence.

The old couple, unable to coax any response from the uncommunicative Hackett, were told he suffered from deep shock and could not talk. The couple soon disembarked and the three men continued on their way alone. In Ede the car stopped in front of a small, three-storey red-brick house at Torenstraat 5. Here the three De Nooy sisters were waiting to take over with maidenly care the administration of Hackett's private life. They undressed the brigadier and disregarding every protest, bundled him into bed in an upstairs room. He presented no serious obstacle to the three determined ladies, who were physically bigger and stronger than the brigadier. The reserves of emotional and physical strength that had sustained Hackett for so long now drained away from his mind and body. He yielded to the attentions of the women in the security of his new home. They placed his walking stick carefully in the cupboard.

Lieutenant Colonel David Dobie felt uncertain what to do next but he knew he must immediately leave Arnhem. After two weeks of hiding in the home of H. B. Bakker next to the St. Elisabeth Hospital, Dobie set out westward with the sixteen-year-old boy Jan Bolte as guide, following the general direction to Ede. Bolte, one of Bakker's evacuees, had promised to lead the colonel safely through the twisting streets of the town into the safety of the countryside. Dobie, always terribly impatient, quickly wished to leave behind the endless maze of bombed-out houses. Once in the open country he intended to reach the Rhine somehow, cross over and rejoin his own troops. Dobie's impatience was not shared by his youthful guide, who proceeded warily in country with which he seemed unfamiliar. He cautioned the tough, ruthless officer to be careful if he wished to reach his lines. The two travellers had already been stopped three times by roadblocks put up on country lanes and had bluffed their way through with Bolte doing the talking. Eventually they reached the fields north of the dropping zone at Ginkel Heath. Here Dobie bade good-bye to Bolte and decided he would go on alone south to the river.

Dobie waited in the woods until nightfall under the erroneous impression he could still find isolated pockets of his own troops fighting north of the Rhine. He did not fully comprehend the idea that all the airborne had been withdrawn eighteen days before he set out on his lonely passage. But Dobie was endowed with tremendous energy and will and he had the reputation for driving himself and his men ruthlessly. His officer casualties in battle were always known to be higher than other battalion commanders. He might not have spared his men but neither did he spare himself.

With no moon to brighten the fields he carefully crossed the deserted dropping zones stepping around burned-out gliders, bits of parachutes and scraps of unrecognizable debris. The skeletal remains of his division, laid out over this silent wasteland, made Dobie feel strange and uncomfortable. There were too many ghosts and memories. A few minutes later he had a frightening experience. He stumbled and almost fell over the edge of an open communal grave filled with dead paratroopers. At the last moment he had caught his balance and then hurried on, anxious to depart from this melancholy scene.

South of the Arnhem-Renkum road, the houses were also deserted. Oosterbeek had become a ghost town. Only a sense of desperate purpose suppressed the overpowering urge to turn around and flee. Occasionally, he heard the distant boom of artillery. But the shells were landing a considerable distance to the east.

In Oosterbeek Dobie took one of the paths used by the troops on their withdrawal to the river. Shreds of white tennis tape fluttered eerily from bushes and trees once used to mark the road down to the Rhine. He passed a house where he heard for the first time in two days a human voice. Ready to draw attention to himself by knocking on the window, he suddenly saw the kitchen full of German troops drinking and eating and hurriedly withdrew, perplexed by the sight.

For two weeks Dobie had been without news of any kind. The colonel had no idea how far Allied troops advanced during the last three weeks or where the headquarters of the 1st Division had gone. However, he did know from the battle plan, now three weeks old, that XXX Corps and American airborne troops should be south of the Rhine. Dobie also recalled that his old friend Robert Strayer commanded one of the battalions of the American 101st Division. They had gone on war games together in England. Dobie pushed on quickly in the dark to the river, slightly confused and disoriented by his discovery of German troops. Five hundred yards from the Rhine a German at his machine-gun post suddenly challenged the Englishman. When he did not answer the German's call, the Spandau fired a quick burst that ripped with deafening sound through the silence. Dobie dived for cover into a ditch of rainwater. Then in the dark he ran back in the direction he came from until he reached the deserted houses of Oosterbeek. With the moon now fully up and with the obvious prospect of meeting a heavily defended line of German defences on the Rhine should he continue with his plan, the colonel retraced his steps as far as the road leading to Ede. Here in a clump of bushes he lay down wet and exhausted and fell asleep in the undergrowth.

At first light Dobie took to the road northward, miserable, depressed, wondering where the route would finally lead, but hoping to have better luck than last night. Presently the sun came up and dried his wet clothes. In his legs he had cramps and pain that radiated back to his hip joint. (These first pains, felt in the full power of his youth, were the symptoms of rheumatoid arthritis that would eventually kill Dobie while still a young man.) After a few minutes the colonel was surprised to find himself overtaken by a pretty Dutch maiden carrying a basket of vegetables. She began a voluble conversation with the good-looking colonel, while they walked together down the road to Ede. Dobie, normally a talkative person himself, felt frustrated at his inability to converse. He answered with frequent "yas" and "nays," and nodded agreeably. It became obvious that the pretty girl had taken a fancy to Dobie and wanted to pick him up and take him home. It became just as clear to Dobie that as much as he would like to accept the invitation, this was neither the time nor place for such an adventure. His freedom and perhaps his life depended upon making contact as soon as possible with a member of the Resistance. The situation became more complicated when the girl took a new route onto a road filled with several passing German battalions of motorized infantry. The troops were young and looked rested and well-armed with their considerable transport. When the Englishman, by accident, looked down at his feet he had a sudden fright. Beneath his civilian trousers he still wore his dreaded hobnailed British army boots; but no one noticed. When the Germans passed by, Dobie at last broke his silence. He spoke a few words of English to identify himself. The girl became so excited that the colonel had to restrain the rush of emotion that overcame her. Almost at the same time another small German infantry column came down the road in the opposite direction and marched by the excitable Dutch girl, who unlike Dobie, paid no attention to the troops. By the time her excitement subsided they already had entered the town and arrived at her home. She explained to her parents the true identity of the handsome stranger.

That night the colonel slept at the house. Early next morning October 16, Menno de Nooy visited Dobie and closely questioned him. Satisfied with his identity, de Nooy conducted the colonel to his own house on Brouwersstraat, where Dobie was amazed to find Lathbury, comfortably settled in, his wounds healing well. While Dobie recounted his story the two men watched a rather bizarre sight from the front window of the house. Across the street the Germans had a workshop where the jeeps from Lathbury's brigade were being repaired and put back into service. The vehicles raced through the streets, the blue Pegasus insignia of the division prominently displayed on the rear.

That same day Dobie strolled with de Nooy over to the house of Wildeboer on Lunterseweg where he joined his fellow officers for their regular morning coffee at 11.0 a.m. After his frightening three weeks of wandering, Dobie was amazed to see the casual manner in which Tatham-Warter conducted his business. Present that morning were some of the officers of Tatham-Warter's escape headquarters: Tony Franks, Tony Hibbert and the dependable Sergeant Major Robert Grainger. Dobie, overjoyed at the the sight of his fellow officers, was pleased to learn of the large number of airborne troops hiding in the Ede district. Tatham-Warter explained the links of communication with their own troops.

Alex Hartmann continued to operate his PGEM telephone connection from the house of Van der Deure in Bennekom to the British Intelligence Section at Nijmegen. And hovering in the background, operating from clandestine locations, was Kirschen of the SAS, who kept airborne headquarters in Moor Park, and indeed, the Allied Army informed of the welfare of the evaders. Tatham-Warter only knew the SAS officer by the name of "King." Kirschen's reluctance for publicity had already become well known.

Then the major explained to the astonished Dobie the amazing manner in which he cruised daily around the countryside on bicycle visiting his airborne community. There were enough soldiers in the vicinity to form a small army which could harass the enemy – about two hundred. Dobie saw the detailed plans drawn up to coordinate an attack with the Resistance against the Germans that would coincide with the Second Army's crossing of the Rhine. All roads leading to any future Allied bridgehead would be mined and ambushed. Arms were already being dropped by the RAF and hidden deep in the countryside. The colonel found it difficult to believe the extent to which Tatham-Warter had organized the evaders. However, the expected push of the Second Army did not look as if it would materialize for a long time. Too many days had passed since they first landed on September 17 without any Allied signs of preparation for an offensive. Tatham-Warter told Dobie that the need for all of them to escape was now imperative. It had first priority. Someone had to reach the Allied lines and prepare the crossing of the evaders from the south shore as soon as possible. An individual familiar with the plans of the soldiers must make the hazardous journey over the one known escape route across two rivers to the Allied troops. The moment the irrepressible Dobie strode in to de Nooy's house that morning Tatham-Warter knew this was his man.

That afternoon Dobie learned the news of Hackett's presence in the town. He had believed the brigadier had died at the St. Elisabeth Hospital of his wounds. The existence of Hackett – even though incapacitated – and Lathbury seemed to give the airborne evaders a strong unifying sense of purpose. Hackett let it be known through Lathbury that the campaign the evaders now embarked upon behind the line was as important as the one they had fought and lost. The idea of mass escape appealed to the imaginative brigadier. He was convinced the survivors were now embarking upon the most formidable exploit of their careers.

The airborne occupation of Ede also gave new confidence to the Resistance, and although the people of the town did not know exactly what was happening, they were aware of many new and strange faces among the population. With the arrival of Dobie the plans for escape took definite shape.

*

We had made progress. In the early morning hours of September 30, clouds of heavy mist hung unmoving above the ground. I awoke in a damp patch of woods several hundred yards square surrounded on three sides by fields and on the fourth by a narrow dirt road. Beside me were the dirty, ugly, unshaven faces of Kettley and Banwell. At the end of the road smoke rose from the chimney of a small wooden cottage into a bleak sky. My companions were awake, shivering in the penetrating cold. Our bones ached as we gazed longingly at the warm house where a fire must be burning on the hearth. Carefully I folded my blanket, which had kept us from freezing during the night. Then we watched the woodsman's cottage for some sign of life. But nothing moved in this early hour. Buckets and a few logs were scattered in the yard where a couple of scrawny hens pecked away at the earth. Presently the front door opened and an old lady in a black dress, a black shawl draped around her shoulders, chased the hens with surprising agility. She caught them all and took them inside. Cautiously we approached the house and knocked softly on the door. After a few minutes a child whimpered, then silence. Some women were whispering to each other but no one moved. Presently, the door parted an inch or two and through the opening the old lady looked without astonishment at me and my companions. The interior of the shack was squalid and smelled of boiled milk that simmered on the stove. The door opened all the way and we were quickly beckoned within. Two half-dressed children and an older boy about twelve curiously examined us.

Banwell tried with sign language to explain we had floated down from the sky near Arnhem and escaped the Germans. The lady smiled and nodded and we thought she understood. Taking the boiled milk from the stove she poured us each a small cupful. The children looked on as we gratefully drank. She spoke quickly to the boy who put on a pair of heavy clogs and trousers and ran out of the house down the road. After a few more minutes I decided we had to move. We had a long way to go to reach the North Sea. We embraced the little old lady and Banwell kissed her on the cheek as we set off down the road into the empty countryside.

A man in clogs wearing a peaked cap overtook us on his bicycle. We followed him, trudging wearily in the early morning several miles around the edge of a muddy turnip field until we came to a prosperous looking farmhouse. Inside two matronly women waited, smiling, gesturing to the kitchen table where they had prepared a large quantity of food. We restrained ourselves only with great difficulty. After a week without a solid meal we fell finally with thanks upon the plates of fried eggs, stacks of bread and mounds of cheese our hosts kindly provided. It would be some days before we could really sate our deep and gnawing hunger. Civilian clothes were brought out and the grandmother who governed this house, singularly absent of menfolk, buried the uniforms in the garden. I still clung to my rubber boots; although too small for my large feet, they seemed particularly well-suited to the muddy Dutch countryside.

Piet Oosterbroek entered the household and stood looking us over as we consumed the last of our meal. This burly, un-smiling Dutchman nodded, shook our hands in turn and said he had known of our presence since dawn. Mistakenly, we had been identified as German deserters by the little old lady in black at the woodsman's cottage. But Oosterbroek did not doubt where we came from.

Some weeks ago the Germans had shot Oosterbroek in the back when he escaped from a routine roundup of Dutchmen in a nearby village. The wound had not healed properly and had affected his left leg. He walked with a pronounced limp. A dedicated member of the Communist Party, the Resistance man asked us to follow him to his own farm a few miles away. It would be more secure at his home. Teams of Germans were searching for evaders with Alsatian dogs in the meadows north of Barneveld according to Oosterbroek. It would not be long before the farmhouses around Putten were also searched.

Late morning we followed the square, powerful, limping figure of Oosterbroek to his farmhouse just outside the village of Putten. A cobblestone courtyard separated the two-storey farmhouse from the barn, well stocked with hay. Although Oosterbroek understood hardly any English, our objective was clear. We wanted to find the quickest way back to our own lines. Banwell and Kettley were very easy, agreeable companions, perfect for a dangerous undertaking. Unhurried, calm, both men showed little anxiety during our days together. After we were fed once more by the charming Mrs. Oosterbroek, she led us to the barn. We climbed the ladder into the hayloft, pulled it up after us and fell asleep in the warm, prickly straw.

Darkness came early and we slept soundly, with a feeling of

protection. I awoke to the quiet, persistent calls of Mrs. Ooster-broek, hastening us to rise and come down from the hayloft immediately. In her hand she held three silver coins of Phillip II dug from her garden. A small souvenir. She handed one to myself, Banwell and Kettley and the bond between us was sealed for all time. Mrs. Oosterbroek then led us over a field of ripening wheat that rose as high as my waist. We waded on through ploughed ground until in the darkness we stumbled onto a cottage where two men on motorcycles expected us. One was Oosterbroek, the other a local policeman named Witvoet. We asked no questions. Oosterbroek quickly motioned me to mount the rear seat of his 1934 Harley-Davidson. Kettley and Banwell squeezed together behind the policeman. Oosterbroek kicked down the starter pedal and we set out, leading the way.

The engines of the two old machines pounded thunderously in the dead silence of the night. We bounced and skidded across the turnip patches, cut deep swaths through barley fields, roared up muddy embankments and raced over narrow bicycle paths at full throttle. I could see nothing, but I held on grimly and was immensely relieved when we finally stopped about an hour later outside an unpainted chicken coop in a deserted field. A thin man in a worn tweed jacket and plus fours stood waiting by the door. The chicken coop belonged to young Henk Pouw's farm at Ennyshoeve – a well-known stopover for evaders. Pouw loaned his farm to the Resistance while he attended to his banking business in Amsterdam, where his father still played an important role in the Dutch banking system. The Ennyshoeve was an isolated, seldom-visited place. Otherwise the shocking noise of our motorcycles would have awakened every German for miles.

When the door of the chicken coop closed behind me I saw a single candle flickering on a table surrounded by four silent men. The slim, dark-haired individual in golfing pants intro-duced himself as Rengers Hora Sikkama, a Dutch baronet who came from an old family in Frisia. Once he had been a cavalry officer. His father, a professor at Utrecht University and married to a German woman, was pro-German. When Sikkama's fellow officers became prisoners in 1940, he had gone into hiding at Putten and joined the Resistance. He had not seen his father for four years. (Before spring came, Sikkama and Pouw would both be killed by the Germans.) Van Geen, another one of the group, was the farmer son of the Burgomaster of the village of Putten. The third man, dressed in dirty blue jeans, taught mathematics at Apeldoorn while the fourth, clothed in a thick black business suit, was a councillor in a nearby village.

Sikkama showed me two Dutch SS soldiers, imprisoned in a tiny adjoining room, who had been taken a week ago in a raid on a police station to free a number of Resistance men. Then the baronet brought out a Bren gun and put it on the table. It had arrived on an RAF drop two nights ago and Sikkama wanted to know how it worked. Banwell, a former instructor, proudly went through the drill of dismantling and putting the weapon together again in the prescribed time of two minutes, to the amazement of the four Resistance men. Late that night Sikkama took me aside and asked if it might be possible for Banwell to remain and fight with them. They desperately needed someone experienced in weapons and explosives to help. Banwell, a professional soldier since 1931, would undoubtedly be a greater asset to the Putten group than Kettley or myself. (Banwell's choice initiated the disastrous chain of events that led him eventually to Auschwitz concentration camp.) That evening I expected Banwell to follow me in a few weeks.

On the morning of October 1 Roelof van Valkenburg arrived to guide me and Kettley further south. I left Banwell that day with a certain amount of unconscious anxiety. We followed the Dutchman on bicycles at a swift pace through the small villages of Terschuur and Achterveld. Van Valkenburg never slackened speed as we plunged from main thoroughfares crowded with Germans back into wooded paths and out again into open countryside. The relentless giant, whose long legs pedalled on, piston-like, worked for the RD, or Radio Dienst, the Resistance communication network under command of Jan Tijssen, Lange Jan of Hilversum. Tijssen operated a cleverly organized system of strategic sites about the country-side manned by girls and boys who passed intelligence back to his headquarters. Van Valkenburg formed an important part of the ingenious Tijssen organization. The girl couriers covered as much as a hundred miles or more a day by bicycle, forging the links that kept the communication system alive. Van Valkenburg, a former third-year medical student at Utrecht University, left school to join the Resistance in March 1943 – on the day all students who wished to study were ordered to take a loyalty pledge to the German occupation authorities. When the Dutchman went underground, he took his blonde girl friend Bep Labouchère, with him.

Although we followed our guide with difficulty, van Valken-burg was really very tired. His legs pumped automatically. All the previous night he had waited at the secret dropping zone known as Bertus, outside the little village of Voorthuizen, for the RAF Stirling to appear. But the plane did not come. At dawn van Valkenburg and his men left the field and returned to the Wuf Langerwey farm to report to Kirschen. Then the Dutchman cycled fifteen more miles to the Ennyshoeve to fetch Kettley and myself. Now he was taking us another fifteen miles back to the Langerwey farm, where I had been sum-moned by his superior. Van Valkenburg had been on his bicycle for almost twenty-four hours.

In late morning of October 2 we arrived at our destination at the farm of Langerwey, about three miles to the west of Barneveld. Van Valkenburg pointed to the middle one of three unpainted chicken coops that appeared unattended in the over-grown grass. We hid our vehicles on the field and walked over the last hundred feet to our destination and knocked several times on the door. From within I could hear a faint tapping sound, like a woodpecker at work. The door opened and a small, athletic man in uniform, Corporal Jean Moyse, motioned us to enter quickly. Moyse's companion, signaller René Pietquin, also in uniform, had just tapped out a message to London on the new Jedburgh wireless set. A hand-powered generator lay on the floor with two Thompson sub-machine-guns, ammunition and an opened box of food stacked beside it. The interior of the building had a dazzling effect on me. The walls were finished in bright, freshly painted acoustic panelling. The living quarters looked exceptionally orderly, clean, immaculate. Gilbert Sadi-Kirschen entered neatly dressed from an adjoining room and shook my hand heartily. The Belgian wore thick, black, horn-rimmed glasses, a clean battledress and a Colt .45 strapped to his waist. Through the doorway to his room I observed a large bed covered with an eiderdown quilt. But one person from the four-man Belgian team was absent. Corporal Jules Regner had been sent on a fruitless mission through the lines with the guide van Een to Oosterbeek. Since the War Office had been without any information for four days on Arnhem, Kirschen was ordered to find out what was happening and report back. (Regner eventually reached the airborne division in time to be evacuated across the Rhine with the survivors.)

We exchanged news and gossip. I told Kirschen that Kettley and I would like to reach the Allied lines without delay. He said so would everyone else. A large traffic jam of evaders was building up with which he did not feel equipped to deal. (However, he agreed to facilitate my departure after some persistent persuasion.) Then Kirschen looked at my feet as I fidgeted uncomfortably in my undersized rubber boots. I explained walking had been difficult and the Dutch had no shoes to fit me. The Belgian said he would ask the RAF to send me a pair of civilian boots on the next drop. With new boots I would be capable once again of walking in comfort. We sipped coffee over the kitchen table and talked about the battle. Fortunately I could give him considerable information. Kirschen said I was the second evader he had met from Arnhem. The first, a doctor, Donald Olliff, had been found wandering in circles about the forest with twenty-nine unarmed medical orderlies. Olliff had been brought to the chicken coop a few days ago by van Valkenburg. Orders received from Moor Park instructed the doctor and his men to remain in hiding until further information became available.

I politely declined Kirschen's persistent invitations to remain in Holland for more than a few days. If no arrangements could be made with the Resistance, Kettley and I intended to make our own way out. Kirschen listened patiently and said he understood. In a few days he hoped preparations would be ready. If they were not, then no one could stop me from leaving – although the Belgian did not think I would go far alone. On the other hand, he thought, maybe I would serve a useful function. If I was willing, I could test the route out for others who, he hoped, would be following.

Our meeting created a deep impression on me. Something ruthlessly efficient dominated all Kirschen's activity. Competent, carefully unemotional, the Belgian performed his duty with the will of a man who would finish any job he started whatever the cost. The chicken coop seemed to reflect Kirschen's character. It had the crisp, efficient atmosphere of a military barracks. The complex system of intelligence gathering, which began with the couriers, had its essence distilled in Kirschen's hideout. The SAS officer told me that the list of evaders had grown so large that he could not take up the limited transmission time and send it off by wireless for normal identification. On the next drop two carrier pigeons would be sent so all the known names could be sent back to England. The pigeons were already christened in advance – Puce and Zig.

At the comfortable clubhouse on the golf course at Moor Park, Lieutenant Colonel Ian Collins received his latest communiqué from Kirschen. The large number of evaders began to disturb Collins, who had no idea what to do with so many people milling around behind the enemy lines. He arranged for the appropriate information to be made known in the highest circles of the army. A full report on the evaders would be sent by the GSO 1 to the Under-Secretary of State, Supreme Headquarters Allied Expeditionary Force, Headquarters 21st Army Group and Headquarters 1st Allied Airborne Army.

*

Plans for the ambush were complete.

Late evening on October 2 Tex Banwell, Piet Denkaart, Rengers Sikkama, Chris Helsdingen, Willem van Helsen, Piet Oosterbroek, Ab Witvoet and Frans Slotboom rode their bicycles to a wooded fringe not far from the Oldenaller bridge that led into the village of Putten. All eight men hid their bicycles in the bushes beside the road. The Resistance had also parked a stolen lorry on a side lane which would flash its headlights into the first oncoming vehicle, blinding the driver. A few minutes before midnight the men crept from the shelter of the woods onto the grassy verge and took up final positions. Twenty yards away they could see the sixteen-foot-wide wooden bridge supported by thick timber trestles. Beyond lay the beginning of Putten. Banwell set up his Bren gun and practised moving the weapon through his intended arc of fire. Then he cocked the weapon. Piet Denkaart, the leader of the group, known to everyone as Dikke Ben, crouched in the soft grass near the Englishman. Besides Banwell, whom he had only met for the first time that day, Denkaart thought he had with him six good men who had fought the Germans from the beginning of the war. They could be trusted. The presence of Banwell, a professional soldier, gave Denkaart additional confidence. The sergeant not only knew his business but also knew how to take orders without questioning them – a rare quality in the Resistance.

At quarter past midnight Banwell heard the motor from the first of the German vehicles approaching from the south. Someone flashed the prearranged signal from a lamp. All the Englishman knew about the ambush was what Denkaart told him a few hours earlier. The occupants of several German vehicles were to be annihilated. A German officer in a staff car would be carrying important documents which were to be captured. They would eventually pass through other hands all the way back to England.

The nervous Resistance men waited with their Sten guns as the noise of the vehicles grew louder. The only man who seemed without nerves that night was Banwell, who squinted through the gun sights at the first lorry and curled his finger around the trigger. Then he squeezed. Nothing happened. Banwell's gun jammed. He cleared it and began firing a few seconds later. Denkaart flashed on the headlights from the Resistance vehicle and the first German lorry rolled onto the side of the road and burst into flame. Banwell saw several Resistance men fleeing in panic. At long intervals several more enemy trucks passed by. When no German opposition materialized, the Dutchmen returned to the roadside. The sergeant figured he must have killed all the occupants of the first two vehicles. But he was not certain since he did not bother to investigate. But somehow a stray unexplainable bullet fired by one of the Germans lodged in Slotboom's stomach.

A large sealed envelope marked "top secret" was removed from the dispatch case of the single German officer they found alive on the side of the ditch. From his case Banwell took a small steel mechanism that probably formed some part of a V-2 rocket. Although the German lived, his right knee cap had been blown off and Denkaart feared he would bleed to death if left alone. The men, their mission accomplished, carried the wounded officer and the dying Slotboom back to the farmhouse of Henk Pouw an Ennyshoeve in the early hours of the morning on October 3. Here they bandaged the German's wounds. At the farm Denkaart and Banwell favoured killing the dying German but this was overruled by the others. On the night following the ambush the German officer was put into a wheelbarrow and rolled to within a hundred yards of an army post near the village of Stroe and left in a conspicuous place by the side of the road where he would be easily discovered. Next day a German patrol found him. This act of clemency did not spare the village of Putten. On the contrary, this living evidence of the ambush inflamed the enemy.

On October 5 German revenge against the citizens of the village began at dawn without warning. A large part of the village of a thousand inhabitants was put to the torch, razed to the ground. Several of the male population were shot. The remainder, 590 men, were deported and sent to concentration camps in Germany where 541 died. That same day the Germans burned down the farmhouse of Pouw at the Ennyshoeve where Banwell hid in the concrete cellar. From the charred remains of the building the scorched sergeant emerged after the fire, his clothes in tatters, almost asphyxiated by smoke. He struggled out through the ruins and fled into the safety of the woods.

Digby Tatham-Warter's daily life functioned with a regular rhythm. From October 4, the day he arrived at Bill Wildeboer's house, Tatham-Warter adopted a routine that changed very little until the day he left.

After dinner each night Wildeboer would put his guest to bed in a dug-out shelter beneath a wood pile in the backyard. The shelter had a cot and a few pieces of furniture and aside from being a little damp was reasonably comfortable and warm. Wildeboer had used it himself numerous times over the years when on the run from the Gestapo. In the early morning the logs would be removed and Tatham-Warter would be let out. After a shave he would breakfast with the family, which consisted of Wildeboer's wife and their two small daughters. About 10.0 a.m. the British major would visit Lathbury at Menno de Nooy's house on Brouwersstraat where usually Tony Hibbert would be in attendance; sometimes joined by Captain Tom Wainwright or Sergeant Major Robert Grainger. They would take morning coffee and then convene their headquarters meeting with their Resistance comrades. Plans for individual escapes or the formation of joint battle teams made up of both Dutch and British would be discussed. But every plan depended on news from the elusive Second Army, or upon instructions relayed from Kirschen.

At the conclusion of their morning "O" group, Tatham-Warter set out either in the company of Wildeboer, de Nooy or one of the other Resistance men to inspect new airborne arrivals in the Ede area. Every evader within twenty miles of Ede at one time or another gained confidence by the casual, unexpected appearance of the wandering major, who travelled with complete disregard for the German presence. Twice weekly Tatham-Warter met with Kirschen in his chicken coop. Reports of the eleven men sent individually at different times through the Maurik-Tiel route, referred to only by code "W," were awaited with intense interest.

On October 7 Kirschen arranged for his fourth supply mission at "Bertus," the secret dropping zone north of Barneveld. This drop provided much needed arms, cigarettes and a little food for the evaders. A few nights later Bertus became unusable when the Germans surrounded the field. But they were several days too late. Bertus had served its purpose. Meanwhile Tatham-Warter had a full-time job trying to restrain the confident Resistance from carrying out any foolhardy raids with their new weapons that could compromise the British. Putten had already caused incalculable agony to the population. Wildeboer, that former tough sergeant of the Netherlands Army, had an unquenched thirst for killing Germans. The presence of the British major made him more manageable.

Several times a week after curfew Wildeboer would conduct Tatham-Warter to Bennekom, where Alex Hartmann continued to furtively operate the PGEM telephone line to his counterpart at Nijmegen in liberated Holland. At prearranged times Tatham-Warter would speak to Hugh Fraser, the SAS major based south of the Rhine. Briefly the two men – one deep in enemy territory, the other in the gay atmosphere in free Holland – exchanged news and pleasantries. Once his business was concluded, Tatham-Warter would bicycle home.

Back at Wildeboer's house before bedtime, the major would take a glass of home-brewed gin before descending for the night into his shelter beneath the wood pile in the garden. The Macostan paint factory, owned by the de Nooy family, still had a few barrels of alcohol for paint making carefully hidden away. Some tasty but strong drinks were concocted from this well-guarded cache. Early in October three German officers were billeted upstairs in Wildeboer's home. At night, while Tatham-Warter discussed his plans – sipping a drink and smoking home-made cigarettes – he could hear the Germans talking and moving about above him in the living room.

*

Bep Labouchère came for me at the Termaten farmhouse. By bicycle she guided me to Kirschen's chicken coop. My boots had arrived. They were dropped the previous night by a Stirling bomber at Bertus a week before its discovery. They fitted perfectly and were carefully broken in and sufficiently soiled so as not to appear too new. In addition to the boots, Kirschen handed me a detailed map, elaborately prepared by Piet Rombout, the local Resistance cartographer, showing German troop concentrations in a wide area of northern Holland. A second document gave the routes of enemy troop movements eastward across the country. I tucked them both safely into my new boots and said farewell. Kirschen had become a friend. We had forged a deep, life-long association. As I left, Moyse tapped out a message to Moor Park announcing my departure.

We picked up Kettley at the farm. After a sentimental good-bye with our generous hosts, Mr. and Mrs. Termaten, we cycled southward towards the Rhine. The red-faced farmer Termaten had insisted I become a fellow countryman. He had grown fond and offered to adopt me. I said one day I would be back to give him my decision. Bep, riding a hundred feet ahead, led us on towards our rendezvous in the woods eight miles away near the village of Maarn. Between tall beech trees, on narrow, wooded paths spongy with pine cones and moss, we rode on until a meadow appeared which faced the Utrecht-Arnhem route. German troops and transport almost crowded us off the road as we followed Bep, threading her way through the massive column of infantry going eastward. Half an hour later we were at our rendezvous, a small knoll in the woods at a crossroads near Maarn. A smiling, blond-haired man and a girl stood by their bicycles watching. Mies, Bep's sister, would accompany her back the way she came. The blond Dutchman, Jen de Bloois, known to his friends only as Piet de Springer (the parachutist), would take us to the next post. (De Bloois, a peasant from Maasland, had escaped to England in 1941 and joined the Free Netherlands Forces. He had been parachuted near Breda in May 1944. He had been very active as a radio operator. Now he was a guide, one of the best.)

De Bloois spoke no English but we understood each other. He would lead Kettley and me south to the north bank of the Rhine at the Maurik crossing. We shook hands with the girls in the middle of the pine forest as the charming Labouchère sisters took their leave. De Bloois made it clear we had to hurry. We were late for our next meeting. Suddenly, a few minutes later, quite breathless from the exertion, the sisters overtook us. Bep thrust two presents at me. One was the woollen, chequered scarf she wore over her blonde hair, the other a small Dutch–English dictionary. Then the laughing girls were off, as suddenly as they came, driving hard around the curving path, disappearing in the woods.

De Bloois allowed us to break our journey at the farmhouse of van Kleef, where a hot meal had been prepared. While we lunched our guide left without explanation. In his absence a tall, quiet Dutchman took his place at the table. E. Preys spoke fluent English and introduced himself as an agent from the Special Forces. Out of his stocking he produced a map giving us an up-to-date summary of German positions along the Rhine and Waal. Apparently the way down to the river was free. We listened to what he had to say suspiciously in de Bloois's absence. A few minutes later our guide burst into the room and saw the stranger. His hand rested nervously on the gun stuck into his belt beneath his coat. He would not have hesitated to kill if he thought we were in danger. But the stranger explained his identity. The tension eased. De Bloois then presented Kettley and myself with a .38 pistol which he had just removed from a local arms cache. We stuck the guns in our trousers feeling a little more secure.

An hour later we came to the winter dike and walked our

bicycles across several hundred yards of deserted fields to the Rhine. All land within a mile of the river was out of bounds to civilians. At three o'clock that afternoon we finally reached the water's edge without incident. On the far shore two boys sat on the grass idly looking at us. Then a Dutch peasant in clogs, dirty blue denims and smoking a small clay pipe suddenly appeared from behind a tree and told us to follow him to his row boat hidden among the reeds. We cast off for the village of Maurik. The blond de Bloois waved good-bye for the last time as he climbed back up the river bank, disappearing into the fields.

(One day, some months later, Jan de Bloois made his last jump. It was four days after Christmas and a fresh snowfall lay on the ground. De Bloois peacefully waited his turn for a haircut in the barber shop of de Jong, a Resistance meeting place in the village of Langbroek. Without warning the Dutchman was suddenly confronted by several members of the German Green Police who had come by chance to arrest de Jong for refusing to cut their hair. Outside leaning against the building rested de Bloois's bicycle with important documents that he had to deliver hidden under the seat. De Bloois vowed long ago that he would never be taken alive. Immensely strong and quick, he pushed aside several of the Germans and leapt out of the door and managed to reach his vehicle. If the bicycle had not skidded on the wet ground he would have escaped, but instead he fell. As he rose to run he was shot in the back and died, bleeding to death in the falling snow. No one in the village of Langbroek had paid much attention to de Bloois while he lived. No one knew much about him. But as de Boeree reports, a strange thing happened that day. The Germans allowed no one to approach the body. But suddenly everyone knew the name of the tall, blond boy lying dead in the blue raincoat and what he did. The whole village paid homage to him. Six days later and Germans carted de Bloois off and the corpse was tossed into an unmarked grave.)

At Maurik, Henk Kok – who was waiting for us on the south bank – took us to the house of the widow Kok, a large, bosomy woman with twelve devoted children. In the neighbourhood people knew her fondly as "moeke," a familiar term for mother. We would stay with the friendly widow until the route to Tiel was ready.

*

By the middle of October Moose Heyliger had come up many times to the Rhine and gazed across in the hazy light of dusk. The sight of the sombre, black river made Moose feel melancholy and yearn for his country home in New England. The north bank looked deserted, although the American paratrooper knew otherwise. German troops, bored by the prospect of a long winter, were dug in like the Americans, waiting for something to happen. While men of Lieutenant Colonel Robert Strayer's 2nd Battalion paddled silently across the water in rubber dinghies in the night to determine German strength or to take prisoners, the enemy lethargically retaliated. They probed the front-line position of the 506th Regiment, that most-northerly, slender spearhead of the Allied Army in Holland. Moose and the men of his headquarters platoon hated the boredom, the cold, the misery they endured along the frozen river line. Almost as insufferable as the deadly boredom was the British food. Under command of the Second British Army the Americans ate the infamous compo rations. Tasteless steak and kidney pie, glutinous oxtail soup and spam came in unending streams as if fed by pipeline from the ordnance depots at Nijmegen. British cigarettes brought more powerful howls of protest from the American paratroopers than the monstrous food. Wet, cold and lonely in their muddy slit trenches on the bank of the Rhine, Moose and his men waited for a break in the tedium.

The job of foraging for food took up a good deal of time in the platoons. The hasty evacuation of the civilian population left many houses in the neighbourhood completely furnished, liveable and in some cases the tables still set and the larders stacked. South of Opheusden lay the small, almost-deserted village of Dodewaard. In the five-mile-wide slender waist between the Rhine and Waal, these two villages were part of the western front line. The empty Dodewaard jam factory still contained barrels of many flavoured jams. The American troops of the 2nd Battalion, sometimes with little else to do, brought back buckets of apple jam to the refuge of their slit trenches. Unmilked cows with swollen udders roamed the fields. Farm boys from Wisconsin milked them, and as the British rations continued to arrive with unrelived monotony, succulent steaks were added to the menus of the American troopers. The occasional squeal of a lost pig often became the first sign of a future pork chop served in the slit trenches beneath the dikes. Bad British food fathered front-line culinary invention, for which the infantry-paratrooper of the 506th Regiment became renowned during these cold, grey, misty days on the river. A shake of a tree in an apple orchard would bring down a rain of apples. Food played a big part in the life of Strayer's 2nd Battalion. Moose and his men began to eat better than they thought possible when they first went up the icy river that winter of 1944.

The land known as "The Island" defined the Allied occupied area, enclosed by the Rhine on the north and the Waal on the south. At the western wasp waist of Opheusden and Dodewaard, the line ran along the river ten miles east to Arnhem. Then it ran south along the Arnhem–Nijmegen road. American and German troops opposed one another on the west, the north and the east in a stalemate.

From the living room of his farmhouse at Hemmen, Strayer commanded the three depleted companies of his battalion with his officers, Lieutenant Lewis Nixon, the S3, Captain McMillan of D Company, Lieutenant Van Dyke of E Company, Captain Spear of F Company and the sad-faced Heyliger of Headquarters Company. This constituted his effective command. The forward sections were in position within a hundred feet of the Rhine. Most of the men had been with Strayer since the Normandy landing on June 6, 1944. Links between men and officers were close. Strayer and his regimental commander, Sink, had known each other from the days of the formation of the regiment in 1942. They were old friends. Heyliger seemed to enjoy a special relationship with his commander, often acting as a kind of troubleshooter. Men and officers went through the dreary, daily routine with little enthusiasm, always wet from sleeping on the sodden earth, always tired, always cynical. On those wet, grassy dikes facing the Rhine the sun hardly ever shone. Clothes never dried out completely, your feet were always sopping and no amount of shaving made one feel clean. Nothing dispelled the sense of deadly, dirty monotony that ate steadily away at morale and discipline.

To Strayer the north shore looked calm enough. It was hard to understand that a few miles back the Resistance worked continuously to safeguard several hundred Allied soldiers. Their preservation demanded constant attention. He imagined that the Resistance, their food resources taxed to breaking point, would have gladly welcomed all the uneaten compo rations that were left lying in the fields. Nor could Strayer know that while his men watched this water barrier silently in the night, shooting up their flares, Tatham-Warter, Wainwright, de Nooy and Driekus van de Pol probed for an opening in the enemy's defence that could lead them down to the Rhine. Around Wageningen and Renkum it was entirely possible that Strayer's men could have met with Tatham-Warter on their occasional reconnaissance across the river. Neither could the colonel have any way of finding out that Wainwright had finally reached the shore of the river, detecting at last a small undefended opening between two enemy posts.

Meanwhile, Strayer and his wet, weary GIs shuffled around in the shadow of the dikes, ignorant of the intense activity taking place three hundred yards away. The men looked like those caricatures of the war artist Bill Mauldin – hands in pocket, sleeping as they stood, gazing with glazed eyes through the never-ending grey drizzle out over the water. Once in a while Strayer thought of his old friend David Dobie, who had landed at Oosterbeek, and wondered whatever became of him.

Between October 5 and 9, six men tried to escape across the Rhine to the home of the buxom widow Kok at Maurik. The party consisted of two Dutchmen guiding four paratroopers. One of the Dutchmen, Siem van den Bent, and three of the paratroopers were captured. The remaining guide fled north into hiding at Apeldoorn. The captured van den Bent was shot for his part in the attempt on October 10 and buried in the cemetery at Utrecht. The news of the failure spread within hours by word of mouth and was picked up by Kirschen. He passed back the warning to Ede that the Maurik route might be finished. For a large body of men there was only one dangerous alternative to Maurik: straight acrosss the Rhine through the densest part of the enemy's defences.

Kirschen became a clearing house. In addition to locating the sites of V-2 rockets aimed at London and reporting enemy troop movements, much of his transmission time was taken up with the activities of the evaders. After two weeks at the chicken coop, he reluctantly, against orders, changed from his uniform to civilian clothes, since his movements among the Dutch population made his instructions obsolete. He would have to risk shedding his miliary immunity and suffer the consequences. Meanwhile Van Valkenburg managed Kirschen's affairs with immaculate skill, supervising the evergrowing Intelligence network. The Belgian's obsession with security probably saved him from capture on more than one occasion.

The SAS officer maintained a discreet distance between himself and the locals, insisting at all times on the strictest attention to minute detail. This strictness and constant concern with security annoyed the Resistance men, many of whom in this fifth year of war had grown careless. In the attractive girl courier, Bep Labouchère, and her unsmiling boyfriend, Van Valkenburg, Kirschen had found the perfect team to assist him. Certainly the Belgian must have been one of the shrewdest agents of the SAS brigade. His prudish appearance, accented by his horn-rimmed glasses, was deceptive. Kirschen's agility of mind allowed him quickly to adjust to new and dangerous situations. (On November 3 an accidental fire burned out Kirschen's second hideout in a hut at the Evers's fruit farm north of Tiel. It destroyed all his equipment as well as his code book. With a spare wireless set hidden at the home of Mrs. Vera Hoogeweegen at Maarn, Kirschen radioed in clear language for a new manual. One arrived safely on the next RAF drop two nights later and he continued to transmit.)

Kirschen hardly missed a daily transmission in six months. When he did it was because he was busy escaping from the Germans.

The doctor, Donald Olliff, and his wandering medical orderlies were just settling down comfortably to their new life in the forest at Mossel when Menno de Nooy suddenly visited them. He told Olliff they had to move quickly to a safer place in the nearby woods at Jagersveld. A horse and cart stood by to transport them. The men were to depart in two groups at suitable intervals. Fifteen of Olliff's men were restrained from going at once when they learned the Germans were digging a large artillery emplacement a few hundred feet away. When the enemy stopped digging and took up their positions, the first group of soldiers would leave. However, the Germans took their time. They appeared in no hurry. They dug and drank "Schnapps" and then dug some more. Because of the delay the medical orderlies were unable to use the horse and cart which had to be returned to the owner. Always ready to improvise, the flexible de Nooy borrowed a fire engine from the local brigade at Ede and thus transported the first lot with their uniforms and equipment to Jagersveld. The fifteen men who stayed behind were safely removed by the horse and cart when it returned for them next day.

But the Germans followed Olliff to Jagersveld and billeted themselves in the farmer's house near the sheep pen where the doctor and the orderlies hid. The doctor, a very tall, sensitive individual, was offended by the putrid stench of the sheep with which he had to share his quarters. However, it was better than being a prisoner or shot as a spy in civilian clothes. When the German troops left next day, Olliff felt immensely relieved.

During the Arnhem battle de Nooy and his group had captured five SS soldiers who they put in the sheep pen with the medical men for lack of a better place. The closely guarded SS prisoners posed a difficult problem for de Nooy. The German prisoners now knew of the presence of the medical men and the complicity of the Dutch. It also meant extra mouths to feed, and if the prisoners escaped the farmer would be executed and mass reprisals would follow for the local population. Olliff felt a revulsion at the only apparent solution. He was not a killer. The small pistol he carried had still not been fired and he was not anxious to use it. His men were all of similar disposition and they had no illusions about the glory of war.

De Nooy did not deliberate very long. He asked Olliff to show him the quickest and most effective way to kill a man. Olliff pointed to a spot on the forehead. An hour later the Resistance men took the five Germans behind the sheep pen and shot them. That night Olliff slept on the ground over the graves of the dead men. He claimed he deliberately did this to prove the decision to kill had been right, however repulsive. This memory and one other haunted Olliff all his life. The second memory was a sound. The agonized squeal of pigs the Germans shot with their machine pistols. This almost-human screech came to Olliff over the farmlands like the dying howl of some soldier in his last moments of mortal agony.

A few days later a small, rotund Russian whose ambling gait and appearance reminded Olliff of a bear, joined the group. The Resistance had found Vladimir Kapustin at Deelen wandering around quite lost. He had escaped while digging slit trenches for the German defences after being captured on the eastern front early in 1942 and sent from one slave labour camp to another ever since. No one knew how he had arrived in Holland, but he was genuine. He only spoke Russian. His single means of communication was to grin with his short teeth at Olliff, who would grin back hospitably. The Russian attached himself to Olliff, following him wherever he went.

(When the time came Kapustin would follow Olliff to the Rhine, take a wrong turn and be made a prisoner once more.)

One day as he made his rounds towards the middle of October, Tatham-Warter rode up to the sheep pen at Jagersveld, parked his bicycle against the wall and approached the British doctor. Neither man had met before. Tatham-Warter, attired in a white mackintosh and dark glasses, introduced himself to the suspicious Olliff. After a small chat during which the major reassured the doctor that his credientials were in order, he climbed onto a table in the shed and addressed the astounded medical orderlies and the uncomprehending Russian. He told them they were all going to escape. A bold plan was now being prepared by the airborne headquarters in Ede in cooperation with the Allied Army on the south side of the Rhine. They should forget about the Second Army coming to rescue them. It would not happen. The medical orderlies, on the run for almost four weeks – dirty, wet, unwashed – accepted the news in amazingly good humour, albeit sceptically. The idea seemed far-fetched. Olliff's men had been running from one forest to another, constantly chased by Germans whom they had no desire to fight. All they wanted to do was to go home. Olliff did not feel entirely confident that the man standing on the table with the dark glasses could lead them all out of this wilderness. But Olliff did not know Tatham-Warter very well. In the following week he visited Ollif once again and the doctor grew increasingly confident that the major might just do what he said he would.

The wooded triangle of land bounded by Arnhem, Apeldoorn and Ede was a blessing for the evaders. It represented an area of about 256 square miles threaded with cart tracks, bicycle paths, interspersed with sheep pens, woodsmen huts, isolated farmhouses and small, scrubby sand dunes. While the terrain may not have been ideal for an organized fight, it was an excellent place to hide. To the west of Ede were open meadows and polder fields all the way south to the Rhine.

Before any plans for escape could be hatched, one had to

feed two hundred or more hungry soldiers. Whole families of couriers like the Steenbergens at Krommesteeg, the de Nooys of Ede, the Van der Vens, the Nijhoffs and countless others took to the roads and bicycle paths with sacks of bread, butter, potatoes and cheese for their supply missions. Forged ration coupons added to the availability of foodstuffs given by friendly farmers. Forged identity documents were turned out in wholesale lots. Never had the people of Ede seen such a large number of young deaf-mutes of military age circulating through the area. While Hackett was posing for an identity card photo, the electrical current diverted by the Resistance for the purpose blacked out the town for an hour.

The master food supplier was Marcel Herz, a Jew, who people knew only by his code name, "Rinus". He controlled most of the distribution. Each day he would collect fifty large loaves from the baker, Evers, in Ede and pay for them with forged coupons and stolen money. Twenty bushels of potatoes, twenty-eight pounds of jam and butter, twenty litres of milk from the farm at Otten and innumerable sacks of vegetables in season were the daily quota taken by cart and bicycle to evaders hiding around the Ede countryside. Several times a week a cow was slaughtered and divided up. Sometimes as a luxury Herz located an occasional sack of sugar. English books were collected to allay boredom among the soldiers confined to their cramped quarters underground or in tiny bedrooms. Herz supervised his supply system closely from a different base each day at a time when Dutchmen themselves scarcely had enough to eat. It was a memorable feat and his success did much to suppress the constant anxiety felt by the listless troops. The lack of physical activity for young men used to constant exertion caused in some a growing apathy, dependency and often deep depression. A few were driven to try ill-conceived escapes. The attempt of four impatient airborne led by Pardu van den Bent ended in disaster and death. This demonstrated to the evader headquarters staff that in addition to luck one required patience and meticulous planning. But a large number of soldiers could not be kept hidden for very long in an area overcrowded with passing German troops and Gestapo agents. Sooner or later someone would talk to the wrong person or confide in the wrong farmer, or a Dutch informer would infiltrate and the delicately linked system of supply and information would be penetrated. The effect would be disastrous for the population.

As the position of the Germans grew more precarious, their actions became crueller, more uncontrolled, more anonymous. Rumours of many hundreds of Englishmen hiding in northern Holland made the Germans unsure whether bands of sabo-teurs had landed to prevent their escape east, or whether the rumoured enemy among them represented a prelude to a new invasion from the south. The Gestapo, Green Police, the Dutch SS – indeed the full apparatus of the German Army – became alerted in October to the invisible enemy in their midst.

While the Germans stepped up their search for the evaders, Tatham-Warter went about his business unconcerned. How-ever, at the house of Bill Wildeboer certain incidents for Tatham-Warter were becoming distinctly embarrassing. The major had a problem that occupied him every evening and whose resolution had now become a question of principle. When he returned before curfew from his long bicycle tours he would often find the doorway blocked by the simultaneous arrival of German officers billeted at the house. At the begin-ning he made way for them, but his attitude gradually changed. A discreet individual would unquestionably have allowed the Germans to pass first. But the major decided otherwise. He thought the moment had come to assert his pride. The first time he tried to cut off the enemy in the battle of the doorway a brief jostling took place and then stopped. To his surprise, the Germans reacted with unexpected courtesy and allowed Tatham-Warter to go in ahead. Eventually the Englishman developed a nodding acquaintance with the officers billeted in the big room upstairs, some of the Germans actually giving the major a friendly pat on the back at their frequent meetings on the front doorstep. In the evening, while they ate their nightly bowl of porridge, downstairs in the living room Wildeboer and Tatham-Warter plotted means of sabotage and destruction against the enemy.

Not far away the house of Aart Roelofsen in the village of Lunteren became a transit post well known to more than fifty evaders and frequently visited by the major. Uncle Aart, as he was fondly called, found many friendly homes in the neighbourhood where the soldiers could be quietly dispersed in small numbers. There were dozens of hiding places – part of the delicately linked chain of protection held together by the continual coming and going of couriers who carried information, instructions and equipment. The Steenbergens, the Van der Vens and Captain van Tynen and his Carol Group near Barneveld all helped to hide the airborne soldiers. One of the helpers, Colonel Jansen, a former Dutch officer, was picked up one day by the Green Police. In October the Gestapo took him to the extermination camp at Natzweiler where he was soundly beaten, then placed at the top of a high stairway and kicked down to his death by a Dutch stormtrooper.

But every Dutchman did not prove helpful to the Arnhem survivors. Tony Deane-Drummond had half a dozen doors slammed in his face after he escaped from his cupboard at Velp. Wip Zeilmaker, a burgomaster of the Renkum area, could not be relied upon and represented a constant source of danger in the Planken Wambuis woods near Wolfheze, where the Resistance had hidden many men. More than one Dutchman might have died and several evaders been captured because of the Dutch informer Ries Jansen, who worked for the Gestapo.* In Apeldoorn, Buitenhuis, the bicycle dealer, not only ingeniously rebuilt antique bicycles for the Englishmen from an odd assortment of spare parts, but also smuggled several dozen airborne out of the Apeldoorn hospital. From here they were taken south to the home of Roelofsen at Lunteren. In Lunteren the houses of T. Hendriks, A. S. Hollenberg, J. C. Herz, G. V. D. Berkt and many others made the place at times seem more like an airborne transit camp than a Dutch village. When

*Ries Jansen was sentenced to death after the war and executed.

the village of Lunteren reached saturation point, Jacob Heg at Barneveld hid the evaders in his house and sheds.

The airborne troops turned up in all sorts of ways and in varying conditions. Just before dark one day at the end of September, two tattered soldiers came out of the woods into a meadow at the Nieuw Reemst farm looking for food. They had been living on beetroots and raw turnips for a week. They were dirty, tired, and one man was continually vomiting. The farmer at Nieuw Reemst had watched them unnoticed on several previous evenings leaving their hiding place. Fortunately, the farmer was friendly and knew where to go for assistance. Menno de Nooy and Bertus van der Post were informed and picked up the soldiers.

De Nooy discovered there were nine evaders hiding close to the first group, some of whom were wounded and required immediate medical treatment. Doctor Krayenbrink, whose fake bandages, generously splashed with red ink, were always available for these events, came to attend the men. With the doctor's help, the Resistance formed a Red Cross convoy to transport the British to safety. The weapons of the eleven soldiers were put onto a cart and covered with straw. In civilian clothes, the evaders sat on top while a farmhand drove the cart at a slow trot, jogging over the country tracks. The doctor led the way on his bicycle to warn any inquisitive Germans that his patients were very sick and could not be molested. To complete the camouflage, two old ladies were picked up and warned not to attempt conversation with the men. The patients were in a daze, hit by shells from attacking Typhoons a few days ago. By coincidence they were also deaf and dumb. Jan Andrius, who sat on the cart beside the wounded men, had rehearsed his story well. It was not the first time he used it. Before the cart came to the house of Van der Fliert at the Jagersveld forest, the puzzled old ladies were gently disembarked and thanked. At the destination the weapons and equipment were hidden and the wounded were left in the care of a Mrs. Dulfer. The healthy soldiers were moved close to Ede and put in a hen house where they were fed mashed potatoes, jam, bread, cheese and pails of ersatz coffee from Herz's supply organization.

Gerrie van Wijhe, about the same time, accidentally came across Privates George Watt and Jack Spruce, who were aimlessly wandering along the Bunschoterweg at Amersfoort. They had been stranded by a frightened guide who could find no friendly haven for them in the town. The men over a period of three days had walked twenty-five miles south to the Rhine and returned when they only saw enemy troops. Fortunately, Van Wijhe met the men before the Germans did and took them to his home next to his hardware shop. To feed his guests he exchanged all the hardware utensils he had left for food. And when Watt had his birthday in October a fabulous meal was prepared to which the local Resistance were invited. The two soldiers lived in an enviable comfort at Van Wijhe's until the night of October twenty-first.

The enterprising paratroop corporal, Jimmy James, constantly baffled Harry Montfroy by his activities. Jeanne Lamberts, proprietor of De Lange Hut, had also run across James when he lived in an ingeniously constructed shelter in the nearby woods. James had a radio at the time with which he and his men listened to the BBC news every day. Almost every night he would enter Arnhem, walking ten miles alone, dodging the enemy patrols and reappearing at Van der Ven's farm before dawn laden with food for his men.

To relieve the boredom Brigadier Lathbury took up the study of Dutch, but the learning of the language seemed beyond him. He had identified every bird he could see from the limited view of his window and read all the books brought to him – some twice. The continued sitting and waiting began to wear on the brigadier's nerves. The atmosphere had a shoddy, theatrical quality as he watched the Germans racing around the streets in his brigade's jeeps. Even the danger seemed unreal. The occasional bicycle ride from his house to Hackett's residence a few blocks away on Torenstraat helped somewhat to break the bleak monotony. He found Hackett weak of body but extremely strong of mind. Although Hackett could not move more than a few steps, he appeared considerably less bored than Lathbury. The little man listened to Lathbury's plans to break out south to the Allied lines with some scepticism. It would require more luck than skill, he thought. His own plans for escape were still a long way off.

Above Hackett's bed one of the de Nooy sisters had embroidered a picture of Sleeping Beauty with the inscription: "And so she slept for a hundred years." It reminded him that no matter how impatient he felt, he could do nothing to hurry his departure. He still had several months' convalescence ahead. The attic in Torenstraat was a long way from Aleppo, where he had roamed alone on a mule with an Arab helper in the desert taking notes for his thesis on the twelfth-century Syrian conqueror, Saladin. But Hackett had come to terms with his environment. It became a period of significant philosophical development. He had somehow touched upon new intellectual horizons in these strange, isolated quarters that would affect him profoundly for the rest of his life.

A marked difference in temperament separated Hackett from Lathbury. Hackett was self-contained. He could live with himself for long periods and be sustained by inner resources that enabled him to flourish in solitude. He had an elaborate defence, difficult for strangers to penetrate. Only time eroded away Hackett's personal awkwardness, but underneath the effort to be social, one always felt the presence of the stiff, eclectic personality of the classical scholar. Indeed, as Hackett once announced, he had joined the army in the hope it would give him time to continue his studies. He always had the knack, under the most bloody of circumstances, to examine events with a kind of scholarly detachment – even when he became the victim himself. In Ede, beneath the woven figure of Sleeping Beauty, Hackett realized that nothing could be taken too seriously, least of all his own predicament. Lathbury was not only a foot taller in height and totally dissimilar in appearance but also given to the grand gesture. He liked to work in teams where he became the team coordinator. Lathbury would never be disturbed by the same profound philosophical problems that engaged his friend. Nor would danger have the same intellectual fascination. However, in spite of the wide differences, the friendship between these two dissimilar brigadiers ripened and deepened in Ede.

Tatham-Warter differed from both these men. His reactions were spontaneous, completely physical. At the time he had neither the charm of Lathbury nor the intellectual preoccupations of Hackett. He controlled the details of his safaris in Kenya in later life with the same calm, purposeful authority as he demonstrated in Ede. The major had a well-established reputation in his battalion for independence at any cost.

When Lathbury's brigade major Tony Hibbert showed up in Ede in his green plus fours, white stockings and grey-and-white checkered coat the brigadier was overjoyed. When the divisional signal officer, Deane-Drummond, appeared on October 7, followed by the commander of the 1st Battalion, David Dobie, men with enough experience to plan any major operation were now present. The mass escape, which had become an accepted fact, would be organized like any other campaign. A little more unorthodox and complex perhaps than most, but nevertheless conceived by soldiers who had already been in many dangerous situations together. By October 10 a detailed plan for a series of ambushes against the enemy was drawn up. Lathbury wished to coordinate the activities of the Resistance and evaders with the hoped-for attack across the Rhine by the Second Army. When the Second Army definitely decided not to attack, the exclusive preoccupation of the evaders focused on mass escape.

Two routes through the German lines were possible. The long route went across the rivers Rhine and Waal by way of Maurik. Although still open, this way grew daily more precarious. Lathbury had played with the idea of taking the long route himself when news came suddenly from the Resistance that it was too dangerous for the brigadier to attempt. Dobie would be among the last evaders to use it successfully. The choices were thus limited. In fact there would be only one way out for a long column of men walking single file. The route dictated itself. It would have to be eight miles directly due south from Ede to the Rhine and then across the river as quickly as possible. The forty-mile-long Maurik route of dirt tracks, main thoroughfares and river crossings was complicated enough for one man, let alone two hundred. It would have to be discounted. Although heavily defended in depth, the short route had to be the way home. Lathbury gave the code name of "Digby" to the future crossing area.

*

I did not know at the time, but Kirschen shadowed me all the way out. His second message, sent to Moor Park on October 2, read:

"Lieutenant Heaps will cross Rhine at Wijk bringing sketch of German positions North of Rhine."

Lieutenant Colonel Collins optimistically expected to meet me in his office at Airborne Headquarters in Moor Park on October 5.

At the house of the widow Kok at Maurik, we met some of her twelve children. Only her sons Anton, Henk, Chris and two of her daughters, Mina and Annie, were at home that day. Koos Meijer, who had been freed by the Resistance from the concentration camp at Amersfoort several weeks ago, joined us later in the afternoon. I asked him what he thought of our chances of crossing the lines. He drew a nervous finger across his throat and said, in broken English, "It is like killing self dead."

I became further concerned when the widow shook me awake in my chair, trembling with fear. The Germans were coming. One of the daughters led us out to the back fields, where Kettley and I burrowed under a pile of apples. A few minutes later the widow, her huge body shaking with helpless laughter, dug us out. The Germans wanted eggs, not Englishmen. I was not too sure. The farmer Termaten and his wife, who had

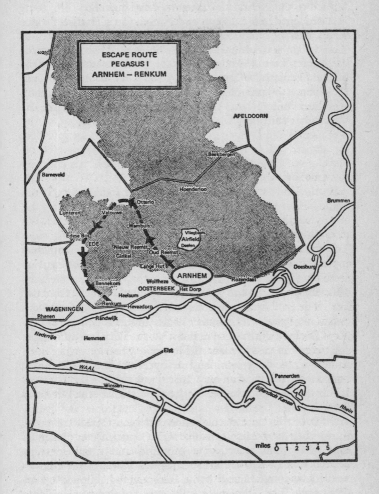

ESCAPE ROUTE
PEGASUS I
ARNHEM — RENKUM

APELDOORN

Beekbergen

Barneveld

Hoenderloo

Brummen

Otterlo

Lunteren   Valouwe

Wambuis

Edese Bos

EDE   Nieuwe Reemst

Ginkel   Oud Reemst

Vliegbaan
Airfield
Deelen

Lange Hut

ARNHEM

Bennekom

Wolfheze

OOSTERBEEK   Het Dorp

Heelsum

Rozendaal

Doesburg

WAGENINGEN

Renkum   Heveadorn

Rhenen

Randwijk

Nederrijn

Hemmen

Elst

WAAL

Pannerden

Winssen

Bijlandsch Kanaal

Rhein

miles 0 1 2 3 4 5

153

sheltered us a few days ago, had been shot and their farm burned to the ground. I wanted to move quickly.

A student, Leo Lamers, and Anton van t'Hart, a former sergeant in the Dutch Artillery, came to dinner. After the meal these two men would take us to the home of a fruit farmer near Tiel. From here we had to reach the Waal. On the other side of the river, Major David De Volpie's squadron of the 7th Canadian Reconnaissance Regiment patrolled the south bank after dark. But Tiel was a supposedly heavily defended barrier. Van t'Hart said that when the moon went down one of the best men of the Betuwe district would be my guide and take me across. Before dark we followed the Resistance men on bicycles southward as the widow Kok standing in her doorway blew me kisses.

Kettley and I cycled between van 't'Hart and Lamers. If the leading rider ran into trouble he would signal back and the others would immediately turn off and make for the fields. We soon left behind a long German convoy parked by the roadside. The fresh fields of the Betuwe smelled of cold, unpicked apples. Two hours later we arrived at the house of Ebbens, our host. The house, set well back in the orchards near the pleasant little village of Drumpt, fortunately could not be seen from the road. The fruit farmer introduced us to his wife and mother-in-law. They were moderately happy to meet us, but did not share Ebben's dutiful conviction that he had a moral obligation to oppose the Germans. Their privacy had long since been crudely violated by too many strangers. In the living room, comfortably settled in an easy chair, I saw Private Ted Bachenheimer, a brash paratrooper from the 101st Airborne Division. Bachenheimer operated a kind of freelance one-man patrol out of Driel, but this time had wandered a considerable distance outside his territory. With him was Captain Peter Baker of IS9, who would shortly be captured and transported to Germany. A British paratrooper captain whose name I never recalled sat immobilized with a fractured leg propped up on a footstool. In the basement Ebbens had stored boxes of ammunition and arms. Outside in the wood half a dozen local men were in hiding from a forced labour call-up. This was not a place to linger.

In the early hours of the morning I awakened. The sound of light, delicate footsteps could be heard outside my door. I went to investigate and saw two frightened, chalk-faced men quietly descending an attic ladder. Each carried a brown paper bag in his hand. Ebbens, in addition to all his other boarders, sheltered a Jewish family. Two of the men tip-toed by me, carrying their shaven whiskers. I smiled at these sad-faced people as they crept down the stairs into new hiding quarters. (When the fatal knock on the door came for Ebbens it would also come for the Jewish family, who would perish with him.)

In the morning Piet Oosterlee waited quietly downstairs in the living room. This thin, blond boy, a former medical student at the University of Groningen, offered me his hand. When Jews were no longer permitted to attend his University, as a personal protest he went underground like many of his fellow students. That was 1941. Today was October 4, 1944, and in two days at the most I wanted to be on my way out of occupied Holland. Oosterlee agreed to help. He would immediately make a reconnaissance of the river around Tiel and arrange for a rowboat. He would be back to fetch me tomorrow.

In the afternoon the smiling, stocky Franz de Vilder, the famous swimmer of the Waal, made his appearance. He immediately suggested I swim the river with him after dark. Politely, I declined the invitation. Instead I gave him Kirschen's maps which he would take that night and hand over to Allied Headquarters in Nijmegen. I also sent a message saying I would follow the next evening, one way or another. (I later learned that the army reacted to my message generously. They sent out a wide alarm along the whole Allied front. My brother waited for me with some incredulity in the Hochwald forest in Germany two hundred miles away, sitting nervously behind his self-propelled gun. He knew I tended to appear in odd places unexpectedly but was still under the impression I had not left England. A friend, Lieutenant Dick Fox stepped out of his slit trench at midnight in the Black Forest and shouted my name across the German lines.)

Next morning Oosterlee returned from his reconnaissance of the river. Arrangements were complete. We would leave tonight as planned. Flight Sergeant Wood, an aerial gunner, newly arrived from Kirschen, joined me. On September 18 he had been one of the two survivors of a Stirling bomber shot down near Barneveld. Two people were the maximum that Oosterlee could take. Under the circumstances Kettley agreed to remain and would attempt to make Ebbens's house a more secure place for future evaders. I told him under no circumstances should he stay more than a week. After the period of the next full moon he must leave. The luck of Ebbens could not last much longer. We left by bicycle in late morning.

An unusual number of Germans were relaxing in the cafés, strolling along the roads with their girls or gathered in small groups on the streets of Tiel. Suddenly in the centre of the town I heard a loud report like a pistol shot. My rear tyre went flat and I came to a halt. My companions left me far behind, unaware I no longer followed. Several Germans were taking photographs, blocking the route as I walked my vehicle. When one of the soliders laid a hand upon my shoulder, I leapt onto the bike and with strength borne of fear pedalled away on the flat tyre with a burst of speed that surprised the Germans and myself. I caught up with Oosterlee about a mile ahead. The Dutchman looked white and nervous. I think he received that day a flash of premonition that comes to men who flirt constantly with danger. Oosterlee knew his luck was running out.

The family Noordzij lived under the shadow of the river dike. My guide always stopped at the house to obtain the latest information. Here we met the bargeman, Geurt van der Zand, a rough-hewn character in a blue peaked hat, peasant tunic and clogs. Van der Zand would take us the last mile along the river to his barge, hide us and return after dark with a rowboat. The bargeman seemed as tense, and uncertain of the outcome, as

Oosterlee. He too felt something would occur to interrupt our passage. I could understand why Franz de Vilder preferred to swim the Waal alone and keep his own company. In some ways it might be preferable. The route we took appeared too vulnerable to last for any length of time. The danger point was the footbridge over the lock, a hundred yards west. A German machine-gun post guarded the approach. If we were challenged and stopped I intended to shoot my way out. I was too close to the end of the journey to be defeated now.

In an hour it would be dusk. Beyond the lock lay the wide summer dike and the river. We set out for the barge of Van der Zand, Oosterlee leading the way, Wood following and myself bringing up the rear. At the footbridge a German guard spoke to me and I smiled back as I chewed viciously one of the several apples I carried in my pocket for these occasions. With a mouthful of apple, anything I said sounded incomprehensible. Meanwhile Oosterlee, the bargeman and Wood were over the bridge waiting nervously in the shelter of the dike for me to appear. The Germans were in fact warning me to stay off the top where I would make an easy target for the British snipers. They urged me to hurry. It became quite simple now as we strolled casually the last hundred yards to the barge and clambered aboard unseen into the dark, deep hold. One of the Germans began firing wild bursts over the river while another dallied with a Dutch girl by the entrance to the footbridge.

After dark Van der Zand came with a little man, crippled in one leg, carrying a heavy briefcase. He had bought his passage across and was not a welcome addition. Then the bargeman left. In a few minutes he unexpectedly returned and excitedly dropped into the hold. A German patrol had suddenly appeared on the river bank and was coming our way. (Whoever informed the Germans of our presence that night would also be responsible for the death of Oosterlee.) Quickly we clambered onto the deck and then lowered ourselves over the side into a waiting rowboat. It took a few minutes longer to help down the cripple. He asked if I could save him if we sank.

He could not swim. I thought this was a bad time to discuss the matter. Besides, I assured him, I would have considerable trouble saving myself. The bargeman cast off and we drifted off into the current out into the cold darkness of the Waal. I could hear soldiers now climbing aboard the barge, searching the boat. The Germans shouted hoarsely, as they smashed their way into the empty cabin looking for us. Oosterlee rowed with powerful strokes into the middle of the stream. Several Spandau bursts sprayed blindly over the river. Far off red tracers fanned across the water. In the bottom of the boat the cripple fearfully crouched beneath my seat, desperately clutching his briefcase. A flare suddenly lit the night like daylight. But I did not care any more. The boat touched bottom and slid over the long reeds and stopped. We got out and pulled it up the mud flats to the top of the summer dike. I gazed thankfully at the long column of tall poplar trees on either side of the road, standing like sentinels. Then that mysterious sense of exaltation that one can feel at twenty, gripped me, held me motionless. A deep sense of rapture, mystical and mysterious, overcame me. I had learned. Strangers had given me their bed, their food, their friendship and risked their lives for my safety. What more could a man ask of a fellow human.

*

Ebbens was betrayed. An informer told the Gestapo that there were Jews hidden in his house and he was doomed. The informer did not know, however, that Ebbens's home was used by the Resistance for a multitude of purposes. On the evening of October 16, three days after Kettley left, there was a quiet knock on the front door. Ebbens that evening had met by coincidence with Van Zanten, the Resistance chief for the Betuwe region. A shipment of arms had by chance been expected momentarily from across the river. When Ebbens answered the door, a German officer and his sergeant asked if they might enter to look at their map in the light of the living room. The German deception worked. The house had already been surrounded. Although the Germans came looking only for the two Jews, they found ten men, two of whom were pilots, the rest Dutchmen avoiding forced labour. Meanwhile the Resistance arrived with their arms shipment from Tiel. A brief, excited exchange of shots followed between the two sides, but the Resistance was ineffectual in its attempt to dislodge the enemy. But one German suffered severe wounds. The Dutchman outside the house fled into the night. Ebbens, trapped within with his two Jewish refugees, became a prisoner, and that same night the Germans took both him and his wife to Utrecht. On November 14 the Gestapo moved the couple to the village of Renswoude. Here Ebbens was placed before a firing squad with several prisoners being shot in reprisal for a railway blown up by the Resistance. Meanwhile, Ebbens's house was plundered and burned down.

The end of Piet Oosterlee came unexpectedly on the night of October 22. Oosterlee and his helper, Van der Zand, were pumping up their rubber boat on the Waal, below the dike in their customary place outside Tiel, preparing to cross over. Without warning they were surrounded by German soldiers with no chance to flee. Old Noordzij, with an American officer ready to cross on another section of the river, was warned by a boy of the arrest of Oosterlee and managed to escape. Oosterlee, Van der Zand, Mrs. Noodzij and one of her sons were taken to the prison in Tiel. Oosterlee knew from the first moment of his capture that he would be shot. He carried a plan on him of German fortifications of the Waal which the Germans took from his pocket. Next day in a house near the prison the blond Dutch student was tried before a court-martial. Rather than wait for the end, Oosterlee leapt out the window of the house and the Germans machine-gunned him down on the street. That night, Theodor de Boeree, the military historian, states, three corpses of three prisoners were taken several miles downstream in a car and dumped into the river.

Sergeant Major Robert Grainger suffered from acute claustrophobia. The fear he felt living covered up in a trench two and a half feet high, four feet wide and five a half feet long was enormous. The fear mounted daily, until only by the greatest display of willpower did the sergeant major manage to restrain the urge to break out. Every day for eighteen hours a lid covered with earth emtombed Grainger in the field. He managed to see a glimmer of light through a tiny peephole and thus keep his sanity.

Within a period of three days Grainger had been wounded in the leg, pretended to be insane at the Wolfheze Mental Home and now lived shut up in the darkness totally disoriented and possessed with a new kind of terror he never believed existed. Today, September 27, in his hole in the ground, would be a date he would not forget. In spite of the grotesque images of fear playing on his mind he endured his entombment for four interminable days and nights. The agony became far greater than anything he had ever experienced in war.

At dawn next day, Edith Nijhoff rumbled up over the field driving her old cart and horse and took the blinded Grainger out of his hole and put him on the back of the ramshackle wagon under some straw. She covered the soldier with a canvas tarpaulin and drove him to her semidetached brick cottage on Berkenlaan 16, next to the German barracks in Ede. Here Grainger could roam the house freely, but always kept in mind the trapdoor in the attic between the two floors where he could hide instantly on a given signal. The trapdoor had been used dozens of times before Grainger arrived and it would be used again by many other evaders.

In early October Mrs. Nijhoff's daughter, Geraldine, came to her mother's home with a message from Tatham-Warter addressed to the sergeant major. The bold Edith Nijhoff had to curb her open contempt for the enemy. It could endanger the evaders. Grainger was instructed to tighten up the security arrangements in the crowded household. Although the Nijhoff luck held out until the end, Tatham-Warter had started to alter some of the Dutch security arrangements, which he found to be too careless. There were too many Germans in Ede and too many airborne evaders. One slip could destroy the organization the major patiently attempted to build up. In the future the Nijhoffs would have to be a good deal more careful. But no one could really control the defiance of Edith Nijhoff.

Grainger continued to stay at Berkenlaan 16. One day as he took a stroll with Geraldine through the crowded streets of Ede he heard behind him the familiar cadence of hobnailed boots on the cobbles. As he turned he saw a group of airborne prisoners, some wounded, most of them in ragged battledress, marching smartly in step down the street led by an ex-guards' sergeant. The ragged soldiers marched with a parade square precision. In silent, frustrated rage the sergeant major kicked the wheel of a parked motorbike, which toppled into a ditch. Realizing what he had done, he hastily picked it up, while the frightened Geraldine quickly apologized to the angry German dispatch rider. The next day Tatham-Warter and Franks visited the sergeant major. They were looking for another man to accompany them down to the Rhine on their reconnaissance mission along the river. Grainger's reputation and experience as a permanent army man would prove valuable.

By October 16 Lathbury felt particularly miserable and unhappy in his restricted surroundings. He sought relief from his depression by completing his brigade records and preparing lists of recommendations of awards for bravery. One evening the monotony was broken by a visit from a Dutch correspondent of the clandestine press who wanted an interview with the brigadier. Soon Lathbury's charm and vitality had the correspondent captivated. Although the conditions for the interview might have been more auspicious than a tiny bedroom in a small house in enemy territory, nevertheless Lathbury enjoyed every moment. It felt good to express freely feelings on subjects that had been suppressed within him for so long. When the correspondent at the end gave Lathbury two fine, pre-War Dutch cigars in payment, the brigadier felt he received the most precious gifts. He liked good cigars almost as much as he enjoyed the company of attractive women.

Later that night, however, his mood of well-being suddenly disappeared at news brought by a courier. The Germans had started a reign of terror in Apeldoorn and Amersfoort. All males between the ages of seventeen and fifty were being immediately conscripted to dig defences. Objectors were shot on the spot. Men were dragged from their homes in a house-to-house search. A house-to-house search in Ede would be disastrous. That night a German officer came to billet himself with Lathbury at the De Nooys dwelling in Brouwersstraat. But the persuasive Mrs. de Nooy convinced the soldier that the house was so full of refugees she had no more room, and he left.

The next night Lathbury felt the need to see his fellow brigadier Hackett before curfew to discuss the state of affairs of the evaders. That evening he needed to talk to someone, more, it seemed, than on any other occasion. His nerves were on edge. The waiting, the boredom, the tension were taking their toll. By contrast Hackett appeared unusually calm, almost contented, detached. Already he had embarked on his reading campaign with the help of the old maids and consumed a Shakespearian tragedy a day. As well as Shakespeare, the aunts had provided as reading material *Christ on the Indian Road, Dombey and Son, One Thousand and One Gems of English Poetry* and the Bible. Hackett had started out to read them all. While Lathbury and Tatham-Warter were concerned with discovering new routes out through the German lines, Hackett made other exploratory journeys of a more literary nature. His most important, he confessed later, was the discovery that Wordsworth was a great poet. Thackeray refreshed him "like deep and grateful draughts", while *Vanity Fair* provided "coolness, compassion, humility." As Freddy Gough, that wild, overaged, white-haired leader of the reconnaissance squadron said, Hackett had only joined the army because he wanted to read more. And at last he had the time. Lathbury felt he had suddenly entered the small, sparsely furnished room of a rather sickly Oxford don – removed from all the real cares of the outside world.

When Lathbury later stepped back out into the night and returned home, the sense of danger became immediate once again. Tatham-Warter had returned with Alex Hartmann from the power station after speaking to Nijmegen. Dobie, still on his way through the Allied lines, was unreported. If the evaders were to leave Ede, Dobie must succeed soon. Rumours had filtered back through the Resistance that Dobie had experienced agonizing delays on the long route to Maurik, already broken several times by the Germans. It was possible the enemy could break it once again, but no one knew for certain. And the fear persisted in Lathbury's mind that his colonel might have failed. One could not hold several hundred men together in a small town full of German troops for very long before someone, somewhere, was discovered. The end could not be far off. A single informer could break the organization. Lathbury hated to think of the consequences that would follow. In Apeldoorn and Amersfoort, squads of Germans were killing disobedient members of the population at random. And Ede was less than twenty miles away from either town.

On October 17 the brigadier observed a glorious sunset and a double rainbow. More than ever he longed to be on his way. The next morning Tatham-Warter brought the brigadier the sad news that any plans they might have had for his personal departure were delayed indefinitely. The long route had been seriously penetrated in several places. Now everything depended on the fateful message from Dobie.

*

David Dobie began his trip on October 16 from the house of Bill Wildeboer at 32 Lunterseweg in Ede, after a detailed briefing from Tatham-Warter. The essence of success was speed. That afternoon the Resistance links were working satisfactorily. Each station waited to pass Dobie on, but no one could plan for the unexpected. Tiel would be evacuated within a week. Any passage through the town by a civilian after that time would be almost impossible. The Germans also gave warning of more impending civilian evacuations at Renkum and along the Rhine. In three days Tatham-Warter hoped to be speaking to Dobie through the PGEM power station cable from Nijmegen. Dobie had carefully memorized the plan prepared for the escape, which he would write down in detail once he reached Allied lines.

The Colonel had begun his journey from Ede somewhat dangerously. On the first day south of Veenondaal, riding around the corner of a dirt track on his bicycle, Dobie smashed into a parked German staff car where some officers were enjoying lunch. In unseemly haste he backed away and went off in the opposite direction, followed by his guide. On the next day he was passed on to the tall, blonde Bep Labouchère, who took Dobie to the chicken coop of Captain Kirschen at the farm of Wuf Langerwey. Although Dobie disclosed the plan to Kirschen, it was doubtful whether the Belgian grasped fully the magnitude of the operation. That night, after a good meal, Dobie slept in Kirschen's large feather bed between clean sheets. Next morning Bep led the colonel south, cycling into the mouth of a full gale that bent the tall pine trees and made progress difficult. The gale-force wind blew with such fury that it toppled Dobie once from his bicycle. For the Englishman, that ride through the storm seemed as if it would never come to an end. Dobie's legs ached and his breath came in short gasps as he endeavoured to keep up with the furious pace set by the Dutch girl. Over fields, dirt tracks, past marching Germans, alongside canals, into a wood, over a railway embankment, into another wood, and finally Bep stopped. Dobie felt half-dead by the time they came to the clearing in the wood where Jan de Bloois (Piet de Springer) waited at the Van Kleef's farm. (Dobie would be the last evader de Bloois would escort before his death.) After a glass of port and a good lunch the colonel, refreshed, pushed on again south.

At the unguarded Rhine at Maurik, de Bloois rowed the

Englishman across in a steel rowboat he had hidden in the rushes. Koos Meijer waited at the house of the widow Kok in Maurik. The atmosphere had grown extremely tense since Kettley and I had been there almost two weeks before. Ebbens's home less than four miles away had already been burned to the ground and the occupants imprisoned. Meijer had been one of the Resistance men who fought the Germans as he returned from Tiel with a shipment of arms. Dobie now learned of the events of that night. Two Germans were killed and several of the Resistance wounded. All the roads leading down to Tiel were heavily patrolled. He could not have chosen a worse time to be taken across the Waal.

That night the Englishman hardly slept. He worried whether there would actually be anyone to take him further, and felt deeply concerned about the men who waited in Ede. In his mind he kept thinking about the warning given by Tatham-Warter and Lathbury. Time was of the essence. The next morning he awoke very early. Another gale howled in from the south and rain squalls splattered the country roads. He thought this would be a good day to go. The more he persisted in his desire to leave, the more reticent and noncommittal the Dutch became. Then quite unexpectedly the news arrived from Tiel on the morning of October 18 that Dobie could leave at five o'clock that same evening. He left Maurik with his face bowed into fierce head winds, pedalling his cycle behind Meijer. They reached Tiel without mishap. From the house of Noordzij he was conducted before dusk to the river barge of Guert van der Zand. Here the swimmer Franz de Vilder had been waiting since early afternoon.

The crossing of the Waal, which began that night with so much foreboding, would have been quite uneventful except for an unforeseen accident. At eight that evening, de Vilder cast off their wooden rowboat from the barge with Dobie handling one oar and himself the other. They began to pull with powerful strokes. Suddenly, de Vilder's oar slipped from his grasp and swiftly vanished on the water in the dark. With only one oar to guide the boat it began drifting down in the direction of the lock towards the German machine-gun post. Although the moon was still down it would not be for long, and the shape of the boat as it drew close to the bank would be quite visible. Dobie quickly tore out one of the seats and using it as a paddle with de Vilder pulling on the remaining oar, managed to manoeuvre the boat in the right direction. Meanwhile, de Vilder – who never liked boats – told Dobie, "it was for swimming", and began to undress, throwing away his clothes. Dobie said he could not swim with all the valuable documents he carried. Also, the sight at close quarters of the swift, cold river was uninviting. He restrained de Vilder from diving in. The Colonel, struggling alone with one oar and the seat, managed to manoeuvre the boat close to the south bank. Fear and desperation had given him more strength than he knew. He had the impression he struggled in the current for half the night, but he and de Vilder were on the water for scarcely an hour when the boat glided into the deep grass on the summer dike and stuck fast. Dobie jumped out in a state of elation and exhaustion.

They walked over the dikes and came after a mile to the village of Beneden-Leeuwen. Here the old 1937 Buick of Doctor Van Hoeke used by the Resistance reception committee waited. From this no-man's-land Dobie would be taken by Franz de Vilder to a tiny duck-shooting house several miles back from the marshes near the village of Wamel. I had been waiting for him since midnight.

Dobie rose next day after a few hours' sleep feeling rested but thoroughly disoriented. He had asked me the previous night to help him. We would work together. Now he only had one thought on his mind – to seek the support of the commander of the Second Army for his plans to bring back the evaders. Nothing else mattered. We left the duck shoot in my jeep and started to move back down the long chain of command to the comfortable caravans of the Second Army staff officers. Our journey was slowed by stops for leisurely whiskies and casual conversations that irritated Dobie. The atmosphere felt throroughly unreal. No one seemed to understand the purpose of his mission, as the desperate colonel was guided further down the endless convoys of army vehicles, from major to colonel to brigadier. The total absence of any urgency was unnerving as the well-dressed liaison officers listened politely to the incomprehensible story. By the late afternoon word reached the Army Commander himself that Dobie had arrived.

In the presence of Lieutenant General Miles Dempsey, at Eindhoven, Dobie's tension lessened sufficiently so that he could properly gather his thoughts. Dempsey's caravan was luxurious. The Army Commander greeted the Colonel warmly and put him at ease immediately. He did not permit him to speak until his servant brought tea and sandwiches. Then he listened patiently for more than an hour while Dobie poured forth his amazing tale. Words tumbled out about the two wounded brigadiers, the two hundred men living as civilians, the hideouts, the help of the Dutch Resistance, the secret telephone line and finally the daring plan to cross the Rhine at Renkum. This would need Dempsey's approval. When Dobie finished there was a silence that seemed interminable. But it could not have lasted more than several seconds. Then Dempsey only said three words: "Get them out."

*

I had been in my quaint, thatch-roofed cottage on the marshes for a week before Lieutenant Colonel David Dobie arrived. But before I met Dobie I met Major Airey Neave of IS9, Major Hugh Fraser of the SAS and Captain Maurice Mac-Millan, a communications officer from Phantom. They seemed to work together. Neave maintained an unusual sense of independence, while Fraser had as his superior Lieutenant Colonel Collins, the GSO 1 at Moor Park who did not always take kindly to the somewhat haughty mannerisms of his subordinate. But all three had one trait in common: the capacity to enjoy life and a freedom of action that I thought even more unique than my own.

On my first introduction to Neave in Nijmegen the night after I returned, he asked whether I would care to work for IS9 in Holland. The idea appealed to me. Also, I had nothing else to do. On my way back to London I caught my first glimpse of the headquarters of the rescue organization and its charming, one-armed Lieutenant Colonel, Jimmy Langley, dining in his luxurious apartment in Brussels. Champagne and oysters were being consumed in quantity by the chief for breakfast when I dropped in shortly before noon. Langley between oysters, agreed I could serve a useful purpose in bringing back airborne survivors and establishing escape routes over the rivers of northern Holland. I did not know much about IS9 but I was certainly willing to learn. The languorous, affluent life-style impressed me. I would not be fighting the grubby, filthy, tedious war of the masses but the elite, sophisticated war of the few who ate with clean cutlery. I did not anticipate there would be objections to working for IS9 from my commander. There was not really very much of a battalion to go back to. Two officers out of forty and ten men from eight hundred were all that remained.

At Airborne Headquarters in Moor Park I paid my respects to the elegant Lieutenant Colonel Ian Collins and reported on the state of the Belgian SAS Captain Kirschen. Evidently Kirschen had fled his chicken coop but his daily messages seldom failed to come in on time. Collins told me that the General expected to see me at the War Office and a car waited outside to take me to Urquhart. At the war office the General greeted me with his usual warmth. He seemed genuinely glad to have me back. However, he did explain that he never expected to see me again alive. Reports had circulated several times that I had been killed. When we met the last time at Hartenstein he thought I would never reappear, I assured the General that the reports of my death, were, like Mark Twain's obituary, highly exaggerated. However, I was the first evader to come back. I told Urquhart that I might be only one of many who would follow. When I asked permission to return to Holland the General gave me his consent, but I never thought I would see Dobie again or that we would be working together to bring back our comrades. There would be other occasions when I would report to the General in England on my progress, but he always seemed too polite to ask the one question which constantly perplexed him. (Thirty years later in a request for information I asked whether he remembered me. He replied by saying, "Of course, I remember you well. But I still don't know what you were doing in the First Airborne Division.") I returned to Brussels, reported to Neave and took up residence in the duck shoot.

*

General Miles Dempsey delegated General Brian Horrocks, XXX Corps, to supervise the Pegasus operation. The execution in turn went down the line to General Maxwell Taylor of the 101st American Airborne Division, which was in position between the Waal and Rhine rivers. The planning officer at the division sent the orders to Colonel Robert Sink of the 506th Parachute Regiment. Sink examined carefully the position of his battalions and concluded the second, under command of Lieutenant-Colonel Robert Strayer, about a mile and a half back from the Rhine opposite Wageningen, would be the logical unit for the job. The composition of German defences along the north shore of the Rhine were best known to Strayer from the active patrolling of his battalion. Sink was not overly optimistic about a plan aimed at the rescue of a large number of men who in some incomprehensible manner were to gather in the midst of the enemy and then penetrate his lines. He retained to the end a healthy scepticism about the operation. To Sink and Strayer the task seemed almost impossible. But it was worth the risk, however slim. No one had any way of knowing the industrious preparation that took place unseen across the water. Sink and Strayer would help in every way they could. From their side they would set to work immediately constructing every possible safeguard for the night the evaders were scheduled to cross the Rhine.

From his headquarters in his battered farmhouse at Hemmen, Strayer started to plan. Major Clarence Hestor, the Regimental Plans and Training officer of the 506th Regiment, began to work out the details. D-Day would be October 23 at midnight. Strayer received the news on October 19 that he would soon meet a British paratroop colonel who would command the rescue party. He had no idea that that man would be his old friend, Dobie. On the afternoon of 19 October, Strayer held a briefing at his shell-battered farmhouse. Present were the S3 of the 2nd Battalion, Lieutenant Lewis Nixon, Captain Joseph McMillan of D Company, Lieutenant Van Dyke of E Company, Captain Ronald Spear of F Company and Lieutenant Fred (Moose) Heyliger of Headquarters Company, which would accompany the assault boats over the Rhine. Strayer's officers accepted their task without undue comment. The risks were only a routine part of the day's work, but the idea of rescuing fellow airborne troops cut off behind the enemy lines for almost a month appealed immensely to everyone. The operation would be a welcome relief from the massive boredom from which most of the troops suffered. When the company commanders returned to their units and asked for volunteers to cross the river, everyone wanted to go.

On the morning of October 21 Strayer, to his great surprise, came face to face with Dobie in his headquarters at Hemmen. The two men were delighted to see each other once again. They set to work immediately to coordinate their efforts. Dobie by this time had spoken twice to Tatham-Warter at prearranged times from the PGEM terminal in Nijmegen and exchanged vital information.

Two machine gunners and twelve riflemen were chosen to protect the flanks of the assault craft landings on the beachhead "Digby." There were to be two crossings, one at Wageningen, another twelve miles further east at Oosterbeek. However, when Dobie spoke that evening for the third time to Tatham-Warter from the brightly lit little room at the power station, plans were dramatically changed. A "razzia" was in progress. Germans were in panic rounding up all people on the streets between sixteen and sixty for forced labour and transporting them east of the Ijssel River to build defences. Due to this high state of German alert, Pegasus was advanced one day. It would now begin on the evening of Sunday, October 22. The lines of advance of the evaders would be at a position on the river where they would see an arc of ten red tracer shells fired by a Bofors gun slightly east of Wageningen commencing exactly at midnight. The signal would be repeated every hour. XXX Corps mortars and artillery would be ready for protection to box in an area four hundred yards square with the open side facing the Rhine. When the column of evaders reached the river they would flash a "V" for victory sign with a red light. At this signal twenty-five paddle-powered assault boats with two sappers in each boat and fourteen paratroopers under Heyliger for flank protection would be launched into the stream. Tatham-Warter had instructed Dobie to prepare to evacuate 140 men from beachhead Digby. That would be all they could safely bring. On Saturday, October 21, Dobie and I moved into Strayer's farmhouse at Hemmen.

*

Shortly after dawn on October 17 Menno de Nooy led Captain Thomas Wainwright and Sergeant Major Robert Grainger down to the German front-line area east of Wageningen. They stopped at the home of farmer Jochemsen, who was still permitted by the Germans to work his land on the river. Here de Nooy went back the way he came and the two paratroopers were left on their own. These were Lathbury's instructions. The final risk had to be taken by the British. In Jochemsen's barn Wainwright and Grainger put on their own uniforms and began their reconnaissance. By five o'clock on that cold, grey morning they had extensively probed the German positions over a distance of several miles between the villages of Wageningen and Grebbeberg. This was not the evaders' first river reconnaissance, nor would it be the last. The men found a narrow pathway through a grove of trees that would be passable for a small group but might be extremely hazardous for 140 men. Every three hundred feet a German machine-gun post blocked the way to the Rhine. Every half hour a patrol of five soldiers walked between the posts. The situation did not look very good. Under the best conditions it would be a gamble. At seven o'clock that same morning, de Nooy came for the two men at the barn, who changed back into civilian clothes and returned to Ede to report their findings.

Several evenings later before curfew an excited Tatham-Warter pedalled his bicycle furiously from the secret telephone terminal at Bennekom to Lathbury's house on Brouwersstraat. He had good news to report to the brigadier. Dobie had the situation under control and was now completing the final arrangements from his side of the Rhine. The gathering of the evaders must begin at full speed. Hibbert, Olliff, Franks, Wainwright, Wildeboer, Grainger and the other key people were immediately notified by couriers that Pegasus would definitely take place on the night of October 22. All the indecision and wavering was over Although the reconnaissance carried out by Grainger and Wainwright had produced uncertain results, the operation would go ahead. No alternative existed. By one means or another the evaders had to be brought to the woods at Renkum, where the final march to the crossing point would begin.

Lathbury would dress suitably for the occasion. His host, Marie de Nooy had presented him with a black, clerical suit which was the only one in town that could be found to fit his tall figure. As he told Tatham-Warter, "he had the appearance of a rather seedy don." However, he looked a gentleman compared with Hibbert, still outrageously attired like a vaudeville comedian with his white stockings, gym shoes, plus fours that hung below his calves and green sports jacket. Fortunately there were very few well-dressed civilians on the streets and the weird outfits of the evaders brought only passing glances from other members of the population who guessed the true identity of these healthy-looking young strangers. Although many hundreds of citizens of Ede were aware of the evaders in their town, they did not know where they were hidden. They kept their silence mainly out of sympathy. But there was another reason for it. Betrayal would not only mean death to the protector but also the informer. The Resistance made this fact well known. They were well acquainted with the names of most of the German informers.

Tatham-Warter prepared the brief operation order, which was transmitted to every group by courier. On the first day evaders in hiding to the north and east of Ede were to be moved after dark in four lorries or other transport (provided by Wildeboer and Kruyff) as close as possible to the concentration centre. From here they must continue on foot, uniformed and armed, with orders to fight if stopped.

On the second day, all evaders in the area of Ede were to move by foot and bicycle in ones and twos with Dutch guides by main roads in daylight. They were to be taken to the concentration area three miles directly north of the crossing place at Renkum. The woods would offer a temporary hiding place. Food for one day, one blanket per man and all arms and ammunition were to be conveyed to the area by horse, cart and bicycle, hidden under vegetables or similar camouflage.

Lathbury and Tatham-Warter hopefully planned to have the entire force on the shore of the Rhine at least half an hour before the zero hour at midnight on D-Day. The troops were impressed again with the need to fight, if necessary on their way to the crossing at Digby. The majority of men meeting in the night at the concentration point would be strangers to one another, but with the exception of a few Dutchmen and the Russian pilot, Kapustin, everyone spoke the same language. A month of extreme inactivity, however, had physically weakened the men and made many of them listless and unusually nervous. Some soldiers had not moved further than the distance from one side of a cramped room to the other for thirty days. The majority lived outside in holes in the ground in the rain-soaked woods, only coming out at night for a breath of air. The darkness, constant damp, the confinement had an acutely demoralizing effect. The weather and the state of alertness of German defences on the river on the evening of October 22 would govern everything.

The total count of evaders that could be gathered in the required time would be limited to 15 officers and 124 men. More than a hundred more were hidden in inaccessible districts or unknown to Tatham-Warter. A daylight reconnaissance and two night patrols had satisfied both Lathbury and Tatham-Warter that with good luck they would have a fighting chance of reaching the exact rendezvous. Dobie had defined it clearly when he communicated by telephone from Nijmegen. From a distance of several miles, Dobie and Tatham-Warter both thought the evaders should be able to see the ten red balls of tracers arcing above the river from the Bofors gun at midnight. Only Lathbury had reservations about the use of a Bofors. He told Tatham-Warter that one could not measure distance in the night from tracer shells. His fears would be justified.

Hibbert was summoned on the morning of October 21 from his comfortable lodging at the home of Anna Aartsen Strijbos at 28 Lunterseweg in Ede. Tatham-Warter waited for him at Wildeboer's house. He outlined the plan. The preposterous idea of a column of more than company strength, walking right through heavily fortified German positions, seemed on the surface suicidal. With sufficient nerve everything appeared possible to Tatham-Warter. The more cautious Hibbert saw that the alternatives were grim. At any moment the fragile, gossamerlike web of protection the Resistance had woven around the evaders could be torn away. Hibbert was delegated to command the rear party that would be the last to arrive at Renkum. Under him would be those men who were in the vicinity of Velp east of Arnhem. They would have to be transported fifteen miles to the rear rendezvous at Oud Reemst. From here Hibbert was told he would be given an hour to drive a minimum of sixty soldiers in two ancient lorries to Renkum. The trucks under normal conditions could take about ten men apiece. Hibbert wondered how he would squeeze sixty men into the back of vans designed for a third of the number. He decided he would worry about the problem when it arose. Meanwhile Hibbert hollowed out the heel of his boot. Inside he hid the complete list of all the prisoners taken at the bridge at Arnhem and plans of German gun emplacements north of the Rhine. The brigade major, always meticulous and painstaking, was a valuable asset to the Lathbury staff in Brouwersstraat. On the night of October 21 Hibbert sent messages to all the evaders hiding east of Arnhem to be ready to move out immediately. Among the groups contacted were the enterprising Corporal Jimmy James and his ten paratroopers. James had collected a small arsenal of arms. He had five Mark IV anti-tank mines, a Bren gun with ammunition, four Stens, three rifles and twelve hand grenades. He would take it all with him.

The day before, October 20, Tatham-Warter, Bill Wildeboer, Flip van der Pol, Menno de Nooy and a Dutchman called Max met at Wildeboer's house in the Lunterseweg. They had come to determine within a few yards the precise place where the evaders should penetrate the German lines. Less than forty-eight hours remained in which to make the decision. A stroke of luck occurred suddenly that same day. The event was tragic for the Dutch population but favourable for the evaders. All residents of Bennekom and adjacent areas on the Rhine were forced to evacuate, creating chaos on the roads. There would now be few serious checks and the movement of the soldiers would not be conspicuous among so many fleeing refugees.

Van der Pol, a teacher at a school in Bennekom, suggested that under the chaotic conditions prevailing, everyone should now concentrate at the house called Oranje Nassau Oord in the woods south of Renkum – about a mile from the river. It would be easy to identify. Lathbury hoped that strong patrols from the U.S. 101st Airborne would cross over from the south and protect the British soldiers until they reached the waiting boats. Tatham-Warter had the fear until the very end that some of the more headstrong among the Resistance might engage the enemy before the evaders made contact with the

Americans. While the Dutch were excellent performing brave acts of sabotage with their small groups, they were ill-equipped or insufficiently experienced to engage in organized warfare. Events moved quickly, dangerously to a conclusion in the last forty-eight hours before D-Day. Never had the Resistance mounted such a complex operation in which the stakes were so great for everyone.

On Friday evening, October 20, Wildeboer sent several messages by courier. All men and women in the Lunteren Resistance were to go immediately to De Groote Voort on the Postweg to await orders. The de Vries group were to meet in Stroombergen's barn on the Ede outskirts, where a few evaders were hidden; while the Maanderbuurt squad under "Uncle Jan" received instructions to go to the Schaapskooi – the sheep pen where Olliff and his medical orderlies were ready to leave. Menno de Nooy headed for Ede, where he had some unfinished business. Lathbury and Tatham-Warter were waiting for his latest information on German troop strength before they left. De Nooy estimated there were about 2,500 Germans including Gestapo in Ede, quartered in barracks a few houses down the street from Edith Nijhoff. Lunteren had a gendarmerie consisting of Dutch Nazis and Germans, about 115 strong.

Mrs. Nijhoff dressed in her all-purpose nurse's uniform, reported that morning for duty at nine o'clock to a group of Red Cross workers gathering on the Keijenberg in Ede. Meanwhile Olliff's group at the sheep pen had moved off that Saturday in three's and four's following their guides at seventy-five-foot intervals to the Keijenberg, where the Red Cross volunteers took over. From here the medical men were led to the river at Nol in 't Bosch where Maarten van den Bent made himself conspicuous in the knee-deep grass of the field, continuing all the while to chop wood. As each small group of soldiers reached the wood cutter they would be approached by a guide and taken to their final hiding place in a particular section of the forest. Red Cross workers at Nol in 't Bosch had a hot meal ready for the men when they arrived. So far the refugees moving with their belongings in push carts and bicycles along the roads out of Bennekom had drawn attention away from the many evaders going the opposite way. The chaos was helping.

On Saturday morning Wim Peelen and Kees de Belg drove up to Olliff's empty sheep pen with a horse and wagon to pick up uniforms, arms and ammunition left hidden in the straw. These items were loaded on to the wagon and transported to the forward rendezvous. No one bothered to search under the piles of old sacks in the back. The horse-drawn vehicle attracted no notice. The Germans pushing their way through the refugees on the blocked roads appeared as confused as anyone else. Some of the evaders lost their guides in the heavy traffic. Wout Evertsen became separated from his party that were loosely strung out behind, cut off from view in the milling crowds of dispossessed civilians pouring out of their homes. Evertsen spent most of the day looking for his evaders. By an amazing coincidence the soldiers stopped at Evertsen's father's house in Ede to ask the way and the guide found the paratroops waiting for him when he returned home. De Nooy almost forgot to pick up a group of six evaders which included Captain George Sykes, the daring American Typhoon pilot who crash-landed his P-51 fighter onto a field near Ede, narrowly missing several cows, on September 17 after forty-nine missions (the riddled plane was still on the field where it landed). Sykes and his men were hidden in the churchyard at Wageningen among the tombstones.

By noon on Sunday, October 22, fifty men had reached the Renkum woods. This included another Russian whom the Resistance had accidentally found at Bennekom. No one knew his name or how he got there. Like his compatriot Kapustin, who still patiently followed Olliff in another sector of the hideaway, the second Russian soldier was baffled by the feverish activity going on around him. No one could explain they were all engaged in a desperate plan to escape.

All through Sunday afternoon stragglers accompanied by their guides added to the growing number of soldiers, Red

Cross workers and Resistance men. Evaders came from as far north as Barneveld and Voorthuizen, twenty-one miles away. Through fields and narrow bicycle paths, under the constant scrutiny of the enemy, the twenty-one miles from Barneveld felt to the Dutch guides more like a hundred. The count of heads taken before dusk showed eight-five evaders present, from the western group. Neither Tatham-Warter, Lathbury nor Hibbert's contingent had yet arrived.

Hibbert's contingent represented all those in hiding roughly east of a line drawn from Otterloo through Oud Reemst to Oosterbeek. Piet Kruyff reckoned he could bring sixty-five men to Hibbert in several wood-powered automobiles that had been carefully preserved for the occasion. Some of the cars had been covered under several feet of hay for years in isolated barns. It would be a miracle if any of them worked. But somehow they did. So far no one had offered a better idea how to transport the men quickly. Hibbert set up his headquarters in a hut in a wooded clearing outside Oud Reemst and prepared for the worst. He dreaded what was to come, but he was ready. During the day he watched with incredulity a model T Ford, an ancient Mercedes and a Chevrolet with solid rubber tyres rattling into the clearing with their shaken cargo of soldiers. The bewildered passengers were discharged and the antique vehicles left the clearing in the woods. Everything so far was going according to plan.

By Saturday evening Hibbert's hut in the wood filled with weapons, uniforms and men, while at the same time Kruyff with Menno Liefstink and Albert Horstman and others travelled on to Otterloo with more guns and ammunition. Sergeant Pat Glover acted as Hibbert's quartermaster and began distributing the equipment to the evaders as they came in. Everyone had a uniform or part of one to wear. Tony Deane-Drummond stepped out from the comparative luxury of a small Red Cross van and surprised the brigade major, whom he had not seen since they fought together at the Arnhem bridge. Then a swarthy Dutch naval officer, Charles Douw van der Krap, joined the British. This would be the Dutchman's thirteenth escape attempt. His first took place as long ago as 1942 in Colditz. He had eluded his captors in Germany and later in Poland, where he fought as a member of the Polish Resistance in the Warsaw uprising. Now he hoped at last to be free. Half Indonesian, half Dutch, Van de Krap was determined to return to the Free Netherlands Navy. The resolute character of the naval officer left a most profound impression upon Hibbert.

At dusk two old Chevrolet trucks, patched up with dozens of homemade spare parts, clattered into the clearing. The trucks were to take Hibbert's contingent on the final stage of the journey. They were the only vehicles considered suitable for the last twenty miles. Perhaps once these trucks had been members of the Chevrolet family, but now an assortment of additional parts made their origin unrecognizable. Wooden side boards about a foot high enclosed the rear of the lorries. Hibbert could only think of one way to fit sixty men into them. Fifteen men would lie on the bottom of each vehicle and on top of them would go the officers and soldiers carrying guns. No one seemed particularly anxious to be the bottom layer and act as a cushion on twenty miles of country lanes. An argument took place among the men as to who should form the bottom layer. No one volunteered. But the matter resolved itself quickly when an explosive burst of machine-gun fire echoed nearby in the woods. Several more bursts followed, then silence, which settled the argument. Without further coaxing the evaders tumbled into the back of the vehicles. Hibbert never did discover who fired the machine guns. But it happened at exactly the right time.

Kruyff, in a stolen sedan, stood by to lead the overloaded lorries to their destination. The weird journey began at 5.0 p.m. on Sunday over a rough dirt track north to Otterloo. Kruyff then turned in a southerly direction through Ede towards Bennekom. This circuitous detour avoided German roadblocks and troop movements. Resistance men were positioned as lookouts every fifteen hundred feet on bicycles. If the way ahead was dangerous, they would stand in the middle of the road with their bicycles blocking the way. Van der Pol accompanied the driver of the first lorry and Zweurs de Nooy sat beside the driver of the second. When they reached Ede at 6.0 p.m. the first driver grew hesitant and decided suddenly his job was too dangerous to continue and halted. Van der Pol took out his pistol and held it against the temple of the reluctant man and the convoy went on. Kruyff left them at the Hotel Neder-Veluwe in Bennekom so he could return the stolen sedan to the owner before curfew.

The lorries jolted precariously on to the forward rendezvous south at Renqum without further incident. When the evaders disembarked they did so by slowly disentangling themselves in the dark, cursing, stiff, bruised and shaken after almost three hours of silent punishment that felt like slow suffocation for those on the bottom. As Hibbert's evaders noisily assembled on the road, a peculiar incident took place that no one quite understood or questioned. Two annoyed Germans on bicycles carrying Schmeisser machine pistols on their backs rode down the track frantically ringing their bells for right of way. The astounded paratroopers politely parted, clearing a path for the enemy who passed on through and vanished into the woods. This strange meeting took place at 7.30 p.m. four and a half hours before the Bofors gun was due to fire its red tracers over the crossing on the river. After the Germans left Hibbert assembled the men into sections and in single file each section, led by a guide, headed south through the dark woods towards the Rhine. In fifteen minutes they should meet the main force who waited for them.

On Sunday morning at eleven o'clock, Tatham-Warter with Menno de Nooy and Van der Pol collected Lathbury from Mrs. de Nooy's house on Brouwersstraat. Lathbury, after an emotional farewell to his host, left in his black clerical dress and mounted his bicycle. He had said his farewell to Hackett the day before, doubting whether he would ever again see the brigadier. The bicycle, as well as his suit, was reputed to be the largest available in Ede. The fifth member of the party,

Snor Top, carried the officer's uniform and weapons on his delivery cycle. As the five men joined the stream of refugees forced from their homes near the river, German SS troops stationed along the road scarcely paid attention to them. Refugees were not only trudging east, west and north but also continually going back and forth to their houses picking up belongings and starting out again on their push carts and bicycles. The Germans had unwittingly provided the perfect cover for the fleeing airborne evaders.

One of the last groups to be taken by Van der Pol that day followed a small footpath deep into the woods west of Renkum. He was very tired. It was his fourth trip and, he hoped, his last. It took Van der Pol half an hour before he found the forward rendezvous in the midst of thick pine trees. The evaders lay still, sprawled out on the shaded floor of the forest in their camouflaged smocks. The bicycles used by Van der Pol's group were handed to other guides who took them back to be reused by other men in a continuous shuttle service. As the final groups arrived, Tatham-Warter began organizing the waiting soldiers into small platoons under command of NCO's and officers. Less than a hundred yards from the rendezvous were artillery enplacements and slit trenches manned by the enemy.

Hardly a cloud appeared in the sky. Lathbury prayed the weather would turn foul and it would rain, but for the time being it remained a clear, crisp autumn day. But as the end of the afternoon approached, Lathbury was unexpectedly granted his wish. The sun suddenly clouded over and the air became colder. Fine, wet mist slowly rose from the damp ground so that by dusk a welcome fog shrouded the tense men waiting for the signal to move. At 9.0 p.m. Tatham-Warter and Maarten van den Bent returned from a short reconnaissance. They had approached to within a few hundred yards of the Rhine. No one had challenged them. The omens looked favourable, but it was still too early to tell. Then the guide shook hands with the major and silently left him in the night. Tatham-Warter now made the decision to go.

It had grown so dark that visibility was limited to a few yards. The column lined up in single file. At the head stood the only remaining guide, Jan Peelen. Behind him was Wainwright and then came Tatham-Warter. Lathbury in position near the middle found it so black in the woods that he could not see the man immediately ahead. The major raised his hand, pointing ahead, and the long column surged forward. From the time Wainwright moved at the front it took almost five minutes before the last man made his first step. The marching men crunched in their boots over snapping twigs, stumbling over unseen branches and frequently falling on the boggy ground. The column bunched up and spread out in turn like a caterpillar, travelling very slowly. A rope was passed back so that the Indian file could keep some semblance of unity as it wound its way cautiously between the trees, up small embankments, sliding down wet, grassy slopes. Except for the few in front none of the evaders had any idea where they were going.

Eventually the column halted at the intersection of two bicycle tracks. Word went back down the line that they had arrived at a particularly hazardous part of the journey. They were now on the outer edge of German forward river defences. Two hundred feet further a paved road about twenty feet wide ran east and west. The column must somehow silently cross the road and find a gate through which they would pass. Beyond the gate were two paths. The wrong path would take them to German billets used by the artillery and the correct one would lead to the meadow. Beyond the meadow lay the Rhine. Although Peelen had never been to the river at night he said he would bring the column to the meadow, but each man must move silently with caution. The news was whispered back down the five-hundred-foot column.

On the paved road, even wound with rags, the army boots made a shattering noise. Lathbury felt convinced they would be detected at any second. But nothing happened. The rope the brigadier held was snatched from his hands as he came to the road and it disappeared into the darkness. Meanwhile,

Hibbert could hear German sentries coughing and talking. This feeling of imminent disaster overcame Lathbury several times during that night until he could no longer understand why the enemy did not shoot. Breaking branches, crunching boots, shouts from lost Dutchmen seemed to come from every side. To his amazement, the deadly fire Lathbury anticipated at every step continued to be withheld.

Tatham-Warter was later to compare the magnified sounds in the still night to a stampeding herd of wild elephants. Olliff slipped on one occasion and tumbled into a slit trench on top of a fellow officer, who had the odd presence of mind to ask for his name, rank and number. Olliff disentangled himself, climbed out and started searching for the column. He found one of his medical orderlies in the blackness and held on to his jacket tail, hoping they were both heading in the right direction. The Russian Kapustin had long since vanished from his position behind Olliff. Not until much later did the doctor discover he had wandered into a German gun emplacement and was made prisoner.

The appearance of this great, serpentine, apparently endless column of men blindly stumbling onto the river was much less formidable than it looked to the few stunned Germans who actually saw it. When it came to a halt, as it often did, those behind frequently tripped over those in front. The entangled bodies resembled several scrimmages simultaneously fighting it out on a football field. At each pile-up the evaders would sort themselves our and surge on again. The cursing and shouting could be heard for several hundred feet. Discipline became increasingly difficult to maintain as the night wore on and midnight approached. More and more men were accidentally falling behind or wandering off on their own in the dark. But somehow or other, with the exception of the one lost Russian, the column held together as the river drew near.

Hibbert considered every moment they went undetected as an undeserved blessing. Any second he expected to hear a sickening burst of fire cutting through the ranks. He prayed for a sight of the river as did Lathbury. A cold, dense, ground mist drifted in patches over the woods and added to the already poor visibility. Suddenly Peelen stepped out from what must have seemed like an unending forest into the meadow. On the meadow the mist clung to the ground.

Tatham-Warter gave the order for every man to crawl through the meadow to the protection of the river bank two hundred yards away. At five-feet intervals the evaders slid on their bellies over the grass and vanished into the mud below the embankment. Here they would not be seen. From the top of the embankment they could be easily silhouetted against the night sky if they stood. Dug in under the shadow of the forest at the edge of the meadow were the German machine gun emplacements.

For the first time Lathbury saw a red glow in the sky from burning buildings in Wageningen, less than a mile away. Wainwright, who had gone ahead to scout the river bank, returned with the disturbing news that he had seen unidentified lights moving on the meadow. It could be Germans searching with lanterns. There was little doubt the enemy were aware of the column, but it had no idea where it was going or what it was doing. Tatham-Warter prepared the soldiers for a battle which could begin at any time. Then the column halted and waited while fighting patrols were sent out for the first time on the flanks. When no attack immediately materialized, the advance continued. Progress became very slow. Every hundred feet the evaders halted as the patrols reported back to Lathbury and Tatham-Warter. Short, sharp bursts of a German Spandau ripped through the night, answered by the slower explosions of Sten guns from one of the patrols. Then, suddenly the firing halted as swiftly as it began. One of the patrols returned with news. They had engaged several of the enemy, who retreated after a brief skirmish back into the woods. Tatham-Warter could not account for the timidity of the enemy. The evaders were completely exposed. Every time the major looked back he marvelled that the long chain of evaders, stretching back much further than he could see, was unbroken.

In the almost complete silence a pig squealed from the far

bank of the river. The time was noted at five minutes before midnight. Then came ten sharp cracks like the powerful snap of a whip. The sound shattered the night. Some of the men dropped to the ground. Ahead to the west balls of red tracers like a flaming necklace arched through the sky. A sigh seemed to run from one end of the Indian file to the other. The pre-arranged crossing at "Digby" had almost been reached. Then it occurred to Tatham-Warter that he did not really know how far they were from the Bofors. Lathbury had already warned him of the difficulty in judging the distance of tracers in the night. The crossing could be a hundred yards ahead, a thousand, or even more. No spark lingered in the black sky to indicate where the shells came from. The momentary joy at seeing the signal quickly faded as the men marched on. The Bofors would not fire again before another hour. In fact the column was more than two miles east of the prearranged crossing.

Tatham-Warter had immediately replied to the Bofors with the prearranged 'V'' signal on his red torch. At least two of the men that night on the north bank knew the hopeless feeling of waiting for boats to take them off a hostile shore. Both Lathbury and Hibbert had been trapped on the beaches of Dunkirk. Now once again they would be waiting to be rescued, feeling the same fearful sense of uncertainty. At regular intervals, in growing desperation, Tatham-Warter flashed his red "V" for victory signal as he walked. No reply came from across the wide expanse of hostile water.

*

A pig squealed. The hands of my watch stood at exactly five minutes to midnight. The shrill, almost human, cry pierced the unnatural silence. Lieutenant Colonel Dobie had put me in charge of the twenty-four assault boats that were in position a little distance back from the river in the shadow of the summer dike. The sappers from the engineers of the Forty-third Wessex Division, who manned the boats, waited for my signal.

Colonel Bob Sink and Lieutenant-Colonel Robert Strayer stood on the road above the dike looking through their night binoculars at the far shore. They saw nothing. In five minutes the Bofors, two miles back from the Rhine, would fire a string of tracers directly over their heads across to Wageningen. That same day General Brian Horrocks had come himself to the river to put his approval personally on the plan. The 101st U.S. Airborne Division had prepared the evaders' reception with great care. Rows of white tennis tape ran back from the shore to an emergency medical aid station and a temporary canteen which would serve hot drinks and food. Lorries and jeeps were parked just over the dike to transport the men to the army base hospital at Nijmegen. Paratroop medical orderlies stood by with stretchers to carry those unable to walk. Dobi and the Moose were crouched near the river with a radio operator ready to go as soon as they saw the red "V" signal. Two machine gunners would come with me to protect the flanks. An artillery observation officer from XXX Corps stood nearby with a map talking to his rear gunner who controlled the fire of the medium artillery. I hoped it would not be necessary to use it.

All day Dobie had been in a mood of nervous anticipation, of high tension and purpose. If devotion to friends could bring the men back, they would return. As midnight approached the tension mounted. Everyone's gaze was riveted on the far shore directly across the river in the direction of Wageningen. Near the forward slopes of the dike, the Majors Airey Neave and Hugh Fraser, wrapped in long greatcoats, quietly observed the operation.

The river current ran east from Arnhem and consequently the boats would be set in that direction. The assault craft were positioned in a rank along the shore to allow for the swift flow of the river. If the operation was to be successful I thought the evaders should by now be making their way over the last few hundred feet down to crossing point at Digby. Several salvos of German rockets flamed up from their firing pods in the Renkum woods and screeched down a few hundred yards to our rear. A flare soared up over the water, lit the river with a terrible brightness, then died. The tension grew unbearable. Dobie and I synchronized watches with the Moose's and waited the remaining seconds for zero hour.

Midnight came unexpectedly. The Bofors cracked out ten times. The gun seemed very close. Ten red balls of tracers, one after the other, spun above the river and dwindled into the blackness of enemy territory. Automatically our gaze followed the line of shells, expecting some immediate response from that direction. But none came. At ten minutes after midnight the far shore still seemed deserted. From hope my mood changed to one of fear as if something definitely had gone wrong. No one for a moment thought the timing of the evaders could be less exacting then the precision-organized reception prepared by the 101st Airborne Division.

West of Arnhem the Rhine curves north and south in a series of bends. From our sector of shoreline on the south an advancing column of men could easily be lost from view if they hugged the far bank. No one had thought of this possibility, nor did anyone anticipate it. Nor did Tatham-Warter realize the poor visibility of his signal light. By chance, about half and hour after midnight, I looked in the direction of the bridge for the first time. I thought I saw a tiny light flicker on and off. I raced down to Dobie to tell him. We watched again together. After a few minutes a faint, red pinpoint of light signalled the "V" for victory symbol. No one could possibly judge the distance. But it seemed several miles east of the prearranged rendezvous. Dobie did not wait any longer. He and the Moose excitedly pushed off and with a weird cry vanished from sight on the river. I shouted to the sappers to drag their boats along the shore another hundred yards east. Every yard would count. The closer we landed to the evaders the less distance they would have to walk. Ten minutes later all the boats were launched.

The current seemed to carry me several hundred yards further eastward than I planned. Other boats had already landed with their crews who rested under the protection of the embankment, ready to quickly push back out again into the stream at a moment's notice. The American machine gunners under Lieutenant Frank Reese had taken up their covering positions on the flank in the long grass of the meadow. With Sergeant Linwood Belisle, one of Heyliger's men, I went searching eastward for the evaders. Several hundred feet further up the river, I found Dobie under the embankment with Heyliger, where he had set up his headquarters. Dobie was already in radio communication with the 2nd Battalion link on the south shore. I left him and with Belisle continued east in the direction of Arnhem towards the place I thought I saw the red light. A flare shot up from behind the trees a few hundred yards north, illuminating the water. We stopped. Then in a few seconds, enveloped again by the darkness, we went on. After a little time I heard a strange sound like wind rustling through the meadow. But there was no wind. We advanced a few feet further, listened and waited. The distant rustle of grass changed slowly, imperceptibly to a multitude of shuffling feet. But I saw no one. Belisle set up his light machine gun. The sound started and stopped several times and then gradually became louder. The origin was now unmistakable. A grey, amorphous column took shape in the dark, shuffling slowly over the meadow. The column seemed to have no end. We let the first few men pass. And then I saw they were the evaders.

I rose with a shout and ran to the front. The leader, a tall, thin man with the rank of major, held up his hand for the tired line of men to halt. Beside the major stood a stoop-shouldered brigadier with a gaunt, sorrowful face. He asked wearily where the boats were. I told him the exact place where the assault craft waited under the embankment with Dobie. The ragged file surged on, possessed with new energy. At half past one that morning, the last of the stragglers and wounded were boarded the last of the boats. Not a shot had been fired during the entire time I wandered over enemy territory. I do not know definitely whether I was the last man who went back across the Rhine that night, but I would like to think so. As I went down to the river I looked with Belisle both ways over the silent meadow for some sign of life. I could see none. Below me the urging sappers held the last boat in readiness as I stepped aboard.

The exuberance of the returning soldiers was considerable. The mournful-looking Heyliger, not known among his fellows as a particularly handsome man, was hugged by the doctor Olliff and kissed gratefully on both cheeks. Olliff thought Heyliger "the most beautiful man he had ever seen." The only casualty that night was Hibbert. He rode joyfully to the reception area on the bumper of an overcrowded jeep from which he accidentally fell, breaking both legs.

The 101st Airborne Division, founded on August 16, 1942, at Camp Claiborne, Louisiana, had, according to its first commanding officer, Major General William O. Lee, "a rendezvous with destiny." For the men of the 1st British Airborne Division that rendezvous had been kept.

On October 28, on the 9.0 p.m. British Home Service, which could be heard in occupied Holland, the broadcaster prefaced the evening news with a prosaic announcement "Message for Bill. Everything is well. All our thanks." Lathbury had sent his promised communication to Bill Wildeboer.

*

A few evaders trickled out from Apeldoorn on their own more by accident than intention. On October 16 at nine o'clock on a dark, rainy evening that irrepressible Catholic priest, Daniel McGowan, looked out of the first floor window of the hospital in Queen Wilhelmina's old palace at Apeldoorn. Lieutenant Colonel Martin Herford, a doctor from XXX Corps who on his own initiative crossed the river into Arnhem on a mercy mission on September 24, stood beside him. After deliberation with Graeme Warrack, the senior medical officer, the two men decided the time had come to escape. Warrack had already assembled all the noncombatants which consisted of clergy and medical staff on that same day and told them their responsibility to the wounded airborne had now come to an end. Those who wished were free to leave, if they dared. In a few days everyone would be transported to Germany.

In pairs or singly most of the men decided that day to escape as soon as they could. But some, like Lieutenant Colonel A. T. Marrable, made the decision to remain with the wounded and would accompany them into prisoner-of-war camps in Germany. While the doctors Lipmann Kessel, Shorty Longland, Graeme Warrack, Theo Redman and Private Leslie Davison would be taking their leave before too long.

Herford had one of the doctors hold onto the end of a blanket and then slid down it from a window to the hospital grounds. McGowan followed. His plumpness caused some difficulty, as he barely squeezed out the small window and followed Herford below into the bushes of the garden. A driving rain in the black night gave this first escape attempt from Apeldoorn a good chance of success. They crawled past the patrolling guards and dug their way out of the hospital compound under the barbed-wire perimeter. Altogether they had to cover twenty-five miles of wooded terrain interlaced with countless drainage ditches, canals and meadows before they reached the Rhine. They aimed for the river near Renkum where, they had been told by the Dutch, American troops were on the south shore. Herford carried a prismatic compass from which they followed an irregular course south by west. On one occasion in the night when Herford thought he had come to a particularly smooth, paved road he dropped from view into the water of a drainage ditch and was fished out by his companion. At last when they came to Otterloo a family of simple Dutch peasants gave the tired men bread and coffee. From here they went on to a wood where they slept for a few hours before continuing their journey towards the river.

On the second day of their travels, the reserved Herford introduced himself to McGowan as a confirmed pacifist. He explained he had served with a Quaker unit in the Spanish Civil War and later as a volunteer doctor for the Finns in their struggle against Russia in 1940. To McGowan, his companion appeared to be a champion of lost causes. He had an intuitive feeling that this new companionship might not augur well. Fortunately, by the time they came to Wolfheze, McGowan was on familiar territory. He knew the area from the days when he searched for the airborne wounded.

The two men had to walk across the landing zone in order to reach the river. Hundreds of SS troops, in black forage hats and camouflaged rain capes, were poking through the wrecked gliders and containers looking for souvenirs. McGowan and Herford turned their red berets inside out, knocked them into the shape of forage caps and then put on their own camouflage capes which fortunately they had taken with them. They boldly stepped out into the dropping zone, jabbering pigeon German. In this way, after midnight on October 18, after twenty-five wet, weary, exhausting miles, Herford and McGowan arrived to within a hundred yards of the Rhine. At daylight they removed most of their clothes and wrapped them in their rain capes, prepared to swim to the far shore. After a liberal swig of whisky from McGowan's flask that had served to buoy up the morale of both men on their travels, they were ready for the plunge. Neither of them saw nearby the camouflaged, slit trenches that formed part of a German company guarding the Rhine. As a precaution, Herford volunteered to reconnoitre the river to determine the best place to cross. McGowan, who waited patiently for him under a bush near the water's edge, suddenly froze with fear. A German unexpectedly rose from a slit trench and came towards the bush where he lay hidden. The German looked casually at the crouching object as he began to pee over the priest and then stopped. "Karl," he asked in amazement. "Nein," replied the polite McGowan. With the point of a bayonet the unlucky priest was pried out from his bush. He then took a final swig from his canteen, draining the last of the whisky and threw the container away. In this obsequious posture stained with German urine, McGowan was made prisoner.

Some time later Herford returned to the place where he left

the priest. He waited in vain for his companion to show up, fearful some misfortune had befallen him. After an hour Herford crawled back alone through the mud to the water's edge and slipped quietly into the Rhine. A patrol of paratroopers from the 506th Regiment of the 101st Airborne Division picked up the shivering doctor near a deserted brick factory on the south shore later in the day. The naked Herford had the audacity to challenge the Americans before being happily escorted away. Thus the splendid McGowan, accidentally trapped by a German who chose to pee at a most inopportune time, spent the remainder of the war in captivity.

*

The success of Pegasus had prompted Airey Neave of IS9 to attempt a rescue operation of his own on a similar scale. He hoped that a hundred and twenty British, Dutch and American evaders would be able to come out of hiding by employing the same techniques that had been used before. Neave's own imaginative escape from Colditz two years earlier had been the performance of an outstanding impresario. However, the planning of an intricately coordinated mass escape required different talents. Also, the old adage of not trying the same trick twice in succession could have been well heeded. Life in IS9 bore little resemblance to conditions under which hunted men lived in enemy territory. Boeree in his *Chronicles of Ede* claimed Pegasus II was a disaster from beginning to end.

The conscientious Dick Kragt, the IS9 agent in occupied Holland, also opposed the idea. And much depended upon him. Kragt never had much of a chance to succeed without the wireless set he had lost in his May 1943 parachute drop. The man whom IS9 sent to help Kragt arrived drunk according to Joop Piller, and proved a disastrous security risk for the Resistance. Eventually he was sent back to England. Kragt was heavily dependent upon Kirschen of the SAS for reliable radio transmission. And the two men were not on very good terms. All the land within ten miles of the Rhine had been evacuated of civilians and occupied by Germans. On November 16 the Germans found the secret PGEM telephone cable which connected Bennekom with Nijmegen and cut it. All messages after that date had to be routed the long way through Kirschen to Moor Park and back back to Holland.

The evaders gathered by Kragt, Piller and the Resistance helpers were fragmented groups, unlike the close-knit band that had operated out of Ede. No Tatham-Warter emerged to control and coordinate the plans. There was no Dobie with a compelling sense of urgency to organize the reception with the American 101st Airborne Division. In occupied Holland, Wildeboer and other important Resistance figures were being ruthlessly hunted by the Gestapo for their role in Pegasus and were constantly on the run. One further calamitous event occurred. In the London *News Chronicle* of Monday, November 20, 1944, a feature article appeared. It gave a reasonably detailed account by Lathbury and Deane-Drummond of their successful escape. Although the article appeared three days after Pegasus II was due to begin, the interviews were given many days before so that most of Fleet Street knew of the successful Rhine crossing by the evaders before the second attempt began. Any German agent possessing some of the details about Lathbury's or Deane-Drummond's story could easily deduce how and where the crossing of the Rhine took place. From the very beginning the entire operation seemed to be designed for disaster.

Major Hugh Maguire, the GSO 2 Intelligence of the 1st Airborne Division would be in command of Pegasus II. The way out once again led through Renkum down to the Rhine where the red balls of tracers at midnight would mark the crossing. On the night of November 17, Maguire led a march of 160 men to the river. In the column were the doctors Longland, Allenby, Redman, Warrack and Kessel. Not far behind Maguire, Tex Banwell – carrying a Sten gun – acted as a mobile patrol. The rain poured down and the wind howled. It had blown hard for two days. The column lost itself constantly, then split up in the dark so that small, detached bands bumped frequently into German emplacements, were challenged by sentries and sometimes fled for their lives. Every so often unexplainable shooting broke out in the woods.

Warrack and his little group wandered around in circles and after an hour of walking they returned their starting place. Several couriers were caught. Didi Roos, one of the captured couriers, knew all the minute details and addresses of the helpers as well as all Resistance headquarters locations. About 2.0 a.m. on the morning of November 18, the evaders were in disastrous circumstances. Guides left the column without notice. Before light that day Maguire saw the red tracers from the Bofors about two miles south. But he could do nothing about it. About the same time the shocked Warrack, going in the opposite direction, bumped into a monstrous naval gun camouflaged in the forest. Banwell wondered how he could leave the column so he could seek the relative safety of his friends in the Resistance. On the south side of the Rhine the 506th Regiment once more having organized the reception with painstaking care, waited patiently. They were assisted now by that stolid, imperturbable Canadian, Major Mike Tucker and his 23rd Field Company of Canadian Engineers with their Evinrude-powered storm boats. It was only two months since Tucker's men had rescued the Arnhem survivors.

I stood with Tucker in the cold dawn of November 17, by the shore waiting for some sign of life from the water. As the morning mist rolled in from the river we heard excited shouts. A lone voice in English yelled, "tomorrow night." We did not know then that only three survivors waited to be taken off on the far shore. We learned later that one of the three had his finger blown off and bled profusely. This paratrooper had miraculously reached the Rhine guided by Wouter van den Brink.

All next day the few surviving evaders hid in the wet grass on the north shore and waited for dark. That night a certain Lieutenant Dixon of the 506th Regiment, who grew up on the bayous of Florida, volunteered to pick up the survivors. He had often made reconnaissance missions on his own in a small light canoe he found in one of the abandoned houses. "I can handle anything with a paddle that floats," he said that night to Colonel Sink. And probably he could in the bayous, but the Rhine in a November flood was not exactly the same as the creeks of Florida. Sink gave him permission to cross the river alone in his canoe. When Dixon arrived on the far shore, he picked up the wounded evader with the blown off finger and they tried to return. I spoke to him for a few minutes on the walkie talkie before it went dead. About half an hour later the lieutenant's canoe turned over in the wild stream with its occupants and we could hear the cries for help in the night as the overturned craft swept swiftly westward and beyond our positions. No one ever heard of Dixon again. His canoe was found on the river bank twenty miles further west by Canadian troops in the spring.

Tucker meanwhile had crossed the Rhine before midnight in a single storm boat with two sappers. A strong wind whined through the trees and the rain pelted down. Tucker came back in what seemed like a few minutes with two men held at gun point. One was the Dutch guide, Van den Brink, the second a trade union official H. Leeuw and the third an Irish paratrooper called Tim O'Casey, who passed out after drinking a large glass of rum. Nobody else showed up that night. The hopelessness, the wastefulness of the task oppressed everyone. Colonel Sink came out of the cellar of the house we occupied on the river, looked at me sadly, shook his head and then walked off without a word. He had made it clear that he could not be responsible for the haphazard organization.

Most of the evading doctors returned into hiding. But Longland was wounded in the thigh and captured. Allenby and Maguire were caught and sent to Germany. Major John Coke of the King's Own Scottish Borderers was killed and buried in the garden of the house of Schriek not far from Bennekom. Most of the Dutchmen were captured, killed or wounded. The Ede Resistance group had its organization badly maimed from Pegasus II and never fully recovered from the shattering experience.

But Kragt, that enterprising IS9 agent, carried on independently with his good work, improvising with the same sense of ingenuity as he had done since the day he arrived in Holland twenty months before. He would continue to help evaders in small numbers to reach their own lines through the one route that remained open.

Banwell's amazing odyssey began on the night of November 19. Since his escape from the burned out Ennyshoeve farmhouse of Pouw in early October, he had travelled to Amerongen and Tiel on missions with the Resistance. There were numerous opportunites to reach his own lines but he never took them. Now as he lay in the frozen brickyard at Wageningen in the company of an American pilot whose name he never learned, Banwell knew he was in deep trouble. Snow fell all day covering the two men as the brickyard became blanketed in the blizzard. Movement was impossible. Every footprint could be seen and when the snow stopped it grew very cold. On the morning of November 21, a German SS patrol came to the brickyard. The shivering American pilot rose to his feet and shouted "I'm an American pilot. Don't shoot." He was cut down by machine-gun fire and left dying on the snow while Banwell, so cold he could hardly walk, was made prisoner.

The Germans marched Banwell to Velp, an eastern suburb of Arnhem. They interrogated him closely. He might have ended up like any other prisoner, except when they stripped him the interrogators were surprised to see he wore clean underwear unlike the rest of the evaders. Then the Gestapo produced a dossier which gave a surprisingly accurate picture of the sergeant's background. After that Banwell received very special attention. Late in November 1944 a Gestapo escort took Banwell to an airport near Apeldoorn, where a twin engined Focke Wulf flew the prisoner to Berlin. At Gestapo headquarters on Prinz Albrecht Strasse, the sergeant went through further long interrogations. Unless he divulged the names of his Resistance contacts he would be shot. The Gestapo placed him twice, on two successive mornings, before a firing squad, but Banwell somehow managed to remain cool until the last moment. On each occasion when he heard the the order to load rifles and aim he was prepared to die for the only kind of life he had ever known. But he did not die. The Gestapo were bluffing. The order to fire never came. Two days later a car drove Banwell to Auschwitz concentration camp where he was imprisoned. He lived on sauerkraut and water served once a week. (When the Russians found the sergeant in March 1945 he weighed less than ninety pounds – one half his normal weight.)

Meanwhile Hackett still lay most of the time in bed, weak but slowly recovering. As news of the success of the first escape and the failure of the second reached him, he thought of the day when he would set out himself. When he did, he decided it would be alone.

*

Before Christmas, Sergeant Alan Kettley and Lieutenant Ronald Adams joined me on the Waal. They had come from England. We settled down in the village of Dreumel in a large, white house across from the town of Tiel – a kind of bizarre no-man's-land where troops from either side came and went in the night. The cold winter of 1944 was punishing for the Dutch in occupied Holland without adequate fuel and food. Snow lay everywhere deep over the ground. Even the swift-flowing Waal sometimes froze so that our mechanically powered canoes had to break through the thin ice that covered the water. The Dutch who accompanied us to the far shore into the now-evacuated town of Tiel set up radio links and brought supplies to evaders and Resistance groups so they could hold on during this period of wild German brutality. Two of our Dutch agents were Leo Wilkens and Piet Westdorp.

After our first failure to infiltrate these two Dutchmen into Tiel on the night of December 20, we tried again three nights later. It was bitterly cold weather. An icy wind drove the snow in flurries over the exposed dikes while the rubberized canoes, with their incongruous Polynesian outriggers, had to break through ice crust to reach the mainstream. The agents took with them the new "S" phone which transmitted on an ultra-high frequency to a Mosquito bomber circling ten thousand feet overhead. I never thought this job, ordered by the Majors Neave and Fraser, was worth the effort for the return. The day before I had flown on a small aerial reconnaissance plane above the river and saw only frozen fields flooded by the broached dikes and a single puff of antiaircraft smoke several hundred feet above me. Probably the failure of Pegasus II and the uneasy feeling of putting other men's lives in jeopardy, while I lived in a kind of wartime luxury in my large white house, was beginning to disturb me. Also news had been brought that my friend, Eric Davies, was lying dangerously wounded in a house north of Barneveld, deep in enemy territory. He had been shot through both legs and taken prisoner when he had led an attack on the outskirts of Arnhem on September 18. In October he had jumped to freedom from a hospital train, hobbling into a Dutch home, where he had received kindness and protection. Now gangrene had infected one leg and his life was in danger. Somehow I had to help him. In a few days I would be meeting a Dutchman in Nijmegen who would be able to carry a package of life-giving penicillin to Davies. Meanwhile, the sad winter of 1944 on the river was made sadder by the knowledge that a good friend lay close to death.

Wilkens – tall, with smooth white skin and red cheeks – wore steel-rimmed spectacles. To function effectively he required the additional courage and calmness of his companion, West-dorp. Wilkens had been recruited by IS9 as a spy and accepted his role as a matter of duty. From the beginning when he volunteered to serve he was a most unlikely candidate. To make sure they reached their destination on the night of December 23, Kettley and I decided to escort the two men to the Tiel shore. In this way we would make absolutely certain they arrived in enemy territory. We set out with our small armada of three canoes between the flooded winter and summer dikes to the river. Our one motorized canoe with retractable pontoons was driven by one of Tucker's Canadian sappers, a dour-faced prairie farmer named Newton.

I steered from the front cockpit by means of two guide cables attached to the rudder. Since there were only two cockpits, Kettley balanced on the narrow stern with his boots dangling in the water. On our return journey the previous night I had retracted the pontoons a little too early and we capsized between the dikes. Kettley and I surfaced caked in ice. But no one seriously suffered after we thawed out before a great log fire in our white house. Tonight there would be no mistakes. The outriggers would remain in position. At the summer dike we pulled the boats up the embankment and waited. Lieutenant Johnny Cronyn, another of Tucker's engineers, would patrol the summer dike with an ultraviolet light to guide us back from Tiel. A special pair of dark glasses Kettley wore could pick up the signal. Visibility was poor, not more than fifty feet. Thick mist hung as usual above the water. We welcomed it as we launched the outrigger followed by the Dutchmen's frail canoe. The sound of the motor, muffled by fog, did not carry far. Soon the figure of Cronyn standing on the embankment faded into the night.

About an hour later we pierced the mist and drifted into the deserted Tiel waterfront among the empty barges and cast off the canoe. In a moment the powerful current swept the Dutchmen into shore. Then, with an unexpected shudder, our boat went aground and the engine stopped. Kettley slipped off his perch on the stern and in waist-deep water pushed us free. Somehow in the blinding river mist Newton restarted the petrol engine and we chugged back home in our strange little outrigger.

The next night Wilkens came on the air with the "S" phone strapped to his chest as he stood back from the window of his parent's home at Burg Bönhofflaan 6 in Tiel. At ten thousand feet over the town, a plywood Mosquito tuned successfully into Cormorant – the code name for the Dutchmen. In the Mosquito, Leo Fleskens spoke freely on his radio set to the two men on the ground far below. A stream of intelligence – not always used, mostly irrelevant – came from Cormorant until its sudden abrupt cessation some weeks later. Neither of these Dutch agents would ever be in a position to help the evaders.

In a few days the two Dutchmen for reasons of security moved their base further north to the village of Kerk-Avezaath where they lived in the house of the Daalderop family not far from Westdorp's home. Near by a quaint village bridge spanned the picturesque Linge River. From this scene of pastoral winter beauty the Dutchmen continued to transmit.

On January 15, Westdorp was arrested on a visit to his father's home. A trap set up by the German Green Police was really meant to apprehend the father, one of the leaders of the illegal railway strike that paralysed communications and supplies. But when the young Westdorp wandered into the house by accident, the police decided that both son and father should be imprisoned. The Germans did not know that Westdorp Junior was an IS9 agent. On the twenty-five mile march to the prison at Utrecht, the column passed Wilkens standing by the side of the road. Unfortunately Wilkens did not recognize his friend in the long procession of prisoners. This would be the last time Wilkens would be seen alive.

The nervous Wilkens, feeling forlorn and hunted, returned to Tiel and ceased to transmit. He hid his "S" phone in a windmill near the town. Without his comrade Westdorp, he felt lost, without direction. Although Wilkens really had nothing to fear and the Germans were not searching for him, he suffered from all the imagined delusions of the hunted. He believed Westdorp under questioning or torture would break down and reveal everything, and that it would not be long before the Gestapo found him. In early March the miserable Wilkens became so depressed that he scarcely moved out of his hiding place at Burg Bönhofflaan 6, in Tiel. Desperate, driven by fear and his nerve gone, he went to the river one dark night. A poor swimmer, the Dutchman inflated a thin bicycle tube and wrapped it around his body. He hoped this would keep him afloat until he reached the south shore. Wilkens was not fated to be a survivor as he plunged fearfully into the freezing waters of the Waal.

In the liberated village of Hurwenen, about two miles west down the curving bend of the river from Tiel, a decomposing body surfaced face first through the thin ice in the last days of March. For some time it lay bobbing about near the slope of the dike until a small boy discovered the corpse. A half-inflated bicycle tube entwined the unrecognizable figure. They buried the unknown man in the village. The Burgomaster of Murwenen kept the single object of identification found on the body. The watch was of military origin and unmarked except for some initials scratched on the back. They were mine.

Shortly after the discovery of Wilkens's corpse, I heard what had happened to the Dutchman who had brought news of Eric Davies. He had reached Davies with the penicillin and a personal note from me. The penicillin I was able to supply saved my friend's life, but he would be forever crippled.

In January I went west to the last avenue of escape still open to the Arnhem survivors – the Biesbosch.

*

November 5 was Guy Fawkes Day in England and Hackett's thirty-third birthday. The de Nooy sisters had quietly extracted this information from the brigadier some weeks earlier. On Guy Fawkes morning, the three maids washed and dressed their patient. Then loudly from the living room below, the brigadier heard his favourite hymns being played on the harmonium. The music ended with a stirring refrain from "God Save the King," which Hackett thought a little risky, considering twenty yards away were billeted German Military Police.

The flour for the birthday cake came from a hoarded supply in the Macostan paint factory of Menno de Nooy and labelled as unfit for human consumption. From the last of this dwindling mound of flour the sisters prepared their cake, on top of which stood a Union Jack made of stiff cardboard, painted with the inscription in Gothic characters: "Right or wrong, my country." The flag originated from the historian Colonel Theodor A. de Boeree, who even in those days, at the age of sixty-five, spent almost all his time minutely cataloguing every event of the Arnhem battle.

Some days after the birthday party, the Resistance, from the house in Torenstraat, began publishing a small newspaper called *Pro Patria*. Hackett became the military correspondent of this foolscap sheet of news printed on both sides and distributed by the young Marie Snoek on her bicycle. The two hundred issues were eagerly passed by hand to many thousands of people throughout the Ede area. The radio hidden under the floor-boards in the de Nooys' living room provided, through the BBC, a regular source of information. The military correspondent filled in the gaps from his own wide personal experience.

Late in November Wildeboer decided Hackett had to move temporarily from Torenstraat. He might not be safe anymore at the de Nooys', as *Pro Patria* had put the household in jeopardy. For the first time since he had been brought here in early October, the brigadier dressed and prepared to change his residence. One evening with the help of two of the de Nooy sisters he walked shakily through the streets of Ede to the "De Bonte Specht" – the villa of the industrious de Boeree on Stationsweg 98. Here Hackett found a certain amount of tranquillity and a partner with whom he could discuss many learned matters. The brigadier spent long, pleasant hours answering endless inquiries about the Arnhem campaign. After a week the Germans' interest in Pro Patria subsided and Hackett returned to his familiar lodgings upstairs at Torenstraat, once more under the matronly care of the three maids.

Next door to the old maid's house was billeted a section of Panzer troops who had requisitioned a large grey goose from a local farmer. Hackett from time to time surreptitiously observed the well-being of the goose as the Germans fattened the bird for their approaching Christmas dinner. The prospects of the meagre Christmas that faced his hosts disturbed the brigadier. He decided he must steal that succulent grey goose so that he and the maids could have it for their own Christmas. However, when he confided his plan to Cor de Nooy she sternly forbade any such foolishness. The sick brigadier would not be permitted to steal the Germans' grey goose. Hackett, rebuked but undefeated, decided that in one way or another the goose would fly from captivity. He told the maids, with a sense of poetic justice, that he would even the score in another way. When the moment came to depart, Hackett would not forget the Germans who would be feasting on that fat goose at Christmastime.

Hackett, a lone evader in Ede with all the others gone, grew restless and suddenly uncertain of his future. He yearned to leave as his health improved and he felt well enough to undertake the journey through the German lines. After Christmas, when Johan Snoek suggested they might try a route out through southern Holland, Hackett readily agreed.

THE GREY GOOSE

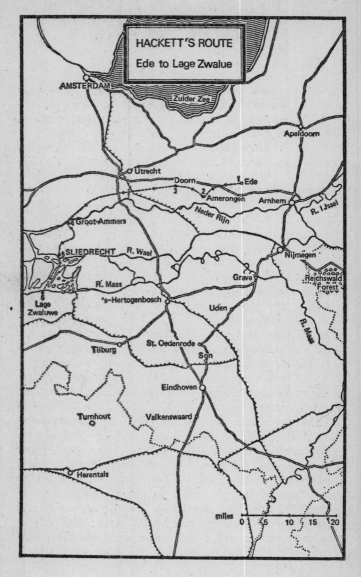

HACKETT'S ROUTE
Ede to Lage Zwalue

AMSTERDAM

Zuider Zee

Apeldoorn

Utrecht   Doorn   1 Ede
                    3   2
                Amerongen   Arnhem
                Neder Rijn   R. IJssel

Groot-Ammers

SLIEDRECHT   R. Waal
                              Nijmegen
                                        Reichswald
                                        Forest
        R. Maas   Grave
's-Hertogenbosch   Uden

Laga
Zwaluwe
                              R. Maas

Tilburg   St. Oedenrode
                    Son

            Eindhoven

Turnhout   Valkenswaard

Herentals

miles
0   5   10   15   20

The creeks of the Biesbosch twist and turn, come to a dead end, lose themselves among the tall willows or thrust out into tongue-like lagoons that become part of the shapeless swamps of this hundred-mile-square watershed. The great veinwork of muddy water is constantly pumped in and out by the powerful tides that run down the Merwede River. The only signs of human life were some isolated huts once used for duck hunting in more peaceful times. But now the huts were derelict, deserted except for the occasional fugitive fleeing the Germans. A man could be swallowed up by the Biesbosch without a trace. Bogs and quicksand made walking treacherous, almost impossible. Only small canoes of shallow draft would slide across the reeds and penetrate the small gaps between the overhanging willow trees. In winter the place was an icy quagmire shrouded in almost continual fog.

A small group of men who grew up on the waters of the Merwede decided in October, 1944, to form their own clandestine transportation system through the Biesbosch. When the moon and tide were favourable, they paddled their canoes from Sliedrecht to Lage Zwaluwe, carrying evaders out of occupied Holland. Normally, the journey one way took four hours, but sometimes it could take days. German machine-gun posts and sunken cables at the Kop van 'tLand did little to deter the river men, who became known as "the crossers." They dressed alike in thick woollen sweaters and scarves, heavy coats and boots, caps and gloves. By the end of October snow and sleet, the river often whipped up by a strong northwest wind, made the canoe crossing more hazardous than usual. But the ferrying service continued regardless of the weather. Only the tide dictated the hour of departure.

Jan van der Ley (Lange Jan), a tall, blond man with an Australian mother and Dutch father, knew the river since childhood. Jan Visser (Grey Jan), a road contractor from Sliedrecht with premature grey hair, spent his youth hunting geese in the swamps. Cheerful Jan Landgraaf (Deaf Jan), a flat-nosed, mechanical engineer, had one great advantage over everyone else. Born deaf, he heard nothing on his canoe journeys and therefore always thought everything was fine. Koos Meijer (Koos), operated a river boat since 1923, named *Janna* after his wife, and figured he knew the river as well as anyone. For safety in the fog he wore a compass strapped to his wrist. Cornelis van Woerkom (Bald Kees), a quiet, bespectacled marine surveyor, preferred to travel alone. Jan Rombout, another river captain, took the name of Staat while Ko Bakker became Alblas. These were the guides who went up and down twenty-five miles of river night after night. Only the river men would be able to bring out the last of the evaders.

*

At dusk on February 5, 1945, Simon Kadijk, a farmer, walked down to a particularly prominent poplar tree that towered on the edge of his riverside property on the Beneden Merwede. With a mallet he tapped a long spike a few inches into the tree so that even in the darkness a man could feel the protruding iron with his fingers. The spike represented a signal to the Resistance. If the farmer had hammered it all the way in it meant Germans patrolled the river that night. If the spike protruded the road over the dike to the river was clear. The low, slope-roofed buildings of Kadijk's farmhouse fronted on the south bank of the river across from the town of Sliedrecht. About a mile further south the Nieuwe Merwede curved back westward on the narrow-pointed peninsula which enclosed the farmer's land. Protected by high dikes, the farm was set into the middle of the swamps of the Biesbosch. The river surrounded Kadijk. He lived on an island. The tides rustled through the reeds all night, the sound broken only by the honking of thousands of wild geese who took flight whenever they were disturbed.

In late January I towed Kees van Woerkom five miles up the

208

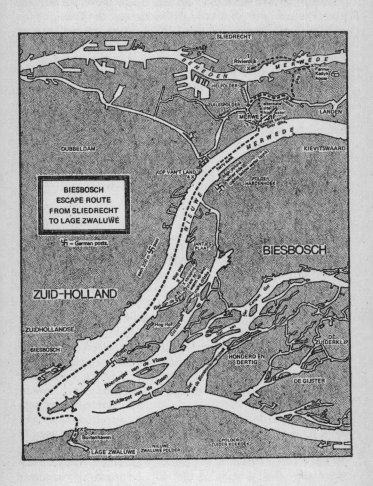

BIESBOSCH
ESCAPE ROUTE
FROM SLIEDRECHT
TO LAGE ZWALUWË

᛭ – German posts.

ZUID-HOLLAND

BIESBOSCH

Merwede River from Lage Zwaluwe in our motor-powered kayak. I cast him off at the Kop van 'tLand. Beyond this point the Germans were vigilantly patrolling and the sound of the engine could be easily located. Paul Hood, another one of Tucker's sappers, had let go the towrope some time before midnight. Van Woerkom waved goodbye in the darkness. He promised he would be back in a few days with some evaders when the moon and tide were right. We expected as usual to meet some of the river men at our rendezvous in the Central Hotel in Lage Zwaluwe shortly after dawn on February 5. Deaf Jan Landgraaf, who had gone up the river to Sliedrecht ahead of Van Woerkom, had made the appointment. This resolute man seldom made a mistake. He also told me to expect some doctors who had come all the way from Apeldoorn. And perhaps a brigadier. But his information about the brigadier was nothing more than rumour.

*

The brigadier, still in more pain from his stomach wound than he expected, finally set out by bicycle from Ede with Johan Snoek on the morning of January 30 after a large breakfast and fond farewells from the three maids. The de Nooy sisters were both sad and happy at Hackett's departure. They did not know whether they would ever see him again. With an early snowfall on the ground, his abdomen wound still unhealed, Hackett, an indifferent bicycle rider at the best of times, rode very unsteadily. The sisters had worried like mothers about their frail patient. The brigadier looked very wan and thin. Before he left the house on Torenstraat, Cor had presented him with some hand-knitted underwear darned with precious wool. The only wool they could find was white and blue. The front of Hackett's new underwear was in blue, the rear in white. But he felt warm. Among his last words to the sisters was his insistence they should listen to the BBC Overseas Service every night at 9.0 p.m., commencing three days hence. If he succeeded in reaching the Allied lines he would send back the message "the grey goose has flown." He had not forgotten the grey goose.

Four months at Torenstraat represented a lifetime of experience for both the brigadier and the de Nooy sisters. None of them would ever forget it as long as they lived. On his lapel Hackett wore a small button with the initials SH (Slecht Horend) – the sign of deafness. If anyone spoke he would not answer but smile and politely doff his hat. Snoek carried the brigadier's uniform wrapped in paper on his bicycle, while Hackett kept his walking stick.

In the evening, after a tortuous fifteen miles over icy roads, Snoek finally led the exhausted brigadier into the large grounds of the estate, Huis te Maarn. The two cyclers followed a curving, mile-long driveway, passed overgrown shrubbery until they came to the deserted mansion of the Blijdensteins. Three miles north from the house lay the village of Maarn itself. In the servants' quarters adjoining the main building Hackett met Cornelis Idenburg, the caretaker, his wife, his son Henny and the doctor Lipmann Kessel.

The next day Kessel, who never wasted much time, took a quick look at the brigadier's stomach wound and decided corrective surgery would be immediately necessary. Henny travelled to the local doctor at Maarn returning with gut and loaned surgical instruments for Kessel to tidy up surgery performed over four months ago at the St. Elizabeth Hospital in Arnhem. With the borrowed instruments the doctor resutured Hackett's wound on the Idenburgs' kitchen table.

For several years the Idenburg household had been a safe place for evaders to hide. They were not only host to Kessel and Hackett at the time but also to the doctors Theo Redman, Graeme Warrack and the dentist, Derek Ridler, all of whom once more sought a way out of occupied Holland after the catastrophe of Pegasus II. They had been led to the Huis te Maarn by Dick Kragt. A Russian officer called Badalian, who had escaped from a forced labour camp in Germany, had also been part of the household for six months. The Idenburgs were happy enough to put up the Russian for this length of time in the common cause, but his private visits to women in near-by villages in the middle of the night proved a security risk. He had also contracted gonorrhea. The Resistance finally curbed him of his excesses by threatening to shoot him. However, while the family had been willing to suffer through the Russian's love affairs for a long time, they did not have much patience with his other shortcomings. In common with many other Russian and Rumanian evaders, he constantly fell off his bicycle. He never learned to ride one properly. For the Dutch this was an unseemly hazard. But he had one other unpardonable fault. He cheated at cards. Eventually Badalian was moved to more supervised surroundings further north.

Hackett made himself useful at the Huis te Maarn by washing the dishes after mealtime. But he was terribly nervous and impatient to leave this busy place. The doctors had come two days ago from Scherpenzeel, where Gilbert Sadi-Kirschen hid with his signalman Moyse and Pietquin. The doctors arrived at Maarn after unsuccessfully attempting a crossing at Tiel a few days before. Like Hackett, they were also very impatient to move. The small medical contingent, with the help of the careful Kragt of IS9, hoped to reach the Biesbosch in forty-eight hours. But Hackett still preferred to keep his own company. A deep snowfall that February covered the gables and lawns around the Idenburg bungalow, conveying an atmosphere of wintry peace and tranquillity.

Elsa Caspers, a businesslike nineteen-year-old schoolgirl, arrived by bicycle at precisely 8.0 a.m. on the morning of February 3 at the Idenburg home to fetch Hackett. The Resistance had used her for several years as a courier to move Jewish children to safe accommodation to prevent them being deported to concentration camps. Since September Elsa had served as one of the girls in Kirschen's unit. All she knew that morning was that she and Johan Snoek would take a high-ranking British officer to Ammerstol, where they would cross the Lek to Groot Ammers. Here her journey must end before night came. On the icy paths with bitterly cold head winds, the trip would take most of the day if the man was in good physical condition. After Elsa was informed that the evader had still not recovered from a serious abdominal wound, she wondered how they would ever manage to cover seventy miles by bicycle over ice and mud before evening. She doubted it. To arrive before 6.0 p.m. curfew in Ammerstol they would have to hurry. For Elsa the ride was routine. She cycled an average of a hundred miles a day from 5.0 a.m. until dark carrying messages, explosives or leading evaders to new hideouts. On this particular Saturday morning she noticed the man who would accompany her to Groot Ammers seemed to be treated with special deference by the other members of the household. When she packed the Englishman's uniform, she saw it was heavily blood-stained. The little man with the moustache appeared to have some high military rank. For Elsa this made no difference. He appeared sombre, uncommunicative, somewhat reserved but not completely unfriendly. Elsa thought the soldier must have been very nervous about the journey. She took from Hackett the walking stick with the "U" carved into the handle and tied it alongside the parcel on the back of her bicycle. The stick seemed to have a special meaning for the soldier, who let it out of his hands only reluctantly. Elsa did not truthfully look forward to the prospect of this particular trip. In addition to the ailing man, she would have to cope with her new bicycle seat over six inches too high. There was no way of lowering it. Her thighs and back ached from the additional exertion this caused. Elsa had instructions to leave the grounds of the Huis te Maarn at 9.0 a.m. promptly. She would obey, leading the way with the soldier in the middle and Snoek in the rear of the small convoy. She noticed Hackett's identity card bore the name of Van Daalen, deaf from childhood. He wore the deaf button on his lapel.

They set out on time and continued all morning, making surprisingly good progress, better than Elsa hoped. They stopped before the bridge at Nieuwegein and lunched in a small café before one o'clock. After the meal Elsa inconspicuously caught up to a horse and cart full of Germans that happened to be going the same way. To ease the journey she told Hackett to hold onto the wagon. Snoek and Elsa, holding onto the cart, kept up a polite conversation with the German soldiers for fifteen miles. By midafternoon they came to Ammerstol, where it took two hours to find a boatman willing to row the three travellers across the Lek. Only the bribe of a precious ball of darning wool belonging to Snoek convinced the boatman to take the three with their bicycles over the river to Groot Ammers.

On February 4 three men, Koos Meijer, Jan Visser and Ko Bakker, left the gas works at Sliedrecht at dusk and rowed through the powerful crosscurrents to the south shore of the Beneden Merwede. There they pulled their heavy wooden row-boat up over the steep dike. From here they were only a few hundred feet from the Kadijk farmhouse. The wind had come up gradually all that day from the northwest and the sky at sunset flamed a deep red. For Meijer, a weather-beaten river captain, the cold evening had all the signs of an approaching storm. Flights of wild geese rose from the white sand banks and soared overhead in clouds, southward to their refuge in the swamps of the Biesbosch. The men walked eastward along the top of the dike in the gathering dusk for a few hundred yards and then descended towards a small creek. Hidden in the tall rushes were two slender wood canoes, especially adapted to carry an electric motor driven by two twelve-volt batteries. The motors were soundless. After inspecting their boats, testing the batteries, the craft were once again covered with rushes and left. The three river men climbed back along the dike in the darkness towards the Kadijk farmhouse, where they intended to spend the night. On the following day at the same time they hoped to be manoeuvring through the narrow creeks of the Biesbosch out into the main river.

Gerrit Hakkesteeg, the busy beadle of the Dutch Reformed Church in Groot Ammers, looked out of the entrance, up and down the street, and then shut and bolted the door of the empty church. The last of the congregation had long since gone that

Sunday after the sermon by the Reverend Tukker. Behind the pulpit the beadle followed some narrow stone stairs up to the organ loft and sat down behind the organ. Instead of playing the instrument he opened a secret panel above the keyboard and switched the radio in time for the 9.0 p.m. BBC news from London. Sitting on the floor in the loft and also waiting for the evening broadcast were Flying Officers Kenneth Parsons, Eric Blakemore, James Branford of the RAF, and Captains Angus Low and Charles Barlow of the American Air Force. After the news broadcast, the beadle closed the loft door and went out a side entrance to his house on the Burgemeester Fortuynplein 3. Here the tired Hackett had arrived with his two guides from Maarn just before curfew. Soon the other men in the loft would surreptitiously come and join the brigadier to exchange news and gossip and have a drink of egg flip.

Hackett's bloodstained uniform and walking stick were transferred from Elsa Caspers's bicycle to that of Heine van Leeuwen, a nurse who lived and worked with her doctor father in Sliedrecht. From Groot Ammers on February 5, she conducted Hackett another ten miles south to Sliedrecht without incident. Unbeknown to the brigadier, Hein had safely deposited the four British doctors in Sliedrecht at the house of Kees van Woerkom on Rivierdijk 486 on the previous day. Heine lived next door to her friend Van Woerkom, separated only by a small hedge. Both houses had an imposing view of the river, fifty feet away.

Hackett arrived at Van Woerkom's house at Rivierdijk on a windy Monday afternoon. From the rear living room window, the brigadier could see the wide Merwede at the end of the garden. The journey from Groot Ammers had not been too difficult and gave the brigadier confidence. When Hackett saw the river that afternoon his excitement mounted. Across the north arm of the Merwede he could just see the Kadijk's farm and the beginning of the creeks and marshes of the Biesbosch. The stormy sky and the sight of this wild panorama represented the final stage of a long and arduous journey that filled the deeply religious Hackett with a kind of spiritual exaltation. Nothing could stop him now. While he rested, Heine – who kept the brigadier's possessions – tried on Hackett's uniform and then climbed over the garden fence to show it off to her neighbour. It was a little small for her, but even with the bloodstains it did not look too bad. Heine cleaned it up the best she could and then told Hackett from here on he had to wear the uniform. This was the custom. An oversized raincoat that fell to the brigadier's ankles would cover it up.

When the university student, Jan van de Ley, appeared that evening with the schoolmaster, Johannes Lanser, Hackett followed the two Resistance men to Middeldiepstraat 131, Lanser's home. Suze Lanser fed the brigadier a large bowl of steaming pea soup laced with small pieces of roast pork meant to sustain him through his long night on the river. After the meal Van der Ley and Lanser walked the last thousand yards to the gas works where the brigadier would be rowed across the upper branch of the Merwede. By an odd coincidence, that evening Hackett passed Graeme Warrack with his guide, Jan Rombout, on the dike at Sliedrecht. The brigadier politely doffed his hat and wished the surprised doctor a good day in Dutch, as if their meeting was a casual daily occurrence. At the gas works where the rowboat lay moored, Hackett put his walking stick into the craft and stepped in after. Van der Ley and Lanser then rowed to the Kadijk farmhouse where Koos Meijer waited for the three men before sundown.

Meijer had decided to wait at the farm until 6 p.m. for Lanser and Van der Ley to show up If they did not arrive by then with the evader, he would descend the river that night to Lage Zwaluwe with his friends, Jan Visser and Ko Bakker. Meijer could not delay his departure as he had an important meeting with Lieutenant-Colonel Jahannes Somer of the Dutch Intelligence service in Eindhoven in forty-eight hours. But the evader had come and all was ready. On the giant poplar tree the spike indicated that the route along the dike was not patrolled by the enemy. Without further delay, the brigadier accompanied Meijer over the half-mile of polder to the creek at the Kikvorskil where the electric-powered canoes were hidden in the rushes. The slight Hackett slipped easily into the small front cockpit of the first craft while Meijer took up his position in the rear. Bakker and Visser then squeezed with their heavy, winter clothing into the cockpits of the second craft and they set off.

Down at the bottom of the winding creek they reached the launching place at the dam where the boats were dragged over the top and slid into a small inlet. Through the black night the wind screamed in the willows, driving snow flurries before it. Black, foreboding clouds scudded across a sky that displayed a tiny sliver of a golden moon. Meijer waited in the sheltered inlet for the clouds to totally envelop the moon. Another hundred feet further on was the main river. By ten o'clock the guide hoped to be on his way as planned. The wind rose steadily to gale force as the poplar trees bent in the moaning gusts.

*

Almost every night Hood and I left the deserted lagoon near Hooge Zwaluwe, where our boats were hidden, to begin our patrol on the Merwede as far as the Kop van 'tLand. On a freezing night we had escorted Koos Meijer part of the way back to Sliedrecht. He promised to return on February 5 with a number of evaders. Twice weekly I could count on Meijer and his friends meeting me for our great pre-dawn feasts in the Central Hotel in Lage Zwaluwe. I did not know then I would be unable to keep my next appointment.

After dark on February 5, Hood, Anthony Knipping – my interpreter – and myself left the lagoon at Lage Zwaluwe in our blue German speedboat. Mounted forward were a pair of twin Vickers machine guns, each loaded with two-hundred-round drums of 303 ammunition. We found the blue boat one afternoon unmanned, drifting helplessly at the juncture of the Maas and Merwede rivers, not far from the twisted girders of the blown Moerdijk bridge. Remote controlled and loaded with several hundred pounds of explosives, it had evidently missed its target and run out of fuel. One of our engineers rendered the charges harmless and the speedboat joined our small fleet. Under full power it could do forty knots.

Our charts of the river were rudimentary and although we usually managed to miss German posts, we frequently ran into uncharted marshes or dead-end creeks. But the power and swiftness of our speedboat always brought us back home safely. The two cylinder German patrol boats and the occasional flares the enemy shot up over the river never worried us. We could twist and turn and run at high speeds over the two-mile-wide Merwede, feeling as if we owned the Biesbosch. The enemy knew we had their speedboat. Frequently in the bewildering confusion of our steaming wake and the thunderous noise we made, the river men slipped silently through the Kop van 'tLand unnoticed and crossed to Lage Zwaluwe before dawn came.

We left the lagoon at slack water on February 5 and glided slowly through the reeds and willows out into the Merwede. I hoped to arrive at the Kop van t'Land – about ten miles up river – by midnight and meet some evaders. As we turned the point of Anna Jacomina Plaat, wet fog suddenly clamped down and blinded us. Ploughing slowly ahead we could see no further than the front of the boat. About an hour later the fog momentarily lifted and we observed a small unfamiliar-looking canoe dart into one of the creeks directly ahead. Foolishly we gave chase. It seemed only seconds before we were lost in the swamps. The canoe meanwhile had vanished. Then the speedboat shuddered to a halt on the bottom, trapped in a forest of dense reeds, locked in deep mud on a falling tide that meant a five-hour wait before we could refloat. Not before dawn would there be sufficient water to lift the boat free. All that night up to our knees in mud and slime we heaved, shoved, pulled and strained to free the land-locked craft, but it refused to budge. Thousands of wild geese rose about us in the reeds, shrieking and honking, announcing our presence. I had no idea of our position except we were stuck fast somewhere in the heart of the Biesbosch north of our base. There was not much we could do. Soon Koos Meijer and his evaders would be coming down from Sliedrecht on the same ebbing tide that trapped me, hoping to meet us.

*

The canoes slowly slid over the last dam at the Katse Gat into the Merwede and were quickly swept along the shore by the current. The brigadier, muffled in his greatcoat, cap and scarf, was further encumbered by his walking stick and a Colt .45 automatic stuck in his trousers. Everything about the Merwede on that wild and stormy night looked majestic. For someone who had never before seen the turbulent expanse of river, the white glimmering sandbanks and the almost total blackness of the sky the sight was awesome, frightening. Through the turning miles of water the electric boats purred along in the current. Meijer steered into the middle of the stream to avoid the Ottersluis where the Germans moored their patrol boats. But he need not have worried. In the black night one could barely see ten feet ahead and the howling wind killed almost all sound. Jan Visser and Jan Staat followed less than a dozen yards behind the first boat. Three-quarters of a mile beyond the Ottersluis the Germans had dropped a cable across the river and sunk barges to deter the crossers. But the canoes only had a draft of six inches and could easily skim over the sunken obstacles.

Every now and then a wave several times the height of the craft crashed over the bow and soaked the occupants. As the wind continued to rise, the waves grew larger. Only the tight-fitting cockpits prevented the canoes from being swamped and capsizing. There were times when Hackett feared his boatman might turn back in the face of the weather. At the Kop van 'tLand the Germans automatically fired machine-gun bursts over the water at regular intervals. Meijer steered from one side of the Merwede to the other to disguise the thin line of translucent foam that followed in the wake of the boat. From the shore long tongues of smooth, white sand thrust out into the stream. The guide seemed to recognize every contour of land, every shift of the current, each small promontory that lay half sunk in the bubbling river.

About one o'clock on the morning of February 6, Meijer and Hackett, wet, miserably cold, became absolutely still. The German post at Deene Plaat Keet – a partially submerged marshy island – shot up a white parachute flare, brilliantly illuminating the canoe for several seconds. As the flare died out directly above the heads of Hackett and Meijer, the men waited for the burst of machine-gun fire that must immediately follow. Nothing happened. Perhaps they were too far out on the river to be seen or no one looked their way at the right time. But whatever the reason, the occupants miraculously escaped detection. About forty-five minutes later Meijer reached the point of Anna Jacomina Plaat and entered the rough, two-mile wide Hollandsch Diep at the confluence of the Merwede and Maas rivers. At two o'clock in the morning he turned sharp east around the point into the safety of the lagoon in Lage Zwaluwe.

Waiting in the early morning mist along the quay-side of the harbour with a bottle of whisky in his hand was Major Tony Crankshaw, commander of B Squadron of the Eleventh Hussars. He greeted his old friend, Hackett, warmly. Crankshaw had expected him and gave the frozen brigadier a stiff drink. The bizarre coincidence of that meeting created such a startling effect on both officers that they accepted the incident with the casual fraternity reserved for men who might have met the day before. The last time they saw each other had been in Cairo in 1938.

The doctors, Redman and Warrack, had also arrived. Eventually I showed up in my limping speedboat after dawn when the tide had lifted us off the mud bank, long after the evaders were comfortably asleep in their beds. I met the smiling Meijer, who waited for me at the Central Hotel. Out of the pocket of his wet coat he took a box of Players cigarettes signed by the evader he brought down that night from Sliedrecht. Hackett's name was scribbled across the crumpled package.

In England Hackett went into the maternity ward of the Radcliffe Infirmary where his wounds were attended. The move was deliberate for security reasons and to allow him time to recuperate away from the glare of the press. After his discharge the brigadier left for his country home at Oakham near Rutland. Urquhart, not standing on ceremonies, came to see his convalescing commander, happy to welcome him back. Urquhart, now a general without a division, talked about the campaign, the reasons for defeat, their dead comrades and the soldiers who distinguished themselves during and after the battle in occupied Holland. The meeting ended cordially, warmly, any suggested differences now forgotten, buried forever. Before Urquhart left, Hackett said he had a present for him. From a rack in the hallway he removed the carefully preserved ash walking stick with the initial "U" carved into the handle. Urquhart, greatly surprised, immediately recognized the stick, perhaps slightly more worn than he recalled, but his beyond a doubt. The brigadier explained how it had remained with him ever since he escaped from the St. Elisabeth Hospital in Arnhem. He now presented the stick to his general with his pride and compliments. "Here it is, sir," he said. "Mission accomplished."

Urquhart broke into a warm smile at the sentimental gesture, but with a gentle firmness, he refused the prize. "No, you've earned it. The stick now belongs to you," he said.

After a cold, desolate winter, spring came beautifully to London in 1945, warmly, with sunshine and blue skies. One bright day in early May, Hackett stepped out of a taxi in Piccadilly on his way to the Cavalry Club. Somewhat preoccupied, he paid the driver and then stopped suddenly in his tracks. He had left something behind. Helplessly he watched the taxi in the distance disappearing into the traffic. Inside was his treasured walking stick.

On the evening of February 10, at Torenstraat 5 in Ede, Johan Snoek took out the radio receiver from under the floorboards in the living room and tuned in to the BBC news. Big Ben resonantly chimed nine o'clock. Cor, Mien and Rie de Nooy sat around the small radio set listening intently. Before the news the broadcaster announced he had a special message for friends in occupied Holland. He read his message twice. Slowly and clearly. It simply said: "The grey goose has flown."

Triumphantly, the three old maids joined hands and danced a small jig of joy.

AFTERWORD

Some people have asked if the war ended for me and some of my friends when John Hackett returned to the Allied lines, and the de Nooy sisters received the news of the brigadier's escape. I will tell you. It did not. I still travelled on, this time into northern Holland to witness an ambush of a long, plodding column of German infantry trying to flee into Germany. My friend, Major Henry Druce, who headed the ambush with his six SAS jeeps each mounted with four Vickers machine guns, was dressed in corduroy trousers and a black silk top hat for the occasion. He had picked up the top hat in some deserted house. In one terrible moment of slaughter, the several hundred Germans in the ambush were all killed and wounded. Then I went east into Germany with my jeep driver, Stimson, a dry, old, gnarled western Canadian of twenty-four. We were among the first people to enter Bergen Belsen concentration camp. Here I saw another kind of horror, more profound and incomprehensible than the first. I only mention these events because I think they must have had a lasting effect upon me. It often takes a while for the meaning of these experiences to settle below the numbed conscience of a soldier – sometimes decades. When I went home to Canada it was difficult to return like many others to the kind of youthful innocence which I left behind. Some years later a strange thought came to me and it gave me a feeling of hope. I do not know its significance. But I realized suddenly that I had never killed a man.

The evaders, in almost all cases, turned out to be unusual human beings. Some, clinging to the wheel of fortune which Machiavelli believed takes us around only once during life, became rich and famous. Others died young, prematurely. Some even perished of a broken heart. A close friend killed himself.

But to satisfy the curiosity of those who may be interested I have set out a minute biography on the lives of many of the people who have appeared in the pages of this book.

*

ADAMS, Ronald, is the head lawyer of one of England's largest banks.

BANWELL, Keith (Tex), only recently left the army, but he still jumps regularly out of airplanes, free falling. He says it keeps him mentally alert.

CASPERS, Elsa, is a doctor practising near The Hague in Holland.

COLLINS, Ian, has sadly recently died. He had retired from his position as chairman of the large publishing house that bears his family name.

CRONYN, Johnny, became a chief executive of a large multi-national company. He now devotes his time to his political interests.

DEANE-DRUMMOND, Anthony, Major [1st Airborne], ended up as a general and Assistant Chief of the Defence Staff (Operations). In 1957 he became British Glider Champion.

DE BOEREE, Theodor A., Lt. Col., died at eighty-eight quite a few years ago, still working to his last days as a military historian.

DE NOOY, COR, Mien and Rie, the three old maids, and their red-brick house on Torenstraat in Ede no longer exist.

DOBIE, David, became a business tycoon in Kenya before his sad death from a lingering illness.

Frost, John D., Lt. Col. [1st Airborne], became a general and eventually retired to a farming life in the south of England.

Gough, Freddy, Major [1st Airborne], has retired after a distinguished career as a British Member of Parliament.

Grainger, Robert E., Co. Sgt. Major [1st Airborne], after a lifetime of service in the army as a Regimental Sergeant Major, has retired quietly to a small cottage in the north of England.

Hackett, John, Brigadier [1st Airborne], was knighted, became a high-ranking general, Commander of the British Army of the Rhine, and later principal of one of England's leading universities.

Hibbert, Anthony, Major [1st Airborne], made his fortune in business and lives in comfortable eighteenth-century surroundings not far from the English southwest coast.

Kennedy, Russel, a leading professor in a large Canadian university.

Kessel, Lipmann, Capt., is a renowned surgeon in London.

Knottenbelt, Maarten Jan, moved to Australia, where he wrote treatises and became a philosopher, and then went to live in Holland.

Kragt, Dick, has suffered some personal misfortune, but like the courageous person he is, has triumphed over adversity.

Kruyff, Pieter, went to work in America as a chemical engineer. He died in 1963.

Labouchère, Charles, became a key figure in the Dutch Intelligence Service and enjoys a quiet life these days in his lovely garden outside the Hague.

LABOUCHÈRE, Bep, married her wartime sweetheart, Roelof van Valkenburg, and lives in a stately Dutch manor house with her children and grandchildren.

LANDGRAAF, (Deaf) Jan, still lives in Sliedrecht and canoes down the Biesbosch for amusement. He is a successful civil engineer.

LATHBURY, Gerald, Brig. [1st Airborne], became a distinguished general and was Knighted and also became Governor General of Gibraltar.

LONSDALE, Dicky, Major [1st Airborne], lives a quiet, retired life near the town of Salisbury, after a turbulent career in business and politics.

McGOWAN, Daniel, after a long struggle to physically rehabilitate himself, now works among the poor and unfortunate to improve their lot in life.

MEIJER, Koos, lives in Sliedrecht near the Merwede River, the source of his memories and his life.

NEAVE, Airey, went into politics and became a prominent Member of Parliament.

NIJHOFF, Edith, still lives in her house on Berkenlaan in Ede, which is a museum of mementos of all the people she helped. I would always like to think of her as one of the grand old ladies of the Resistance movement.

OLLIFF, Donald, is a country doctor and practises medicine with his wife, also a doctor, from a charming eleventh-century home deep in the Cotswold forest.

SADI-KIRSCHEN, Gilbert, lives in his native Brussels and is a distinguished Belgium lawyer.

SNOEK, Johannes M., is a clergyman who devotes his life to the World Council of Churches.

STRAYER, Robert L., Lt. Col. [101st Airborne], is an insurance executive in Philadelphia.

SYKES, George, became a general and lives in Texas.

TATHAM-WARTER, Digby, went to live in Kenya and became a famous hunter. His safaris are renowned around the world.

TUCKER, Michael, became the mayor of his home town in Canada, and a chief executive of a large engineering company until his recent retirement.

URQUHART, Robert Elliott (Roy), Maj. Gen. [1st Airborne], commanded the 1st Airborne Division. He retired to his native Scotland, where he seems to have lost none of his vigour or his charm.

VAN VALKENBURG, Roelof, is a doctor and the head of a large hospital in Holland. He lives happily with his wife, the former Bep Labouchère.

WILDEBOER, Bill, is dead. One of the forgotten men who was confused by the devious politics of peace.

WILSON, Boy, fifty years old when he led the parachute drop into Arnhem, quietly vanished in his latter years and died. Hardly anyone ever heard from him again after 1945.

VAN WOERKOM, Kees, still lives in Sliedrecht in his house on Moerdijk and practises his profession as a marine surveyor.

BIBLIOGRAPHY

Unpublished Documents

Adams, Ronald. Personal Account, 1945.
de Boeree, Theodor A. Personal Letters, 1947–48.
Dobie, David. Personal Diary, 1944.
Hibbert, Anthony. Diary of Events, 1944.
Jenkins, John Howard. Contemporary.
Lathbury, Gerald. Personal Diary, 1944.
McGowan, Daniel. Personal Account, 1945.
Redman, Theo. Personal Account, 1945.
Strayer, Robert. Contemporary.
Tatham-Warter, Digby. Personal Account, 1944.
Terrett, Peter. Personal Account, 1944.
Tucker, Michael. Personal Account, 1945.
Van Woerkom, Kees. Personal Account, 1945.

Main Published Sources

Arnhem: September 1944. Arnhem: Gemeentearchief, 1969.
Bauer, Cornelis. *The Battle of Arnhem*. London: Hodder and
　Stoughton, 1966; New York: Stein and Day, 1967.
Brammall, R. *The Tenth: A Record of the 10th Battalion, The
　Parachute Regiment*. Ipswich: Eastgate Publications, 1965.
Collins, Lieutenant Colonel Ian. *Special Air Service Reports on
　"Fabian," Gilbert Sadi-Kirschen*. London: Airborne Head-
　quarters, 1944.
Deane-Drummond, Anthony. *Return Ticket*. London: Collins,
　1953.
Farmer-Hockley, Anthony. *Airborne Carpet: Operation Market-
　Garden*. Ballantine's Illustrated History of World War II,
　Battle Book #9. New York. Ballantine Books, 1969.

Heaps, Captain Leo. *Escape from Arnhem*. Toronto: Macmillan 1945.

Herford, M.E.M. "All in a Day's Work." (Parts 1 and 2), *The Journal of the Royal Army Medical Corps*, April, 1952.

Herford, M.E.M. "Campaigning Notes." *Bristo Medico Chirurgical Journal*, Vol. LXIII (1946).

Hibbert, Christopher. *The Battle of Arnhem*. London: B.T. Batsford, 1962; New York: Macmillan, 1962.

Horrocks, Lt. Gen. Sir Brian, Ed. *The Red Devils: The Story of the British Airborne Forces*. London: Leo Cooper, 1971.

Kessel, Lipmann and St. George, John. *Surgeon at Arms*. London: William Heinemann, 1958.

Rapport and Northwood. *Rendezvous with Destiny: A History of the 101st Airborne Division*. London: Infantry Journal Press, 1948.

Sadi-Kirschen, Gilbert. *Six Amis Viendront ce Soir*. Chartres: Maison d'Editions Wesmael, 1946.

Saunders, Hilary St. George. *The Red Beret*. London: Michael Joseph, Ltd., 1950.

Sosabowski, Maj. Gen Stanislaw. *Freely I Served*. London: William Kimber, 1960.

Urquhart, Maj. Gen. R. E. *Arnhem*. London: Cassell, 1958; New York: W. W. Norton, 1958.

Warsack, Graeme. *Travel By Dark After Arnhem*. London: Harvill Press, 1963.

Zeno, pseud. *The Cauldron*. London: Macmillan, 1966; New York: Stein & Day, 1967.

ACKNOWLEDGEMENTS

A unique diary, hardly known and seldom if ever seen, came into my possession. It belonged to Tony Hibbert, the Brigade Major of the 1st Parachute Brigade and one of the men who fought at the bridge at Arnhem. The diary is remarkable because Hibbert was an unusually meticulous man and one of the important evaders after the battle. He kept an hourly account of every event in excruciating detail. What he could not write down during intervals in the battle he completed at Tjeenk Willink's house in Brummen where he waited for his escape plans to mature. Later he hid the diary under the floor of the Protestant Church in Ede and picked it up at the liberation of Holland in May, 1945.

General Sir Gerald Lathbury's diary also remained hidden in Ede until the end of the war. Much of what this sensitive soldier could not set down at the time he recounted to me later. On the other hand, the diary of my late commander of the 1st Parachute Battalion, Lieutenant Colonel David Dobie, communicated but a small part of the restless, tormented spirit that eventually drove Dobie to his death. His former Intelligence officer, Tsyphe Britneff, filled in many of the important gaps that helped me to understand Dobie better.

The 49th British Infantry Division under command of General Rawlings captured Arnhem in April, 1945. The Intelligence officer of the Royal Scots Fusiliers who entered the devastated town came across a Dutchman who handed him a thin sheaf of papers. Smudged, written in faded pencil, they were almost indecipherable. General Rawlings, realizing their importance, had the pages typed and sent them to his old friend, General Roy Urquhart, who had commanded the airborne force at Arnhem. The signature on the report seemed to belong to a man called "Taitham-Waites." But Urquhart knew the signature. Digby Tatham-Warter, the chief archi-

230

tect of the evasion plan, had written the report and given it to a Dutch Resistance leader for safekeeping. "Bill' Wildeboer had waited on the Arnhem side of the bridge as the Allies poured across looking for someone to whom he could hand over Tatham-Warter's report as he promised to do. That report, written in a covered dugout behind Wildeboer's house on Lunterseweg in Ede in September and October of 1944, contained important information. Until recently this musty document lay in a suitcase in the English countryside. Some of the information is pertinent to my story.

The shorthand notes of Tony Cotterill, the only correspondent to reach the Arnhem bridge, might also have presented much that is new, but Cotterill was executed by the Germans in an escape attempt in which only Hibbert survived. Neither Cotterill's notebooks nor his body have ever been found.

I owe a special debt to the late Dutch Colonel Theodoer de Boeree, who spent almost all his days after 1944 correlating information about events surrounding Arnhem. His *Chronicles of Ede* and other voluminous notes put at my disposal by K. Schaap and P. R. A. Van Iddekinge of the Gemeentearchief, Arnhem, have enabled me to pick out important facts helpful to the narrative. When, many years ago, I wrote a small book about my own experiences at Arnhem, it was De Boeree in 1948 who sent a long letter in which he corrected errors, gave names of people and places and filled in omissions.

Certain individuals among many should be singled out for their contributions. Theo Tromp offered me his considerable support and help. Colonel Robert Strayer of the 101st U.S. Airborne Division, whose battalion organized the reception party for the first big escape over the Rhine, gave generous assistance. Major General Anthony Deane-Drummond helped me with some of the background of certain people. Danny Morgans led the way to many former evaders. Ted Lough of Pegasus, Doctors Theo Redman and Lipmann Kessel, General Sir Roy Urquhart and General John Frost all responded graciously to innumerable questions. Jimmy Edwards, comedian and actor, recalled, with the assistance of his log-book, vital incidents of his memorable last flight over Arnhem.

I have shied away from dialogue. None of it can be accurately remembered after thirty years. Since I set out to write a true story about true people I have used only dialogue recorded up to the end of 1946 – two years after Arnhem.

In Holland my list of thanks is very long. Professor L. de Jong, Director of the Rijks Instituut voor Oorlogs Documentatie, Amsterdam, put his office at my disposal. The Gemeentearchief, Arnhem, and its entire staff supplied me not only with the personal notes and the works of De Boeree that were pertinent to this book but also with additional information. Piet van Iddekinge gave much of his time and always offered his constant cooperation. Charles Labouchère, Edith Nijhoff, Harry Montfroy, Elsa Caspers, Kees Meyer, Kees van Woerkom all pointed me in the right direction. Charles Labouchère supplied vital documents, as did Harry Montfroy, that related to the Resistance in the months of September and October, 1944. The children of Jan Visser took me down the creeks of the Biesbosch so that I could trace the route of the river men. Piet Westdorp supplied the story of what happened to himself and Leo Wilkens on their mission. Dozens of other Dutchmen and former evaders gave their help in numerous small but important ways essential to this work and formed part of the more than one hundred and fifty men and women whom I personally interviewed.

Hans Smith did the considerable Dutch translations, and John McGrath filled in many details on the modern use of the Hercules aircraft.

Last of all, I should like to thank General Sir John Hackett, who gave me so many hours of his time and answered tolerantly, patiently, many impertinent questions.

INDEX

Adams, Ronald, 69–70, 197, 224
Alblas. *See* Bakker, Ko
Allenby, 193, 195
Amersfoort, 152, 163
Andrius, Jan, 148
Apeldoorn, 115, 163
Apeldoorn hospital, 147
Araghdale, Lord, 57
Arnhem
  battle for, 19–20, 31–35, 47,
    52–54
  burning of, 34, 53
  evacuation of, 75
  radio communication at,
    41–42
Arnhem bridge, 18, 36–39
Arnhem Resistance, 99–100,
  115–18. *See also* Dutch
  Resistance
Auschwitz concentration camp,
  127, 197

Bachenheimer, Ted, 154
Badalian, 211–12
Baker, Peter, 154
Bakker, H. B. 75–76, 118
Bakker, Ko, 208, 214, 216, 217
Banwell, Keith (Tex), 13–15,
  61–62, 82, 105–108, 123–127,
  131–133, 194, 196–197, 224
Barlow, Charles, 215
Barnett, 51
Bartholomew, John, 95
BBC, 202, 210, 215, 222
Belg, Kees de, 177
Belisle, Linwood, 188
Bennekom, 134, 175
Benson, B. J., 95
Bent, Maarten van den, 176
Bent, Pardu van den, 145
Bent, Siem van den, 141
Bergen Belsen concentration
  camp, 223
Berkt, G. V. D., 147

Bernhard, Prince, 108
Bertus (RAF drop zone), 128,
  135
Beusekom, Van, 75
Biesbosch, 207–209, 212
Bittrich, Wilhelm, 51
Blakemore, Eric, 215
Blok, Leo, 116
Bloois, Jan de (Piet de
  Springer), 136–137, 164–165
"Blue Johnny." *See* Nooij,
  Zwerus de
Bode, Nicolaas de, 116
Boeree, Theodor A. de, 137,
  159, 202, 224
Bofors, 185, 187, 194
Bold Kees. *See* Woerkom,
  Cornelis van
Bolte, Jan, 118–119
Bowe, 78
Braafhart, 111
Branford, James, 215
Briggs, B., 51
Brink, Van den, 195
Brown, Fred, 112

Cairns, G., 51
Carol Group, 147
Carrier pigeons, 74, 130
Caspers, Elsa, 212–214, 215, 224
Casualties, 18, 32, 48, 50, 52,
  56, 60, 65–66, 69, 74
Cauldron, The, 26
Clarke, Knobby, 43
Cleminson, Jeremy, 82
Coke, John, 195
Collins, Ian, 25, 130, 152, 168,
  224
Communist Party, 125
Cormorant, *See* Wilkins, Leo
Cotterell, Anthony, 53, 102–103,
  104, 105
Courtney, Brian, 76
Crankshaw, Tony, 220

233

234

237

238

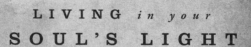

LIVING *in your*

SOUL'S LIGHT

UNDERSTANDING YOUR ETERNAL SELF

RICHARD WEBSTER

About the Author

Richard Webster was born and raised in New Zealand, where he still resides with his wife and three children. He travels widely every year, lecturing and conducting workshops around the world.

Richard has been interested in the psychic world since he was nine years old and is the author of over a hundred books. His bestselling books include *Spirit Guides & Angel Guardians* and *Creative Visualization for Beginners*.

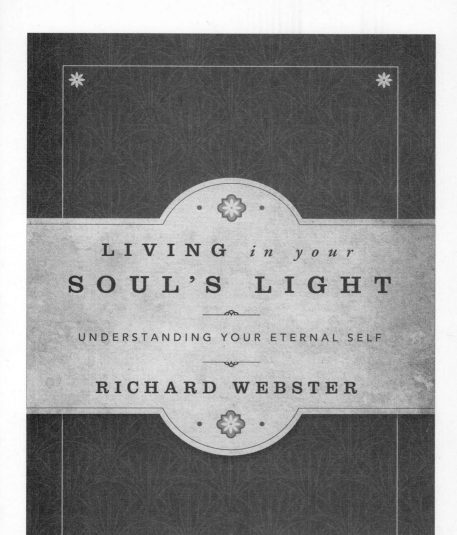

LIVING *in your* SOUL'S LIGHT

UNDERSTANDING YOUR ETERNAL SELF

RICHARD WEBSTER

Llewellyn Publications
Woodbury, Minnesota

FIRST EDITION
First Printing, 2012

Book design by Donna Burch
Cover art ©: Background pattern: iStockphoto.com/Olga Dmitrishena
           Mandala: iStockphoto.com/Heidi Kalyani
Cover design by Kevin R. Brown
Editing by Andrea Neff
Interior illustrations by the Llewellyn Art Department

Llewellyn Publications is a registered trademark of Llewellyn Worldwide Ltd.

Library of Congress Cataloging-in-Publication Data
Webster, Richard, 1946–
  Living in your soul's light : understanding your eternal self / by Richard Webster.
 — 1st ed.
     p. cm.
  Includes bibliographical references and index.
  ISBN 978-0-7387-3249-7
1. Reincarnation. 2. Soul. 3. Future life. I. Title.
BL515.W384 2012
133.901'35—dc23

                      2012010693

Llewellyn Worldwide Ltd. does not participate in, endorse, or have any authority or responsibility concerning private business transactions between our authors and the public.
    All mail addressed to the author is forwarded, but the publisher cannot, unless specifically instructed by the author, give out an address or phone number.
    Any Internet references contained in this work are current at publication time, but the publisher cannot guarantee that a specific location will continue to be maintained. Please refer to the publisher's website for links to authors' websites and other sources.

Llewellyn Publications
A Division of Llewellyn Worldwide Ltd.
2143 Wooddale Drive
Woodbury, MN 55125-2989
www.llewellyn.com

Printed in the United States of America

Other Books by Richard Webster

Dedication

For my good friends
Paul and Natalie Romhany

Contents

INTRODUCTION

A COUPLE OF YEARS ago I was rushed to the hospital
late one evening. I had felt well all day, and my wife and I
had enjoyed a barbecue dinner that evening. However, after
dinner I noticed a slight discomfort on my left side. This
gradually got worse, and after a few hours I started having
problems with my breathing, so my wife called an ambulance. I was misdiagnosed twice before the doctors discovered I had two large blood clots in my lungs.

I remember nothing of the following two days. On the
third evening I woke up in the middle of the night with
tubes attached to both arms and a small box on my chest
that transmitted information about me to a computer
somewhere else in the building. Five doctors and nurses
surrounded the bed. I stared at the five pairs of eyes gazing

down on me and thought, *I must be sick.* I immediately fell back to sleep.

When I woke up the following morning, I was disappointed that I hadn't seen any tunnels leading to the light or any other signs of a near-death experience. All the same, I was grateful to be alive. I also woke up with the title of this book in my mind, and the thought refused to go away. I spent another week in the hospital before being allowed to return home. It was a frustrating time, as all I wanted to do was leave the hospital and start writing.

Of course, it wasn't as simple as that. It took time to get my energy back, and then I had to finish the project I'd been working on before going to the hospital. Consequently, more than three months passed before I was able to start work on this book.

I also had time in the hospital to think about life and death. I was extremely fortunate. Apparently, sixty percent of the people who suffer from a pulmonary embolism are dead within twenty-four hours, and a large number of the survivors suffer from strokes and heart attacks.

I have no fear of death, as I don't believe death is the end. It simply marks the end of one stage of existence and the start of the next. I came to this conclusion for five main reasons:

1. For many years I worked as a hypnotherapist and helped many people recover memories of their past lives. Some people's lives were rather vague, but others provided detailed accounts of their previous incarna-

tions. In a few cases the people were able to revisit the places where they had lived before, and instantly felt at home.

2. The research of Dr. Ian Stevenson, and many other researchers, into children who remember their past lives has produced convincing evidence of reincarnation. I have a small personal example of this, too. For as long as I can remember, I've had a memory of being a small child, with a full stomach, lying in front of a huge fire with large red circles revolving around it. Years before becoming interested in reincarnation, I accidentally knocked a volume from a set of encyclopedias onto the floor. The book opened at a photograph of Russian peasant women dancing around an open fire. Although their skirts were black, the interior lining was red, and it must have been this that I remembered.

3. Although I haven't had a near-death experience myself, I've read many books about people's near-death experiences and am fascinated with what they saw, felt, and experienced on the "other side." I also find it convincing that very similar near-death experiences have been recorded from all around the world.

4. There is ample evidence of life after death provided by mediums who have communicated with people on the other side. This may sound surprising, but for at least 2,500 years thousands of messages have been recorded, all around the world, by people who claim

they have received messages from the other side.[1] One of the most evidential of these was William Stainton Moses (1839–1892), an English clergyman who was unhappy with the un-Christian teachings that came through him in the form of automatic writing. Automatic writing occurs when the person's mind is at ease, and the writing does not come from his or her conscious mind. William Stainton Moses wrote four books, including *Spirit Teachings*.[2]

5. Most major religions teach that life continues after death. Christians, for instance, teach that believers in God will go to heaven, but agnostics, atheists, and members of other religions will not. In Islam, the righteous will experience all the joys and pleasures of paradise, but everyone else will go to hell. Hindus also have a heaven and a hell. Reincarnation is an integral part of Buddhist belief, and everyone has to experience many lifetimes before they can return home. Judaism is the only major religion that is vague about what happens after death. However, it teaches that good people will be rewarded and evil people punished.

Obviously, we leave our body behind when we die. However, our soul carries on.

The soul is the immortal or divine aspect of our being. It is present in every cell of our body and continues to exist after the physical body dies. The soul could be described as the software that enables a computer to function. In this instance, the computer would be the physical body that is lifeless unless it contains a soul (software). Many religious people believe the soul is the presence of God inside each and every one of us.

People have been preoccupied with death, and the possibility of life after death, for thousands of years. Most early civilizations believed in life after death, and that belief is just as popular today as it ever was. When someone died, the ancient Neanderthals buried food and weapons with the body, as they believed the person's soul would need those items in the next world.

The ancient Greeks believed that to be fully alive, you needed a soul. The Greek word *psyche* means both "alive" and "possessing a soul."

The soul played an important role in Orphism, a Greek religion said to have been founded by the legendary musician, poet, and prophet Orpheus. Practitioners believed the physical body was dirty and corrupt, but the soul was perfect and part of the Divine. The soul became truly alive only after the death of the body. To achieve total freedom, the soul had to reincarnate many times. Depending on the quality of the person's life, the soul would be reborn in either a higher or lower form of life.

Pythagoras (c. 570–c. 490 BCE) was a Greek philosopher, numerologist, and teacher who believed that the cosmos followed certain moral and numerological principles. He was best known for his teachings on the soul. According to Pythagoras, who claimed to remember his own past lives, the soul was immortal and underwent a series of reincarnations.

Xenophanes (c. 570–c. 480 BCE), the Greek poet and philosopher, wrote of an occasion when Pythagoras heard the yelping of a puppy who was being punished. He ordered the beating to cease, as he realized the dog possessed the soul of a deceased friend. This shows that Pythagoras believed human souls could be reincarnated into plants, animals, or humans, a belief called *metempsychosis*. Not surprisingly, Pythagoras was a vegetarian.

Herodotus (c. 485–425 BCE), the Greek historian, wrote that the ancient Egyptians believed the soul was reborn time and time again until it had lived a lifetime as every possible animal before returning to human form three thousand years later. However, there is no evidence, apart from his writings, to confirm this. Herodotus also wrote that the bodies of dead Athenians who were killed at the siege of Potidaea were committed to the ground, but their souls flew upward.[3]

Plato (c. 428–347 BCE) recorded and developed the teachings of his mentor, Socrates (469–399 BCE). Plato believed the soul was the person's spiritual essence. It survived the person's death and was reincarnated inside another body. Plato and Socrates both thought that no harm could come to someone who kept his or her integrity, as this person's soul remained unharmed. Someone who deliberately hurt others damaged his or her soul. Consequently, it was better to be a victim of injustice than to commit an act of injustice.

In his dialogue *Phaedo*, Plato wrote that both the *psyche* (the life force) and the *nous* (the mind) were immortal. Together, the psyche and the nous formed the soul. In *Phaedrus*, another of his dialogues, the soul, released from the dead body, raced heavenward but failed to reach the home of the gods. It fell back to Earth and was reincarnated. The soul continued to do this until it was finally reunited with the Divine. This reveals Plato's belief that everything possesses a strong desire to return home to the ultimate life force. Even the earth itself (the "world-soul") longs to return home.

Aristotle (384–322 BCE) considered the soul to be the essential essence or nature of a person, but did not accept that it could continue to exist separate from the physical body. He believed the soul provided the person's personality and intellect while he or she was alive, but did not carry on after the person had died. In his treatise *De Anima (On the Soul)*, Aristotle argued that although the soul was the essential essence of a living organism and was necessary for life to exist, it did not possess a shape and consequently could not be measured or seen. Aristotle believed the soul took on the form of the body. However, by this he meant that the soul existed in every cell of the body.

Posidonius (c. 135–c. 51 BCE) was a Greek philosopher, historian, and Stoic. Most Stoics believed that the soul died with the body, but Posidonius had a different point of view. He believed that the soul continued to live in the air until the next major world calamity occurred. There was no hell in his system, but evil people did not fare as well as good people. Any sin affected the soul and discolored it, making it impossible for a sinful soul to rise as high as a pure soul. The souls of extremely evil people remained close to Earth and were reincarnated. Conversely, the souls of extremely virtuous people rose so high that they could watch the movements of the stars. From this position, they could help other souls.[4]

Plotinus (c. 205–270), the Greek philosopher and founder of Neoplatonism, developed a concept of "One" that he considered the essential underlying structure of all existence. As "One" was spiritual and nonmaterial, it could not be understood or fully explained. Plotinus claimed that "One" was both all things and nothing. Consequently, it could live both within and outside the world at the same time. "One" also provided humans with minds, intellects, and souls. The soul was, in effect, trapped inside the body, as it constantly sought union with the "One." Although this was the soul's true destiny, many people focused on their sensual desires, which caused the soul to descend, or move further away from the "One." When this occurred, the soul did not return to the "One," and entered another body. Plotinus had a strong influence on early Christian theology.

Avicenna (c. 980–1037), the Persian philosopher and physician, is best known today for his *Canon of Medicine*, which is arguably the most famous book in the history of medicine. However, in addition to this, he wrote more than two hundred works on a variety of topics, including philosophy and religion. He was deeply interested in Aristotle's ideas, and introduced many of them to the Islamic world. He agreed with Aristotle that the soul originated from the heart. He believed that, although the soul was immortal, this was purely an aspect of its nature rather than its prime purpose.

Avicenna lived in difficult times and was imprisoned on at least two occasions. While in prison, Avicenna wrote about an experiment his readers could try for themselves. This has become known as the "flying man" experiment. Avicenna told his readers to imagine they were suspended in space, temporarily blind and totally isolated from any sensation, including their own bodies. In this instance, Avicenna wrote that the person would not be able to affirm the existence of his or her own body but would still possess consciousness. This, he concluded, demonstrated that the soul was an essential part of humankind's nature, and everyone possessed it from birth.

St. Thomas Aquinas (1225–1274), the Italian philosopher and theologian, was a prolific author who tried to harmonize Aristotle's philosophical rationalism with Christianity. He claimed that the soul was the first principle of life and that people possessed both a body and a soul. He argued that, because the soul was not composed of matter, it could continue to exist outside a human body.[5] St. Thomas Aquinas agreed with Aristotle that the soul was present in every part of the body.

Immanuel Kant (1724–1804), the German philosopher, believed that perfect good could exist only if the soul was immortal. He believed in *unendlichen progressus*, the unending progression of the soul through countless incarnations.

Sir Edward Tylor (1832–1917) was the first professor of anthropology at Oxford University. In his two-volume work *Primitive Culture*, he demonstrated that human culture constantly grows and develops, following specific laws of evolutionary development. He developed a theory of animism, which he described as "the doctrine of souls and other spiritual beings in general." Animism is derived from the Latin word *anima*, which means "breath" or "soul." Tylor described the soul as:

> … a thin insubstantial image, in its nature a sort of vapour, film or shadow; the cause of life and thought in the individual it animates; independently possessing the personal consciousness and volition of its corporeal owner, past or present; capable of leaving the body far behind, to flash swiftly from place to place; mostly impalpable and invisible, yet also manifesting physical power, and especially appearing to man walking or asleep as a phantasm separate from the body of which it bears the likeness; continuing to exist and appear to man after the death of that body; able to enter into, possess, and act in the bodies of other men, of animals, and even of things.[6]

Carl Jung (1875–1961), the Swiss psychiatrist and psychologist, described the soul as "the greatest of all cosmic miracles."[7]

Belief in the soul is probably more common in the East than in the West, and the concepts of reincarnation and karma are accepted more readily there than in the West. Reincarnation requires a soul, as it is the belief that the soul is eternal and is reborn into a new personality once the current life has ended. The soul learns from every incarnation as it progresses on its journey to oneness with God.

In chapter 1 we'll look into the concept of reincarnation and learn three methods you can use to examine your past lives.

CHAPTER ONE

HAVE I MET YOU BEFORE?

REINCARNATION IS THE BELIEF that after death some part of the self, usually the soul, is reborn in a new body.

My interest in the soul began many years ago, when I was working as a hypnotherapist. Many of my clients requested a past-life regression to help them remember information about their previous lives. I was fascinated with the amount of detail some people were able to recall. A few of my clients traveled overseas to visit the places where they had lived in a previous lifetime. Some of them returned with information that confirmed, at least in their minds, that they had lived in that place at some time in the past.

Some people came for a past-life regression out of curiosity. Without exception, all of them found the experience helpful in explaining factors in their current life. Someone who was terrified of water, for instance, learned that she'd drowned in a previous lifetime. A man who loved the works of Franz Joseph Haydn learned that he'd worked in the court of Prince Miklós Esterházy at the same time as the great composer, and was introduced to his music there. Someone who was abused by his father when he was a child discovered that he had been the abuser in a previous lifetime.

Many people ask for a past-life regression to see if certain people in this lifetime figured in previous incarnations. Often this is the case, even though the nature of the relationship, and even the gender of the people involved, sometimes change.

Many of my clients discovered that the person they love the most in this lifetime is a true soul mate, as they have been together in a number of previous lifetimes. Interestingly, they may not have been together in every incarnation. Usually some impediment prevented them from being together in a particular lifetime. One person may have already been married, for instance. I recall one sad example where the man was a priest and unable to enter into a relationship.

It seems that people who share a deep spiritual and emotional bond are always together, both while in a relationship on earth and in the period between lives. These people also incarnate at approximately the same time and are exposed to opportunities where they can meet and carry on their relationship. One couple I regressed had almost met on several occasions, in three different countries, before finally meeting (or re-meeting) each other. It seems the universe works to enable soul mates to meet and continue their relationship in each incarnation.

I have met a number of people who dislike the idea of reincarnation. "I don't want to be reborn," they tell me. "Once is enough!"

Fortunately, people do not reincarnate as the people they are today. Their physical body, mind, and emotions die. It is their soul that carries on and reincarnates into a new body and personality.

Another common question is "Why can't I remember my past lives?" I think it's fortunate that we can't. If we remembered details from all our previous lifetimes, we'd never be able to progress in this incarnation. Some people spontaneously remember incidents from their past lives, and many instances of these have been recorded.[1] Many people have a vague sense that they have lived before. The poem "Sudden Light" by Dante Gabriel Rossetti (1828–1882) captures these feelings extremely well:

I have been here before,
But when or how I cannot tell:
I know the grass beyond the door,
The sweet keen smell,
The sighing sound, the lights around the shore.

You have been mine before,—
How long ago I may not know:

But just when at the swallow's soar
Your neck turned so,
Some veil did fall,—I knew it all of yore.

Another logical question is "Why do we reincarnate?" Even people who lead outwardly happy lives sometimes feel there must be more to life than constantly striving for worldly success. What's the point of living for five, six, or seven decades if you, and everything you've accomplished, are forgotten in a few generations?

Reincarnation enables us to experience a wide range of possibilities as we progress from one lifetime to the next and become increasingly aware of our divine nature. It is impossible to do this in just one lifetime, as we all face various limitations, including gender, family circumstances, race, color, intelligence, natural skills, and personality. Hopefully we progress spiritually in each incarnation until we eventually return to our "source," which is God.

William Wordsworth refers to "God, who is our home" in his ode "Intimations of Immortality":

Our birth is but a sleep and a forgetting:
The Soul that rises with us, our life's Star,
Hath had elsewhere its setting,
And cometh from afar:
Not in entire forgetfulness,
And not in utter nakedness,
But trailing clouds of glory do we come
From God, who is our home.

There have been many recorded instances of people remembering their previous incarnations. Dr. Ian Stevenson (1918–2007), former head of the Division of Perceptual Studies at the University of Virginia, investigated more than three thousand cases of children who appeared to remember their past lives. He traveled extensively to research these cases and wrote several books about his findings.

One of the many examples Dr. Stevenson collected was told to him by Ravi Shankar, an Indian boy who vividly recalled his previous life as Munna Prasad. On January 19, 1951, Munna Prasad was lured away from his friends by two neighbors who killed him with a knife or razor. His head and body were buried separately. Munna was only six years old.

One of the alleged murderers, a barber named Jawahar, apparently killed Munna because he was the only son of Sri Jageshwar Prasad. This meant that Jawahar would inherit property that would otherwise have been left to Munna. Neighbors had seen Munna being taken away by the two men, and they were arrested. One of them, a washerman named Chaturi, confessed to the murder but then retracted his confession after being officially charged. As there were no witnesses to the murder, the case was dropped and the two men were released from custody.

A few years later, the dead boy's father heard about a boy who had been born six months after Munna's death. This boy, Ravi Shankar, said he was the son of Jageshwar and could clearly remember his life and death as Munna. He was even able to name the murderers and describe the place where he had been killed.

Ravi Shankar's mother and his older sister remembered that when he was two years old he repeatedly asked for toys that he remembered having in his previous life. When he was five years old, he described his murder in great detail to his schoolteacher, who recorded the conversation in a letter. He told the teacher he had eaten some guavas before meeting his friends, when he was enticed away by two men who killed him in an orchard near the river by the Chinta-mani Temple and then buried him in the sand. He knew his throat had been cut with a razor.

Naturally, Sri Jageshwar Prasad, Munna's father, wanted to learn more. He visited the home of Ravi Shankar, but Ravi's father, fearing that Jageshwar might take his son, refused to talk with him. Fortunately, Ravi's mother allowed Jageshwar to talk with Ravi, who provided a full account of the murder. He recognized Munna's watch and asked what had happened to his ring. He also recognized Munna's maternal grandmother, who was with a group of other women.

Ravi was born with a strange birthmark on his neck. When Dr. Stevenson saw it in 1964, he described it as looking "much like an old scar of a healed knife wound."[2]

Ravi's father was concerned about his son's constant fixation on his previous lifetime, and beat him severely whenever he talked about it. After this, Ravi became afraid to talk about his experiences. However, he was overcome with fear when he happened to see one of the men who had allegedly killed Munna. He was also afraid of barbers and washermen. When Ravi continued to discuss certain aspects of his murder with his neighbors, his father sent him away for a year.

By the time he was eleven, Ravi had forgotten most of the events of his previous life. However, he still became frightened whenever he saw Chaturi or Jawahar, the two men who allegedly murdered Munna.[3]

It is common for children who remember their previous lives to gradually forget them as they grow up. It is less common for spontaneous past-life memories to unexpectedly return.

This happened to General George S. Patton (1885–1945), the famous American hero of World War II. When he arrived at the French town of Langres, his driver offered to show him around the well-preserved Roman ruins. "You don't have to," the general replied. "I know this place. I know it well."[4]

He then took the driver on a tour of the Roman remains, indicating the drill ground, the forum, the amphitheatre, and the temples of Mars and Apollo. Visiting Langres brought back memories of General Patton's past life as a legionary in Caesar's army.

Not surprisingly, General Patton believed in reincarnation, and remembered several previous lifetimes. He remembered fighting with Alexander the Great. He spent a lifetime as the great Carthaginian general Hannibal. He also recalled being part of a Greek contingent that met the Persian conqueror Cyrus II around 500 BCE. He remembered fighting in the Hundred Years' War, and served as a general with Joachim Murat, one of Napoleon's most honored marshals.

One year before he died, General Patton wrote a poem called "Through a Glass, Darkly," which clearly illustrated his Christian faith as well as his belief in reincarnation. Here is one verse from the poem:

So as through a glass, and darkly
The age-long strife I see
Where I fought in many guises,
Many names, but always me.[5]

Most reincarnation memories are faint and fragmentary. However, a few accounts are incredibly detailed and convincing. The story of Corliss Chotkin Jr. is a good example.

Victor Vincent was a full-blooded Tlingit Indian who lived in Angoon, Alaska. He had a close relationship with his niece, Mrs. Corliss Chotkin. One year before he died in 1946, Victor told his niece that he would return as her next son. She would recognize him, he said, because the baby would have two scars on his body that matched surgical scars he had received. Eighteen months after Victor died, his niece gave birth to a son who was named after his father, Corliss Chotkin. The baby had two birthmarks that were identical to the two scars Victor had had.

When Corliss was thirteen months old and starting to talk, his family tried to teach him his name. Corliss suddenly spoke in a Tlingit accent: "Don't you know me? I'm Kahkody." This was Victor Vincent's tribal name.

When Corliss was two, he was out with his mother when they came across a woman he hadn't met before. He immediately became excited, saying, "There's my Susie." Susie was Victor Vincent's stepdaughter. Corliss hugged her, called her by her Tlingit name, and kept saying, "My Susie, my Susie!"

A few weeks later, Corliss and his mother were out for a walk, and Corliss said, "There is William, my son." Mrs. Chotkin hadn't noticed William Vincent, Victor's son, until Corliss pointed to him.

A year later, when Corliss was three, he and his mother went to a meeting, and Corliss called out, "There's Rose" and "That's the old lady." Rose was Victor Vincent's widow, and he'd always called her "the old lady." Corliss's mother had not known Rose was at the meeting until Corliss said her name.

In addition to recognizing family members, Corliss frequently recognized Victor Vincent's friends, and spoke of various incidents that had occurred in his previous life. On one occasion, he and his mother visited a house that Mrs. Chotkin had lived in while Victor Vincent was alive. Corliss pointed out the room that he and "the old lady" had slept in when they had stayed overnight.

One day Corliss told his parents about an incident that had happened in his previous life. He (Victor) was out fishing when his engine broke down. This was potentially life-threatening in the cold waters of southeast Alaska. Victor was a part-time worker for the Salvation Army. He changed into his uniform to help attract attention and got into a small rowboat. His unusual clothing, plus the fact that he was in a small dinghy, caused a passing ship, the North Star, to rescue him. Corliss's mother had heard Victor tell this story and was amazed to hear it again, in complete detail, from her young son.

By the time Corliss was nine, memories of his previous life started to fade. When Dr. Ian Stevenson met him in 1962, the fifteen-year-old told him he remembered nothing of his previous life.[6]

Edgar Cayce (1877–1945) was the most famous American psychic of the twentieth century. At the age of sixteen, he injured his spine. While in a coma, he suddenly spoke in a strong, clear voice, prescribing himself an herbal remedy. The attending doctor agreed to give this alternative medicine a try, and when Cayce woke up the following morning, he was fit and well again.

When he was twenty-four, Cayce lost his voice, and doctors were unable to do anything to help. Cayce was desperate and asked a friend to put him into a hypnotic trance. In this state Cayce prescribed himself a cure, which worked just as well as the herbal remedy he'd prescribed himself before. Gradually word spread about this unusual ability, and before long local physicians started asking him for help in diagnosing and treating difficult cases. His fame increased dramatically when the *New York Times* wrote an article about him in October 1910.

Cayce's workload increased so much that he was forced to hire a stenographer, who wrote down everything he said while in a trance state. On August 10, 1923, Cayce, a fundamentalist Christian, was alarmed to read that he had proclaimed the reality of reincarnation while in trance. At that time he had no interest in the subject, and considered it anti-Christian.

Two months later, on October 11, 1923, Cayce mentioned a client's previous incarnation. "Third appearance on this plane," he said while in trance. "He was once a monk."[7]

Cayce gradually reconciled reincarnation with his Christian faith, and his readings frequently traced people's problems back to previous lifetimes. In fact, he talked about people's previous lives in more than 1,900 of his life readings. Cayce even uncovered two of his own past incarnations. In about 10,500 BCE, he had been a Carpathian priest named Ra-Ta at the time his tribe conquered Egypt. In 1742, he was born again as John Bainbridge in Cornwall, England. He led a highly adventurous life in America, and died on a raft floating down the Ohio River while helping a group of people escape from an Indian attack.[8]

Although there is no way to prove reincarnation, the numerous accounts of people remembering their past lives have created a huge body of anecdotal evidence that cannot be ignored.

Many famous people throughout history have believed in reincarnation. Benjamin Franklin is a good example. When he was just twenty-two, Franklin wrote his epitaph:

The body of B. Franklin,
Printer,
Like the Cover of an old Book,
Its Contents Torn Out
And
Stripped of its Lettering and Gilding,
Lies Here
Food for Worms,
But the Work shall not be Lost,
For it Will as He Believed
Appear Once More
In a New and more Elegant Edition
Revised and Corrected
By the Author.

Charles C. Emerson (1808–1836), Ralph Waldo Emerson's younger brother, was, like his brother, a strong believer in reincarnation. He wrote:

The reason why Homer is to me like a dewy morning is because I too lived while Troy was, and sailed in the hollow ships of the Grecians to sack the devoted town. The rosy-fingered dawn as it crimsoned the tops of Ida, the broad seashore covered with tents, the Trojan hosts in their painted armor, and the rushing chariots of Diomede and Idomeneus,—all these I too saw: my ghost animated the frame of some nameless Argive ... We forget that we have been drugged by the sleepy bowl of the present.

But when a lively chord in the soul is struck, when the windows for a moment are unbarred, the long and varied past is recovered. We recognize it all; we are not mere brief ignoble creatures; we seize our immortality and bind together the related parts of our secular beings ... Something there is in the spirit which changes not, neither is weary, but ever returns into itself, and partakes the eternity of God.[9]

How to Experience Your Past Lives

You can explore your own past lives. Some people find this difficult to do, but in my experience, everyone can learn to do it. Once you've returned to a past lifetime, you'll have no difficulty repeating it whenever you wish. The method I prefer is hypnosis. If you've had no previous experience with hypnosis, you might want to find a competent hypnotherapist in your area who performs past-life regressions. You may have to phone a few people, as not all hypnotherapists are interested in doing these. Once you've been hypnotized by a certified hypnotherapist and relived a few incidents from a previous lifetime, you'll have no difficulty hypnotizing yourself and learning more about that lifetime, or possibly looking at other previous lives.

If you're unable to find a competent hypnotherapist or prefer to experiment on your own, you'll need to hypnotize yourself. This is called self-hypnosis, and is a useful skill to learn.

Hypnosis is not something to be afraid of. Like everyone else, you go into and out of hypnosis many times every day. Every time you have a daydream, for instance, you are in a state of hypnosis. I'm sure you know people who get hypnotized whenever they watch television. You can speak to them and they don't hear a word you're saying, because they're in a state of hypnosis. Many people cry at sad movies. In every case, they were hypnotized. The fact that they cried shows they were emotionally involved in the movie, even though they knew it was simply a picture on a screen. I can get lost in a book. This means I've been hypnotized by the words I'm reading.

Possibly the most common form of unconscious hypnosis occurs when you're driving your car along a route that you know extremely well. When you arrive at your destination, you may wonder how you got there, as you have no conscious memory of the trip you've just completed. This is known as "wild" hypnosis. Fortunately, although you're in a state of hypnosis, you'd instantly come out of it if anything happened that needed your attention.

Hypnosis is similar to meditation. You are physically relaxed in both meditation and hypnosis. However, in hypnosis your mind is focused on a particular goal, such as retrieving memories of a previous lifetime. Here is a past-life regression script you can experiment with. You can use it in three different ways.

1. You can record the script and play it back when you are ready to experience a past life.

2. You can familiarize yourself with the script and then use your own words to silently guide you through the past life.

3. You can ask a friend to read the script out loud while you relive a past life. Afterwards, you can change roles.

There are advantages and disadvantages with each of these options. A recording may rush you through different scenes more rapidly than you would like. However, a recording is convenient, as all you need to do is relax and follow the instructions.

The second scenario has advantages, too, but it's easy for random thoughts to get in the way. It's also easy to forget what you're supposed to think next.

The third scenario is ideal, as long as you have a good friend who is also interested in exploring his or her past lives. Your friend won't rush you through the session and will let you stay at certain places for as long as you're continuing to tell him or her about them. However, you'll need to say your responses out loud, to let your friend know when to move forward.

With all three scenarios, you'll need to make yourself as comfortable as possible. I like to do this while relaxing in a recliner chair, as I tend to fall asleep when lying on a bed. I'm also happy to do this while lying on the floor. I can relax there, but I don't fall asleep. Cover yourself with a blanket, as you lose one or two degrees of body heat when you're in a state of hypnosis.

You should also wear loose-fitting clothes and ensure the room is warm enough. Once you're comfortable, close your eyes and start listening to the script.

Past-Life Regression Script

"Take a nice, deep breath, and exhale slowly. Allow all the muscles of your body to relax. Each breath makes you more and more relaxed, taking you deeper and deeper into pleasant relaxation. Allow the relaxation to spread through your body each time you inhale, and allow the tension and stress to dissolve and disappear each time you exhale.

"Relax more and more as you listen to the sound of my voice. Nothing need bother or disturb you, as you go deeper and deeper into pleasant relaxation.

"Soon you'll notice your feet are becoming relaxed. They'll feel loose and limp and so, so relaxed. Allow that pleasant feeling of relaxation to drift up into your legs now, and become aware of how relaxed they are. Relax your arms and hands, and feel all the stress and strain of the day slipping away from you. Soon you'll experience the wonderful sensation of complete and total relaxation throughout your entire body.

"Allow the pleasant feeling of total peace and tranquility to start in your feet and drift up through your entire body. Feel it moving up through your legs and thighs, and notice they're relaxing even more than before. Feel it drifting up into your abdomen and carrying on into your chest, your shoulders, your arms, and your neck. Allow it to drift into your head and face. Notice how relaxed the fine muscles around your eyes are becoming. Feel the relaxation drift right up to the top of your head. You feel totally loose, limp, and relaxed.

"In this nice, calm, relaxed state, become aware of your breathing. Each breath helps you drift even deeper into pleasant relaxation. It's a wonderful, soothing, peaceful sensation, and you enjoy noticing this incredible feeling of complete and total relaxation spreading all through you.

"As you let go more and more, you find yourself drifting even deeper into a peaceful state where nothing can disturb or bother you. You want to feel this pleasant relaxation in every cell of your body, and you can do this by letting go completely, letting go, and allowing the relaxation to spread through you again, all the way from the tips of your toes to the top of your head.

"Enjoy the sensation of complete and total relaxation for a moment. It's so peaceful and pleasant that you want to go even deeper, and you find you can go even deeper than you are now. Your whole body is becoming loose, limp, and so, so relaxed. Allow the relaxation in your feet to drift up into your legs, your thighs, your abdomen, your chest, and your neck. Allow it to drift down your arms to the very tips of your fingers. And allow this wonderful relaxation to drift into your head and face.

"It's a wonderful feeling to be so relaxed, and in this nice, calm, peaceful, relaxed state, your only desire is to recapture memories of one of your many past lives. In your inner mind, your subconscious mind, are all the memories of your previous lives, and in this nice, calm, peaceful, relaxed state you'll be able to unlock those memories and relive them.

"In your imagination now, visualize a beautiful staircase that leads down to what appears to be a large ballroom. Place your hand on the handrail, and allow yourself to double your relaxation with each step you take as you go down this beautiful staircase.

"Ten. Moving down one step and doubling your relaxation.

"Nine. Every breath you take is making you more and more relaxed. Drifting even deeper as you take another step.

"Eight. You are so relaxed now as you take another step down into a world of total and complete relaxation.

"Seven. Taking another step and feeling so peaceful, and calm, and relaxed.

"Six. Going even deeper now, and floating down as you quietly listen. Floating gently down one more step.

"Five. You're halfway down this beautiful staircase and feeling so, so relaxed as you take another step.

"Four. You're almost there now. Drifting down deeper and deeper with each easy breath you take.

"Three. S-o-o-o-o r-e-l-a-x-e-d. Taking another step down and doubling your relaxation once again.

"Two. Almost there. Almost at the bottom of this beautiful staircase.

"One. Taking one more step and moving into the beautiful room. Feeling good and so totally relaxed.

"And now it's time for you to explore this beautiful room. It's the most beautiful room you've ever been in, and you marvel at the beautiful carpet, the luxurious furnishings, the artwork, and the soft, gentle lighting. You even look up and admire the gorgeous ceiling. It really is an unbelievably beautiful room.

"As you walk around the room, notice all the closed doors. All the doors are different, yet they harmonize perfectly with the décor of your special room. You realize that each door lets you experience one of your many past lives. Allow yourself to take as long as you wish to decide which door you want to open. If you have a particular past life that you wish to explore, allow yourself to be guided to the correct door. If you've visited here before and want to explore a particular lifetime in greater depth, you'll instinctively know which door to open. If you haven't visited this room before and have no specific lifetime to examine, simply allow yourself to choose a door that appeals to you. When you open it, memories of the past life that has the most relevance to you in your present incarnation will come into your mind.

"There's no hurry. Take all the time you need to choose a door. [Pause for ten seconds.] Now you're looking at the door you've chosen. Take three slow, deep breaths. One. That's right. Nice, even, deep breaths. Two. Gaining confidence and strength. Three. Relaxing totally.

"You're now ready to open the door and experience some important incidents from one of your past lives. You'll remain calm and detached. Your emotions will not be affected, no matter what you experience. You can move away from any scenes you find disturbing, and if in your imagination you request a happy scene, you'll instantly find yourself there. You can return to your present life any time you wish by simply counting from one to five and opening your eyes.

"And now it's time to open the door. You'll walk in and find yourself in a situation that tells you how you spend most of your time. Walk in and familiarize yourself with the situation you find yourself in.

"Look down at your feet and see what you're wearing. Look at your clothes and your hands. Gradually become accustomed to where you are and what you're doing. [Pause for sixty seconds.]

[If someone is reading the script to you, he or she can start asking questions at this stage. Typical questions are: "Are you indoors or outside?" "Are other people here with you?" "Are you male or female?" "What is your name?" "What are you doing?" "Are you happy?"]

"Now it's time to move into a situation with the person who is most important to you in this lifetime we're exploring. On the count of three, vivid memories will return. One … two … three. [Pause for sixty seconds.]

[If someone is reading the script to you, he or she can ask questions at this stage, such as: "Describe the person." "What relationship do the two of you have?" "Why is this person so special?" "What is his/her name?"]

"And now we'll move on to a family scene. On the count of three, vivid memories will return relating to your home and family life. One ... two ... three. [Pause for sixty seconds.]

"Now it's time to relive a scene in which you were honored or felt proud. On the count of three. One ... two ... three. [Pause for sixty seconds.]

"And now it's time to find out where you lived and in what time period. If you don't know, simply allow letters and numbers to come into your mind. One ... two ... three. [Pause for sixty seconds.]

"On the count of three, you'll find yourself on the very last day of the lifetime you're now exploring. You will not have passed over into spirit, and you'll see yourself in a totally detached way. You won't experience any emotion or pain. One ... two ... three. [Pause for sixty seconds.]

[If someone is reading the script, he or she can ask questions, such as: "What are you wearing?" "Who is there with you?" "How old are you?"]

"On the count of three again, it will be just a few moments after you've passed over into spirit in this lifetime we're exploring. One ... two ... three. [Pause for sixty seconds.]

"And now I'd like you to think about the lifetime you've been exploring and see what karma, or anything else, from that lifetime is affecting your current life. On the count of three, all sorts of thoughts will come into your conscious mind. One ... two ... three. [Pause for sixty seconds.]

"Now it's time to leave this past life and return to your current life. I'm going to count from one to five, and you'll be back in the present, relaxing quietly with your eyes closed. You'll return to your current life, remembering everything that happened during this lifetime, and more memories will come into your conscious mind over the next few days. It's time to return to the present on the count of five. One... two... three... four... five.

"You're now back in your current life and I'm going to count from one to five again. When I reach number five, you'll open your eyes feeling relaxed and refreshed, as if you've just enjoyed a really good night's sleep. However, this session will not affect your sleep tonight. You'll sleep extremely well. Gradually coming up now on the count of five. One. Gaining energy, and feeling fine. Two. Feeling good. Very, very good. Three. Recalling who you are, and where you are. Four. Almost there. And five. Eyes opening, and feeling wonderful."

Lie quietly for a minute or two before stretching and getting up. If possible, have something to eat or drink within ten minutes of completing the regression.

Everyone responds to a past-life regression in their own way. Some people feel slightly sad, especially if the past life was an unhappy one. Some people are excited, as the experience has explained certain things that have happened in their current life. Some people recognize important people in their current life as figures in their previous life. The relationships, and even genders, might have changed, but these people were clearly recognizable. These people are soul mates who appear in many, if not all, of the person's past lives.

As you can see, listening to a recording is not always the best way to experience a past life. Sixty seconds may be too long, or too short, to spend examining a certain scene. However, there is no reason you can't record a different tape and revisit the same past life with different questions.

When I used to do one-on-one past-life regressions, I would sometimes take people to their funeral, or to visit their burial site, so they could read what was on the headstone. This clarified dates of birth and death. Hundreds of years ago, most people were illiterate and never traveled far from home. Consequently, they often did not know the name of the country they lived in or the time period. Seeing their headstone sometimes answered these questions.

Once you've experienced a past-life regression, you'll find you'll be able to repeat it whenever you wish.

There's no danger in doing this. I find it fascinating that you can be in the middle of a past-life regression and still be aware of sounds and smells from your present life. The phone may ring, a noisy car may pass your home, and you may smell dinner cooking in the kitchen. Despite remaining aware of these, you are still vividly reliving a past life. Sounds and smells from your present life do not interfere with reliving a past life. In fact, it's good that you remain aware of everything that's going on. If an emergency occurred in your present life, you'd instantly return to your current life and be able to deal with it.

Other Methods of Retrieving Past-Life Memories

There are many other techniques that can be used to retrieve memories of your past lives.[10] You can dowse for your past lives, you can use astrology and numerology to provide insight into your past lives, you can meditate, and you can even experience dreams about your past lives. You can also use your memory to go back before your birth in this lifetime. This is known as "far memory."

Far memory and dreaming are the only methods, apart from hypnosis, that allow you to relive experiences from your past lives. Because of that, we'll discuss them briefly here.

Far Memory

An elderly friend named Stephen taught me this technique more than thirty years ago. Stephen suffered from insomnia and filled in the hours waiting for sleep to come by thinking about different experiences he'd had. He tried to remember every detail of every experience. Over a period of time, he went further and further into his past until he was reliving experiences from his early childhood.

He was brought up in the east end of London and remembered being taken out shopping with his mother. Stephen discovered that, with practice, he was able to recall the name of every shop on the street. In fact, in his mind's eye he was able to "see" the entire street and all the shops exactly as they were when he was a small boy.

Stephen decided to go back even further, and recalled an incident when he was one year old and his mother rushed him to the hospital. He was fascinated to discover that he had memories dating back that far, and tried to go back even further.

After experiencing feelings of comfort and security, which made him think he'd returned to the womb, Stephen suddenly saw himself as an adult again. As he knew nothing about reincarnation, this experience terrified him, and he returned to the present.

A few nights later, Stephen decided to see what would happen if he tried again. He took himself back to the womb, and suddenly found himself as a young man hiding in a swamp while men and dogs searched for him. They failed to find his hiding place, but the young man froze to death during the night.

Stephen became obsessed with this young man, and tried to learn more about him every night. He had planned to write a book about his earlier life but unfortunately died before he could do so. Stephen was initially reluctant to accept that he was reliving a past life. I encouraged him to go back even further, but he refused to do so, as he was so fascinated with the lifetime he had uncovered.

Far memory is a deceptively easy way to experience past lives. However, most people find that it takes a great deal of practice to achieve success. My friend Stephen spent months reliving experiences from his current life before he suddenly found himself in a past life. Consequently, it is a good idea to have several sessions to see how far back you can go in this lifetime before trying to return to a past life.

Stephen suffered from insomnia, which is why he could do this lying in bed. Whenever I've tried to do this in bed at night, I've fallen asleep before returning to a past life. Consequently, I usually relax in a comfortable chair, or lie on the floor, when doing this. In the summer months, I enjoy doing this experiment outdoors. However, I've met many people who are able to do this in bed before falling asleep. They are extremely fortunate, as they can easily fall asleep afterwards no matter what the outcome is.

Once you're comfortable, start by taking several deep breaths and relaxing as much as you can. Visualize an important event that occurred within the last few years. As people see things in different ways, you may see the event clearly in your mind. This means you're a visual person. You may be an auditory person and hear what is occurring as you relive the experience. If you're a kinesthetic person, you'll feel or sense the experience. There is no right or wrong way to visualize an experience.

Once you've relived the event in your mind, let it go, and allow yourself to drift back further to another experience. Continue doing this until you've gone as far back as you can in this lifetime.

At this point, think of your desire to experience one of your past lives, and see if you can go back even further. If you're successful, explore the past life for as long as you wish, and then return to the present. It's more likely, especially on your first few attempts, that you'll either go back to a forgotten incident from your current life or will experience nothing at all.

Patience is required when learning this method. Although the far memory technique sounds easy, most people find it can take months before they achieve success. The most important part of the exercise is to simply relax and allow it to happen.

Lucid Dreaming

A lucid dream occurs when you are in a dream and become aware that you are dreaming. Most people have experienced this sensation. Usually the dream takes over again and the conscious mind returns to sleep. However, it's possible in this situation to direct the dream anywhere you wish using your conscious mind.

Edgar Cayce, the famous American psychic, experienced a lucid dream during World War I. In 1910, his wife had given birth to their second son, but sadly the baby lived for only two months. Some years later, Edgar dreamed that he had met and talked with some of his Sunday school pupils who had been killed during the war. While still dreaming, Edgar thought that as he had been able to see these young soldiers, even though they were dead, there had to be a way to see his son. Instantly he found himself in a room full of babies, one of whom was smiling at him. This was his son. This dream provided consolation for the grieving father, and afterwards Edgar was able to move forward again.[11]

Although virtually everyone has experienced an involuntary lucid dream, it takes practice to be able to have one when you want to. Fortunately, there are a number of things you can do to increase the chances of experiencing a lucid dream.

As you're drifting off to sleep, tell yourself that you will experience a lucid dream. You need to say this to yourself in a casual, nonchalant manner. If you demand a lucid dream, you can almost guarantee that it won't happen. You might say: "Tonight, as I dream, I'll realize I'm dreaming and will immediately go back to an important experience that occurred in a past life."

If you happen to wake up during the night and feel that you're dropping straight back to sleep, again request a lucid dream.

You probably won't experience a lucid dream the first time you try, but if you persevere you'll suddenly find yourself experiencing a past life. You'll be able to move backwards and forwards in this past life. If anything unpleasant occurs, you'll be able to move back and observe what is happening in a detached manner from a distance. You'll also be able to move closer to any event, if you wish. While you're experiencing this past life, try to discover what your main purpose was in this incarnation. Experience situations that enable you to spend time with the people who were closest to you, and also find out what you enjoyed doing most.

You can return to the present any time you wish while you're lucid dreaming. Although you may be experiencing a lifetime that occurred hundreds or even thousands of years ago, you remain aware that you are lucid dreaming. Once you've experienced enough of the past life, you can return to the present and drift back to sleep.

When you wake up in the morning, record everything you can remember about your past life. You can gain further information by returning to that past life as many times as you wish. Over a period of time, you'll build up a valuable record of many of your past lives.

The common factor in all of your past lives is your soul. Although your physical body dies and decays, your soul continues to learn and grow as it experiences incarnation after incarnation. We'll look at the soul in the next chapter.

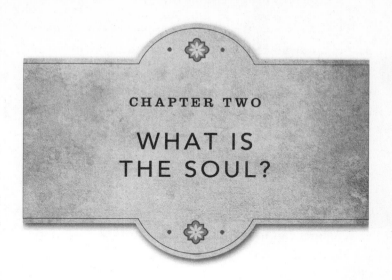

CHAPTER TWO

WHAT IS THE SOUL?

IN HIS ACCEPTANCE SPEECH, Nobel Prize winner William Faulkner (1897–1962) said:

> I believe man will not merely endure, he will prevail. He is immortal, not because he, alone among creatures, has an inexhaustible voice but because he has a soul, a spirit capable of compassion and sacrifice and endurance.[1]

Faulkner obviously had a strong belief in the soul and knew that it provided humankind with many positive qualities, such as compassion, sacrifice, and endurance. However, powerful though his words are, they do not define the soul.

The soul is often described as the spiritual and immortal part of a human being. It is a distinct entity that is separate from the physical body. The soul is the person's essential essence. It is the animating principle that enables the physical body to live. It is also the person's life force, the seat of his or her personality, and the spark of the Divine that is found within each cell of the body. The soul is eternal. It existed before the person was born and continues to exist after he or she dies. The personality is the part that is born and ultimately dies, but the soul is immortal. The soul is your connection to the ultimate life force. Unfortunately, the word *soul* is also frequently used as a synonym for *mind* or *self*.

In his book *Wisdom of the Ages*, Dr. Wayne W. Dyer writes: "Your soul has no boundaries, no form, no dimensions to measure. Yet it is the very core of your being. When you are able to experience that space, you will know the peace and joy that comes from a life fully lived and fully appreciated."[2]

Belief in the soul has been a common phenomenon throughout the world for thousands of years, even though people have struggled to define it. The soul is often considered to be an invisible substance that is present in people who are alive but absent in people who have died. Many people also believe that the soul can temporarily leave the body, especially when the person is asleep. Memories of dreams in which someone traveled widely, yet woke up safely in bed, are probably the reason behind this belief. In their minds, the person's soul made the trip, while his or her physical body remained asleep, and temporarily soulless, in bed.

It is not simply good manners to cover your mouth when yawning. In the past, people believed that when someone died, the soul left the body with the person's final breath. Consequently, covering the mouth when yawning prevented the soul from accidentally leaving the body prematurely.

The English poet John Keats (1795–1821) had a keen interest in philosophy and believed everyone was born with "sparks of the divinity." However, these did not become souls until the person acquired an identity. Keats wrote about this in a letter to his brother and sister, George and Georgiana, on February 14, 1819:

> Call the world if you please "The vale of Soul-making" ... I say "Soul making" Soul as distinguished from an Intelligence—There may be intelligences or sparks of the divinity in millions—but they are not Souls till they acquire identities, till each one is personally itself. I[n]telligences are atoms of perception—they know and they see and they are pure, in short they are God—How then are Souls to be made? ... This is effected by three grand materials acting the one upon the other for a series of years. These three Materials are the Intelligence—the human heart (as distinguished from intelligence or Mind) and the World or Elemental space suited for the proper action of Mind and Heart on each other

for the purpose of forming the Soul or Intelligence destined to possess the sense of Identity.[3]

Ralph Waldo Emerson (1803–1882) wrote in his *Journals:*

The soul is an emanation of the Divinity, a part of the soul of the world, a ray from the source of light. It comes from without into the human body, as into a temporary abode, it goes out of it anew; it wanders in ethereal regions, it returns to visit it ... it passes into other habitations, for the soul is immortal.[4]

These definitions of the soul might sound rather technical. However, the reality is quite different, and I'm sure you've seen the souls of other people at different times in your life. Whenever you see someone totally lost in an awe-inspiring, magical, or tender moment, you'll see his or her soul. You'll see the person in a completely different, almost incandescent way. Here's an example.

My daughter, Charlotte, married her longtime boyfriend, Jeff, about twelve years ago. They chose to get married at a beautiful vineyard on a beautiful island that offered magnificent views back to the mainland, where they lived. It was a gorgeous, sunny afternoon, and after the wedding the bridal couple went down to a beach for the wedding photographs. As Charlotte turned to look at Jeff, I saw an emanation of light completely surrounding her. It was so magnificent it brought tears to my eyes. When I could see properly again, the moment had passed, and Charlotte was her normal self again.

I have seen this on other occasions, too. My sister is involved with a group called Riding for the Disabled. They use horses to increase the confidence of people with physical or intellectual difficulties. On one occasion I was there when a small, physically disabled boy was placed on a horse. He was terrified for the first few seconds, but gradually became used to the sensation of sitting on a large animal. After a few minutes, one of the helpers led the horse around a quarter-mile circuit. When they returned, the boy was ecstatic. He had a huge grin on his face, and light shone from every cell of his body.

As these moments come and go in a matter of seconds, they can easily be missed. However, when you happen to see one, it becomes an experience you'll remember for the rest of your life.

The Christian View of the Soul

The term *immortal soul* appears nowhere in the New Testament or in the writings of early Christian theologians. This is because early Christians followed the Jewish belief that union with God meant a union involving the whole person, and this meant both body and soul.[5] They believed that the body and the soul were separate entities.

Gradually, over a period of time, the Christian church came to accept two apparently opposing ideas: the resurrection of the body as well as the immortality of the soul. St.

Paul must have been thinking about this when he wrote, "There is a natural body, and there is a spiritual body" (1 Corinthians 15:44). He was also writing for any of his readers who may have been influenced by the Gnostics.

For the first two hundred years of its existence, Christianity was divided into two main groups. Christian Gnosticism was influenced by Judaism, Persian teachings, and Platonist philosophy. The Gnostics believed in dualism, as they accepted the Devil as a deity who was opposed to God. They considered the body to be unclean and a prison for the soul. In their teachings, the soul is liberated at death and ascends heavenwards to become reunited with God.

Orthodox Christians opposed the Gnostic teachings, as they believed in monism (one God) and the resurrection of the body. They did not accept that the soul had existed before someone was born, or that it reincarnated into another body after the person's death.

In the third century CE, Greek philosophical ideas about the superiority of the soul began playing a role in theological thought. Influenced more by Plato than Aristotle, the Christian fathers started teaching the concept that the soul survived even though the physical body died.

Origen (c. 185–c. 254), a prolific writer and biblical scholar, believed the soul was immortal, and existed before the current lifetime and survived the person's physical death. However, this was an exceptional point of view. St. Augustine (354–430) suggested a more limited view of the soul. He wrote that the soul mirrored the Trinity, as it contained the three qualities of memory, understanding, and will. However, like the physical body, the soul was created by God, and could not exist without Him.

St. Thomas Aquinas (1225–1274) thought that God made each soul expressly for a specific body, but that it could live independently from the body, as the soul survived from the time of the person's death until his or her resurrection.

St. Teresa of Ávila (1515–1582) had an extremely clear image of the soul. She wrote: "I began to think of the soul as if it were a castle made of a single diamond or of very clear crystal, in which there are many rooms, just as in heaven there are many mansions … some above, others below, others at each side; and in the center and midst of them all is the chiefest mansion where the most secret things pass between God and the soul."[6]

Many Christians believe in a soul-body dualism. Humans are made in the image of God, and the soul is a gift from God. In 1869, the Roman Catholic Church declared that the soul is present at the moment of conception. Many people, especially Roman Catholics, believe this today. Ralph McInerny, the Michael P. Grace Professor of Medieval Studies at the University of Notre Dame and an eminent Catholic scholar, wrote: "A soul is not produced from matter but breathed into the conceptum by God."[7] Today, a more common Christian point of view is to consider people as spiritual beings who have gradually developed both subjectivity and self-transcendence.

The Jewish View of the Soul

Jewish people consider the body and the soul to be united. After death, the soul goes to Gehenna to be cleansed and purified. This can take, in extreme cases, up to eleven months. This is why Jewish people recite the kaddish, a prayer of memory, for eleven months after a parent dies.

In the first century CE, the Jewish soldier and historian Flavius Josephus (c. 37–?) wrote that the Essenes, an ascetic Jewish sect, believed that the soul was preexistent and immortal. He also wrote that the Pharisees believed the souls of evil people were punished after death. However, the souls of good people were reincarnated into other bodies. As there is no evidence that Jewish people believed in reincarnation, it's possible that Josephus meant "resurrection" rather than "reincarnation."

The Talmud, a compilation of rabbinical thought, dates back to about the fourth century CE. It discusses *gilgul neshamot*, which means "the judgment of the revolutions of the souls." In the revolutions of the souls, people who had been particularly evil had the opportunity to reincarnate and lead worthwhile lives. Moses and Jethro, for instance, were believed to be the gilgulim (reincarnations) of Cain and Abel.

In the seventeenth century, Rabbi Menasseh ben Israel (1604–1657) wrote *Nishmat Hayyim (The Soul of Life)*, in which he claimed that "the belief or the doctrine of the transmigration of souls is a firm and infallible dogma accepted by the whole assemblage of our church."[8]

Today, Orthodox Jews believe in the resurrection. However, many non-Orthodox Jews believe that we possess immortal souls.

The Islamic View of the Soul

In Islam, there are two Arabic words for the soul. The first of these is *nafs,* which means "the independent soul." It equates to the Greek word *psyche.* Nafs sometimes represents the unperfected soul that needs to be nurtured and guided until it becomes a soul at peace. The other Arabic word for soul is *ruh,* which means "spirit," or "the non-independent soul." Ruh is synonymous with the Greek word *nous.* Ruh is the central part of a human being and contains the spirit of God.

Nafs and ruh are, respectively, the lower and higher, or the human and divine, levels of the soul.

The Hindu View of the Soul

The nearest Hindu equivalent to the soul is *atman,* which is the person's real self. The word atman originally meant "breath," but it now has a wide range of meanings taught by different branches of Hinduism.

The Upanishads discuss *paramatman,* or universal soul. This is identical to the individual atmans, which ultimately merge with it. This concept is known as *nirguna brahman,* which means an absolute reality that is impersonal and free from all human qualities. The individual atmans remain in limbo for a period of time and then reincarnate into another person. They continue reincarnating until the atman, or soul, becomes perfect and becomes one with Brahman (the Divine). This is called *moksha* and is the ultimate goal of all Hindus.

The Bhagavad Gita, the sacred Hindu text, says: "Just as a man discards worn out clothes and puts on new clothes, the soul discards worn out bodies and wears new ones" (2:22).

The Buddhist View of the Soul

Buddhists believe in reincarnation and karma. They believe that the soul will be born again, and that it will carry with it all the karma and lessons it has learned from previous incarnations. They believe that by following the teachings of Buddha in this life, they will progress in their next incarnation.

Buddhists and Hindus share the doctrine of *samsara*. This is the cycle of birth, death, and rebirth that continues until the person is liberated from it. However, there is an important difference between the two religions. Hindus believe that humans possess a changeless soul, which transmigrates from person to person during different incarnations. Buddhists believe that everything is impermanent. This means the soul is also impermanent, and cannot be fixed and unchangeable. Buddha rejected the idea of an immortal soul, as he considered it to be, like God, wishful thinking created by people who sought immortality.[9]

The Tibetan Book of the Dead explains the *bardos*, or the space between lives, that the consciousness of the deceased person must experience before being born again. Bardos usually last forty-nine days. During the first twenty-one days the soul is dealing with the karma from the lifetime that has just ended, and in the remaining twenty-eight days it is working toward its rebirth. Buddhists believe that the person's consciousness is extremely clairvoyant during its bardo state, and consequently family and friends of the deceased think about, pray for, and send best wishes to the deceased person at this time, as they believe it will help him or her make a positive rebirth. In Tibet, family members also read *The Tibetan Book of the Dead* out loud to help provide guidance to the person's consciousness while it is in the bardo state.

The Chinese View of the Soul

In China, the Taoists and Confucians believe in two kinds of soul, known as the *hun* and the *po*. Varying sources claim that humans have different numbers of hun and po souls. However, everyone has at least one hun soul and one po soul. The hun soul is made up of yang energy and looks after the person's spiritual and intellectual aspects, while the hun comprises yin energy, which provides life to the body. When the person dies, the souls leave the body. The hun souls ascend, and the po souls sink into the person's grave. Special rituals are performed to encourage the hun souls to move into the family's ancestral tablets. The same rituals ensure the po souls remain peacefully in the grave with the body.

As well as becoming used to their new homes in the grave, the po souls also descend into the Chinese version of hell, where their deeds are judged by the Ten Magistrates who preside over the Ten Tribunals. Each tribunal tries different types of offenses. The magistrates are appointed by Yama, the king of hell. What happens next depends on the person's karma (good deeds compared with bad deeds). There are a number of punishment levels in hell, and the soul spends enough time in each of these to balance its karma before reaching the final court to make sure the soul has fully atoned for its actions. Only then can it be reincarnated into another body.

Multiple Souls

The ancient Egyptians believed that they had seven souls given to them at birth by the Seven Hathors, the goddesses of fate. The Hathors, usually depicted as seven beautiful women, were present at every birth and predicted the baby's destiny. The Hathors were sometimes depicted as seven cows, but they appeared in this form mainly at funerals accompanied by the Sky Bull. The Hathors were called upon for help in matters concerning love and protection from evil. The Seven Hathors also protected the heavenly spheres in the sky.

The seven Egyptian souls are:[10]

1. aakhu: the life spirit, located in the blood.

2. ab: the heart, created from the heart blood of the person's mother.

3. **ba:** a birdlike ghost that appeared after death and flew into and out of the person's grave.

4. **ka:** the person's reflection.

5. **khaibut:** the person's shadow.

6. **khat:** the person's physical body.

7. **ren:** the person's secret soul-name.

The poet and mystic Gerald Massey (1828–1907) wrote and lectured on the subject of seven souls and noted the similarities between the systems of seven souls developed in India and Egypt. Here are his versions of the seven souls.[11] Note that his version of the Egyptian souls is slightly different from the one just given.

Indian

1. **rupa:** the body, or element of form.

2. **prana, or jiva:** the breath of life.

3. **astral:** body.

4. **manus:** intelligence.

5. **khama-rupa:** animal soul.

6. **buddhi:** spiritual soul.

7. **atma:** pure spirit.

Egyptian

1. **kha:** body.

2. **ba:** the soul of breath.

3. **khabs:** the shade.

4. **akhu:** intelligence or perception.

5. **seb:** ancestral soul.

6. **putah:** the first intellectual father.

7. **atmu:** divine, or eternal, soul.

Gnostic Christianity adopted the Egyptian concept of seven souls, and reduced it to a single soul that was modified and influenced by the seven known planets as it passed through each of them in turn on its journey from heaven to the body of a newly born baby. Consequently, the purity of the soul was weakened as it learned the seven deadly sins. Fortunately, this situation was reversed when the soul left the body after death and returned to heaven. Although most Christians accepted the concept of a single soul, some Gnostics believed that everyone possessed two souls: one from the person's mind and the other from God.

Members of the Menomini tribe of American Indians believe that the head and the heart each contain a soul. The Bagobo people in the Philippines believe there is one soul for the left side of the body and another soul for the right. After death, one of these souls joins its ancestors, while the other becomes a ghost.

Some concepts of multiple souls appear strange to outsiders. The Jívaro people of Ecuador believe that everyone has three souls. The first is a soul you have from birth, called *wakani.* When you die, this soul returns to the place where you were born and turns into a demon. The demon then dies and transforms into a giant moth, which becomes a fine mist when it dies. The second soul is called *arutam*. You can gain this soul by fasting, bathing under a waterfall, and imbibing a hallucinogenic juice. Unfortunately, this soul makes you feel capable of doing anything but temporarily leaves you when it is really needed. The third soul is an avenging soul, known as *muisak*. This soul attempts to leave the head of anyone who has been murdered so it can avenge the person's death. Consequently, if you kill someone, it is important to shrink that person's head.[12]

In Indian mysticism there are three main bodies: the physical, the astral, and the causal. Naturally, everyone is aware of the physical body, but few people are aware of their astral and causal bodies. The astral body is the same form as the physical body, but is composed of a form of subtle matter known as prana. The causal body is egg-shaped and is a body of light. These three bodies can be related to the body, mind, and soul.

The Causal Body

In Hindu mysticism, the causal body is considered to be the body of the soul. In the nineteenth century, the Theosophical Society introduced this concept to the Western world, and today it is accepted by many people interested in New Age concepts.

The causal body contains everything you have experienced and learned in previous incarnations. It is where your consciousness comes from. It provides the divine spark that gives you life. It also provides you with your personality. When your life ends, your personality returns to the causal body and adds its love and knowledge to everything that was learned in earlier lifetimes.

As the person evolves spiritually, the causal body contacts other souls who are at the same level. They are able to communicate with each other without the assistance of the human bodies that are their temporary homes in this lifetime. By doing this, the causal body helps the person develop positive qualities, such as love, unity, wisdom, and a sense of purpose.

Soul Awareness Exercise

Many years ago, a friend of mine experienced a dramatic change in his life. He was a successful businessman, but his endless pursuit of money and possessions had brought him little pleasure or satisfaction. Eventually he started thinking, *There must be more to life than this.* We had a number of discussions about better ways of living, and he became interested in the concept of the soul.

"Something is missing in my life," he told me. "I don't even know what it is, but I've a deep longing for it. Is it possible that I'm missing my soul?"

Of course, he wasn't missing a soul, but he did need to learn how to connect with it. He'd spent most of his life living through his head, but next to no time connecting with his heart. People who live in their heads always find it hard to connect with their soul, as they try to make the connection intellectually. Fortunately, once my friend became aware of his divine soul, and experienced it, he was able to progress again, but as a markedly different man. He is still successful in business, but is now equally well known as a philanthropist. This is the exercise I taught him.

You can do this exercise whenever you wish to connect with your soul. If you are familiar with relaxation techniques, you'll be able to contact your soul in a matter of seconds. If you have not yet learned how to relax quickly, you should allow about thirty minutes to complete the exercise. With practice, you'll find it easier and easier to relax completely and will be able to perform this exercise in a matter of minutes.

You should wear comfortable, loose-fitting clothing. Make sure the room is pleasantly warm but not hot. Temporarily disconnect the phone so you won't be disturbed or interrupted while you are doing the exercise.

You can sit in a comfortable recliner chair, or lie down on a bed or the floor. I prefer lying on the floor, as I tend to go to sleep when doing this exercise on a bed. Cover yourself with a blanket, because you're likely to lose a couple of degrees of body heat while doing the exercise.

Make yourself as comfortable as you can. When you feel ready, close your eyes and take ten slow, deep breaths. Hold each inhalation of breath for a couple of seconds before exhaling. Each time you exhale, say to yourself, "Relax, relax, relax."

Once you've completed the ten deep breaths, forget about your breathing and allow your attention to focus on the toes of your left foot. Allow these toes to relax as much as possible. You might feel a slight tingling sensation in your toes as you do this. When you feel your toes have relaxed, allow the relaxation to spread into your left foot, and up to your ankle.

Take as long as necessary to make sure your left foot is totally relaxed, and then repeat this with the toes of your right foot. Once these toes are relaxed, allow the relaxation to drift into your right foot, up to the ankle.

Both feet should be completely relaxed now. Allow the relaxation to drift up one leg. Imagine it relaxing every cell as it slowly moves up your leg, relaxing your calf, knee, and thigh. When one leg feels totally relaxed, allow the relaxation to drift up the other leg.

Allow the relaxation to drift up your abdomen, into your stomach and up to your chest. Let your shoulders relax, and then let the pleasant relaxation drift down one arm to the tips of your fingers. Repeat with the other arm.

When you feel both arms are relaxed, focus on your neck, and allow all the muscles in your neck to relax. Gradually allow the relaxation to drift up into your face. Pay special attention to the muscles around your eyes. These are the finest muscles in your whole body. Once these muscles are completely relaxed, allow the relaxation to drift up to the top of your head.

You are now completely relaxed. Mentally scan your body to make sure this is the case. Focus on any areas that do not feel totally relaxed, and allow all the muscles in the area to dissolve and relax.

Take another three slow, deep breaths, and then visualize yourself in the most peaceful and beautiful setting you can imagine. People visualize in different ways. Some people are able to clearly "see" the scene in their imagination. Others "see" it faintly. Others experience the scene in different ways. They might feel a pleasant warmth, hear sounds, or simply know they're in a comfortable, tranquil paradise created by their imagination.

Allow yourself to become familiar with the situation and the magnificent surroundings you find yourself in. You might feel the pleasant sunlight on your body. You might hear the sounds of birds or the lapping of waves on a beach. You'll certainly find yourself relaxing even more as you go deeper and deeper into your own special, personal paradise.

Notice how calm and relaxed you feel. See yourself as the wonderful creation you are. You are special. You are important. You are a vital, integral part of the universe. You have a right to be happy, to experience all the good things life has to offer. As you relax even further, become aware that this special, secret, magical world has been created by your soul. You are basking in the rich, protective glow of your soul.

Allow yourself to feel this with every breath you take, as you drift even deeper into complete and total relaxation. Feel the beautiful, comforting warmth all around you, and feel appreciated, loved, and nurtured by your soul. Allow this energizing warmth to nurture and heal every part of your mind, body, and soul.

As you're relaxing in the magical kingdom of your soul, allow yourself to receive all the love the universe is willingly giving you. Accept this love, because you deserve it. You deserve nothing but the best. When you feel completely full of love, allow it to spill over and spread throughout your magical world and out to the room you're lying in. Once the room is full of love, allow it to spread throughout the building and continue to spread on and on, until the whole world is full of your love.

Bask in this love for as long as you wish. See yourself as a happy, loving, confident, strong, powerful, generous, protective, and loving person. Your immortal soul has created this magical world purely for you, and you can return here as often as you wish. Whenever you want to feel loved, appreciated, and blessed, all you need do is relax and return to your own special world.

Remain in this special place for as long as you wish. When you feel ready to return to your everyday world, take five slow, deep breaths, mentally counting from one to five. When you reach five, open your eyes, become familiar with the situation around you, stretch, and relax for a few moments before getting up. If you're doing this exercise in bed at night, you can remain in your pleasant paradise until you drift off to sleep.

Some people find it easy to relax, but others find it difficult. Even if you find it easy to relax, it's a good idea to go through the complete relaxation process before visualizing your personal paradise, for at least the first three or four times. Once you've become used to the procedure, you'll be able to use whatever method you wish to relax.

If you find it difficult to relax, you'll find this exercise a useful way to learn progressive relaxation. With practice, it will gradually become easier and easier to relax. In time, you'll find you'll be able to spend most of your time inside your personal paradise rather than on the process of relaxing your physical body.

Layers of the Soul

The soul is present in every cell of the human body. This must be the case, as the soul animates every part of the body. However, the soul is also a spirit, which means it has no form and cannot be located and identified like any of the other essential organs of the body. It may well exist outside the physical body.

Alvin Plantinga, the John A. O'Brien Professor of Philosophy at the University of Notre Dame, believes this is the case. He demonstrates the existence of the soul in an interesting way. He argues that if every part of his body was immediately replaced by other body parts while he remained conscious, and the original body parts were destroyed, he would continue to exist, even though his original body had ceased to exist. Consequently, the soul exists separately from the physical body.[13]

If this is the case, where is the soul located? The most logical place is in the subtle body, the invisible electromagnetic energy field, or aura, that surrounds all living things. We'll look at the aura more closely in the next chapter.

CHAPTER THREE

YOU ARE
A RAINBOW

MOST PEOPLE ARE UNAWARE that their physical body is just one of several bodies they possess. This is because it usually takes time and effort to learn how to see the other bodies. This is unfortunate, as people's lives would change overnight if they could see the potential that is visible in their aura.

I know a young man who disassociated himself from his former friends after developing the ability to see auras. "They were all losers," he told me. "And I'd have been a loser, too, if I'd stayed with them. We were doing drugs and other things. My life changed once I started seeing auras and discovered how incredible everyone is. Most people have no idea how great their potential is. Once I saw that I could achieve virtually anything, it seemed almost criminal not to act on it."

This former high-school dropout is now in his third year of college.

Dictionaries describe the aura as an electromagnetic energy field that surrounds all living things. The word aura is derived from the Greek word *avra,* which means "air" or "a breeze." It is often described as an egg-shaped ball of energy that surrounds the body. Ursula Roberts, the British medium and author, described the aura as "a magnetic field of vibration which surrounds every person, in the same way that light surrounds a lighted candle or perfume surrounds a flower."[1] This is only partially correct. As the aura is part of every cell in the body, it is an extension of the body that in an average person extends for eight to ten feet in all directions. Some highly spiritual people have extremely large auras that are said to extend for several miles. Gautama Buddha's early followers claimed his aura extended two hundred miles.[2]

The aura expands and contracts in size depending on the health, vitality, and mental state of the person. Someone who is reasonably fit and full of the joys of life will have a much larger aura than someone who is unwell or has a negative outlook on life. The person with the larger aura will feel more in control of his or her life than the person with the smaller aura.

Anxiety, stress, frustration, anger, hostility, low self-esteem, and poor social skills weaken the aura. Friends, a loving family, happiness, humanitarian ideals, love, hobbies, and enjoyable work all strengthen the aura.

Your aura constantly interacts with the auras of others. Consequently, your aura expands and contracts as you go through each day. It expands when you meet positive people and contracts when you spend time with negative people.

It is also affected by encounters with people you like and dislike. Like everyone else, you absorb and pass out aura energy everywhere you go. This is why you feel depleted and drained of energy after spending time with negative people. Fortunately, this works the other way, too, and you feel invigorated and restored after spending time with positive people.

Anticipation also affects the size of the aura. Someone who is waiting to meet his or her lover will have a large, expansive aura, while someone expecting a rebuke or set-back will have a small aura.

Auras contain all the colors of the rainbow. Auras also change color to reveal people's moods and emotions. Someone who is "in the pink" is likely to be happier than someone who is "green with envy" or "red with rage." Someone in a "black hole" is depressed, while a coward is said to be "yellow." All of these expressions came into being because people noticed these colors in people's auras and discovered they consistently described the person's emotional state.

Even if you haven't yet seen an aura, you'll have been affected by other people's life force energy from the moment you were born. Recently, my wife and I met a friend while we were walking along a beach. He called out a cheery hello and joined us for a few minutes. After he left, my wife said, "He's such a nice man. He radiates charm." On the same walk, she described someone else as "glowing with happiness." In both instances, my wife was describing the person's aura.

People have been interested in the aura for thousands of years. There are at least three passages in the Bible that appear to relate to auras.[3] In the Beatitudes, Jesus taught something that appears to relate to auras: "Let your light so shine before men, that they may see your good works" (Matthew 5:16). The halos that Christian artists draw around Jesus Christ, the apostles, saints, martyrs, and angels are their depictions of auras that show their spiritually evolved state. It's interesting to note that artists in ancient Egypt, Greece, Rome, and India also used halos to illustrate this well before Christian times.

The aura provides a clear picture of the person's character, emotional state, attitude, values, habitual thoughts, health, vitality, and mood. It reveals his or her physical, mental, emotional, and spiritual energy. Positive and negative experiences from the past are shown in the aura. It also reveals the soul's journey through many past incarnations to the present. People who see auras are often able to detect illnesses in the aura well before they become apparent in the physical body.

Layers of the Aura

The aura consists of a number of layers known as *subtle bodies*. In the East, these layers are known as *koshas*, or "sheaths." This is a good name, as people who are able to see the aura often remark that the layers look like sheaths.

Most people, with practice, are able to feel three layers (the etheric double, the astral body, and the mental body), but many highly intuitive people can feel a number of other layers, even if they can't see them.

Many clairvoyants can feel seven layers of the aura (figure 1):

1. The physical etheric plane

2. The astral (or emotional) plane

3. The lower mental plane

4. The higher mental plane

5. The spiritual plane

6. The intuitional plane

7. The absolute plane

These seven layers relate to the seven chakras, which we'll discuss in the next chapter. In the past, the seven layers of the aura were looked at individually. The astral plane related to emotions, for instance, while the mental bodies related to thought. However, thoughts affect our emotions, and emotions affect our thoughts. Consequently, today most people look at the aura as a whole.

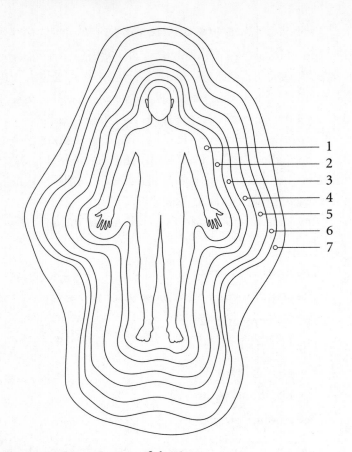

Figure 1: Seven Layers of the Aura

1. The physical plane (etheric double)

2. The astral (or emotional) plane

3. The lower mental plane

4. The higher mental plane

5. The spiritual plane

6. The intuitional plane

7. The absolute plane

Although the layers of the aura can be felt individually, the aura as a whole appears to be a gridlike matrix of swirling energy, in which all the layers mix and interact with each other.

The Physical Plane (Etheric Double)

The physical plane, or etheric double, is a fine, almost invisible layer that extends between a quarter inch and half an inch around the body. The etheric double appears to be a type of battery that recharges itself when the person is asleep. This is because it expands during sleep and contracts during the waking hours.

When people first start seeing auras, they see the etheric double as a clear space between the physical body and the aura. However, as their skills develop, they notice that the etheric double has a grayish tinge that is constantly shimmering and moving. This movement creates a variety of delicate, almost luminous, constantly changing colors that range from white to blue.

The etheric double is often called the health aura, as ill health is revealed as a dark smudge or a break in the movements inside the etheric double. Illnesses can often be detected in the etheric double long before the person realizes something is wrong. Medical intuitives who examine the etheric double can see past health problems as well as present and future concerns inside this layer.

You can also see someone's basic nature in the etheric double. Someone who constantly thinks negative thoughts has a dull etheric double, especially when compared to the beautiful, bright, and radiant etheric double that belongs to someone who looks mainly on the bright side of life.

The Astral Plane

The astral plane, sometimes called the emotional layer, relates to feelings, emotions, and desires. It is sometimes referred to as the "animal soul," as it is concerned with the person's subconscious mind. All the person's emotional experiences, good and bad, are stored here.

The Lower Mental Plane

The lower mental plane relates to reason, thought, ideas, and the conscious mind. This is where most people spend their waking hours. The lower mental plane expands when the person is involved in study or deep thought. The person's beliefs, values, and ideals are stored here.

The Higher Mental Plane

The higher mental plane, sometimes known as the causal plane, relates to the higher mind, love for self and others, and unconditional love. The higher mental plane connects the lower mental plane (conscious mind) to the spiritual plane.

The Spiritual Plane

The spiritual plane, sometimes known as the etheric plane, is the home of the person's spirituality. It connects the person with the universe.

The prophet Ezekiel described the spiritual plane as a throne: "Over their heads was the likeness of a throne, as the appearance of a sapphire stone: and upon the likeness of the throne was the likeness as the appearance of a man above upon it. And I saw as the color of amber, as the appearance of fire round about within it, from the appearance of his loins even upward, and from the appearance of his loins even downward, I saw as it were the appearance of fire, and it had brightness round about. As the appearance of the bow that is in the cloud in the day of rain, so was the appearance of the brightness round about" (Ezekiel 1:26–28).

The Intuitional Plane

The intuitional plane, sometimes known as the celestial plane, relates to the person's dreams, intuitions, and spiritual awareness. Every connection ever made to the universal life force is visible here. This plane also relates to forgiveness and acceptance.

The Absolute Plane

The absolute plane, sometimes known as the ketheric plane, balances and harmonizes all the other layers. It contains all the experiences of the person's soul. It connects the person with the universal life force. It also contains a blueprint of the person's spiritual development and potential.

Other Layers of the Aura

When I was living in India, a guru told me the aura consisted of eighty-nine layers. I was impressed, until other gurus gave me different numbers. Most said there were between seven and ten layers. As it's unusual to find people who can feel more than three layers, it's impossible to say how many layers there might be. The names given to the other layers vary enormously, too. These include the soul layer, memory layer, eternal layer, and universal layer.

The Seven Rays

The seven rays have been discussed and written about for more than two thousand years.[4] They are not part of the aura. They are universal energies that, according to ancient esoteric teachings, are expressed by the universal life force and have a profound effect and influence on the soul. Each ray has its own particular energy that produces one of seven different types of souls. Theosophists, members of the Theosophical Society, the worldwide organization formed by Madame Blavatsky in 1876, believe that everything in the entire solar system belongs to one of the seven rays. Alice A. Bailey (1880–1949), the American occultist and founder of the Arcane School, wrote: "Each vibrating unit of energy can say: I am part of a divine whole, which in its septenary [sevenfold] nature expresses to love and life of the One Reality, coloured by one of the seven qualities of love of Deity and responsive to other qualities."[5]

The seven rays were little known in the West until the nineteenth century. Once the Theosophical Society started teaching the principles of the seven rays, knowledge of them spread quickly.

Theosophists associate these rays with the seven spiritual masters (also known as *chohans*, or Lords of the Rays) of the Great White Brotherhood. According to Theosophical lore, these masters secretly govern the world, and encourage its spiritual development.

Theosophists believe the universe is evolving along seven paths, known as rays, and every person is associated with a particular ray. Because of this, the seven rays can be used to determine each person's personality and purpose in life.

Many people believe that every person's soul is attuned to a particular ray to help it achieve its purpose in this incarnation. However, it is more likely that our souls use the energy of one or two particular rays most of the time, but have access to the qualities and energies of the other rays when we need them. Some people naturally use the energies of three or four of the rays, while others, equally as naturally, focus on just one. The particular focus enables the soul to potentially make as much progress as possible in each incarnation.

Here is a description of the seven rays.

First Ray: Ray of Power and Will
Color: Red
Master: El Morya
Gem: Diamond

The first ray is the Ray of Power and Will. It is sometimes called the Ray of Deity, as the purpose of this ray is to confirm the existence of the Divine on a physical level.

This ray provides courage, self-reliance, willpower, and ambition. It gives leadership qualities, a sense of purpose and direction, and the ability to come up with good ideas and make them happen. This ray also provides ultimate wisdom.

Each ray has a negative side to it. Some people on the first ray are arrogant, overly proud, impatient, and domineering. They seek power and will do anything to achieve it. Because of this, negative first ray people are usually egotistical.

Second Ray: Ray of Love-Wisdom
Color: Blue
Master: Kuthumi
Gem: Sapphire

The second ray is the Ray of Love-Wisdom. People on this ray can see themselves from the perspective of the Divine, and this enables kindness, love, and ultimately wisdom to develop. People on this ray are able to send positive and negative feelings and emotions to the Divine for healing and growth.

This ray also provides insight, wisdom, generosity, diplomacy, sympathy, and compassion. People on this ray are empathetic, sensitive, loving, tactful, and tolerant. They are also naturally intuitive and possess healing capabilities.

Most people on the second ray have a positive outlook on life. However, some show the negative qualities of fear, codependency, oversensitivity, indifference, and overprotectiveness. They frequently possess an inferiority complex.

Third Ray: Ray of Active Intelligence

Color: Yellow

Master: Venetian Chohan

Gem: Emerald

The third ray is the Ray of Active Intelligence. This ray enables the Divine to send thoughts and ideas to people on this ray. These people then need to decide whether they will act on them. This ray also enables their decisions, results, and actions to go back to the Divine.

This ray provides creativity, comprehension, understanding, adaptability, and perception. It also gives people on this ray the ability to plan ahead and communicate well with others. People on this ray are good with financial matters and often do well in business. Once they have achieved success, they gain pleasure from using their wealth to help others.

People who operate on the negative side of the third ray are critical, careless with details, manipulative, and devious. They are sometimes absent-minded and find it hard to say no. This can lead to failure, caused by trying to do too many things at once.

Fourth Ray: Ray of Harmony, Beauty, and Art

Color: Green

Master: Serapis

Gem: Jasper

The fourth ray is the Ray of Harmony, Beauty, and Art. This essential harmony usually comes about through conflict. This ray enables the Divine to send people on this ray the heart's desires they need to manifest. It also allows any harmonies or disharmonies to return to the Divine for healing and development.

The fourth ray provides balance, harmony, and stability. It provides inner peace, too, though this usually occurs after a struggle. These people have the ability to captivate and entertain others with various forms of self-expression. They have a good sense of humor and enjoy making people laugh. They have a strong aesthetic sense and enjoy expressing themselves creatively. They possess a strong sense of color, and many utilize this in their careers. Even if it is not being used in this way, their sense of color will be obvious to others. Over a lifetime they develop spiritually, but their faith is always hard won.

The negative qualities of this ray are stress, worry, moodiness, self-absorption, unreliability, indecision, and a lack of confidence. These people usually experience a great deal of turmoil in their lives.

Fifth Ray: Ray of Concrete Knowledge and Science

Color: Orange

Master: Hilarion

Gem: Topaz

The fifth ray is the Ray of Concrete Knowledge and Science. People on this ray have access to knowledge from the past, present, and future, and hopefully make good use of it. This ray also enables them to instill this information into their everyday lives.

The fifth ray provides patience, logic, and the ability to analyze and discern. People on this ray are inventive, precise, and accurate. They enjoy using their brains to analyze, research, and solve complex problems.

The negative aspects of the fifth ray are rigidity, narrow-mindedness, a critical approach, intolerance, overanalysis, and skepticism. These people are usually loners, as they find it hard to fit in and relate well with others.

Sixth Ray: Ray of Devotion and Idealism
Color: Violet
Master: Jesus
Gem: Ruby

The sixth ray is the Ray of Devotion and Idealism. It enters the body as intuition, enabling the Divine to send pure, unconditional love and support to the person. It encourages people on this ray to investigate what is hidden or unknown.

The sixth ray gives enthusiasm, optimism, loyalty, sincerity, humility, and devotion. It gives people on this ray the potential to motivate and inspire others. It also gives them drive and persistence. People on this ray are idealistic and devout.

People operating on the negative side of the sixth ray are impractical, overly emotional, insecure, selfish, and gullible. They are rigid and take everything to extremes.

Seventh Ray: Ray of Order and Ceremonial Magic
Color: Indigo
Master: Comte de Saint-Germain
Gem: Amethyst

The seventh ray is the Ray of Order and Ceremonial Magic. People on this ray have the potential to express themselves effectively, create order out of chaos, and turn their dreams into action. These people also have the qualities of grace, dignity, nobility, and chivalry. They pay attention to detail. They are good organizers and are able to motivate others to achieve worthwhile goals.

People working on the negative side of this ray are materialistic, unoriginal, rigid, and intolerant. They enjoy routine and like to follow the rules. They are often frustrated perfectionists, as perfection is impossible to achieve.

In the next chapter we'll return to the aura and discuss the seven chakras, or energy centers, that are located along the spine.

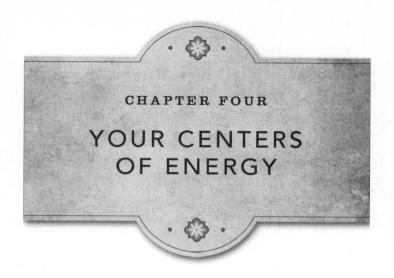

CHAPTER FOUR

YOUR CENTERS
OF ENERGY

INSIDE THE AURA, SITUATED in a vertical line in the center of the body in line with the spine, are seven revolving, wheel-like circles of subtle energy called *chakras* (figure 2). The word chakra comes from the Sanskrit word for wheel. In the East, chakras are often depicted as lotus flowers, each with a different number of petals. These petals open and close, reflecting the moods, feelings, and experiences of the person.

The chakras absorb the higher energies, including the universal life force, and transform them into energy that the body can use. They are, in effect, batteries that stimulate the physical and subtle bodies they connect and look after. The universal life force is said to enter the aura through the chakra at the top of the head. It then energizes and stimulates each

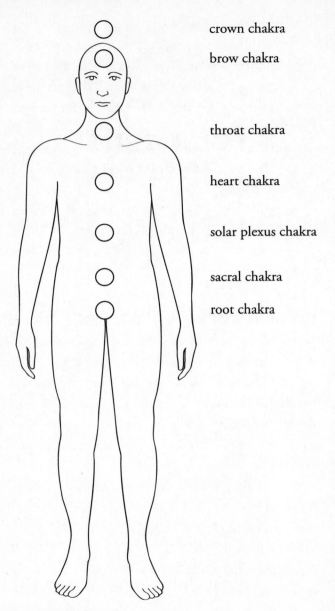

crown chakra

brow chakra

throat chakra

heart chakra

solar plexus chakra

sacral chakra

root chakra

Figure 2: Seven Chakras

chakra as it moves downward through the *nadis*, the channels of energy that connect all the chakras to each other. The word nadi means "flowing water." Six of the chakras are situated on the Sushumna, the main nadi that starts at the base of the spine and ends between the eyebrows at the level of the third eye.

Intertwined with the Sushumna are two other nadis known as Ida and Pingala. They carry the person's male and female energies.

Although most people are not aware of them, the chakras play a vital role in a person's physical, emotional, and mental health. They are powerful batteries that stimulate and energize the entire body.

Each chakra has a number of associations, such as a color, an endocrine gland, and a physical system, along with the organs associated with the system. There is a direct relationship between the state of each chakra and the health of the organs associated with it.

Chakras can be open, closed, in or out of balance, and blocked. All of these conditions affect the chakra. Consequently, if an affected chakra is restored to balance, the person will notice an immediate difference in his or her health, and will experience feelings of well-being. It is unusual to meet someone who has every chakra perfectly balanced. This person would feel contented and be full of all the joys of life. Unfortunately, the fears, worries, frustrations, and stresses of everyday life affect the chakras, which is why it is rare to find someone with all seven chakras in balance.

The concept of chakras is thousands of years old, and a great deal of information about them was recorded in the Upanishads (c. 900–400 BCE), the sacred Hindu texts. Even though the chakras have been utilized in the East for thousands of years, Western science showed no interest in them until the 1970s. The chakra system was little known in the West until the Theosophical Society began teaching it in the late nineteenth century.

The Quatern Chakras

The chakras are frequently depicted as a square and a triangle, known as the *quatern* and the *trinity*. The bottom four chakras represent the quatern. They each represent one of the traditional elements of earth, water, fire, and air.

The quatern chakras have a slower vibration than the three trinity chakras. Because of this, some people feel they are of lesser importance than the chakras in the trinity. This is not the case. Each chakra is essential, as it has its own specific purpose. All of the chakras are equally important.

Root Chakra (Muladhara)

Color: Red
Element: Earth
Functions: Survival, grounding
Glands: Adrenals
Petals: Four
Sense: Smell
Desire: Physical contact

Gemstones: Ruby, garnet, hematite
Challenge: To think before acting
Keyword: Physical

Muladhara is the Sanskrit word for the root chakra. It comes from *mula,* meaning "root," and *adhara,* "support." It is often called the base chakra or support chakra.

The root chakra is situated at the base of the spine in the area of the coccyx. It is concerned with self-preservation and keeps us firmly grounded in the earth. It also provides feelings of security and comfort. It provides vitality, enthusiasm, energy, and a sense of being alive. It symbolizes survival and the life force. Emotionally, it provides drive, courage, strength, and persistence. It also controls our fight-or-flight responses.

The root chakra governs our sense of smell and the solid parts of our body, such as teeth, bones, and nails.

Unlike the other chakras, the root chakra faces downward to the earth.

When the root chakra is understimulated, the person will feel nervous and insecure. This triggers digestive problems and causes fear to gather inside the chakra.

When the root chakra is overstimulated, the person will be self-centered, aggressive, and addicted to money, power, and sex.

When the root chakra is not functioning as it should, the person may suffer from hemorrhoids, constipation, skin irritations, and an increase in weight.

The root chakra can be both calmed and stimulated by meditation. Sit in a straight-backed chair with your feet flat on the floor and your knees creating approximately a ninety-degree angle.

To calm the root chakra, hold a piece of rose quartz behind your back at the base of your spine. Close your eyes, take slow deep breaths, and visualize the gentle, cooling energies of the rose quartz soothing and balancing your root chakra.

To stimulate the root chakra, hold a deep red crystal, such as garnet, at the base of your spine, and visualize its stimulating energy revitalizing, energizing, and balancing your root chakra. You can also stimulate your root chakra by doing anything physical, such as walking, swimming, gardening, or even vacuuming the house.

Sacral Chakra (Svadisthana)

Color: Orange
Element: Water
Functions: Sexuality, creativity, pleasure
Glands: Ovaries, testicles
Petals: Six
Sense: Taste
Desires: Respect and acceptance
Gemstones: Coral, carnelian
Challenge: To love and serve others
Keyword: Social

Svadisthana is the Sanskrit word for the sacral chakra. It means "home of the vital force." This chakra is located at the level of the sacrum in the lower abdomen, approximately two inches below the navel.

Because the sacral chakra is associated with the element of water, it is concerned with all the fluidic functions of the body, including our sense of taste. It represents creativity, sexuality, and emotional balance. It stimulates optimism and hope at an emotional level. People who get along well with others usually have a well-balanced sacral chakra, as this gives them the necessary fluidity to interact with other people easily.

When the sacral chakra is not functioning as it should be, the person may suffer from frigidity or impotence or experience problems with the bladder or kidneys.

The sacral chakra can be both calmed and stimulated by meditation. You can stimulate this chakra by lying on your back on the floor. Bend your knees until you can place the soles of your feet together. Slowly spread your arms until they make a forty-five- to sixty-degree angle to your body. Relax as much as possible, and visualize orange energy filling the area of your sacral chakra until it is overflowing. While remaining in this position, allow yourself to meditate on your sacral chakra for two to three minutes. You can also stimulate your sacral chakra by spending time doing something you enjoy. It can be as simple as meeting a friend for a cup of coffee or taking time out to read an enjoyable book.

You can meditate to soothe and calm your sacral chakra. Sit in a straight-backed chair with your feet flat on the floor and your knees creating approximately a ninety-degree angle. Hold a piece of moonstone to the front of your body below your navel and meditate for a minute or two while the moonstone calms and balances your sacral chakra.

Solar Plexus Chakra (Manipura)

Color: Yellow
Element: Fire
Functions: Will, assertiveness, personal power
Gland: Pancreas
Petals: Ten
Sense: Sight
Desire: To understand
Gemstones: Amber, topaz
Challenge: To communicate effectively with loved ones
Keyword: Intellect

The Sanskrit word Manipura means "jewel of the navel." The solar plexus chakra is located between the navel and the sternum.

The solar plexus chakra provides good self-esteem, warmth, confidence, and happiness. It is involved with the emotions and enhances creativity, optimism, and self-respect at an emotional level. The solar plexus chakra also relates to the eyes.

This chakra can cause anger, resentment, and hostility in people with a negative approach to life. If this chakra is overstimulated, the person will be an overly demanding perfectionist. When the solar plexus chakra is understimulated, the person will be overly sensitive and lacking in confidence.

When the solar plexus chakra is not functioning as it should be, the person may suffer from diabetes, digestive disorders, or hypoglycemia.

The solar plexus chakra can be both calmed and stimulated by meditation. To stimulate this chakra, stand on the floor in bare feet, close your eyes, and visualize your solar plexus chakra completely full with a beautiful yellow energy. Visualize this energy gradually spreading throughout your body. With your eyes remaining closed, start marching slowly on the spot while visualizing your solar plexus chakra becoming revitalized and energized with each movement of your legs. You may find it helpful to make exaggerated movements with your arms and legs while doing this. Stop when you feel that your solar plexus chakra is fully energized. You can also stimulate your solar plexus chakra by setting a worthwhile goal for yourself, and then steadily working at it until it is achieved.

The solar plexus can be soothed and quieted with a piece of quartz crystal. Sit in a straight-backed chair with your feet flat on the floor and your knees creating approximately a ninety-degree angle. Hold the quartz against your solar plexus, close your eyes, and visualize the unwanted energy moving from the chakra into the quartz. Repeat once a day for as long as necessary.

Heart Chakra (Anahatha)

Color: Green
Element: Air
Function: Love
Gland: Thymus
Petals: Twelve
Sense: Touch
Desires: To love and be loved
Gemstones: Emerald, jade, tourmaline
Challenge: To gain confidence
Keyword: Emotions

The heart chakra is located in the center of the chest, in line with the heart. The Sanskrit word Anahatha means "unstruck" or "unbroken." This relates to an eternal sound that has not been created by any human instrument.

The heart chakra relates to personal and unconditional love, sympathy, compassion, understanding, empathy, and the sense of touch.

When the heart chakra is overstimulated, the person will be possessive, controlling, and moody. When the heart chakra is understimulated, the person will feel overly sympathetic and overly sensitive. Most codependent people have an understimulated heart chakra.

When the heart chakra is not functioning as well as it should be, the person may suffer from asthma or have problems with the heart or lungs.

The heart chakra can be both calmed and stimulated by meditation. Sit in a straight-backed chair with your feet flat on the floor and your knees creating an approximately ninety-degree angle. To stimulate your heart chakra, close your eyes and visualize the center of your body in the area of your heart as a glowing green orb. Each time you inhale, allow the orb to grow bigger and bigger until your whole body is inside it. Spend a minute or two enjoying the healing, stimulating energy of the green orb before opening your eyes and carrying on with your day. You also stimulate your heart chakra every time you experience a sense of joy and fulfillment.

To calm your heart chakra, close your eyes and visualize your entire body enveloped in a pure white light. In your imagination, allow the white light to enter your body with each inhalation. Allow it to spread to every cell of your body, soothing and cleansing as it goes. Focus on the area of your heart, and allow the white light to soothe and calm your heart chakra. Continue meditating until you feel that all the stress and tension in your body has been released.

The Trinity Chakras

The top three chakras of the trinity vibrate at a higher level than the four chakras of the quatern. They relate to the three quadruplicities of astrology, known as cardinal, fixed, and mutable. The cardinal signs are Aries, Cancer, Libra, and Capricorn. They are all outgoing and energetic. The fixed signs are Taurus, Leo, Scorpio, and Aquarius. They are determined, patient, loyal, and reliable. The mutable signs are Gemini, Virgo, Sagittarius, and Pisces. They are adaptable, resourceful, and communicative.

Highly evolved people make use of all seven chakras. However, most people are unwilling to invest the necessary time and energy to develop their brow and crown chakras, and work mainly with the lower five chakras.

Throat Chakra (Visshudha)

Color: Blue
Element: Sound
Quadruplicity: Fixed
Functions: Communication, creativity
Glands: Thyroid and parathyroid
Petals: Sixteen
Sense: Sound
Desire: Inner peace
Gemstone: Turquoise
Challenge: To risk
Keyword: Concepts

The throat chakra is located at the level of the throat. The Sanskrit word Visshudha means "pure." The throat chakra relates to communication and self-expression, especially when spoken. It constantly searches for the truth in all things.

When the throat chakra is well balanced, the person will feel contented and be kind and considerate to others. When the throat chakra is overstimulated, the person will be overbearing, sarcastic, and arrogant. When the throat chakra is understimulated, the person will be weak, uncommunicative, devious, and unreliable.

When the throat chakra is not functioning as it should be, the person may suffer from sore throats and colds or have problems with the sinuses, thyroid, or ears.

The throat chakra is stimulated whenever you use your voice. Consequently, singing, talking, shouting, and screaming are all effective ways to energize and recharge this chakra.

You will need a piece of moonstone to calm your throat chakra. Sit in a straight-backed chair with your feet flat on the floor and your knees creating approximately a ninety-degree angle. Use both hands to hold the moonstone against your throat. Close your eyes and visualize the unwanted energy being released from your throat chakra and absorbed by the moonstone. Visualize this for at least two minutes, and repeat daily for as long as necessary.

Brow Chakra (Ajna)

Color: Indigo
Element: Light
Quadruplicity: Mutable
Functions: Intuition, thought, perception
Gland: Pituitary
Petals: Ninety-six
Desire: To be in harmony with the universe
Gemstones: Lapis lazuli, quartz
Challenge: To turns one's dreams into reality
Keyword: Intuition

The brow chakra is located in the forehead, just above the eyebrows. The Sanskrit word Ajna means "command."

The brow chakra governs the mind and looks after the other chakras. This chakra is frequently called the "third eye," as it is concerned with psychic and spiritual matters. We can pick up other people's thoughts, feelings, and intuitions with the brow chakra.

When the brow chakra is overstimulated, the person is proud, authoritative, and dogmatic. When it is understimulated, the person is timid, hesitant, and unassertive.

When the brow chakra is not functioning as it should be, the person may suffer from headaches or have problems with his or her vision.

The brow chakra can be stimulated with a piece of amethyst. Sit in a straight-backed chair with your feet flat on the floor and your knees creating approximately a ninety-degree angle. Place the amethyst in the area of your third eye, close your eyes, and visualize energy passing from the amethyst into your brow chakra. Slowly move the amethyst in small circles in a clockwise direction for about sixty seconds.

To calm and soothe your brow chakra, lie on your back, close your eyes, and take slow deep breaths until your body feels totally relaxed. If necessary, visualize all stress and worry leaving your body with each exhalation.

Crown Chakra (Sahasrara)
Color: Violet
Element: Thought
Quadruplicity: Cardinal

Function: Union with the Divine
Gland: Pineal
Petals: Nine hundred and seventy-two
Desire: Universal understanding
Gemstones: Amethyst, diamond
Challenge: To grow in knowledge and wisdom
Keyword: Spirituality

The crown chakra is located at the top of the head and is often depicted as a halo when artists paint someone who is spiritually evolved. The Sanskrit word Sahasrara means "thousand." The symbol of this chakra is the thousand-petaled lotus.

The crown chakra harmonizes and balances the often conflicting sides of our nature. It also helps us gain insight into the interconnectedness of all living things. The crown chakra remains dormant until all the other chakras have been mastered and are in a state of balance. When the crown chakra is balanced, the person experiences enlightenment and gains a sense of being at one with the universe.

When the crown chakra is overstimulated, the person will feel frustrated and depressed. When this chakra is understimulated, the person will be withdrawn and find it hard to experience any joy in life.

When the crown chakra is not functioning as it should be, the person may suffer from apathy, listlessness, or depression.

To stimulate the crown chakra, lie on your back with your eyes closed. Starting with the root chakra, visualize each of your chakras in turn. See them all perfectly balanced, and notice the colors of each one. After visualizing the brow chakra, take a deep breath, hold it for as long as you can, and say "Om" as you slowly exhale.

To calm and soothe the crown chakra, sit in a straight-backed chair with your feet flat on the floor and your knees creating approximately a ninety-degree angle. Cup a piece of rose quartz in your hands and close your eyes. Focus on your breathing for sixty seconds, and then shift your attention to the rose quartz in your hands. Visualize a gentle, relaxing, and cooling energy coming from the crystal and moving into every cell of your body. Conclude the exercise by raising your hands and holding the crystal to the top of your head for a few seconds. Take three slow, deep breaths and open your eyes.

Meditation, prayer, and periods of quietness all help you gain a closer connection with your crown chakra and become aware of your divine nature.

There are seven rays and seven main chakras. We'll look more at the magical and mystical number seven in the next chapter.

CHAPTER FIVE

THE POWER OF SEVEN

THE NUMBER SEVEN HAS appeared many times in this book already. We've discussed the seven main colors of the aura, the seven main chakras, and the seven rays. It would seem that this number is important and significant.

Seven has been considered a sacred and mystical number since well before recorded history. According to the Bible, the creation of the world took seven days. The ancient Babylonians and Egyptians gazed in awe at the seven sacred planets they could see in the sky. The ancient Egyptians also venerated seven Wise Ones. These were seven hawks who flew upwards from the eye of Ra, and looked after knowledge and learning.[1]

The word seven is derived from the Greek word *sebo*, which means "to venerate." The Hebrew word *shaba*, "to swear," comes from the same root as the number seven and can be interpreted as "to come under the influence of seven things."[2] This shows that the number seven was considered so powerful that oaths were made using it. The ancient Greek historian Herodotus wrote that the Arabs made their oaths over seven stones that had been smeared with blood.[3] Another example of this can be found in the first book of the Bible when Abraham and Abimelech met at Beersheba to swear an oath. "And Abraham set seven ewe lambs of the flock by themselves" (Genesis 21:28).

In the second century BCE, the Greek poet Antipater of Sidon listed the Seven Wonders of the World: the Great Pyramid of Giza, the Hanging Gardens of Babylon, the Statue of Zeus at Olympia, the Colossus of Rhodes, the Temple of Artemis at Ephesus, the Mausoleum at Halicarnassus, and the Lighthouse of Alexandria. It's highly likely that he chose seven wonders, rather than six, or eight, or twelve, because of the symbolic qualities of the number seven.

There were also Seven Wise Men of Greece. These were seven sages who lived between 620 and 550 BCE. They were Bias, Chilon, Cleobulus, Periander, Pittacus, Solon, and Thales. However, even when Plato created this list, there was much disagreement about who should be included. Yet again it seems that seven were chosen because of the symbolism of the number.

Seven in Christianity

The number seven appears frequently in the Bible. There were the seven days of Creation. "An on the seventh day God ended his work which he had made; and he rested on the seventh day from all his work which he had made. And God blessed the seventh day, and sanctified it: because that in it he had rested from all his work which God created and made" (Genesis 2:2–3). God told Cain that if anyone killed him, "vengeance shall be taken on him sevenfold" (Genesis 4:15). Pharaoh dreamed about seven plentiful years followed by seven years of famine in Genesis 41.

Seven played an important role in the fall of the walls of Jericho. God said to Joshua: "Seven priests shall bear before the ark seven trumpets of rams' horns: and the seventh day ye shall compass the city seven times, and the priests shall blow with the trumpets. And it shall come to pass, that when they make a long blast with the ram's horn, and when ye hear the sound of the trumpet, all the people shall shout with a great shout; and the wall of the city shall fall down flat" (Joshua 6:4–5).

The first deacons of the early Christian church were "seven men of honest report, full of the Holy Ghost and wisdom" (Acts 6:3).

Jesus turned seven loaves of bread and a few small fish into a feast that fed four thousand people. The meat that was left over filled seven baskets (Matthew 15:34–38).

When Peter asked Jesus if he should forgive his brother seven times, "Jesus saith unto him, I say not unto thee,

Until seven times: but, Until seventy times seven" (Matthew 18:22).

There are also several references to seven in the Book of Revelation, the final book of the Bible. These include the seven churches of Asia (1:11), seven golden candlesticks (1:12), seven stars (1:16), seven lamps of fire (4:5), seven Spirits of God (4:5), seven seals (5:1), a lamb with seven horns and seven eyes (5:6), seven angels with seven trumpets (8:2), seven thunders (10:3), a red dragon with seven heads and seven crowns (12:3), seven plagues (15:6), seven golden vials (15:7), and seven kings (17:10). There are also seven petitions in the Lord's Prayer (Matthew 6:9–13).

Christian interest in the number seven explains the seven joys of the Virgin Mary, the seven sorrows of the Virgin Mary, the seven spiritual works of mercy, and the seven words from the cross.[4] The seven deadly sins—lust, gluttony, greed, sloth, wrath, envy, and pride—were also part of the teachings of the early Church. Pope Gregory is one of many teachers who used this list of sins to help people lead godly lives.

The number seven appears in early Christian literature, too. A fifth-century legend called *The Seven Sleepers of Ephesus* was extremely popular during the Middle Ages, as it affirmed the Christian belief in the resurrection of the dead. In this story, seven Christian soldiers were sealed inside a cave during the persecution of Christians in the time of Emperor Decius (about 250 CE). The soldiers fell into a miraculous sleep that lasted more than 150 years. When the cave was opened during the reign of Theodosius II (408–450 CE), the soldiers woke up. After explaining to the emperor the Christian interpretation of their experience, they died. The emperor was impressed and pardoned all the bishops who had been persecuted for believing in the Resurrection.

In medieval times there were also Seven Champions of Christendom. These were the national saints of seven countries: St. George (England), St. Andrew (Scotland), St. Patrick (Ireland), St. David (Wales), St. Denys (France), St. James, the son of Zebedee (Spain), and St. Anthony of Padua (Italy).

The Most Famous History of the Seven Champions of Christendom by Richard Johnson (1598) was one of the most popular books of its time. It contained heavily embellished stories of the lives and achievements of the seven saints. The number seven features frequently in the book, too. St. George was imprisoned for seven years, and St. Denys lived inside a hart for seven years. St. James was dumb for seven years. St. Anthony was freed of his enchantment when the seven lamps were dowsed using water from an enchanted fountain. St. Andrew rescued six women who had spent seven years as white swans, and St. David slept for seven years in an enchanted garden.

Seven in Islam

The Kabah is a square-shaped building in the center of the great mosque in Mecca. During the Hajj, an annual pilgrimage to Mecca that all devout Muslims intend to make at least once in their lifetime, pilgrims walk around the Kabah seven times in a counterclockwise direction.

In addition to this, pilgrims walk between Mount Safa and Mount Marwah seven times. This is to commemorate Hagar, the mother of Ishmael, who ran between these two hills looking for water to help save the life of her son. Fortunately, an angel arrived, and a well appeared where the angel touched the ground. The water it produced saved both mother and child.

Pilgrims also visit Mina, which is just outside Mecca. Here they throw seven pebbles at each of the three walls that represent the Devil.

In Islam there are seven skies, seven seas, and seven layers of the earth. There are also seven heavens. They are:

1. **Pure silver.** This is the home of Adam and Eve.

2. **Pure gold.** John the Baptist and Jesus are here.

3. **Pearl.** Joseph lives here. Azrael, the Islamic angel of death, also lives here.

4. **White gold.** Enoch, who became Metatron, the king of angels in Christian belief, is called Idris in Islam. He rules the fourth heaven. The Islamic Angel of Tears lives here, too.

5. **Silver.** Aaron, the brother of Moses, rules the fifth heaven. The Islamic Avenging Angel lives here, too.

6. **Ruby and garnet.** This heaven is ruled by Moses. The Guardian Angel of Heaven and Earth lives here. This angel is composed of both snow and fire.

7. **Divine light.** The seventh heaven is ruled by Abraham. Every inhabitant of this heaven has 70,000 heads. Each head has 70,000 faces, each face has 70,000 mouths, each mouth 70,000 tongues, and each tongue can speak 70,000 languages, all of which continually chant the praises of Allah.

There are seven levels of hell and seven doors leading to hell.

There are seven major sins in Islam. These come from a *hadith,* or report, from the Prophet Muhammad. They are polytheism (worship of many gods), witchcraft, killing a soul that Allah has forbidden to be killed, riba (usury), unlawfully taking the money of an orphan, running away from the field of battle, and slandering chaste, innocent women.

Seven in the Bahá'í Faith

Bahá'u'lláh (1817–1892), the founder of the Bahá'í religion, wrote a book called *The Seven Valleys,* which describes the seven mystical stages a follower must go through to find God. The seven valleys are:

1. The Valley of Search
2. The Valley of Love
3. The Valley of Knowledge
4. The Valley of Unity
5. The Valley of Contentment

6. The Valley of Wonderment

7. The Valley of True Poverty and Absolute Nothingness

Seven in Judaism

The *Sepher Yetzirah,* also known as the *Book of Creation* or the *Book of Formation,* is the oldest book of Jewish esotericism. It was probably written between 200 and 500 CE, although Jewish tradition says it was written by Abraham. This book confirms the Jewish belief that seven is an extremely powerful number: "God has loved and blessed the number seven more than anything beneath heaven."[5] The *Sepher Yetzirah* says that God created the seven days of the week, the seven orifices of perception, seven heavens, and seven planets.[6]

The Hebrew word for luck is *gad.* This is equal to the number seven in gematria, a form of numerology in which letters have numerical values. Interestingly, *mazel,* the other Hebrew word for luck, equals 77.[7]

Seven appears in Jewish weddings, too, since there are seven wedding blessings and seven circuits of the groom. There are also seven days of festive meals after the wedding. When someone dies, there are seven days of mourning.

The menorah is the most ancient symbol of Judaism, as God revealed it to Moses. It is a seven-stemmed candleholder, and its shape represents the burning bush (Exodus 3:2–4).

The Talmud contains the Seven Laws of Noah, also known as the Noachide Laws, which are intended for all humankind. According to Jewish belief, any non-Jew who follows these laws will be considered a Righteous Gentile and be guaranteed a place in the world to come. These laws are:

1. Thou shalt not commit idolatry.
2. Thou shalt not blaspheme God's name.
3. Thou shalt not commit bloodshed.
4. Thou shalt not steal.
5. Thou shalt not commit incest or adultery.
6. Thou shalt establish courts of justice.
7. Thou shalt not eat the flesh cut from a living animal.

Seven in Hinduism

In the Hindu tradition, the world mountain has seven faces, and the sun has seven rays. The seventh ray symbolizes the power of God. Surya, the sun god, rides a chariot pulled by seven horses, each symbolizing a color, an energy, and a day of the week.

In Hinduism there are seven truths, which include living peacefully, freedom of thought, respect for nature, respect for all animals, becoming one with Brahman, and the belief that our good and bad actions will ultimately affect us.

There are seven vows or promises in a Hindu wedding. There are also seven holy cities, seven sacred places, seven sacred rivers, and seven famous battlefields.

There are fourteen worlds, or planes of existence. The Earth is the lowest of the seven higher worlds, and beneath it are seven lower worlds (underworlds or hells). When someone dies, the god of death measures the person's good and bad deeds and determines which heaven or hell the soul should go to. The god of death also determines how long the soul has to remain there before being reborn.

The seven higher worlds relate to the chakras and the seven layers of the aura.

Earth is the eighth world and is inhabited by living human beings. It relates to Muladhara (root chakra).

Bhuvarloka, the middle world of air, is the ninth world. It is inhabited by celestial beings. It relates to Svadisthana (sacral chakra).

Suvah, or heavenly world of the sky, is the tenth world. It is inhabited by devas (gods). It relates to Manipura (solar plexus chakra).

Maharloka, or world of radiant beings, is the eleventh world. It relates to Anahatha (heart chakra).

Janaloka, or world of deities, is the twelfth world. It relates to Visshudha (throat chakra).

Tapoloka, or world of pure souls, is the thirteenth world. It relates to Ajna (brow chakra).

Satyaloka, or world of truth, is the fourteenth world. It relates to Sahasrara (crown chakra).

The seven lower worlds (hells) are Atala, Vitala, Sutala, Mahatala, Tatatala, Rasatala, and Patala.

Seven in Buddhism

According to legend, Buddha took seven steps when he was born. In 477 BCE, when Buddha felt that his Nirvana was close, he went to the town of Kusinara and stood on a stone facing south. His feet left an impression on the stone. Copies of his footprints can be found in temples throughout India, China, and Japan. Seven auspicious signs were observed in his footprints, and these are called the Seven Appearances. They are the conch shell, the crown of Brahma, the diamond mace, a fish, a flower vase, a swastika, and the Wheel of the Law.

Seven in Japanese Lore

The Japanese have Seven Gods of Good Luck who bring happiness as well as good fortune. Six of the gods are men, and Benten, the goddess of music, is a woman. They are often depicted traveling on a treasure ship known as Takarabune. The Seven Gods of Good Luck give gifts to honest, worthy people every New Year.

Seven in China

The seventh month of the lunar year is known as the Ghost Month. At this time of year, the ghosts of the dead are able to return and mingle with the living. During this month, people burn paper offerings to the dead. These can depict anything; examples include paper money, paper houses, paper cars, or paper television sets. On the fifteenth day of the month, huge food festivals are held to please and placate the hungry ghosts. Any concerts held at this time contain empty seats for the ghosts to sit in. Any music played at this time is loud, as ghosts appreciate this. By the end of the month, it is hoped that all the ghosts will have returned to the underworld.

In China, young women look forward to the Feast of the Double Seventh, which occurs each year on the seventh day of the seventh lunar month. An ancient tradition says that magpies gather to form a bridge across the Milky Way, so the Weaving Maiden can visit her lover, the Cowherd. The Weaving Maiden is the patroness of unmarried women, and on this day young girls bring her various gifts and have their fortunes told, hoping that this will be the last time they have to do it. The Weaving Maiden and the Cowherd are popular subjects for Chinese artists.

There are many versions of the story of the Weaving Maiden and the Cowherd. One tells of how a young cowherd came across seven girls bathing in a pool. He took the clothing of one of the girls and hid where he could watch them. When the girls finished their swim, they clothed themselves in feathers and flew up into the sky. The one girl without clothes remained behind, and Niulang, the cowherd, discovered she was Zhinu, the seventh daughter of the Goddess of Heaven. The seven sisters had come down to earth in search of fun, as life in heaven was rather boring. Niulang and Zhinu fell in love, married, and had a son.

When the Goddess of Heaven discovered that her seventh daughter had married a mere mortal, she was furious and ordered her to return to heaven. The cowherd was devastated, until one of his cows told him to kill her and use the cow's hide to fly after her. The cowherd did this, and he and his son were reunited with Zhinu in the sky. They were so happy together that Zhinu completely forgot to carry out her daily task of weaving beautiful clouds. The Goddess of Heaven angrily scratched a line through the heavens to separate Niulang and Zhinu. This created the Milky Way. The Goddess decided they should see each other only once a month. She asked a magpie to deliver this message. Unfortunately, the magpie forgot it was once a month and told them they could meet only once a year.

Ever since then, the lovers have met on the evening of the seventh day of the seventh month in the lunar calendar. Magpies gather to create a bridge across the Milky Way. In China, this has become the annual feast day of young girls, one of the biggest events in the Chinese year.

In China, the number seven also plays an important role after someone dies. It takes up to 7 x 7 days for the person's soul to finally leave the body, as it needs to break its connection with the world and the person's family before it can move on. Every seventh day, up to and including the forty-ninth day, sacrifices and rituals are held to ensure that the soul leaves the body and makes its way into the next world.

Seven in Folklore

The Irish hero Cúchulainn had seven fingers on each hand, seven toes on each foot, and seven pupils in each eye. He was seven years old when he was given his first weapons, and his son, Connla, was seven years old when his father killed him.

According to British folklore, the Queen of the Fairies pays a tithe to Hell every seven years. Thomas the Rhymer lived in the world of the faeries for seven years.

The seventh son of a seventh son is traditionally believed to possess special powers. In Ireland, he had the gift of healing. In the United Kingdom, he possessed magical powers and a gift for divination. In Central America, it was believed he would become a werewolf.

Children's fairy tales often use the number seven as well. "Snow White and the Seven Dwarfs," "The Seven Ravens," and "Seven at One Blow" are good examples.

The Seven Wise Masters is a collection of Oriental stories dating from the tenth century. In this book, Prince Lucien returns home after receiving instruction in the seven liberal arts by seven wise masters. His astrological forecast told him that he could die if he spoke in the next seven days. One of the women of the court tried to seduce him, but was turned down. She lied to the king about this, and the prince was condemned to death. The wise masters managed to have the sentence suspended by one day. However, the spurned woman further embroidered her story, and the one-day suspension was disallowed. The wise masters appealed again and again until the seventh day, and Prince Lucien was able to tell the true story of the attempted seduction. The prince was acquitted, and the woman who had attempted to seduce him was condemned to death instead.

One of the most famous examples of the number seven in folklore appears in this traditional children's nursery rhyme:

As I was going to St. Ives
I met a man with seven wives.
Each wife had seven sacks,
Each sack had seven cats,
Each cat had seven kits:
Kits, cats, sacks, wives—
How many were going to St. Ives?

Seven as Superstition

Many craps players refuse to say the word seven while gambling, as they believe it will bring them bad luck. Instead of saying "seven," they refer to it as "the Devil" or "it."

A common superstition says that breaking a mirror will bring seven years of bad luck. This superstition dates back to Roman times. They believed that the mirror reflected the person's soul. If the mirror broke, the person's soul would be trapped inside the remains of the mirror.

The Seven Senses

"It is enough to fright you out of your seven senses."
—*François Rabelais*

"You frighten me out of my seven senses."
—*Jonathan Swift*

"Huzzaed out of my seven senses."
—*Joseph Addison*

"I am almost frightened out of my seven senses."
—*Miguel Cervantes*

The concept of seven senses dates back to the Stoics' philosophy of the soul. The Stoic school of philosophy was established in Athens in 308 BCE. The Stoics believed the soul comprised seven parts, which were housed in different parts of the body. Both Philo of Alexandria (c. 20 BCE–c. 50 CE), the Jewish theologian and philosopher, and Claudius Galen (c. 130–c. 201 CE), the Greek physician, referred to the seven parts of the soul.[8]

An ancient tradition says that the soul, or the "inward holy body," comprises seven properties, which are directed and influenced by the seven visible planets.[9] The properties are:

1. **Fire.** This animates (body movement, sense of balance).

2. **Earth.** This provides feeling.

3. **Water.** This provides speech.

4. **Air.** This provides taste.

5. **Mist.** This provides vision.

6. **Flowers.** These provide hearing.

7. **South Wind.** This provides the sense of smell.

Consequently, the seven senses are animation, feeling, speech, taste, vision, hearing, and smell. These are described in the Apocrypha as: "They received the use of the five operations of the Lord [sight, hearing, taste, smell, and feeling], and in the sixth place he imparted them understanding, and in the seventh speech, an interpreter of the cogitations thereof" (Ecclesiasticus 17:5).[10]

Seven in Numerology

Pythagoras is generally considered to be the father of numerology. He considered seven to be "the vehicle of life," as it consists of a triangle (three) and a square (four). Three and four are also considered auspicious numbers in numerology, and symbolize body and soul, spirit and matter.[11] Seven is also indivisible, which means it's not directly related to any other number between one and ten.

Over time, seven came to symbolize perfection, completeness, and spirituality. It is also the number of introspection, insight, analysis, understanding, and wisdom. In numerology, every number possesses both positive and negative qualities. The negative side of the number seven is aloofness, a critical approach, inability to express one's feelings, lack of trust, uneasiness in social situations, and a strong desire to work on one's own, with little or no input from others.

In the next chapter, we'll combine everything we've learned so far, and start working with the soul.

CHAPTER SIX

WORKING WITH YOUR SOUL

NOW IT'S TIME TO put everything we've discussed together. The first step is to look at the seven rays and determine which ray or rays you resonate to. Here is a questionnaire that will help you discover which rays you are using most in this lifetime. Answer each question with a 0 to 5. A 5 means your answer is a strong "yes," while a 0 means the question is not relevant for you in this lifetime.

Here are the questions:

1. Do you like to be in charge? 0 1 2 3 4 5

2. Are you tactful and diplomatic? 0 1 2 3 4 5

3. Do you enjoy discussing your ideas with others?
   0 1 2 3 4 5

4. Do you find it easy to help others resolve their differences? 0 1 2 3 4 5

5. Are you a clear, logical thinker? 0 1 2 3 4 5

6. Are you loyal? 0 1 2 3 4 5

7. Do you work best in a tidy, well-organized environment? 0 1 2 3 4 5

8. Are you a leader? 0 1 2 3 4 5

9. Are you sympathetic and compassionate? 0 1 2 3 4 5

10. Are you broad-minded? 0 1 2 3 4 5

11. Do you have a good imagination? 0 1 2 3 4 5

12. Did you enjoy mathematics at school? 0 1 2 3 4 5

13. Are you an optimist? 0 1 2 3 4 5

14. Do you enjoy complicated, detailed work? 0 1 2 3 4 5

15. Are you an independent thinker? 0 1 2 3 4 5

16. Are you tolerant of others? 0 1 2 3 4 5

17. Are you good at dealing with money? 0 1 2 3 4 5

18. Do you have an aesthetic sense and appreciate beauty? 0 1 2 3 4 5

19. Do you enjoy researching and analyzing? 0 1 2 3 4 5

20. When you make up your mind to do something, do you persist until you have achieved it? 0 1 2 3 4 5

21. Do you enjoy ritual and ceremony? 0 1 2 3 4 5

22. Do you have a strong sense of where you're going in your life? 0 1 2 3 4 5

23. Do you love humanity as a whole? 0 1 2 3 4 5

24. Do you enjoy analyzing problems and creating effective solutions? 0 1 2 3 4 5

25. Are you growing spiritually as you progress through life? 0 1 2 3 4 5

26. Are you a logical thinker who can put all emotions to one side while working on a problem? 0 1 2 3 4 5

27. Are you an idealist? 0 1 2 3 4 5

28. Are you able to manifest your desires? 0 1 2 3 4 5

29. Are you courageous? 0 1 2 3 4 5

30. Are you able to remain serene and worry-free when problems are occurring in your life? 0 1 2 3 4 5

31. Are you constantly full of ideas? 0 1 2 3 4 5

32. Are you able to captivate others? 0 1 2 3 4 5

33. Are you as good with your hands as you are with your mind? 0 1 2 3 4 5

34. Are you able to focus on a task and carry it all the way through to completion? 0 1 2 3 4 5

35. Do you see yourself as powerful? 0 1 2 3 4 5

36. Do you stand up for what you believe in? 0 1 2 3 4 5

37. Are you good at teaching others the skills that you possess? 0 1 2 3 4 5

38. Are you, or would you make, a good businessperson? 0 1 2 3 4 5

39. Can you express yourself well with words on paper? 0 1 2 3 4 5

40. Do you have many technical skills? 0 1 2 3 4 5

41. Do you have a strong faith? 0 1 2 3 4 5

42. Are you patient, and prepared to wait until the time is right before taking action? 0 1 2 3 4 5

Once you've completed the questionnaire, you can find out which ray or rays you are on.

Questions 1, 8, 15, 22, 29, and 36 relate to the first ray.

Questions 2, 9, 16, 23, 30, and 37 relate to the second ray.

Questions 3, 10, 17, 24, 31, and 38 relate to the third ray.

Questions 4, 11, 18, 25, 32, and 39 relate to the fourth ray.

Questions 5, 12, 19, 26, 33, and 40 relate to the fifth ray.

Questions 6, 13, 20, 27, 34, and 41 relate to the sixth ray.

Questions 7, 14, 21, 28, 35, and 42 relate to the seventh ray.

You may find that one ray is much stronger than the others. This means you are primarily on this ray.

You may find that two or three rays are all stronger than the others. This shows that you are learning the lessons of these rays in this lifetime.

It's possible for all the rays to be approximately equal in strength. This is unusual, but it can happen. If this occurs, read the descriptions of the seven rays in chapter 3 to see if you can determine which is the strongest and consequently your primary ray.

Other Ways to Determine Your Ray

There are several other ways to determine your personal soul ray(s).

Occupation

Your choice of occupation can frequently give you a clue as to your personal ray. This is especially the case if you've always been attracted to a certain type of career. This applies even if you are not currently engaged in that particular career. The armed forces, for instance, are listed under the first ray. If you always wanted to be in the army, navy, or air force, but circumstances prevented you from following this career, it may still indicate that you are a first ray person.

First Ray
Armed forces
Police
Security
Politics
Leader
Entrepreneur

Second Ray
Teacher
Healing professions

Mentor
Philanthropist
Researcher

Third Ray
Philosopher
Economist
Businessperson
Judge
Scholar
Astrologer
Organizer
Banker

Fourth Ray
Mediator
Psychologist
Artist
Musician
Writer
Architect

Fifth Ray
Scientist
Lawyer
Engineer
Inventor
Researcher
Mathematician

Sixth Ray

Evangelist
Missionary
Mystic
Orator
Zealot

Seventh Ray

Administrator
Builder
Producer
Politician
Designer
Magician
Priest

Problem Solving

People on different rays resolve their problems in specific ways.

First Ray

Force
Willpower
Giving orders
Overpowering opposition
Making decisions with little input from others

Second Ray

Negotiation
Intuition

Gentle persuasion
Nonresistance
Creating empathy

Third Ray
Logic
Creating a plan of action
Lengthy thought and analysis
Adaptability
Strategy
Ability with words

Fourth Ray
Charm
Captivating others
Dramatizing the situation
Creating an illusion of vulnerability
Creating harmony
Reconciling the situation

Fifth Ray
Research
Scientific approach
Observation and analysis
Patient review of the facts
Experimentation
Slow, deliberate thought

Sixth Ray

Single-mindedness

Spiritual guidance

Ability to inspire and persuade others

Sacrificial approach

Seventh Ray

Finely tuned, deliberate approach

Good organization

Highly detailed approach

Ability to create order

Magic

Negative Qualities

Everyone possesses a mixture of positive and negative qualities. People who are not living up to their full potential frequently exhibit more of their negative, rather than their positive, potential. Many people fail to recognize their negative traits. If this applies to you, then you may need to ask a friend to help you determine your negative qualities. If you feel you can do this on your own, your negative traits will provide information as to the particular ray or rays you happen to be on in this lifetime.

First Ray

Arrogance

Pride

Impatience

Selfishness

Egotism
Extravagance
Rigidity and obstinacy
Stubbornness
Domination

Second Ray

Impracticality
Unassertiveness
Overprotectiveness
Fearfulness
Inferiority complex
Sentimentality
Self-pity
Self-sacrificing

Third Ray

Indecision
Aloofness
Cunning
Deceit
Cruelty
Opportunism
Overly critical
Carelessness
Dishonesty

Fourth Ray

Lack of confidence
Excessive worry

Rapidly changing moods
Self-indulgence
Impracticality
Moral cowardice
Lack of motivation
Frequent inner conflict

Fifth Ray

Self-centeredness
Critical
Pedantic
Materialism
Coldness
Skepticism
Prejudice
Uneasy in social situation

Sixth Ray

Impulsiveness
Intolerance
Fanaticism
Overly dependent
Overly idealistic
Inability to adapt
Gullibility
Low self-esteem

Seventh Ray

Materialism
Regimentation

Extravagance
Pomposity
Need to conform
Intolerance
Perfectionism

Purpose of the Soul

The soul is guided by the interests and qualities of the particular ray, or rays, it is using in this lifetime. Each soul is different, of course, but here are the main desires and potentials of souls that work with specific rays. If your soul is working on two or more rays, then you'll have to read the potentials of each one.

First Ray Soul Purpose

The purpose of first ray souls is to provide leadership, motivation, and strength to others. These souls work for the benefit of humanity as a whole. They are benevolent, generous, steadfast, and firm when necessary. These souls have enormous vision and are usually concerned with the overall picture rather than the details. Consequently, they sometimes appear detached and unconcerned about problems that other souls consider important. They enjoy freedom and hate being constricted or limited in any way. They have a strong connection with the Divine and constantly strive to uphold spiritual ideals and principles. Their greatest desire is to carry out divine will in this incarnation. Although the latent talents of first ray souls are obvious to everyone who knows them, few of them achieve anywhere near their full potential.

Second Ray Soul Purpose

The purpose of second ray souls is to serve, counsel, teach, and advise others. These souls possess a deep love of human-kind and work hard to help others grow and achieve their full potential. These souls are selfless and tend to put other souls first. As second ray souls work best when helping others, they are frequently found in people who work in humanitarian-type careers. They almost always work best in a partnership, and seek the love, comfort, and security of marriage and friendship, as this gives them security as well as a good base to work from. Second ray souls instinctively sense that all humanity is connected, and we should all love one another. They also have a powerful love for the Divine and enjoy a strong connection with the source of all life.

Third Ray Soul Purpose

The purpose of third ray souls is to encourage the creativity and intellect of others. They enjoy helping people raise their sights and realize what they are truly capable of. These souls gain enormous satisfaction from creating and participating in actions that are in keeping with the divine plan. Third ray souls solve their problems using reason, logic, and analy-sis. Despite working according to a plan, third ray souls are flexible and adaptable and fit in easily with others. Their greatest satisfaction frequently comes from the sheer joy of thinking about a problem and coming up with a good, practical solution. Despite this strong love of logic, third ray souls still have a strong sense of the sacred and desire a closer connection with the Divine.

Fourth Ray Soul Purpose

The purpose of fourth ray souls is to create harmony and unity in the world. These souls enjoy bringing peace and happiness into the lives of others. They are selfless, loving, altruistic, compassionate, and tolerant. They find it easy to fit in and relate well with others, as they take people as they find them. They are able to see both sides of a situation and can empathize with everyone concerned. All souls can speak through the person's conscience, but fourth ray souls seem to do this more effectively than souls on other rays. Fourth ray souls have a strong sense of beauty and try to create it in everything they do. They possess a strong sense of the sacred and see the presence of the Divine in everything that is beautiful, peaceful, and meaningful.

Fifth Ray Soul Purpose

The purpose of fifth ray souls is to make good use of innovation and technology to improve the lives of all humanity. They can lose themselves in scientific and technical research, as they have total faith in their ability to use their inventions and discoveries for the benefit of others. They are happiest when they make a new discovery or experience a revelation as a result of their intellect. They enjoy problems, because they see them as challenges that can be resolved scientifically. They also gain enormous pleasure as a result of successfully solving them. They are fascinated with the mysteries of the world, and hope to be involved in deciphering them. They constantly see the Divine in the wondrous and beautiful natural world. These souls live by the concept that "the world is my church, and life is my prayer."

Sixth Ray Soul Purpose

The purpose of the sixth ray soul is to selflessly inspire and motivate others to live up to their greatest potential. These souls are idealistic and altruistic and possess a great love for humanity. Because they are so idealistic, they refuse to accept anything less than perfection. Sixth ray souls are enthusiastic and encouraging and derive great satisfaction from the success of others. They express their love freely and are devoted to the recipients of their love and friendship. Even if they don't receive love and friendship in return, they still place the objects of their devotion on a figurative pedestal, where they can admire and love them.

Seventh Ray Soul Purpose

The purpose of the seventh ray soul is to help others organize and manage their own lives more effectively. This helps them gain vision and clarity, and they become much more successful as a result. Seventh ray souls are selfless. They invariably play an important role inside groups, teams, and organizations, where their selflessness enables them to work for the benefit of everyone in the group. They respect and value others and treat them with courtesy, friendship, and love. Seventh ray souls gently direct others to become aware of their spiritual nature and to always do what is right. Seventh ray souls enjoy establishing and maintaining system and order, as they are naturally tidy and well organized.

How to Experience the Rays

The following meditations will help you become attuned to the energies of the different rays. Start with the ray that resonates most with you before experimenting with the others.

Relaxation Exercise

You need to be in a quiet, meditative state before you can experience the energies of the different rays. Set aside at least thirty minutes of time during which you will not be disturbed. Make sure the room you are in is pleasantly warm, and wear comfortable, loose-fitting clothes. Make yourself as comfortable as possible. You might like to do this progressive relaxation exercise in a recliner chair, or perhaps lying on the floor. I find it difficult to perform these exercises while lying in or on a bed, as I tend to fall asleep. Consequently, although you need to be warm and comfortable, you don't want to be so relaxed that you drift off to sleep. Temporarily disconnect the phone to avoid being disturbed during the exercise.

Take three slow, deep breaths, holding each breath for a few seconds before exhaling. Close your eyes and allow your body to relax. Become aware of your breathing, and notice how each breath helps you to relax. Focus on your eyes, and allow the fine muscles around your eyes to relax.

Once you have done this, focus on your left foot, and allow the toes on this foot to relax. You may feel a tingling sensation in your toes as you do this. Once your toes are relaxed, allow the pleasant feeling of relaxation to gradually spread throughout your foot, until your entire left foot is relaxed.

Repeat this with your right foot, until both feet are completely relaxed. Focus on your left foot again, and allow the feeling of relaxation to drift upwards, over your ankle and into your calf muscles. Allow the relaxation to drift over your knee and into your thigh. Once you feel your entire left leg is totally relaxed, repeat the process with your right leg.

Both of your legs should now be completely relaxed. Allow the relaxation to drift into your abdomen, your chest, and into your shoulders.

Focus your attention on your left arm, and allow the relaxation to drift down your arm and into your hand and fingers. Repeat with the right arm.

Allow the relaxation to drift into your neck, your face, and all the way up to the top of your head. Focus on your eyes again, and let them relax as much as you possibly can.

Finally, mentally scan your entire body to make sure that every part is completely relaxed. If you find any areas of tension, gently focus your attention on the tension until it dissolves.

You are now completely relaxed, and every muscle in your body is loose and limp. Everyone is different. Some people find it easy to relax, while others need more time. It's not a race, and it doesn't matter how long it takes to relax your body. Although I can now become completely relaxed in a matter of seconds, I usually prefer to take several minutes to complete the process, as I enjoy the sensation of relaxation slowly drifting through my body.

If you haven't performed a progressive relaxation exercise before, you might want to practice this a few times before moving on to the next stage of experiencing the energies of each ray. If you want to finish at this point, for any reason, all you need do is tell yourself that you're returning to your everyday life on the count of five. Slowly count from one to five, open your eyes, and allow yourself to become familiar with your environment again. When you feel ready, get up and carry on with your day. Have something to eat and drink before returning to your everyday tasks. I have a glass of water and a few raw almonds. Although you can return to conscious awareness by simply counting from one to five, you might want to add a few words as well, perhaps along these lines:

"One. Gaining energy and feeling fine. Two. Feeling good about every aspect of my life. Three. Becoming familiar with my surroundings. Four. Almost back. And five. Eyes opening and feeling great."

If you are continuing with the exercise, here are the scripts for exploring the seven rays.

Experiencing the First Ray

"In this nice, calm, peaceful, relaxed state, I can achieve anything I set my mind to, and in this session I'm going to become closer to my soul. I'm going to become aware of my own spiritual energies by experiencing the energies of the seven rays that emanate from the Divine [use whatever word feels right for you, such as God, the universal life force, the Ultimate, Creator, Mother, Father, and so on].

"In this meditation I'm going to feel the energies of the first ray, the Ray of Power and Will. I'll start by experiencing the power and incredible energy of my own personal life force. [Pause, and visualize or imagine your own personal life force. Become aware of it in every cell of your body.] I feel this life force reaching out and connecting with the Divine, enabling me to gain insights into my true purpose in this lifetime. I sense myself moving steadily forward. I'm doing it with greater and greater confidence now as my focus becomes clearer.

"I sense myself working for the greater good of all humankind, working in accord with my divine purpose to further my evolution and growth.

"I feel myself developing the necessary confidence to inspire, motivate, lead, and direct others, to help them find their own path to the Divine. I sense the strength and courage I have deep within to do what is right, to seek what is worthwhile, and to uphold what is true and good.

"I see myself coming up with good ideas, experimenting with new and different concepts, and being prepared to start something new. I feel strong, bold, and unafraid. I feel independent and ready for anything.

"I'm aware of a sense of unbelievable strength that helps me to achieve everything I want to accomplish in this lifetime. I experience physical strength [pause for a couple seconds], mental strength [pause for a couple seconds], and spiritual strength [pause for a couple seconds].

"I have unlimited energy and am aiming higher now, higher than ever before. I will achieve my goals, and the results will be positive for everyone concerned.

"I feel restored, revitalized, and motivated as a result of spending time with the first ray. I'm excited that I can bask in the energies of the first ray whenever I wish. [Pause for as long as you wish.]

"And now it's time to return to my everyday life. I'll open my eyes on the count of five, feeling stimulated and energized. One. Gaining energy and feeling fine. Two. Becoming aware of my surroundings. Three. Gradually returning. Four. Feeling ready for anything. And five. Eyes opening and feeling wonderful."

Experiencing the Second Ray

"In this nice, calm, peaceful, relaxed state, I can achieve anything I set my mind to, and in this session I'm going to become closer to my soul. I'm going to become aware of my own spiritual energies by experiencing the energies of the seven rays that emanate from the Divine [use whatever word feels right for you, such as God, the universal life force, the Ultimate, Creator, Mother, Father, and so on].

"In this meditation I'm going to experience the energies of the second ray, the Ray of Love-Wisdom. I allow myself to become totally surrounded with loving energy from the universe. I feel every cell of my body becoming filled with pure, divine love. And in this nice, peaceful, relaxed state, I consciously let go of all negativity and allow myself to relax completely in this ocean of love.

"I see myself becoming energized. My love for the universe is apparent in everything I do. I'm ready and willing to help others who need love and a helping hand. My love spreads further and further every day as I give and receive radiant love. I am sensitive and compassionate. I can now understand and feel the joy and suffering of others.

"As I'm surrounded with love, I look at life in a different way now. I'm gaining knowledge and wisdom. I understand at a deeper level than ever before. This understanding enables me to see the essentials of any situation. I can hone in on problems and resolve them using the unlimited energies of understanding, wisdom, and love.

"My intuition is growing and expanding. I can sense the immortal soul in everyone I meet, and I love each and every soul.

"I'm developing patience and moving forward in a steady, gradual, easy fashion. Nothing bothers or disturbs me, as I am calm and serene in every type of situation.

"I feel happy and contented with my progress as a result of spending time with the second ray. I know that I'm developing in exactly the way I should be. It's comforting to know I can bask in the energies of the second ray whenever I wish. [Pause for as long as you wish.]

"And now it's time to return to my everyday life. I'll open my eyes on the count of five, feeling stimulated and energized. One. Gaining energy and feeling fine. Two. Becoming aware of my surroundings. Three. Gradually returning. Four. Feeling ready for anything. And five. Eyes opening and feeling wonderful."

Experiencing the Third Ray

"In this nice, calm, peaceful, relaxed state, I can achieve anything I set my mind to, and in this session I'm going to become closer to my soul. I'm going to become aware of my own spiritual energies by experiencing the energies of the seven rays that emanate from the Divine [use whatever word feels right for you, such as God, the universal life force, the Ultimate, Creator, Mother, Father, and so on].

"In this meditation I'm going to experience the energies of the third ray, the Ray of Active Intelligence. I focus on my powerful mind, and everything it does for me. I appreciate my ability to reason and assess, to focus on problems and resolve them analytically, to think thoughts, both great and small, and to create in my mind anything and everything I desire.

"I see myself communicating with others, expressing myself well, grateful for my ability to express my thoughts in conversation as well as in words on paper. I picture myself using my mind and ability to communicate with others in all sorts of situations, such as making plans, expressing my views, directing others, and helping worthwhile causes.

"I visualize myself thinking and acting quickly, even when under pressure. I can handle complex situations and problems effectively because I detach myself from all emotion and work logically and rationally. I enjoy being busy, and my mind can work on several matters simultaneously. I want to know exactly what's going on, in any situation I find myself in.

"I change quickly when situations and circumstances change. I'm adaptable, flexible, and quick to act.

"I handle money well and enjoy being generous with what I have. I have the ability to make more money than I need, as I enjoy helping others who are less fortunate than I am.

"I am economical and try to achieve as much as possible, with as little as possible. I enjoy achieving good results efficiently and economically.

"I am satisfied with my progress as a result of spending time with the third ray. I know I'm learning, growing, and developing in exactly the way I should be. It's comforting to know I can enjoy spending time basking in the energies of the third ray whenever I wish. [Pause for as long as you wish.]

"And now it's time to return to my everyday life. I'll open my eyes on the count of five, feeling stimulated and energized. One. Gaining energy and feeling fine. Two. Becoming aware of my surroundings. Three. Gradually returning. Four. Feeling ready for anything. And five. Eyes opening and feeling wonderful."

Experiencing the Fourth Ray

"In this nice, calm, peaceful, relaxed state, I can achieve anything I set my mind to, and in this session I'm going to become closer to my soul. I'm going to become aware of my own spiritual energies by experiencing the energies of the seven rays that emanate from the Divine [use whatever word feels right for you, such as God, the universal life force, the Ultimate, Creator, Mother, Father, and so on].

"In this meditation I'm going to experience the energies of the fourth ray, the Ray of Harmony, Beauty, and Art. I realize everyone on this planet experiences conflict from time to time. Even though I know and experience this, I remain focused on harmony and unity.

"No matter what situation I find myself in, I continue to grow and develop spiritually. I learn through struggles, crises, setbacks, and occasional disappointments. I experience personal growth in my body, mind, and soul every time these occur.

"I have the ability to create harmony where there was discord before. I can resolve long-standing difficulties and can reconcile people who are unable to reach an agreement on their own.

"I can see both sides of every situation and have the ability to mediate and facilitate resolutions where there was previously conflict and disharmony.

"I keep my feet firmly on the ground and utilize a practical approach that creates harmony and beauty everywhere I go.

"I have a strong aesthetic sense and enjoy living and working in attractive surroundings. I have a good imagination and use it to create beauty in my environment.

"I gain pleasure and satisfaction from using my creative abilities. I have a strong sense of color and harmony, which could be harnessed into art or music, if I wish. I enjoy writing, and this gives my imagination plenty of room to create good ideas and record them on paper.

"I am naturally intuitive and rely on my hunches and feelings to resolve difficulties and achieve my goals.

"I enjoy entertaining and amusing others with my sense of humor and my unique approach to life. I am spontaneous and sometimes surprise people with what I say and do.

"My greatest pleasure comes from creating peace and harmony in the world I live in.

"I am satisfied with my progress as a result of spending time with the fourth ray. I know I'm learning to handle conflict, so I can reconcile and balance not only my life but also the lives of others. I gain strength and satisfaction whenever I spend time inside the energies of the fourth ray. [Pause for as long as you wish.]

"And now it's time to return to my everyday life. I'll open my eyes on the count of five, feeling stimulated and energized. One. Gaining energy and feeling fine. Two. Becoming aware of my surroundings. Three. Gradually returning. Four. Feeling ready for anything. And five. Eyes opening and feeling wonderful."

Experiencing the Fifth Ray

"In this nice, calm, peaceful, relaxed state, I can achieve anything I set my mind to, and in this session I'm going to become closer to my soul. I'm going to become aware of my own spiritual energies by experiencing the energies of the seven rays that emanate from the Divine [use whatever word feels right for you, such as God, the universal life force, the Ultimate, Creator, Mother, Father, and so on].

"In this meditation I'm going to experience the energies of the fifth ray, the Ray of Concrete Knowledge and Science. This gives me the ability to look at situations in a logical and rational manner. I can analyze, dissect, and think deeply, to gain knowledge and wisdom. I can focus on a problem and resolve it using clarity, insight, and practical common sense.

"My mind is so strong and powerful that I can think of something and immediately create an effective plan to turn it into a reality. I enjoy the accuracy and detail that are necessary to make this happen.

"I enjoy getting below the surface of things to work out the true situation that is hidden beneath. I take little at face value, preferring to make up my own mind after analyzing the situation thoroughly.

"I am detached when necessary. I can think calmly and rationally, without involving my emotions in the process.

"I am inquisitive and have a strong sense of curiosity. I enjoy finding answers by asking questions and investigating. I enjoy research and am persistent and rigorous until I find the answers I'm seeking. I take little on trust, preferring to verify the truth in my own time and in my own way.

"I enjoy technology and love keeping up with all the latest advances in the fields I enjoy. I am practical and prefer a hands-on approach.

"I enjoy explaining what I've learned to others, and gain satisfaction when they understand my ideas, take them on board, and start working with them.

"I am satisfied with my progress as a result of spending time with the fifth ray. I know my rigorous scientific approach enhances not only my life but also the lives of others. I gain confirmation and satisfaction whenever I spend time inside the energies of the fifth ray. [Pause for as long as you wish.]

"And now it's time to return to my everyday life. I'll open my eyes on the count of five, feeling stimulated and energized. One. Gaining energy and feeling fine. Two. Becoming aware of my surroundings. Three. Gradually returning. Four. Feeling ready for anything. And five. Eyes opening and feeling wonderful."

Experiencing the Sixth Ray

"In this nice, calm, peaceful, relaxed state, I can achieve anything I set my mind to, and in this session I'm going to become closer to my soul. I'm going to become aware of my own spiritual energies by experiencing the energies of the seven rays that emanate from the Divine [use whatever word feels right for you, such as God, the universal life force, the Ultimate, Creator, Mother, Father, and so on].

"In this meditation I'm going to experience the energies of the sixth ray, the Ray of Devotion and Idealism. I have the ability to transcend my everyday world and spend time communing with the Divine. My devotion has no bounds. Although I'm frequently let down and hurt, my idealism, faith, and optimism keep me moving forward.

"I have a strong vision of what the world should be like, and I focus on the possibilities and potentials rather than the limitations.

"I focus clearly on what I desire and pursue my goals with persistence and determination. Nothing can distract me once I've made up my mind to do something.

"I am loyal to others, and once I've made a friend, this loyalty becomes an integral part of the relationship. I am sincere, honest, and open with my friends. They know they can rely on me whenever necessary, and I value their belief in my willingness to help.

"I have good self-esteem but remain humble, as I have the ability to see myself exactly as I am.

"I have the ability to inspire and motivate others. I am a natural enthusiast and have the ability to sell my ideas to others. I have the potential to be a powerful force for good, especially in spiritual matters.

"I constantly endeavor to develop spiritually and to gain a closer connection with the Divine. When it comes to important matters, I seek divine help and guidance. This plays an increasingly important role in my life.

"In all ways I try to be good, honorable, kind, devoted, and loving.

"I am satisfied with my progress as a result of spending time with the sixth ray. My idealistic approach and love for all humanity enhance not only my life but also the lives of others. I gain spiritual comfort whenever I spend time inside the energies of the sixth ray. [Pause for as long as you wish.]

"And now it's time to return to my everyday life. I'll open my eyes on the count of five, feeling stimulated and energized. One. Gaining energy and feeling fine. Two. Becoming aware of my surroundings. Three. Gradually returning. Four. Feeling ready for anything. And five. Eyes opening and feeling wonderful."

Experiencing the Seventh Ray

"In this nice, calm, peaceful, relaxed state, I can achieve anything I set my mind to, and in this session I'm going to become closer to my soul. I'm going to become aware of my own spiritual energies by experiencing the energies of the seven rays that emanate from the Divine [use whatever word feels right for you, such as God, the universal life force, the Ultimate, Creator, Mother, Father, and so on].

"In this meditation I'm going to experience the energies of the seventh ray, the Ray of Order and Ceremonial Magic. I know I have the ability to create and maintain system and order. I sense a divine plan that is perfect in every way, and although this is far beyond the ability of humankind to see, let alone understand, I feel a faint glimmering of its system and order.

"I have the potential to achieve anything I set my mind to in this incarnation. With the help of the Divine, I can manifest anything I desire, and I'm prepared to do whatever it takes to achieve it. I desire success on a large scale.

"I enjoy structured activities, regular routines, and rituals that help me achieve my goals. I work well with groups of like-minded people, and enjoy rituals and ceremonies that bring us closer together.

"I am a good organizer. I can communicate my ideas to others, handle the details, manage, delegate, and motivate. I am patient and realize that some things need time to incubate before they can be manifested.

"I am growing and developing as a result of spending time with the seventh ray. My personal power and ability to make good use of system and order enhance not only my life but also the lives of others. I gain strength and power whenever I spend time inside the energies of the seventh ray. [Pause for as long as you wish.]

"And now it's time to return to my everyday life. I'll open my eyes on the count of five, feeling stimulated and energized. One. Gaining energy and feeling fine. Two. Becoming aware of my surroundings. Three. Gradually returning. Four. Feeling ready for anything. And five. Eyes opening and feeling wonderful."

You might feel that friends or acquaintances are experiencing more interesting or important rays than you. This is not the case, as no ray is better than any other, and all seven rays are equally important. The particular ray you happen to be on indicates the lessons and experiences you need to learn in this lifetime.

In the next chapter we'll see how the seven rays work with each chakra.

CHAPTER SEVEN

LAYERS OF THE SOUL

THE RAYS ENTER THE physical body and have an energizing, life-giving effect on every cell. They also have a profound effect on the layers of the aura (the subtle body), especially the chakras. Each ray influences and affects each chakra. In effect, each ray splits into seven parts, one part for each chakra. These can be considered layers of the soul.

The chakras are the energy centers inside the subtle body that receive the energies of the universal life force from the particular ray and then distribute these energies around the body.

No one knows how the universal life force enters the body. As a teenager, I was taught that it entered the body through the crown chakra (at the top of the head) and filtered down to the other chakras through the nadi system that connects them. However, there are other possibilities. In her book *The Complete Book of Chakra Healing*, Cyndi Dale suggests that each ray enters the body in a particular place. The first ray enters through the coccyx, for instance, and the second ray enters through the third eye/forehead.[1] Other people suggest that the rays enter the body through the chakra that relates best to each ray. If this is the case, then the rays enter the body through these chakras:

First ray: Crown chakra

Second ray: Heart chakra

Third ray: Throat chakra

Fourth ray: Root chakra

Fifth ray: Brow chakra

Sixth ray: Solar plexus chakra

Seventh ray: Sacral chakra

How the First Ray Stimulates the Seven Chakras

The first ray is the Ray of Power and Will. It relates strongly to the crown chakra. The positive qualities of this ray are courage, strength, honesty, and leadership.

The root chakra is concerned with survival and the will to live. This includes eating the right foods, exercising, sleeping, and even earning money. The root chakra grounds, or "roots," us to the earth. It provides feelings of security and comfort. The positive qualities of the first ray help the root chakra perform its functions, as they help it feel safe and secure.

The sacral chakra is concerned with creativity, sexuality, and emotional balance. The positive qualities of the first ray enhance the sacral chakra's potential in all of these areas.

The solar plexus chakra is concerned with will, power, and strength. These are all qualities shared with the first ray, which is able to add extra power if and when required.

The heart chakra is concerned with compassion, love, and relationships. The first ray adds steadfastness, honesty, and open-mindedness to enhance the positive qualities provided by a balanced heart chakra.

The throat chakra is concerned with communication, self-expression, and creativity. The first ray enables the throat chakra to speak the truth in a confident, fearless manner.

The brow chakra is concerned with the mind as well as intuitive and spiritual matters. The first ray enables the brow chakra to develop intuitive and spiritual insights and look toward the future with confidence.

The crown chakra is concerned with our spirituality and connection with the Divine. The courage, honesty, and strength of the first ray harmonizes well with the purity of the crown chakra, and helps it to grow in knowledge, wisdom, and understanding of the interconnectedness of all life.

How the Second Ray Stimulates the Seven Chakras

The second ray is the Ray of Love-Wisdom. It relates strongly to the heart chakra. The positive qualities of this ray are calmness, patience, endurance, serenity, intuition, and a love of the truth.

The root chakra is concerned with grounding, solidity, and survival. All the positive qualities of the second ray have a positive effect on the root chakra, enabling it to perform its functions with serenity, calmness, and patience.

The sacral chakra is concerned with pleasure, emotional balance, and sexuality. The second ray aids this chakra by providing patience, when necessary, as well as calmness and serenity.

The solar plexus chakra is concerned with will, power, and strength. The second ray can soften any potential aggressiveness and domination by providing calmness, cooperation, and a sympathetic approach.

The heart chakra is concerned with compassion, balance, love, and relationships. The wisdom and love of the second ray harmonizes perfectly with the energies of the heart chakra.

The throat chakra is concerned with communication, self-expression, and creativity. The insight, wisdom, sympathy, and universal love provided by the second ray are all expressed effectively when combined with the throat chakra.

The brow chakra is concerned with intuition, clairvoyance, and the powers of the mind. The second ray is concerned with intuition, too, and also adds qualities of philanthropy, sympathy, understanding, and universal love.

The crown chakra is our connection to the Divine. This harmonizes perfectly with the second ray qualities of humanitarianism, philanthropy, intuition, wisdom, and spirituality.

How the Third Ray Stimulates the Seven Chakras

The third ray is the Ray of Active Intelligence. It relates strongly to the throat chakra. The positive qualities of this ray are a powerful and creative mind, the ability to see the overall picture as well as the details, good communication skills, adaptability, and financial and business acumen.

The root chakra is concerned with grounding, solidity, and survival. All the positive qualities of the third ray have a powerful effect on the root chakra, enabling it to keep the person grounded while at the same time seeing greater opportunities that can be achieved with the unlimited potential of the mind.

The sacral chakra is concerned with pleasure, emotional balance, and sexuality. The third ray aids this chakra by providing adaptability, creativity, and good communication skills. These all help the sacral chakra to realize its potential, too.

The solar plexus chakra is concerned with will, power, and strength. The third ray aids this chakra by adding the qualities of adaptability, abstract thinking, and a powerful mind. These both soften and strengthen the direct approach of this chakra.

The heart chakra is involved with compassion, balance, love, and relationships. These qualities are considerably enhanced by the good mind and excellent communication skills provided by the third ray.

The throat chakra is concerned with communication, self-expression, and creativity. These are all major characteristics of the third ray. All these qualities are all considerably enhanced by this combination.

The brow chakra is concerned with intuition, clairvoyance, and the powers of the mind. These enhance the creative potential of the third ray. The communication skills provided by the third ray enable the person to express his or her intuitive experiences.

The crown chakra is our connection to the Divine. The qualities of the third ray enable the person to enjoy an even closer relationship with the universal life force.

How the Fourth Ray Stimulates the Seven Chakras

The fourth ray is the Ray of Harmony, Beauty, and Art. This ray relates most strongly to the root chakra. The positive qualities of this ray are the ability to reconcile situations and achieve harmony through conflict, artistic and creative potential, and the ability to captivate and entertain others.

The root chakra is concerned with grounding, solidity, and survival. This chakra provides confidence and persistence to people on the fourth ray. This solid foundation also enables them to develop their creativity and people skills.

The sacral chakra is concerned with pleasure, emotional balance, and sexuality. All of these qualities are enhanced by the ability of fourth ray people to harmonize difficult situations and to get on well with others.

The solar plexus chakra is concerned with will, power, and strength. The people skills of the fourth ray enable the solar plexus chakra to express itself more diplomatically and with concern for the well-being of others.

The heart chakra is involved with compassion, balance, love, and relationships. The innate harmony and cooperation provided by the fourth ray enhance all of these qualities.

The throat chakra is concerned with communication, self-expression, and creativity. The people skills, creativity, and aesthetic approach of the fourth ray enhance the communication and self-expression skills of the throat chakra.

The brow chakra is concerned with intuition, clairvoyance, and the powers of the mind. The beauty and harmony expressed by the fourth ray enhance the intuitive qualities of the brow chakra.

The crown chakra is our connection to the Divine. The ability of the fourth ray to grow spiritually through difficulties enhances this connection. The fourth ray's strong aesthetic sense enables the crown chakra to see spirituality in all creation.

How the Fifth Ray Stimulates the Seven Chakras

The fifth ray is the Ray of Concrete Knowledge and Science. It relates strongly to the brow chakra. The positive qualities of this ray are its common sense, powerful intellect, and ability to objectively analyze, discriminate, and assess information in a clear yet detached manner.

The root chakra is concerned with grounding, solidity, and survival. The practical, objective, and precise qualities of the fifth ray enhance the ability of the root chakra not only to survive but to expand and grow.

The sacral chakra is concerned with pleasure, emotional balance, and sexuality. The analytical approach of the fifth ray enhances the sacral chakra's potential for emotional balance.

The solar plexus chakra is concerned with will, power, and strength. The insight, technical capabilities, and commonsense approach of the fifth ray enhance all of the qualities of the solar plexus chakra.

The heart chakra is involved with compassion, balance, love, and relationships. The scientific, analytical approach of the fifth ray enables the heart chakra to remain balanced while expressing love and compassion.

The throat chakra is concerned with communication, self-expression, and creativity. The powerful, discriminating intellect provided by the fifth ray enhances the potential of the throat chakra for creativity and self-expression.

The brow chakra is concerned with intuition, clairvoyance, and the powers of the mind. The powerful intellect and down-to-earth approach of the fifth ray enable the brow chakra to develop its intuition in a balanced, impartial manner.

The crown chakra is our connection to the Divine. The clear, focused, investigative intellect provided by the fifth ray enhances the crown chakra's connection with the universal life force.

How the Sixth Ray
Stimulates the Seven Chakras

The sixth ray is the Ray of Devotion and Idealism. It relates strongly to the solar plexus chakra. The positive qualities of this ray are humility, sincerity, loyalty, idealism, and a strong faith.

The root chakra is concerned with grounding, solidity, and survival. The solidity and grounding of the root chakra are considerably enhanced by the sincere, loyal, humble, and idealistic qualities of the sixth ray. The strong faith provided by this ray is also enhanced by the solidity and grounding effect of the root chakra.

The sacral chakra is concerned with pleasure, emotional balance, and sexuality. The qualities provided by the sixth ray enhance the emotional balance, pleasure, and sexuality of this chakra.

The solar plexus chakra is concerned with will, power, and strength. The idealism, love, and devotion of the sixth ray balance and harmonize the strength, will, and power of the solar plexus chakra, creating a powerful combination. The unyielding persistence of the sixth ray further strengthens this combination.

The heart chakra is involved with compassion, balance, love, and relationships. The idealism and devotion of the sixth ray harmonize perfectly with the energies of the heart chakra.

The throat chakra is concerned with communication, self-expression, and creativity. The sixth ray energies allow the throat chakra to express itself with humility, idealism, love, and devotion.

The brow chakra is concerned with intuition, clairvoyance, and the powers of the mind. The idealism and love of the sixth ray enable the brow chakra to develop and grow in spirituality and wisdom.

The crown chakra is our connection to the Divine. The humility, idealism, and devotion of the sixth ray enhance and strengthen the connection with the Divine. The persistence of the sixth ray helps in this regard, too.

How the Seventh Ray Stimulates the Seven Chakras

The seventh ray is the Ray of Order and Ceremonial Magic. It relates strongly to the sacral chakra. The main quality of this ray is the energy it has to create order. It can plan, organize, pay attention to details, motivate, and manifest whatever it desires.

The root chakra is concerned with grounding, solidity, and survival. The energy and power of the seventh ray motivate and stimulate the root chakra to help it achieve its goals.

The sacral chakra is concerned with pleasure, emotional balance, and sexuality. This is the chakra that relates to the seventh ray, and it uses the energy this ray provides to organize its activities, scheduling time for pleasure as well as hard work.

The solar plexus chakra is concerned with will, power, and strength. This harmonizes well with the seventh ray's practicality and ability to organize, manage, and achieve its goals.

The heart chakra is involved with compassion, balance, love, and relationships. These qualities help the seventh ray achieve order. The organizational skills provided by the seventh ray help the heart chakra achieve harmony and balance in its relationships.

The throat chakra is concerned with communication, self-expression, and creativity. All of these qualities help the seventh ray to create and maintain system and order. The communication skills of the throat chakra enable the seventh ray to express its needs to coordinate, manage, and motivate others.

The brow chakra is concerned with intuition, clairvoyance, and the powers of the mind. The practicality, power, and reasoning ability of the seventh ray broadens and balances the intuition and psychic potential of the brow chakra. This is a powerful combination, as answers can be provided by both logic and intuition.

The crown chakra is our connection to the Divine. The seventh ray has a close connection with the ultimate life force, too, and this enables the ray to use its soul nature to manifest its goals on the physical plane. This is a form of white, or good, magic. This is why the seventh ray is called the Ray of Order and Ceremonial Magic.

A Day with Your Soul

This exercise will help you learn more about your chakras and your soul. You will also gain a closer connection with the Divine.

You will need to set aside some time on your own for this exercise. A whole day would be ideal, but if you can't spare that amount of time, set aside as much time as possible. You can do a great deal in a single hour if that is all the time you have.

If you're going to spend more than an hour on this exercise, you'll need to prepare some food and drink. Choose good, healthy, nourishing food. Pick at least one thing to eat that you consider expensive or a luxury. This could be considered a treat or an extravagance. This will enable you to nurture your body as part of the exercise. You might also like to pack some small snacks, such as raw, unsalted nuts, raisins, and fruit.

The drinks can be anything except for alcohol and soda. Water is the best choice, but you might like to take tea, coffee, or some other beverage with you.

You will also need pen and paper, or some other method to record your experiences.

You should also set an intention for the day. This can be as brief or as long as you wish. Your intention might be to gain a greater connection with the Divine. You might ask to feel the presence of God in your everyday life. You might ask for some indication that you're moving in the right direction. It's a good idea to think about your intention a few days, or a week, before your special day. Write it down and keep it with you, as you may want to enlarge or amend it as different ideas occur to you.

Decide ahead of time where you're going to spend this pleasant day. There may be a spiritual or holy place nearby. If there is, do some research and learn as much as you can about the place before you visit.

You might choose a place you're familiar with, or deliberately decide to visit someplace you haven't visited before. Choose a pleasant setting where you won't be interrupted. If it's a warm day, you may choose to do this exercise outdoors, possibly by a river or the ocean or maybe out in the country. The idea is to do the exercise in pleasant surroundings, away from your normal, everyday life. If possible, do this well away from other people as well. Of course, this may not be possible. It might be mid-winter, or you may not be able to get away from your home. In this situation, you'll obviously have to do the exercise at home.

If you're doing this exercise outdoors, go for a pleasant walk. Take your time and pause to look at anything that interests you. Look for beauty in everything you see. Watch the flight of a bird, the trunk of a tree, the movements of the clouds. Most of the time we're too busy to notice the beauty that surrounds us.

If you're doing this exercise at home, sit in a comfortable place and look at, or hold, something you find attractive. Look at it from different angles and fondle it, if it's something you can hold. Appreciate the work that has gone into the making of it, and remember how and when you obtained it.

When you feel ready, sit or lie down, close your eyes, and think about the beauty you have just experienced. Hold this thought for as long as possible and then become aware of your physical body. Notice if your thoughts of beauty can be felt in any part of your body. You may notice a sensation in the area of your solar plexus, heart, or throat chakras. You may not become aware of any sensation anywhere in your body, and that is fine, too.

The sensation can appear in unusual places. Not long ago, an acquaintance of mine told me that she had noticed a sensation on the tip of her tongue. Someone else told me he'd experienced tingling fingertips on his right hand.

Again, when you feel ready, open your eyes, and have something to eat or drink. Afterwards, write down your thoughts on what you've done so far. If you experienced a sensation in your body, you should write that down. You should also jot down any thoughts that occurred to you while you were communing with nature.

The next stage is to experience the Divine. Whenever possible I like to do this close to running water, such as a stream or the ocean. There is something about the air close to moving water that seems to make it easier for me to make contact. However, this is not always possible, and if I can't do this close to water, I simply imagine myself lying down beside a bubbling brook or listening to waves rolling in to shore.

Make yourself as comfortable as possible. Close your eyes and relax your body as much as possible. One way of doing this is to focus your attention on the fine muscles around your eyes, and to consciously relax them as much as you can. By the time you've done this, you'll find that the rest of your body has also relaxed.

Another method is to consciously relax all the muscles in your body, starting with the toes of one foot and working your way up to the top of your head, relaxing all the muscles in your body in turn.

Once you feel totally relaxed, mentally scan your body to ensure every muscle is as relaxed as possible. Focus on any areas that are not fully relaxed, and allow them to become loose and limp.

Think about your desire to make contact with the architect of the universe, and then let the thought go. Focus on your breathing, and remain quietly expectant. It's natural for your mind to start thinking about matters that are unrelated to what you're trying to do. Buddhists call this "monkey mind." Whenever you notice that your mind has become sidetracked and is thinking about other things, gently bring it back and focus on your breathing again.

The aim is to enter into the quietness and become one with the Divine. This is exactly what holy people do when they practice contemplative prayer. They are not asking God for anything. Their desire, and goal, is to spend time in God's presence.

You may want to communicate with the Divine. Many people have been taught formal prayers that use stilted, formal language. Naturally, you can speak to God in this way, if that is what you want. For most people, there is a better way. Simply open your heart and say whatever you want. When you've finished, stay in the silence for as long as you can before returning to the present.

You may be fortunate and become one with the Divine the first time you try this exercise. It's more likely that you'll experience the frustrating feeling of getting close but not quite reaching your goal. Even if you don't feel you've become closer to the Divine, you'll have learned more than you might think.

When you feel ready, become aware of your physical body and your chakras. Notice what responses they are giving to your quiet contemplation and meditation.

Once you have done this, take three slow, deep breaths and silently count from one to five. Open your eyes and familiarize yourself with your surroundings again. Lie or sit quietly for a minute or two before getting up. Move around for a few minutes, and eat some nuts, raisins, or fruit and drink some water.

Sit down and draw a picture on your pad. There is no need to think about this. Simply pick up your pen and start drawing. When you've finished the drawing, write down everything you can remember about this experiment. If you recall any of the extraneous thoughts that came into your mind during the meditation, write them down, too.

If it's lunchtime, pause and eat your lunch. Pay particular attention to the beauty all around you as you eat.

Once you've finished writing down your thoughts, or have finished your lunch, enjoy some gentle exercise. If you're outdoors, you might go for a walk. If you're indoors, you may have to run in place, do some stretching exercises, or walk up and down a flight or two of stairs.

The next stage is to visualize your soul ray, or rays, coming from the Divine and going into your body, giving you life. After that, you can visualize the ray exerting its influence on all seven main chakras.

Start by making yourself as comfortable as possible. Relax all the muscles in your body. When you feel totally relaxed, visualize yourself sound asleep in bed. Notice your chest rising and falling rhythmically with your breathing. Also become aware of a ray of pure energy that comes from above and totally surrounds you.

As you look at yourself, see yourself gradually stirring. You may stretch and open your eyes for a few seconds. See yourself lying in bed not fully asleep yet not fully awake.

You can look more closely at the ray now. You see that smaller sub-rays head toward each chakra. As you watch, you sense yourself moving along a sub-ray and into your root chakra. You feel totally at peace and relaxed. It makes perfect sense that you are now inside your own root chakra. From this vantage point you can watch your root chakra performing all its functions, and you can also sense the influence your soul ray has on your root chakra. Watch it energize and breathe new life into your root chakra.

You can stay inside your root chakra for as long as you wish. When you're ready, allow your focus to move inside your sacral chakra. Examine all of the chakras in turn. Alternatively, you might want to do this exercise in seven parts, looking at a different chakra each time.

When you've finished, take three slow, deep breaths, count to five, and open your eyes. As before, relax for a minute or two before getting up. Eat some nuts, raisins, or fruit and drink some water.

Make notes of everything you experienced during this meditation. You have visualized your soul in action, and probably have a great deal to think about.

Allow at least half an hour before performing the final exercise. Sometimes I fill in this time by relaxing and thinking about the previous experiments. Usually, though, I do some stretches and then go for a walk, pausing to appreciate anything interesting or beautiful that I see on the way.

When you feel ready, make yourself comfortable and read your intention out loud. Close your eyes and relax. If you're relaxing in a beautiful setting, visualize it in your mind. If you're doing this exercise at home, imagine a pleasant setting. It may be a place you remember, or you might create a pleasant fantasy scene, if you prefer.

Allow your thoughts to come and go. Instead of accepting any of them, let them go as soon as they become conscious. You may like to watch them float up into the sky or perhaps allow them to dissolve. It makes no difference how you let them go, just as long as you pay no attention to any of them. For all intents and purposes, you are a disinterested bystander who pays no attention to these idle thoughts.

It's hard to give an indication of how much time you should allow for this, as everyone is different. However, after a while you'll notice there are fewer and fewer thoughts to discard, and you've entered into a meditative state. Allow yourself to stay in this state for as long as possible. When you notice that extraneous thoughts are starting to appear again, consciously think of your intention. Repeat it to yourself over and over again, like a mantra.

You might like to say your mantra slightly differently with each repetition. You might sing it, place the emphasis on different words, repeat it slowly or quickly, or even say it falsetto. You'll find that the repetition will help you relax even more than before.

When you feel the time is right, stop repeating the mantra and allow yourself to focus on your soul. Take time to think about how it gives life and energizes every single cell of your body. Think of the countless incarnations it has already experienced before deciding to enter your body. Think about the many incarnations it has yet to experience.

Allow yourself to mentally feel your soul in each of the chakras, and thank it for giving you the spark of life, enabling you to take advantage of all the opportunities this lifetime has to offer.

Finally, simply relax for a few minutes, quietly communing with your soul. When you feel ready, take three slow, deep breaths, count to five, and open your eyes.

Before getting up, think about all the things you've accomplished during this special day. When you get up, have something to eat and drink to ground yourself once again.

Before carrying on with your day, write down any notes you wish to make about your experiences.

CHAPTER EIGHT

CONTEMPLATION AND THE SOUL

THROUGHOUT HISTORY, CONTEMPLATION HAS been used to gain wisdom and a closer connection with the Divine. Contemplation played an important role in the teachings of the Greek philosophers. St. Thomas Aquinas wrote: "It is requisite for the good of the human community that there should be persons who devote themselves to the life of contemplation."[1] Contemplation still plays an important role in the lives of Christian mystics.

Contemplation involves thought, but is not exactly the same as thinking. Dictionaries define it as "thoughtful observation." When you're contemplating, your mind is quiet and relaxed, and you're able to observe, reflect, and consider something while remaining in a meditative state.

You will have experienced this state of quiet contemplation while doing many of the exercises in this book.

Contemplation allows you to access information that you could not gain in any other way. Contemplation enables you to draw on your intuition and emotions, as well as your mind. It can help you discover what your heart and soul are trying to tell you.

You can use contemplation to provide answers to a variety of questions. You can ask comparatively simple questions, such as "What can I do to make today a perfect day?" You can also ask more difficult questions, such as "Should I persevere with my difficult relationship?"

You can also use your quiet time to contemplate spiritual matters. This is an excellent way to study spiritual texts, as it enables you to fully appreciate and understand what the writer had in mind. I find it helpful to contemplate writings on the soul. I find it interesting that only small extracts are required. Sometimes a single sentence is all that is necessary, as you quietly contemplate the words, their meaning, and how they relate to you and your everyday life.

You can enter into a contemplative state in many different ways. In fact, you already reach this state on a regular basis without knowing it. Here are two methods I use when contemplating spiritual matters.

Breath Contemplation

Start by choosing a brief passage that appeals to you. (You'll find some quotes on the soul at the end of this chapter.)

Read the passage and then close your eyes. Take three slow, deep breaths and allow your body to relax. Remain aware of your breathing, and allow each breath to quiet your mind.

Open your eyes and read the passage again. Close your eyes and allow the words you've just read to filter through every part of your body. Become aware of your physical body and notice any effects the words have, especially in your throat and heart. Become aware of any sensations you may experience in your chakras. Think about the words you've just read, and ask: "What do they mean to me?"

If necessary, open your eyes and read the passage again. Close your eyes, still your mind by focusing on your breathing, and ponder the words for as long as you wish. Repeat this stage as many times as you wish.

When you feel you've absorbed everything possible from the words you've read, take three slow, deep breaths and open your eyes. If possible, write down your thoughts and any insights you obtained while you were contemplating.

Mandala Contemplation

You will need a pad of paper and some colored pencils, markers, or crayons for the mandala contemplation. Mandalas are designs that were originally drawn to symbolize the universe. Mandala is a Sanskrit word that means "circle." Consequently, mandalas are usually drawn within the confines of a circle. However, mandalas can be drawn in any shape you wish.

Mandalas work well because they enable you to create pictures that come directly from your soul. With a mandala you're able to convert the words you read into picture form. You'll find this revealing and illuminating.

Before starting the mandala contemplation, draw a circle, or any other shape, on your pad of paper. You'll draw your mandala inside this shape. I usually use an upturned plate as a template for my circle.

Start by choosing a text that appeals to you. Close your eyes and focus on your breathing. Allow your mind and body to become completely relaxed.

Open your eyes and read the text again. Close your eyes, breathe slowly and deeply, and meditate on the words you have just read.

When you feel ready, open your eyes and use your intuition to pick up one of the colored pencils. Use it to start drawing whatever you wish inside your mandala. As it's important to draw spontaneously, let your hand draw whatever it wishes. Observe your hand with mild interest, but pay little attention to what is going on. Your hand will know when it's time to put down one pencil and pick up another. Your hand will also know when you're finished.

Read the words again. Close your eyes and meditate on the words for as long as you wish. Open your eyes and see if your hand has a desire to add anything to your mandala. Allow it to pick up a pencil and draw, if that is what it wants to do. The contemplation is over if your hand has no desire to add anything to the mandala.

You need to repeat this last stage of meditation if your hand picked up a pencil and added anything to your mandala.

You may want to study your mandala right away to see what insights it has given you. I occasionally do this, but usually allow a few hours to pass before examining it.

You'll be surprised at the added insights you'll gain from your mandala. If you do this contemplation on a regular basis, you'll build up a valuable collection of mandalas that will provide insights directly from your soul.

Quotes on the Soul

Here are some insights into the soul provided by famous people throughout history.

"Now I was a child good by nature,
and a good soul fell to my lot.
Nay, rather, being good,
I came into a body undefiled."
—*The Wisdom of Solomon 8:19–20 in the Apocrypha*

"The soul is of heavenly origin,
forced down from its home in the highest,
and, so to speak, buried in earth,
a place quite opposed to its divine nature."
—*Cicero,* On Old Age, *translated by E. S. Shuckburgh*

"A man has a soul, and it passes from life to life,
as a traveller from inn to inn,

till at length it is ended in heaven.
But not till he has attained heaven in his heart
will he attain heaven in reality...
Love does not die with the body...
it lives for ever and ever,
through incarnation after incarnation."
—*H. Fielding Hall (1859–1917),* The Soul of a People

"The soul is an emanation of the Divinity,
a part of the soul of the world,
a ray from the source of light.
It comes from without into the human body,
as into a temporary abode, it goes out of it anew;
it wanders in ethereal regions, it returns to visit it;
it passes into other habitations, for the soul is immortal."
—*Ralph Waldo Emerson (1803–1882),* Journals

"Being born twice is no more remarkable
than being born once."
—*Voltaire (1694–1778)*

"Either we have an immortal soul, or we have not. If we
have not, we are beasts; the first and wisest of beasts it may
be; but still beasts. We shall only differ in degree, and not
in kind; just as the elephant differs from the slug. But by
the concession of the materialists, we are not of the same
kind as beasts; and this also we say from our own consciousness. Therefore, methinks, it must be the possession
of a soul within us that makes the difference."
—*Samuel Taylor Coleridge (1772–1834),*
"Materialism" in Table Talk

"I simply believe that some part of the human Self or Soul
is not subject to the laws of space and time."

—Carl Jung (1875–1961)

"Nowhere can man find a quieter
or more untroubled retreat than in his own soul."

—Marcus Aurelius (121–180), Meditations

"You don't have a soul. You are a Soul. You have a body."

—C. S. Lewis (1898–1963), Mere Christianity

"Just as a mirror, which reflects all things, is set in its own
container, so too the rational soul is placed in the fragile
container of the body. In this way, the body is governed in
its earthly life by the soul, and the soul contemplates heavenly things through faith."

—Hildegard of Bingen (1098–1179)
in a letter to the monk Guibert

"One certainly has a soul; but how it came to allow itself
to be enclosed in a body is more than I can imagine. I only
know if once mine gets out, I'll have a bit of a tussle before
I let it get in again to that of any other."

—Lord Byron (1788–1824)

CHAPTER NINE

SOUL MATES

NO BOOK ON THE soul would be complete without at least some mention of soul mates. Even people who do not believe in reincarnation use the term *soul mates* to describe the type of relationship between two people who appear to be made for each other.

For people who believe in reincarnation, a soul mate relationship is one between two people who have been together in a number of previous lifetimes. Usually the attraction is instant as soon as these two people meet, and the friendship that ensues seems natural and familiar.

Of course, not every close friendship is necessarily a soul mate one. Recently, someone told me that her marriage had ended after three years.

"I thought he was my soul mate," she told me. "But he couldn't have been, as he's no longer in my life."

In fact, they may well have been soul mates. Soul mate relationships do not necessarily last for a lifetime. Once the two people have learned everything they need to learn from the relationship in this lifetime, there is no need for it to continue. If the relationship continued, the two people involved might miss out on other important lessons they have to experience in this incarnation.

Soul mate relationships can change from one lifetime to the next, too. Someone who was your brother last time around might be your daughter this time. Even though the relationships and gender have changed, the two souls will instantly recognize each other.

Other people have told me how worried they are that their soul mate might be living in another country and they might not have the opportunity to meet in this lifetime. Fortunately, this is not a problem. Soul mates don't meet by accident, and your soul mate will come into your life at the right spiritual time to enable you to have the experiences you both need to make maximum progress in this lifetime.

In fact, there is more than one soul mate waiting for you. Ancient teachings say that groups of cells gathered together while waiting to be transformed into souls. When they were in human form, these souls would instantly recognize each other if and when they happened to meet. All the other cells in the group that you belonged to are your soul mates, and you will notice a strong immediate attraction and recognition whenever you meet them.

Soul mates meet each other when the time is right. It may seem unfair when one person meets his or her soul mate at the age of, say, twenty, while someone else has to wait another forty or fifty years. I was fortunate enough to meet my soul mate at the age of twenty, and we have been married now for more than forty years.

However, an old school friend of mine married twice and had a string of unhappy relationships before finally meeting his soul mate at the age of fifty-eight.

"I envied you," he told me. "I just didn't seem to get it right. However, it finally worked out, and in many ways I'm grateful for all of my previous relationships. I made lots of mistakes, and learned from each one. I can really appreciate my soul mate now. If I'd met her thirty years ago, I'd probably have lost her again because of my immaturity and self-centeredness."

Obviously, the universe waited until my friend was ready before allowing him to meet his soul mate. Consequently, you'll need to remain patient if you're still waiting for your soul mate to appear. You, and your soul mate, may have a number of things that have to be resolved before you can get together. Remember that there are a number of soul mates waiting for you, and when the time is right, you'll finally meet.

Twin Souls

The concept of soul mates dates back thousands of years. In his *Symposium,* Plato wrote that people had been looking for their soul mate ever since Zeus cut them in half. In his mythical story, Plato tells of a world that contained men, women, and people who were both male and female. Plato told how humans began discussing how they could climb up to heaven and replace the gods. Not surprisingly, the gods were upset when they heard this, and discussed what they should do. The simplest solution was to destroy humankind. Fortunately, Zeus came up with a better idea. He suggested cutting all the people in half. This would, he said, immediately double the number of people making offerings to the gods. It would also weaken the people and prevent them from carrying out their plan.

The gods agreed, and all the people were divided into two. Naturally, the people were upset, and Zeus decided to enable each half to enjoy intercourse with their opposite, symbolically creating a whole. As a result, the males sought other males, the females other females, and the people who had been both male and female also sought their other half.

The concept of twin souls dates back to this story. Your twin soul is your other half, dating from when we were all whole. Although the term *twin souls* is mentioned frequently, it is most unlikely that you'll meet your twin soul in this incarnation. This is because your twin soul comes into your life when you are both experiencing your final lifetime on this earth plane.

A twin soul relationship is a perfect one in every way, because you connect on the physical, mental, emotional, spiritual, and soul levels. You can imagine how incredible this must be when you think that most relationships begin when the partners meet on two levels, and in many relationships there is no connection on any level. You will experience this incredible joy one day, but that day may be many incarnations from now. In the meantime, though, you can experience a deeply rewarding, fulfilling, and joyful relationship with one of your soul mates.

William Shakespeare's *Romeo and Juliet* is a good fictional example of a soul mate relationship. However, you don't have to look far to find true examples of soul mate relationships. One of my favorites, as it involves two poets I love, concerns Robert Browning and Elizabeth Barrett Browning.

Robert Browning (1812–1889) was thirty-three years old when he met Elizabeth Barrett (1806–1861). She was six years older than him, and looked much older than her years. At the time they met, she was bedridden and was looked after by her pious father, who said lengthy prayers at her bedside every night and forbade her from ever marrying. Robert and Elizabeth corresponded for four months before she consented to meet him. She was a recluse and was concerned about the effect her appearance would have on him.

The initial meeting went well, and on the following day Robert wrote her a letter saying that he hoped he hadn't offended her or stayed too long. One day later, he wrote her another letter proclaiming his love.

The relationship developed with daily exchanges of letters that gradually became less formal and more intimate. Before long, Robert was writing to "My own, dearest love." After she told him the sad story of her brother's death by drowning, Robert wrote: "Let me say now—this only once—that I loved you from my soul, and gave you my life."[1]

Because her father was adamant that she should never marry, Elizabeth and Robert were forced to elope. After their marriage, they settled in Florence, Italy, and focused on their writing careers. Their son, Robert Barrett Browning, who later became a well-known sculptor, was born in 1849. One year later, Elizabeth's most famous work, *Sonnets from the Portuguese,* was published. This book of sonnets proclaims her love and devotion to her husband. It was written during their two-year courtship, but she did not present it to him until three years after their wedding. Robert's pet name for Elizabeth was "Little Portuguese." This was because she had written a poem called "Catarina to Camoens," which contained the feelings of a dying Portuguese girl for her absent lover.

Sonnets from the Portuguese includes her most famous sonnet, which describes the intense love and devotion she felt for Robert:

How do I love thee? Let me count the ways.
I love thee to the depth and breadth and height

My soul can reach, when feeling out of sight
For the ends of Being and ideal Grace.
I love thee to the level of everyday's
Most quiet need, by sun and candle-light.
I love thee freely, as men strive for Right;
I love thee purely, as they turn from Praise.
I love thee with the passion put to use
In my old griefs, and with my childhood's faith.
I love thee with a love I seemed to lose
With my lost saints,—I love thee with the breath,
Smiles, tears, of all my life!—and, if God choose,
I shall but love thee better after death.

Elizabeth died in 1861, and Robert returned to London, where he continued his career. He died in 1889 and was buried in Westminster Abbey. Two years after his death, two volumes of the letters Robert and Elizabeth wrote to each other were published. They demonstrate conclusively the incredible love they had for each other.

Some writers have asked how an attractive and popular thirty-three-year-old poet, with a wide circle of female friends, could instantly fall in love with a bedridden invalid several years older than himself. Elizabeth delayed the meeting because of concerns about her appearance, but Robert's soul instantly fell in love with her soul, as they had been together in many previous incarnations.

Their love story has been retold many times. The famous play *The Barretts of Wimpole Street* by Rudolf Besier is just one example.

Clara and Robert Schumann are also a good example of a soul mate relationship. Robert Schumann (1810–1856), the famous German composer and pianist, met Clara Wieck (1819–1896), the daughter of his piano teacher, when she was just nine years old. Clara's father disapproved of their friendship and did everything in his power to prevent their relationship from developing. Robert first proposed to Clara when she was fifteen, and three years later, when Clara was eighteen, the couple took Clara's father to court to receive permission to wed. Robert and Clara married in 1840, and Robert Schumann's creativity blossomed as a result. Over the next few years, he composed his best-known works.

However, a shadow was hanging over them. Within a few years of their marriage, Robert started showing signs of mental illness. He was forced to resign his professorship at Leipzig Conservatory. In 1854, he tried to commit suicide by jumping into the Rhine River and was placed in a mental asylum. Clara was forced to go on concert tours to earn enough money to support their family of seven children. Robert wrote to her every day but was not allowed to see her, as it was thought it would make his illness worse. Finally, after almost two and a half years, Clara persuaded his doctors to let her visit. She wrote in her diary: "He smiled at me and put his arm round me with great difficulty, for he had almost lost all control of his limbs. Never shall I forget that moment. I would not give that embrace for all the treasures on earth."[2] Twenty-four hours later, he died.

Robert Schumann had pleaded with her to marry their mutual friend Johannes Brahms, but she refused to do so. She spent the rest of her life composing and teaching.

The story of Robert and Clara is a desperately sad one. They were obviously brought together to enable them to learn some powerful karmic lessons. In the process, they composed some of the most beautiful music that has ever been written.

In many cases, soul mates share the same ray. However, this does not always occur, as soul mates come together for many purposes. Soul mate relationships always provide opportunities for both people to grow and develop. Consequently, someone on the first ray (willpower, forceful, dogmatic) may well be a soul mate of someone on the fourth ray (charm, harmony, reconciliation). In this example, the person on the first ray may need to learn how to sway others without being overly demanding, while the partner might need to learn to stand up for him- or herself. Seemingly unlikely combinations enable both partners to learn valuable lessons.

Because these lessons are sometimes painful, it's important to love and nurture your soul. We'll look at that in the next chapter.

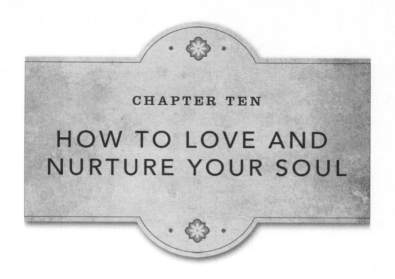

CHAPTER TEN

HOW TO LOVE AND NURTURE YOUR SOUL

CARL JUNG, THE GREAT Swiss psychiatrist, called the soul "the greatest of all cosmic miracles."[1] Yet most people give little if any thought to their immortal souls. The astonishing fact that the soul existed long before the birth of the body, and continues to exist long after the death of the body, is seldom considered. Given this, many people would find it strange to even think about loving and nurturing their soul.

Fortunately, it's not hard to nurture and nourish your soul, and every part of your being will benefit as a result. You'll experience more happiness, joy, and fulfillment in life. You'll gain more pleasure out of everything you do. You'll eliminate stress and negativity and become a more positive, cheerful person. You'll be able to make the most of the present moment, instead of remaining trapped in the past or constantly worrying about the future. You'll also gain a closer connection with the Divine.

I learned the incredible joy of being in the moment from my grandchildren. When they were small, it was impossible to go on a brisk walk with them. They'd stop and gaze, entranced, at the beauty of a spider's web or the flight of a butterfly. They'd watch the movements of a cloud and be absorbed at the different shapes it formed itself into. They'd pick up an acorn or a leaf and enjoy looking at it and handling it. They were, quite naturally, experiencing joy in the present moment.

Every time you allow yourself to experience joy, you're nurturing your soul. There are countless ways of doing this.

Spending time with positive friends who make you laugh nurtures your soul. The laughter provides your physical body with a healthy workout, too. Conversely, spending time gossiping, or discussing grievances with negative people, starves your soul.

Going for a walk, or engaging in any other form of physical activity, is good for your soul. Stay in the moment and try to look at everything as if you were seeing it for the first time. Beauty can be found everywhere, and appreciating and enjoying it does wonders for your soul.

Creating anything is good for your soul, too. Writing and painting are good examples, but what you do doesn't necessarily need to be something that people would term creative. Gardening, cooking, knitting, singing, dancing, playing a musical instrument, humming, journaling, and repairing a broken object are all creative and good for your soul, as long as you enjoy them. I get frustrated doing household repairs, but my son-in-law loves doing them and receives great joy and satisfaction from them. Consequently, he nourishes his soul when engaged in these pursuits, while all I experience is frustration.

Listening to music is a wonderful way to relax and nurture your soul. Reading a good book or watching a good movie also nurtures your soul.

Volunteering your time and/or expertise enables you to help others. Most volunteers report that they get back much more than they give. In addition to the pleasure and satisfaction they receive, their soul benefits, too.

Spending time with the people you love most is one of the best ways to nurture your soul.

You can also nurture your soul by meditating, praying, contemplating, and spending quiet time on your own.

Your soul benefits whenever you do something you enjoy. Consequently, it's impossible to provide a complete list of ways to nurture the soul.

Sometimes people tell me they're too busy to take time out to nurture their soul. I can't imagine why people would choose to starve their soul when all that is necessary is to do something enjoyable.

Here are some specific ways to nurture your soul.

Eye Gazing

If eyes are truly the windows to the soul, it's amazing how few people use them to see the souls of others while at the same time finding a reflection of themselves. Many traditions teach that we are all made in the image of God. Consequently, if you gaze into someone's eyes and see the person's soul, you'll also see God. In the Hindu tradition, eye gazing is called *Darshan,* which means "seeing God, while being seen by God."

Everyone who has been in love has experienced the delight of gazing into the eyes of their partner. By doing this, the two people involved have opened themselves up and revealed their soul to their opposite half. It's a practice that lovers should follow throughout their lives together, but sadly, few people do.

Recently I spoke with a lady who told me about the last few hours of her husband's life. He was dying of cancer and had asked to go home to spend his last days with his loved ones. He could barely speak, and the family made a bed for him in the downstairs living room, as he was incapable of walking up stairs.

At about six in the morning, he called out to his wife in a strong, clear voice. She rushed downstairs, and he greeted her with a big smile on his face. He looked ten years younger than he had the night before. She climbed into bed with him, and for the next three hours they lay together, gazing into each other's eyes. At the end of that time he took a few gasping breaths, and, still gazing into his wife's eyes, he died.

"We gazed into each other's eyes throughout our marriage," she told me. "Whenever times were tough, or one of us needed reassurance or comfort, we'd cuddle and look at each other's soul."

Jalāl ad-Din Muhammad Balkhi (1207–1273), better known as Rumi, is remembered today mainly because of his famous love poems. Rumi was a poet, mystic, theologian, and jurist. He was a keen advocate of eye gazing and wrote: "Whenever two are linked in this way there comes another from the unseen world."[2]

You don't need to be passionately in love to practice eye gazing. All you need is a willing partner who is prepared to experiment with you. Obviously, it needs to be someone who is willing to accept your gaze, and to return it, without feeling awkward or uncomfortable.

Sit facing each other at a distance that feels right for both of you. You might like to start at a distance apart where you cannot quite touch hands. Take a few slow, deep breaths and then gaze at the other person's face. Stay as relaxed as possible, and gradually focus on the other person's eyes. You might like to look at one eye first, and gradually expand your gaze to look into both eyes. You cannot do this for any length of time without absorbing the other person's energy. Your partner will receive your energy in return. Ultimately, you'll become aware of the universal life force, and discover that God, by whichever name you use, is everywhere. This is unlikely to happen the first time you experiment with this, but it will occur when the time is right.

You can also perform eye gazing on your own by sitting in front of a large mirror. You'll find this both healing and restorative. When you do this, gaze at yourself in a loving, compassionate, and gentle way, appreciating yourself for the wonderful creation you are.

Some people have told me they find it hard to gaze into someone's eyes, or even their own eyes, for any length of time. Practice is all that's required to overcome this difficulty.

Some people experience a variety of sensations, even mild pain, in different parts of their bodies. These are the vestigial memories of long-forgotten negative experiences and emotional pain. As you relax and release stress and tension, these sensations will gradually disappear. Because of this, eye gazing can be used to heal yourself, and others, of emotional pain.

Kindness

Most of us give little thought to the needs of the people we encounter as we progress through life. Of course, we pay attention to the needs of friends and loved ones, but we seldom think about the stresses and difficulties other people experience in their lives.

It costs nothing to smile at a stranger. A kind word can make the world of difference to someone who is feeling lonely. The simple act of listening can be a form of kindness.

When we were first married, my wife and I owned a small motel. An elderly lady stayed with us for several months. She was shy, and it took her a while before she'd talk to us freely. Gradually we learned about her sad and lonely life. One day, her nephew arrived and took her home to live with his family. When she left, she thanked us for our kindness. "You're the only people who've ever listened to me," she said. I felt guilty, as sometimes I'd been busy and hadn't wanted to listen to her stories.

An old proverb says you shouldn't criticize others until you've walked a mile in their shoes. You naturally become kinder if you try to imagine what life must be like for the person you are interacting with.

You should also be kind to yourself. Most of us are our own worst enemies, as we constantly sabotage ourselves with negative thoughts.

Your soul benefits from every act of kindness you perform, no matter how small. My boss's secretary, at the first job I had after leaving school, had an office that overlooked a busy street. Several times a day she'd run downstairs and put a coin into a parking meter. When I asked her why she did it, she told me that it made her feel good. She was performing good deeds for people she'd never met and would probably never meet. Putting money in the meter saved these people from receiving a parking ticket, and she hoped they would pass on the favor by doing something to help someone else. It was a good lesson for me, and one I've always remembered.

Another advantage of practicing kindness is that it makes you feel good. That is the whole premise of Charles Dickens's book *A Christmas Carol.* When you feel good, every aspect of your life improves, and you'll start spreading happiness everywhere you go.

The Dalai Lama said: "My religion is very simple. My religion is kindness." Thousands of years ago, Aesop, the Greek writer of fables, wrote: "No act of kindness, however small, is ever wasted."

Make a deliberate effort to be kind for a whole week, and record any changes you experience in your life. At the very least, you'll feel better about yourself, and you'll be more tolerant and understanding of others. If you deliberately practice this for four weeks, you'll find that kindness will become a habit and the benefits will multiply. It would be hard to find a better way to nurture your soul.

Gratitude

Several years ago, I received a letter from a good friend who was dying from cancer. He briefly mentioned the chemotherapy treatment he was undergoing and then told me how grateful he was to have had the gift of life. Because of that, he'd been able to laugh, love, and follow his dreams. He'd built up a good business and married the girl of his dreams, and together they'd had three children. He told me he was sad to be dying decades sooner than he'd expected, but he was full of gratitude for all the gifts and opportunities he'd had. "Life is such a precious gift," he wrote. "I just wish I'd appreciated it more when I was fit and well."

Most of us are too busy with everyday life to pause and think about all the things we should be grateful for. We have the gift of life, for instance. Most of us have family and friends. We possess the necessary skills to earn a living and support our families and lifestyles. We all have skills and talents of various sorts. I have a friend who finds it hard to write a simple sentence but is able to build or repair anything using wood. I admire his practical skills and have called on him many times to fix household problems. In return, I've been able to write letters and reports for him. I'm grateful to have him as a friend.

It is highly beneficial for your soul when you sit down quietly and think about all the things you are grateful for. You'll probably start by thinking about the gifts of life, health, family, and friends. When it comes to people, think about them individually rather than simply expressing thanks for having good friends.

Once you've covered these, you might start expressing gratitude for your job, home, car, hobbies, and the people you work with. However, you can go much further than this. You can think about the person who delivers your daily paper, mows your lawn, and serves you coffee at a local café, and all the other people you interact with. I always include bookstores and libraries, as well as the staff who work at them, when I think about gratitude. After this, I think about the people who write, edit, publish, print, and distribute books.

Can you go even deeper? You can express gratitude for the farmers who provide your food and for the people who built your home, car, and computer. You can think about the people who deliver your mail, collect your garbage, clean the roads and sidewalks, and prepare and serve food at your favorite restaurants. Since my health scare, I include my gratitude for doctors, nurses, and everyone else involved in healthcare. That includes the people who design and develop the latest advances in medicine as well as the hospital orderlies, who also fulfill a vital role.

There is virtually no end to the list of people you could thank for their role in making your world the way it is. When I tried to explain the concept of gratitude to my three-year-old granddaughter, she told me she'd like to thank the person who made the beaches. I agreed with her. We definitely should express our gratitude to the universal life source for providing us with beautiful beaches, mountains, forests, oceans, and everything else that makes this planet such a wonderful place for us to live.

I usually think of all the things I'm grateful for when lying in bed at night. As soon as I start thinking thoughts of gratitude, I feel calm and at peace. I'm sure this helps me enjoy a better night's sleep, since I fall asleep with happy thoughts in my mind.

Generosity

About twenty years ago, I was attending a convention in New Orleans. At the end of the day, four of us walked to a nearby restaurant and enjoyed a good meal. On our way back to our hotel, we were approached by a beggar. Three of us moved away from him, but the fourth stopped and chatted with the man for a couple of minutes. At the end of the conversation, he gave the beggar twenty dollars, and we continued on our way.

One of the others asked him why he'd given the man anything, let alone a significant sum of money. I'll never forget Ken's reply: "Because it made me feel good. I've found that being generous nurtures my soul."

I can't remember much else that happened at that convention, but I'll never forget what Ken did that evening. His actions certainly had an effect on me, and I've been more generous ever since as a result.

Generosity doesn't have to involve money. You can be generous with your time, energy, compassion, and love. When my children were small, one of my son's friends told us that his dad seldom spent time with him, as he was too busy. I thought, at the time, how sad that was. My father was busy, too, but he always made time to watch his children play sports or act in a school play. I sometimes have to make an effort to be generous with my time, but when I do, it always makes me feel good and nurtures my soul.

Be Happy

I was very fortunate to have a wise mentor named Tai L'au. One of his favorite sayings was: "If you want to be happy, be happy." These deceptively simple words are sometimes hard to put into practice. It can be difficult to be happy when everything appears to be going wrong in life, but it can be done. Your soul dislikes negativity and pessimism. It thrives on positivity and joy. Your soul is happy when you're happy. When you're looking ahead with optimism rather than focusing on your problems, your soul feels nourished and fully alive.

Recently I read an article about Dr. Bruce Arroll, a medical professor who was diagnosed with leukemia. He became a patient in a hospital he had regularly visited as a teacher or practitioner. He quickly discovered that "uncertainty is not a good state for the human mind." He decided immediately after the diagnosis that he could choose his attitude. He remained happy throughout the treatment, which was successful. Dr. Arroll said: "I see this as a learning experience. And in some ways I'm grateful to have had it, in a funny sort of way."[3] I'm sure Dr. Arroll's positive attitude and his determination to remain happy no matter what contributed to his full recovery from a life-threatening illness.

I regularly meet people who are going to be happy "one day." They keep postponing happiness until some time in the future, such as when the children leave home or the mortgage is paid off. They're mystified when I tell them they can be happy now if they want to be. It doesn't make sense to postpone happiness. Do yourself, and your soul, a huge favor and resolve to be happy now, no matter what is going on in your life.

Relax

We all know that it's good to relax and unwind, yet few of us consciously relax often enough or even at all. Many people seem to spend most of their lives in a stressed, agitated, and rushed state. If this describes you, you might need to deliberately set aside a few minutes every day in which you simply relax. Let go of all the stresses and worries of your life, and think nothing but pleasant thoughts. You can also relax by doing something you love. My wife relaxes by working in the garden and creating mosaics. I feel totally relaxed when browsing through a used bookstore.

Relaxing restores your body, mind, and soul. I find it much easier to write, for instance, when I'm relaxed, as this allows my thoughts and creativity free play. When I'm stressed out or worried about a particular problem, I find it almost impossible to write. My remedy for this is to go for a walk, listen to some favorite music, or take myself through a relaxation exercise. Once I've taken this time out for myself, I can return to my work and achieve ten times more than I would have if I'd forced myself to continue writing in a stressed state.

Laugh Often

Pablo Neruda (1904–1973), the Chilean poet, wrote: "Laughter is the language of the soul." ("La risa es el lenguaje del alma.") The American poet e. e. cummings (1894–1962) wrote: "The most wasted of all days is one without laughter." Victor Borge (1909–2000), the Danish pianist and humorist, said: "Laughter is the shortest distance between two people."

Laughter is an essential part of life. It's impossible to think about your problems and concerns when you're laughing. It's also highly infectious and brings people together. It relaxes your body, produces endorphins, strengthens your immune system, reduces stress, protects your heart, and nurtures your soul. No wonder people say that "laughter is the best medicine."

Children laugh all the time when they're playing. Adults take life much more seriously. I've even had people tell me they haven't laughed in years.

Fortunately, it's not hard to laugh, if you want to. You can laugh on your own, of course. I laugh out loud when I read something amusing or see something funny on television. When my wife and I travel together, she constantly tells me to keep quiet, as I laugh out loud at comedies I watch on the airplane.

All laughter is good for your soul, but the best laughter occurs when it's shared with others. This is not hard to arrange. All you need do is ask someone if anything funny happened to them recently. Be prepared to reciprocate with a funny story of your own, and you'll both soon be laughing.

Another way to laugh more is to seek out people who laugh frequently. You'll enjoy spending time in their company, and your body and soul will benefit, too.

Laughter is useful in the workplace, too. People who work for someone with a good sense of humor get more work done and suffer less stress than people who work for someone with little or no sense of humor.[4]

Seek out every opportunity you can find to have a good laugh, and your soul will rejoice.

Forgiveness

Everyone has been hurt by others at some time. Sometimes the hurt is deliberate, but it can also be caused unintentionally. Some people are able to forgive and forget easily, but others hang on to the grievance for months, years, or even decades.

I was reminded of this recently when someone sent me an e-mail telling me that a mutual acquaintance had separated from his wife. The e-mail was mischievous, as the person whose marriage had broken up had attacked me on the Internet several years earlier, and the sender thought I'd be pleased to hear the news. Actually, I felt sad, as virtually all marriages begin with love, and it's tragic for both people concerned when those feelings disappear. I was also surprised that it took me several seconds to recall the person he was telling me about. His attacks on me had been hurtful at the time, but I'd forgotten about them years ago.

This was because I'd forgiven him. At the time I was angry and consumed with rage. However, I quickly realized that this created unnecessary stress, made me feel like a victim, and held me back from getting on with my own life. It was a waste of my time and energy. By forgiving him, I didn't condone what he had done. Instead, I released the power this person continued to hold over me as long as I continued to feel resentment and anger. I was slightly surprised that I'd done it so effectively that it took me time to even remember who he was.

Forgiveness may not change the other person, but it will always have a positive effect on you. It will bring peace, serenity, and joy back into your life. Forgiveness is a form of emotional and spiritual healing.

Forgiveness plays a role in every spiritual tradition. The parable of the prodigal son in the Bible (Luke 15:11) is a good example of this. St. Paul wrote about forgiveness in his Epistle to the Colossians: "Forbearing one another, and forgiving one another, if any man have a quarrel against any: even as Christ forgave you, so also do ye" (Colossians 3:13).

A reluctance or inability to forgive has been shown to have a negative effect on a person's health. It creates anxiety, stress, high blood pressure, chronic pain, and depression. It also affects the person's mental health by undermining his or her confidence and self-esteem.

Forgiveness is also good for the soul. Edwin Hubbell Chapin (1814–1880), the American preacher, orator, and author, wrote: "Never does the human soul appear so strong as when it forgoes revenge and dares to forgive an injury."

In the 2009 movie *Invictus*, Morgan Freeman, playing the role of Nelson Mandela, said: "Forgiveness liberates the soul. It removes fear. That is why it is such a powerful weapon." I have no idea if Nelson Mandela ever said this, but he is an outstanding example of someone who practices forgiveness. After twenty-seven years in prison, he was still able to forgive the people who had put him there.

You also should forgive yourself. We've all said and done things that we've regretted later. The feelings of shame and guilt that we impose on ourselves are frequently much greater than the pain we experience when someone hurts us.

If it's possible, make amends. It might be difficult to apologize to someone you've hurt, but it's good for your body, mind, and soul. This is the case even if the other person is unwilling to accept your apology.

By forgiving yourself and others, you'll release all the pain and will be able to move forward in a positive direction and start living again.

Live in the Present

It should be easy to live in the present moment, but most people, myself included, find it hard to do so for any length of time. We're constantly thinking about problems and worries from the past. It's too late now to be concerned about what you should have done or said at some time in the past.

Some people take this to extremes. Some years ago, some-one came to me for help, as he was an insomniac. He found it hard to get to sleep, because the minute he closed his eyes, he'd think about all the silly things he'd done during the day. That would remind him of something he'd done a few days earlier, and that would make him think about how he'd made a fool of himself the week before. Before long, he was think-ing about something he'd done when he was four years old. No wonder he couldn't get to sleep.

Other people do the opposite, and worry about the future. How would I manage if I lost my job? What if that nagging cough is a sign of something serious? Is it safe to allow my daughter to fly across the country on her own? These people are concerned about things that will probably never happen.

It doesn't matter if these people are looking backwards or forwards. In both cases they're preventing themselves from living in the present. They're failing to see and appreciate all the magnificent things that are happening around them at the present moment.

The remedy is to gently tell yourself that you'll worry about whatever the concern happens to be at a certain time in the future. I usually use 7:00 a.m. the following morning. When the time comes, you'll likely find that the worry has vanished, as your concern wasn't as important as you thought it was.

Once you let the concern go, you can live in the present moment. When you think about it, the present moment is the only time you ever have. Yesterday is gone, and although the chances are you'll be here tomorrow, there are no certainties.

As you start spending more and more time in the present, you'll find yourself enjoying life much more and will appreciate everything that is going on around you. It's early spring as I'm writing this. Every day I go for a walk. I live right on the edge of a city, which means I can walk in the countryside. It's a wonderful time of year to do this, as I see newborn lambs, baby ducks, courting birds, and spring flowers every day. Because I make a concerted effort to live in the present moment, I'm able to enjoy all of this. If I went for my daily walk full of concerns and worries, I'd hardly notice any of the beauty of the changing seasons around me. I return home revitalized and ready to get back to work.

Living in the present, and making the most of it, nurtures your soul. Someone told me that living in the present makes her soul sing. I like that image, and often think of it, especially when I find myself stressed or worried about something. I tell myself to allow my soul to sing, and deliberately bring myself into the present moment.

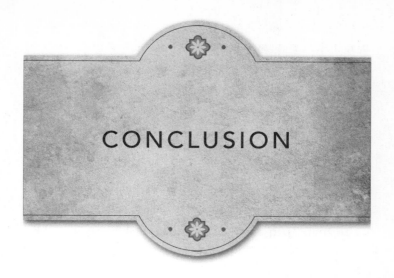

CONCLUSION

I HOPE THIS BOOK has helped you strengthen your connection with your immortal soul and enabled you to appreciate everything it has done, and continues to do for you, in this lifetime, as well as the lives you have already lived and the lifetimes you are yet to live. I also hope this book has made you realize that you cannot die. There is life after death. Although I've met many people who say they don't want to come back again, I think most people—believers, agnostics, and atheists alike—secretly hope that death is not the end.

Many near-death experiences occur when the person is clinically dead. The person is no longer breathing and the heart has stopped beating.[1] Consequently, these people have experienced death and returned to life. Apart from anything else, the near-death experience shows that consciousness can exist despite the absence of a functioning brain.

Many near-death experiences begin with the person traveling rapidly through a dark tube or tunnel toward an incredibly brilliant white light. Frequently, the person sees people he or she knew while alive, has a life review, and experiences feelings of love, forgiveness, and acceptance. Usually the person wants to stay inside the light, but somehow the person knows it is not yet his or her time, and returns to earthly life.

So many people have described this scene in books, magazine articles, TV shows, and movies that it cannot be considered a rare experience. More than 2,500 accounts of near-death experiences have been recorded on the Near Death Experience Research Foundation website alone (www.nderf.org).

I was disappointed not to have had a near-death experience. Because my heart had stopped and then started again, I thought I'd come close enough to death to experience one. However, it became clear to me, after discussing this with many people, that although my heart had stopped and started again, I was in the hands of experts who did this sort of thing on a regular basis. Consequently, although my heart stopped briefly, I was in no real danger of dying from that particular procedure. My experience was completely different from that of someone who may, for instance, have died by drowning or in a car accident but was resuscitated by the expertise of modern-day medicine.

Incidentally, I spoke to a number of people who had been returned to life after a major accident or illness and did not remember having a near-death experience. I also spoke to a few people who had left their bodies and were able to look down dispassionately at the people who were trying to save their lives. These people didn't see a brilliant light or experience moving to "the other side."

I was amazed at the number of people I spoke to who've had a near-death experience. I probably shouldn't have been. In 1992, a Gallup Poll found that five percent of the U.S. population have experienced an NDE. This means approximately fifteen million people in the United States have had one.[2]

In every case it was a life-changing experience that, without exception, changed their lives for the better. They lost all fear of death, became more patient, compassionate, and loving, and became more interested in spirituality. They all became convinced that death is not the end, and that there is life after death. Until they had their NDE, many of these people had never before considered the concept of reincarnation.

One of these people, a former criminal, told me that his near-death experience was the best thing that had ever happened to him. It enabled him to see, for the first time, what he was doing to himself and the people who loved him. He now counsels and helps at-risk teenagers.

Another person I spoke to was a multimillionaire. He told me that making money had been an obsession, and it had brought him no happiness whatsoever. "I realized I didn't have a single true friend," he said. "If I'd died on that operating table, no one would have grieved for me." Five years after his operation he is happily married, with an eighteen-month-old son. He looks after his investments and is involved with several charitable organizations.

Many of the people I spoke to had become interested in religion and spirituality as a result of their near-death experience. Some of them had had no interest in religion in the past. However, this experience taught them that death was not the end, and they had a strong desire to learn more about the spiritual side of life. "I don't think anyone would have thought I'd become a believer in reincarnation," one person told me. "Yet it's become one of the most important aspects of my life. I now believe in God, and also believe I'll come back here again and again."

Not surprisingly, a large number of these people became interested in psychic development, and were exploring areas they considered weird or unusual before their experience. "My husband used to have gut feelings," one lady told me. "Only now he calls them flashes of intuition. He's joined a psychic development circle and attends meetings every week. I didn't think anyone as down-to-earth as my John would ever take the psychic world seriously."

Almost everyone I spoke to was experiencing more joy and love in their lives than they had before their near-death experience. "As well as feeling more joy, I've somehow become much more compassionate," one lady told me. "I seem to be able to empathize with other people and their problems now. I never did that before."

Most near-death experiences were fairly similar. Terry, a good friend of mine, told me about what he called his "attempt to get to the other side":

"I was in the hospital for a hernia operation. It was supposed to be a simple procedure, but something went wrong and I almost died. For a brief moment, I felt I was looking down on the operating table. I could see myself asleep with four people bending over me. Almost as soon as I saw that, I found myself in a long tunnel heading toward an incredibly bright light. It was more powerful than anything I'd seen before, but I could look at it without hurting my eyes. I seemed to be moving at breakneck speed, but I still had time to experience feelings of love, compassion, and forgiveness. I felt totally at peace. I knew I was dying or dead, but it didn't matter, as I'd never experienced such bliss before. All I wanted was to reach the light. I felt as if I was returning home. I had no regrets. I was full of joy and reaching out to the light. I was almost there when I heard a strong, deep voice from inside the light telling me it wasn't my time yet. I felt a wave of sadness, and then in the space of a second I was above my body again, and must have returned to it, though I can't remember any more." Terry beamed at me. "You know, when I regained consciousness, I was able to tell the doctors and nurses exactly what they were doing at that moment. The surgeon told me that near-death experiences were common, and he was no longer surprised when a patient mentioned it to him. I know now, without a shadow of a doubt, that there is more to life than we think. I'm a happy man. I have a good life. But I always had a fear of death. That's gone, as I know death is the doorway to a whole new world."

People experience near-death experiences in different ways. Terry didn't mention noises or music. He didn't see any spirits or deceased family members, nor did he experience a review of his life. These are common features in many people's memories.

Terry felt he was inside a tunnel that led to the light. When people who haven't had a near-death experience think about what it must be like, they usually imagine some sort of tunnel. However, a 1982 Gallup poll found that only three percent of people who have had a near-death experience reported being in a tunnel.[3] However, as others reported a swirling sensation or the feeling of being constantly in motion, three percent is probably on the low side.

Constance, a young woman who's studying to become an Episcopalian minister, told me that she did not experience a tunnel. "It was a road, a bumpy road with many twists and turns," she told me. "It was dark, and I was racing along this road. I was knocked and buffeted all the time, but I felt strangely at peace. Ahead, in the distance, I could sense an amazing light, and I knew I was safe and would soon be home." Although Constance did not experience a tunnel, her experience of traveling at great speed along a road in the dark sounds very much like a tunnel.

Many people who have had a near-death experience do not want to come back to their present lifetime. In her book *The Passionate Years,* Caresse Crosby wrote about the time she almost drowned when she was seven years old. As she was drowning, she saw her father and brothers realize what had happened and attempt to rescue her. "I saw the efforts to bring me back to life and I tried not to come back," she wrote. "It was the most perfect state of easeful joy that I ever experienced, then or since ... One thing I know, that Nirvana does exist between here and the hereafter—a space of delight, for I have been there."[4]

A day or two after telling me about his near-death experience, Terry phoned to tell me that as a result of the experience he now believed in the soul.

"I never gave the soul a moment's thought before," he said. "It seemed to me we could function pretty well without one. But what was it that traveled into the light if it wasn't my soul? It had to be my soul."

If someone experiences a cardiac arrest, the heart stops circulating blood and the brain ceases to function. At this point, the person's consciousness and ability to reason or remember anything should cease. However, there are now thousands of well-documented exceptions to this.

In 1991, a woman named Pam Reynolds was diagnosed with a life-threatening, inoperable brain aneurysm. Fortunately, Dr. Robert Spetzler, a neurosurgeon in Phoenix, Arizona, offered to help. However, in order to perform the operation, Pam Reynolds needed to be clinically dead for more than an hour. Her body temperature had to be lowered to sixty degrees to stop all vital functions, including brain activity. Pam was clinically dead, as her heart had stopped, she was no longer breathing, and there was no measurable activity occurring in the brain.

Despite all of this, Pam was able to hear the sound of the surgical saw that cut open her skull. She "popped" out of her body while this was going on, and rose over the operating table where she could watch the procedure taking place. She felt she was metaphorically sitting on the surgeon's shoulder as he worked. She could also hear the conversation of the nurses in attendance. At some stage, her consciousness was pulled into a tunnel that led her toward a brilliant light. She could hear her dead grandmother calling her. Once she reached the light, she found other deceased friends and relatives waiting for her there. They refused to let her travel further, even though she wanted to continue into the light. After a joyful reunion, her deceased uncle Gene guided her back to her body. She didn't want to reenter it, but her uncle pushed her back in.

Afterwards, Pam was able to tell the nurses the conversation she had heard, and could describe the surgical saw and other tools that had been used during her operation.

The entire operation was conducted while Pam was officially dead. It is generally assumed that the mind is a function of the brain. Yet even though all three medical tests showed that Pam's brain was dead, something remained alive to observe and remember every detail of what occurred. Could this have been her soul?[5]

Throughout history, some people have had the ability to receive messages from people who have died. Mediums and channelers are the best-known examples of people who communicate with "the other side." The messages these people receive provide comfort to the bereaved relatives who are suffering from their loss. Unfortunately, though, most of the information that comes across does not contain enough factual information to prove that it came from someone who is dead.

However, there are exceptions. One of the most famous examples of this is the remarkable story of James L. Chaffin. Mr. Chaffin was a North Carolina farmer who died in 1921. In his will, dating from 1905, he left his farm and everything he owned to his third son, Marshall. His widow and three other sons received nothing. The family was not surprised, as Marshall had always been his father's favorite, and they all already knew the contents of the will. Consequently, Marshall took over the farm.

Almost four years later, in June 1925, James, the second son, woke up in the middle of the night with a vivid memory of a dream. In his dream, his father had appeared wearing the long black overcoat that he frequently wore. His father said nothing, but continually pointed to the inside pocket of the overcoat. The apparition appeared in another dream, and this time James's father spoke: "You will find my will in my overcoat pocket."

The next morning, James's mother told him that she'd given the coat to his older brother, John. James immediately went to John's house, some twenty miles away. John was not in, but his wife found the coat, which was too big for John to wear. They examined the coat and found that the inside pocket had been sewn up. They cut it open and found a roll of paper tied up with string. James recognized his father's handwriting. He had written: "Read the 27th chapter of Genesis in my daddie's old Bible." James and his sister-in-law looked up the passage in her bible. The 27th chapter of Genesis told how Jacob received his father's blessing and his brother Esau's birthright.

The bible was a family heirloom and was kept at the old Chaffin farmhouse. James took his daughter and two other witnesses with him to examine the bible. At the 27th chapter, they found a sheet of paper with a message written in James's father's handwriting. It read:

> After reading the 27th chapter of Genesis, I, James L. Chaffin, do make my last will and testament, and here it is. I want, after giving my body a decent burial, my little property to be equally divided among my four children, if they are living at my death, both personal and real estate divided equal, if not living with share going to their children. And if she is living, you all must take care of your mammy. Now this is my last will and testament. Witness my hand and seal.
>
> James L. Chaffin
> This January 16, 1919

Marshall, who had been the sole beneficiary of the 1905 will, was dead by the time the second will was found. His widow recognized her father-in-law's handwriting and agreed that the second will was valid. However, she and her son contested the will in court. Fortunately for the family, an unwitnessed will was considered valid in North Carolina at that time. One week before the court hearing, James saw his father again in a dream. This time his father asked, "Where is my old will?" James took this as a sign that they'd win the case.

The second will was presented in court, and ten witnesses declared that the handwriting was genuine. The court ordered the first will to be canceled, and the second will was duly probated.[6]

This is a remarkable story. Where did the information that came to James Chaffin in his dreams come from, if not from the soul of his father? It's interesting that the son was directed to the overcoat rather than the will. The apparition in the dream told James that the will was in the overcoat. Obviously, the father's memory was faulty. If anything, this adds credibility to the account. The fact that the father returned one week before the trial shows that he was still concerned about the injustice he had unintentionally caused his family. This must be one of the few occasions in which an apparition caused a court to reverse a previous decision.

The evidence of so many near-death experiences from all around the world strongly indicates that we do not die, but transition to an afterlife. As our physical bodies are discarded and remain, it's our souls that move on and return temporarily to the realm of spirit before coming back to give birth to our new incarnations. I find this an incredibly exciting thought. If everyone accepted this, no one would fear death, as they'd know that the end of this lifetime is merely a transition into a whole new stage of life.

I hope this book has given you insights into your soul and enabled you to utilize it to enhance every aspect of your life. Learning your soul's purpose will help you gain a greater appreciation of your particular skills and talents. You'll be more tolerant of people who are traveling on rays that are different from yours, as you'll be able to recognize the specific ray qualities they have brought into this incarnation. You'll also realize that you are a divine being.

What you learn about your past lifetimes will help you understand why you are the specific person you are today. It may reveal and clarify areas of difficulty you have had. Once you understand them, the problems are much easier to deal with, and frequently resolve themselves.

Most importantly, this book will help you to value, appreciate, and nurture your immortal soul. When you do this, you'll become more accepting and loving, your happiness and self-esteem will grow, and you'll gain insights into how you may progress further in this incarnation. You'll also lose all fear of death, as you'll have complete faith in the process of life.

I wish you all the best as you gain a closer connection with the Divine by exploring the miracle of your eternal soul.

SUGGESTED READING

Aristotle. *De Anima (On the Soul).* Written 350 BCE. Many versions available. Can be found on the Internet at http://classics.mit.edu/Aristotle/soul.html.

Atwater, P. M. H. *Beyond the Light: The Mysteries and Revelations of Near-Death Experiences.* New York: Avon Books, 1994.

———. *We Live Forever: The Real Truth about Death.* Virginia Beach: A.R.E. Press, 2004.

Auerbach, Loyd. *Reincarnation, Channeling and Possession: A Parapsychologist's Handbook.* New York: Warner Books, 1993.

Aurobindo, Sri. *The Problem of Rebirth.* Pondicherry, India: Sri Aurobindo Ashram, 1972.

Bacci, Ingrid, PhD. *The Art of Effortless Living*. London: Bantam Books, 2002.

Baggini, Julian, and Jeremy Stangroom. *Great Thinkers A–Z*. London: Continuum, 2004.

Bailey, Alice A. *A Treatise on the Seven Rays*. New York: Lucis Publishing Company, 1936.

Bertholet, Alfred. *Transmigration of Souls*. London: Harper and Brothers, 1909.

Casey, John. *After Lives: A Guide to Heaven, Hell & Purgatory*. New York: Oxford University Press, 2009.

Cayce, Edgar. *Edgar Cayce on Atlantis*. New York: Paperback Library, 1968.

Cerminara, Gina. *Many Mansions*. New York: William Sloane Associates, 1950.

———. *The World Within*. New York: William Sloane Associates, 1957.

Challoner, H. K. *The Wheel of Rebirth*. Wheaton, IL: Theosophical Publishing House, 1969.

Cornillier, Pierre-Emile. *The Survival of the Soul and Its Evolution after Death*. London: Kegan Paul, Trench, Trubner & Co., 1921.

Crawley, A. E. *The Idea of the Soul*. London: Adam & Charles Black, 1909.

Cullmann, Oscar. *Immortality of the Soul or Resurrection of the Dead?* London: Epworth Press, 1958.

Currie, Ian. *You Cannot Die: The Incredible Findings of a Century of Research on Death*. Toronto: Somerville House

Publishing, 1978. Reprint, Rockport, MA: Element, 1995.

Dale, Cyndi. *The Complete Book of Chakra Healing: Activate the Transformative Power of Your Energy Centers*. Rev. ed. Woodbury, MN: Llewellyn Publications, 2009.

Danelek, J. Allan. *The Mystery of Reincarnation*. Saint Paul, MN: Llewellyn Publications, 2005.

Dennett, Daniel C. *Breaking the Spell: Religion as a Natural Phenomenon*. New York: Viking Penguin, 2006.

Favero, Kevin T. *The Science of the Soul: Scientific Evidence of Human Souls*. Edina, MN: Beaver's Pond Press, 2004.

Fiore, Edith. *You Have Been Here Before*. London: Sphere Books, 1980.

Fisher, Joe. *The Case for Reincarnation*. Toronto: Somerville House Publishing, 1998.

Fodor, Nandor. *Between Two Worlds*. West Nyack, NY: Parker Publishing Co., 1964.

Frazer, J. G. *The Belief in Immortality and the Worship of the Dead*. London: Macmillan and Company, 1929. Reprint, New York: Barnes & Noble, 1969.

Gallup, George, with William Proctor. *Adventures in Immortality*. New York: McGraw-Hill, 1982.

González-Wippler, Migene. *What Happens After Death: Scientific & Personal Evidence for Survival*. Saint Paul, MN: Llewellyn Publications, 1997.

Harpur, Patrick. *A Complete Guide to the Soul*. London: Rider Books, 2010.

Hastings, Adrian, Alistair Mason, and Hugh Pyper, eds. *The Oxford Companion to Christian Thought*. Oxford: Oxford University Press, 2000.

Head, Joseph, and S. L. Cranston, eds. *Reincarnation: An East-West Anthology*. New York: Julian Press, 1961.

Heath, Pamela Rae, and Jon Klimo. *Handbook to the Afterlife*. Berkeley, CA: North Atlantic Books, 2010.

Hodson, Geoffrey. *Reincarnation: Fact or Fallacy?* Wheaton, IL: Theosophical Publishing House, 1967.

Holland, John. *Power of the Soul: Inside Wisdom for an Outside World*. Carlsbad, CA: Hay House, 2007.

Johnson, Raynor. *The Imprisoned Splendour*. London: Hodder & Stoughton, 1953.

Johnson, W. J. *Oxford Dictionary of Hinduism*. Oxford: Oxford University Press, 2009.

Kenny, Dennis. *Promise of the Soul*. New York: John Wiley & Sons, 2002.

Langley, Noel. *Edgar Cayce on Reincarnation*. New York: Paperback Library, 1967.

Long, Jeffrey, MD, with Paul Perry. *Evidence of the Afterlife*. New York: HarperCollins, 2010.

MacGregor, Geddes. *Reincarnation in Christianity*. Wheaton, IL: Quest Books, 1978.

McColman, Carl. *Spirituality: Where Body and Soul Encounter the Sacred*. Georgetown, MA: North Star Publications, 1997.

Merton, Thomas. *Contemplative Prayer*. New York: Doubleday & Company, 1989.

Moody, Raymond. *Life After Life*. Atlanta, GA: Mockingbird Books, 1975.

Moore, Thomas. *Care of the Soul: A Guide for Cultivating Depth and Sacredness in Everyday Life*. New York: HarperCollins, 1992.

———. *The Soul's Religion*. New York: HarperCollins, 2002.

Mumford, Dr. Jonn. *Death: Beginning or End?* Saint Paul, MN: Llewellyn Publications, 1999.

Myss, Caroline. *Anatomy of the Spirit: The Seven Stages of Power and Healing*. New York: Harmony Books, 1996.

Newton, Michael, PhD. *Destiny of Souls: New Case Studies of Life Between Lives*. Saint Paul, MN: Llewellyn Publications, 2000.

———. *Journey of Souls: Case Studies of Life Between Lives*. Saint Paul, MN: Llewellyn Publications, 1994.

———. *Life Between Lives: Hypnotherapy for Spiritual Regression*. Saint Paul, MN: Llewellyn Publications, 2004.

Pond, David. *Western Seeker, Eastern Paths: Exploring Buddhism, Hinduism, Taoism & Tantra*. Saint Paul, MN: Llewellyn Publications, 2003.

Potter, Richard N. *Authentic Spirituality: The Direct Path to Consciousness*. Saint Paul, MN: Llewellyn Publications, 2004.

Rogo, D. Scott. *Life After Death: The Case for Survival of Bodily Death*. Wellingborough: Aquarian Press, 1986.

Russell, Bertrand. *A History of Western Philosophy*. London: George Allen & Unwin, 1946. Revised edition 1961.

Sheed, F. J. *Theology for Beginners*. London: Sheed and Ward, 1958.

Singer, June. *Boundaries of the Soul*. London: Victor Gollancz Limited, 1973.

Steiner, Rudolf. *Life Between Death and Rebirth*. New York: Anthroposophic Press, 1968.

Stevenson, Ian. *Twenty Cases Suggestive of Reincarnation*. Second edition. Charlottesville, VA: University of Virginia Press, 1974.

Thaler, Linda Kaplan, and Robin Koval. *The Power of Nice: How to Conquer the Business World with Kindness*. New York: Doubleday, 2006.

Trainor, Kevin, ed. *Buddhism: The Illustrated Guide*. London: Duncan Baird Publishers, 2001. Revised edition 2004.

Varghese, Roy Abraham, ed. *Great Thinkers on Great Questions*. Oxford: Oneworld Publications, 1998.

Walker, Benjamin. *Encyclopedia of Esoteric Man*. London: Routledge & Kegan Paul, 1977.

Weatherhead, Leslie D. *Psychology in Service of the Soul*. London: Epworth Press, 1929.

Webster, Richard. *The Complete Book of Auras*. Woodbury, MN: Llewellyn Publications, 2010.

————. *Practical Guide to Past-Life Memories: Twelve Proven Methods*. Saint Paul, MN: Llewellyn Publications, 2001.

————. *Soul Mates: Understanding Relationships Across Time*. Saint Paul, MN: Llewellyn Publications, 2001.

Wilson, Colin. *After Life: Survival of the Soul*. Saint Paul, MN: Llewellyn Publications, 2000.

Zukav, Gary. *The Seat of the Soul*. New York: Free Press, 1989.

————. *Soul to Soul: Communications from the Heart*. New York: Free Press, 2007.

NOTES

Introduction

1. Pamela Rae Heath and Jon Klimo, *Handbook to the Afterlife* (Berkeley, CA: North Atlantic Books, 2010), 47.

2. W. Stainton Moses, *Spirit Teachings* (London: Spiritualist Alliance, 1883). *Spirit Teachings* is also available at www.meilach.com/spiritual/books/st/spteach.htm.

3. J. F. Crehan, "Immortality," *Man, Myth & Magic* (London: Marshall Cavendish Corporation, 1970), 4:1413.

4. Bertrand Russell, *A History of Western Philosophy*, rev. ed. (London: George Allen & Unwin, 1961), 249.

5. St. Thomas Aquinas, *Summa Theologica* (*Summary of Theology*)(1264–1274). Many translations are available on the Internet, including www.op.org/summa. Question 75 relates purely to the soul.

6. Edward B. Tylor, *Primitive Culture, Volume 1* (London: John Murray, 1871), 429.

7. Carl Jung quoted in Erwin Schrödinger's *What Is Life? With Mind and Matter and Autobiographical Sketches* (Cambridge: Cambridge University Press, 2006), 119. *What Is Life?* was originally published in 1944.

Chapter One

1. There are many books that recount instances of people remembering their previous incarnations. These include *Reincarnation: Amazing True Cases from Around the World* by Roy Sternman (London: Piatkus Books, 1997) and *Twenty Cases Suggestive of Reincarnation* by Dr. Ian Stevenson, 2nd ed. (Charlottesville, VA: University of Virginia Press, 1974).

2. Stevenson, *Twenty Cases Suggestive of Reincarnation*, 101.

3. Ibid., 91–105.

4. Fred Ayer, Jr., *Before the Colors Fade: Portrait of a Soldier, George S. Patton* (New York: Houghton Mifflin, 1964).

5. This poem can be found in many place on the Internet, including www.mylot.com/w/discussions/1163967.aspx.

6. Stevenson, *Twenty Cases Suggestive of Reincarnation*, 259–69.

7. Edgar Cayce quoted in Benjamin Walker's *Masks of the Soul* (Wellingborough: Aquarian Press, 1981), 50–51.

8. Edgar Cayce, *Edgar Cayce on Atlantis* (New York: Paperback Library, 1968), 150.

9. Charles C. Emerson, "Notes from the Journal of a Scholar," *The Dial*, July 1840. Reprinted in *The Dial: A Magazine for Literature, Philosophy, and Religion*, vol. 1 (Boston, MA: James Munroe and Company, 1841), 14.

10. Richard Webster, *Practical Guide to Past-Life Memories: Twelve Proven Methods* (Saint Paul, MN: Llewellyn Publications, 2001). This book contains a number of different methods to retrieve past-life memories.

11. Noel Langley, *Edgar Cayce on Reincarnation* (New York: Castle Books, 1967), 75.

Chapter Two

1. William Faulkner, speech in *Les Prix Nobel en 1950* (Stockholm, Sweden: P. A. Norstedt & Söner, 1951), 71.

2. Wayne W. Dyer, *Wisdom of the Ages: 60 Days to Enlightenment* (New York: HarperCollins, 1998), 146.

3. Maurice B. Forman, ed., *The Letters of John Keats* (London: Oxford University Press, 1931), 335–36.

4. Ralph Waldo Emerson quoted in *Reincarnation: An East-West Anthology*, compiled and edited by Joseph Head and S. L. Cranston (New York: Julian Press, 1961), 237–38.

5. Jeffrey Burton Russell, *A History of Heaven* (Princeton, NJ: Princeton University Press, 1997), 15.

6. St. Teresa of Ávila quoted in *Interior Castle,* translated from Spanish and edited by E. Allison Peers (London: Sheed & Ward, 1974), I,i,4.

7. Ralph McInerny, "The Existence of the Soul," *Great Thinkers on Great Questions*, edited by Roy Abraham Varghese (Oxford, UK: Oneworld Publications, 1998), 51–52.

8. Joseph Head and S. L. Cranston, eds., *Reincarnation in World Thought* (New York: Julian Press, 1967), 92.

9. Kevin Trainor, ed., *Buddhism: The Illustrated Guide*, rev. ed. (London: Duncan Baird Publishers, 2004), 70.

10. Homer Smith, *Man and His Gods* (Boston, MA: Little, Brown and Company, 1952), 24.

11. Gerald Massey, *The Seven Souls of Man and Their Culmination in Christ* (privately printed, 1900). Available at http://www.africawithin.com/massey/gml1_seven.htm. Also in H. P. Blavatsky, *The Secret Doctrine*, vol. 2 (1888), 632.

12. Daniel C. Dennett, *Breaking the Spell: Religion as a Natural Phenomenon* (New York: Viking Penguin, 2006), 97–98.

13. Alvin Plantinga, "The Existence of the Soul," *Great Thinkers on Great Questions*, edited by Roy Abraham Varghese (Oxford, UK: Oneworld Publications, 1998), 45–46.

Chapter Three

1. Ursula Roberts, *The Mystery of the Human Aura* (London: The Spiritualist Association of Great Britain, 1950), 1.

2. Cassandra Eason, *Encyclopedia of Magic & Ancient Wisdom* (London: Judy Piatkus Ltd., 2000), 11.

3. These three Bible passages appear to relate to auras:

   "And when Aaron and all the children of Israel saw Moses, behold, the skin of his face shone; and they were afraid to come nigh him" (Exodus 34:30).

   At the Transfiguration of Christ, Matthew wrote that Jesus's "face did shine as the sun, and his raiment was white as the light" (Matthew 17:2).

   When Saul was traveling on the road to Damascus "suddenly there shined round about him a light from heaven" (Acts 9:3).

4. Barbara G. Walker, *The Woman's Encyclopedia of Myths and Secrets* (San Francisco, CA: Harper & Row, 1983), 253.

5. Alice A. Bailey, *A Treatise on the Seven Rays* (New York: Lucis Publishing Company, 1936), 42.

Chapter Five

1. Elisabeth Goldsmith, *Ancient Pagan Symbols* (Berwick, ME: Ibis Press, 2003), 206. First published in 1929.

2. W. Wynn Westcott, *Numbers: Their Occult Power and Mystic Virtues* (1890; reprint, London: Theosophical Publishing House, 1974), 73.

3. Rudolph Brasch, *The Supernatural and You!* (Stanmore: Cassell Australia, 1976), 53.

4. Adrian Room, ed., *Brewer's Dictionary of Phrase and Fable* (1870; reprint, London: Cassell & Co, 1999), 1066.

The seven joys of the Virgin Mary are the Annunciation, the Visitation, the Nativity, the Epiphany, the Finding in the Temple, the Resurrection, and the Ascension. The seven sorrows of the Virgin Mary are Simeon's prophecy, the flight into Egypt, the loss of the Holy Child, meeting Jesus Christ on the road to Calvary, the crucifixion, taking Jesus down from the cross, and the entombment. The seven spiritual works of mercy are to tend the sick, feed the hungry, give drink to the thirsty, clothe the naked, befriend the stranger, minister to prisoners, and bury the dead (Matthew 25:35–45). The seven words from the cross are: (1) "Father, forgive them; for they know not what they do" (Luke 23:34); (2) "Today shalt thou be with me in paradise" (Luke 23:43); (3) "Woman, behold thy son! ... Behold thy mother!" (John 19:26–27); (4) "My God, my God, why hast thou forsaken me?" (Matthew 27:46); (5) "I thirst" (John 19:28); (6) "It is finished" (John 19:30); (7) "Father, into thy hands I commend my spirit" (Luke 23:46).

5. *Sepher Yetzirah* quoted in John Michael Greer's *The New Encyclopedia of the Occult* (Saint Paul, MN: Llewellyn Publications, 2003), 431.

6. W. Wynn Westcott, trans., *Sepher Yetzirah* (1887), chapter 4, page 3. Many versions are available. It can also be found at www.sacred-texts.com/jud/yetzirah.htm.

7. Rabbi Geoffrey W. Dennis, *The Encyclopedia of Jewish Myth, Magic and Mysticism* (Woodbury, MN: Llewellyn Publications, 2007), 186.

8. Ute Possekel, *Evidence of Greek Philosophical Concepts in the Writings of Ephrem the Syrian* (Leuven, Belgium: Peeters Publishers, 1999), 191.

9. Adrian Room, ed., *Brewer's Dictionary of Phrase and Fable* (1870; reprint, London: Cassell & Co, 1999), 1068.

10. Ecclesiasticus, also known as The Wisdom of Ben Sira and Sirach, is available in many editions. It can also be found at www.sacred-texts.com/bib/poly/sir.htm.

11. Ernest Busenbark, *Symbols, Sex, and the Stars in Popular Beliefs* (New York: The Truth Seeker Co., 1949), 243.

Chapter Seven

1. Cyndi Dale, *The Complete Book of Chakra Healing: Activate the Transformative Power of Your Energy Centers*, rev. ed. (Woodbury, MN: Llewellyn Publications, 2009), 233.

Chapter Eight

1. St. Thomas Aquinas quoted in James V. Schall's *Roman Catholic Political Philosophy* (Lanham, MD: Lexington Books, 2004), 186.

Chapter Nine

1. Robert Browning quoted in F. E. Halliday's *Robert Browning: His Life and Work* (London: Jupiter Books, 1975), 74.

2. Victor Basch, translated by Catherine Alison Phillips, *Schumann: A Life of Suffering* (New York: Alfred A. Knopf, 1931), 230. This book can be found at http://www.archive.org/stream/schumannalifeofs027254mbp/schumannalifeofs027254mbp_djvu.txt.

Chapter Ten

1. Carl Jung quoted in Erwin Schrödinger's *What Is Life? With Mind and Matter and Autobiographical Sketches* (Cambridge: Cambridge University Press, 2006), 119. *What Is Life?* was originally published in 1944.

2. Will Johnson, *Rumi: Gazing at the Beloved* (Rochester, VT: Inner Traditions, 2003).

3. Dr. Bruce Arroll quoted in Geraldine Johns's "Fighting 'Toxic Uncertainty,'" *New Zealand Listener*, 230, no. 3722 (September 10, 2011): 24–26.

4. Melissa B. Wanzer quoted in "Laughter is the Best Medicine," *ScienceDaily*, January 26, 2008. Also available at www.sciencedaily.com/releases/2008/01/080124200913.htm.

Conclusion

1. Jeffrey Long, MD, with Paul Perry, *Evidence of the Afterlife* (New York: HarperCollins, 2010), 5.

2. Pamela Rae Heath and Jon Klimo, *Handbook to the Afterlife* (Berkeley, CA: North Atlantic Books, 2010), 56.

3. George Gallup, with William Proctor, *Adventures in Immortality* (New York: McGraw-Hill, 1982), 32.

4. Caresse Crosby, *The Passionate Years* (New York: The Dial Press, 1953), 18–19.

5. Michael Sabom, MD, *Light and Death* (Grand Rapids, MI: Zondervan, 1998). See also www.near-death.com /experiences/evidence01.html.

6. *Proceedings of the Society for Psychical Research*, 36, (1927): 517–24. The story of the Chaffin will can be found in many books, including George Nugent Merle Tyrrell's *Science and Psychical Phenomena (Perspectives in Psychical Research)* (Secaucus, NJ: University Books, 1961), 28–30.

INDEX

To Write to the Author

If you wish to contact the author or would like more information about this book, please write to the author in care of Llewellyn Worldwide and we will forward your request. Both the author and the publisher appreciate hearing from you and learning of your enjoyment of this book and how it has helped you. Llewellyn Worldwide cannot guarantee that every letter written to the author can be answered, but all will be forwarded. Please write to:

Richard Webster
℅ Llewellyn Worldwide
2143 Wooddale Drive, Dept. 978-0-7387-3249-7
Woodbury, MN 55125-2989

Please enclose a self-addressed stamped envelope for reply, or $1.00 to cover costs. If outside the U.S.A., enclose an international postal reply coupon.

GET MORE AT LLEWELLYN.COM

Visit us online to browse hundreds of our books and decks, plus sign up to receive our e-newsletters and exclusive online offers.

- **Free tarot readings • Spell-a-Day • Moon phases**
- **Recipes, spells, and tips • Blogs • Encyclopedia**
- **Author interviews, articles, and upcoming events**

GET SOCIAL WITH LLEWELLYN

Find us on Facebook
www.Facebook.com/LlewellynBooks

Follow us on twitter
www.Twitter.com/Llewellynbooks

GET BOOKS AT LLEWELLYN

LLEWELLYN ORDERING INFORMATION

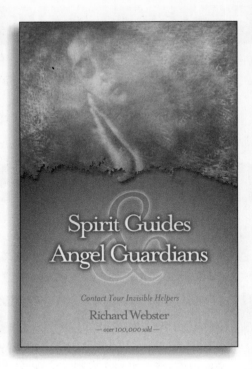

Spirit Guides
&
Angel Guardians

Contact Your Invisible Helpers

Richard Webster

— *over 100,000 sold* —

Spirit Guides & Angel Guardians

Contact Your Invisible Helpers

RICHARD WEBSTER

They come to our aid when we least expect it, and they disappear as soon as their work is done. Invisible helpers are available to all of us; in fact, we all regularly receive messages from our guardian angels and spirit guides but usually fail to recognize them. This book will help you to realize when this occurs. And when you carry out the exercises provided, you will be able to communicate freely with both your guardian angels and spirit guides.

You will see your spiritual and personal growth take a huge leap forward as soon as you welcome your angels and guides into your life. This book contains numerous case studies that show how angels have touched the lives of others, just like yourself. Experience more fun, happiness, and fulfillment than ever before. Other people will also notice the difference as you become calmer, more relaxed, and more loving than ever before.

978-1-56718-795-3, 368 pp., 5³/₁₆ x 8   **$12.95**

Creative
Visualization

For Beginners

Achieve Your Goals & Make Your Dreams Come True

RICHARD WEBSTER

Creative Visualization for Beginners

Achieve Your Goals & Make Your Dreams Come True

RICHARD WEBSTER

Everyone has the natural ability to visualize success, but ordinary methods used to reach fulfillment can be inefficient and unclear. Creative visualization allows anyone to change the direction of his or her life by mentally picturing and altering images of their goals. In his popular conversational style, bestselling author Richard Webster explains the methodology behind creative visualization, and provides readers with the tools and knowledge necessary to achieve their goals in all areas of life, including business, health, self-improvement, relationships, and nurturing and restoring the soul.

Creative Visualization for Beginners includes simple exercises enhanced by real-life situations from the author's personal experiences with creative visualization, and demonstrates how to react when you encounter difficulties along the way. In addition, he gives advice on what to do if you have no predetermined goals in mind, and how to implement positive results while maintaining your natural balance.

978-0-7387-0807-2, 264 pp., 5³/₁₆ x 8   **$13.95**

Pendulum Magic

For Beginners

Tap Into Your Inner Wisdom

RICHARD WEBSTER

Pendulum Magic for Beginners

Tap Into Your Inner Wisdom

RICHARD WEBSTER

The pendulum is a simple, accurate, and versatile device consisting of a weight attached to a chain or thread. Arguably the most underrated item in the magician's arsenal, the pendulum can reveal information not found any other way. It can read energy patterns, extracting information from deep inside our subconscious.

This book will teach you how to perform apparent miracles such as finding lost objects, helping your potted plants grow better, protecting yourself from harmful foods, detecting dishonesty in others, and even choosing the right neighborhood. Explore past lives, recall dreams, release blocks to achieving happiness, and send your wishes out into the universe.

978-0-7387-0192-9, 240 pp., 5³/₁₆ x 8   **$13.95**

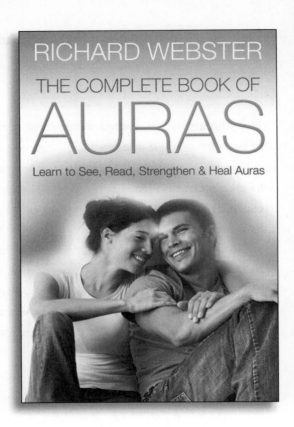

RICHARD WEBSTER

THE COMPLETE BOOK OF

AURAS

Learn to See, Read, Strengthen & Heal Auras

The Complete Book of Auras

Learn to See, Read, Strengthen & Heal Auras

RICHARD WEBSTER

Everything you ever wanted to know about the aura is now in one easy-to-use guidebook!

Bestselling author Richard Webster shares simple, step-by-step techniques for seeing, feeling, strengthening, and cleansing the aura—your personal energetic signature—for better health, psychic protection, and achieving your highest goals. Learn to balance and clear the seven chakras using pendulums and crystals. Practice enjoyable meditations, visualizations, and other practical aura-based methods. Learn to recognize signs of illness, release emotional blockages, and determine anyone's mood, personality, and true nature just by their aura's appearance.

This book also offers expert instruction on giving insightful aura readings—and even how to read the auras of pets.

978-0-7387-2180-4, 216 pp., 6 x 9   **$16.95**